D0373996

To the memory of my parents and grandparents who encouraged my interests in politics and my pursuit of higher education, and to my wife, Cheryl who keeps me steered in the right political direction.

PREFACE

We are just beginning another presidential election cycle. It promises to be the longest and most costly in U.S. history. The 2008 election occurs within a political environment in which the military occupation in Iraq, the implementation of the war on terrorism at home, and a host of other domestic and international economic and social issues have divided Democrats and Republicans, the Bush administration and Congress, and the United States and much of the international community. The presidential campaign will continue the debate on most of these issues. Hopefully, the election will resolve some of them by its selection of new national leaders and by the policies that these new leaders promised to pursue.

But at what cost is the election being conducted? Is it necessary to extend the election cycle for over two years, numbing the electorate, taxing the candidates, and spending hundreds of millions of dollars in the process? Does the current presidential electoral system encourage the most qualified candidates to run? Does it force them to discuss the issues, present feasible policy alternatives, and talk candidly with the American people? Does the electorate get the kind of information it needs to make an enlightened judgment? Will the results of the election fairly and accurately reflect the opinions, interests, and needs of the population as a whole? Is it consistent with principles and practices of a democratic electoral process?

A primary goal of this book is to answer these questions. It does so by describing and evaluating the presidential election system from the perspectives

THE ROAD TO THE WHITE HOUSE 2008

The Politics of Presidential Elections

EIGHTH EDITION

Stephen J. Wayne
Georgetown University

THOMSON

WADSWORTH

Australia • Brazil • Canada • Mexico • Singapore • Spain
United Kingdom • United States

THOMSON

✳ ™

WADSWORTH

The Road to the White House 2008: The Politics of Presidential Elections, Eighth Edition
Stephen J. Wayne

Senior Acquisitions Editor: Carolyn Merrill
Editorial Assistant: Patrick Rheaume
Technology Project Manager: Yevgeny Ioffe
Marketing Manager: Janise Fry
Marketing Communications Manager:
  Heather Baxley
Senior Content Project Manager: Joshua Allen

Creative Director: Rob Hugel
Art Director: Linda Helcher
Print Buyer: Barbara Britton
Production Service: ICC Macmillan Inc.
Cover Designer: Bartay Studios
Cover Image: Blue Line Pictures/Getty
Printer: West Group

© 2008 Thomson Wadsworth, a part of The Thomson Corporation. Thomson, the Star logo, and Wadsworth are trademarks used herein under license.

ALL RIGHTS RESERVED. No part of this work covered by the copyright hereon may be reproduced or used in any form or by any means—graphic, electronic, or mechanical, including photocopying, recording, taping, Web distribution, information storage and retrieval systems, or in any other manner—without the written permission of the publisher.

Printed in the United States of America
1 2 3 4 5 6 7 11 10 09 08 07

Library of Congress Control Number: 2007929141

Student Edition:
ISBN-13: 978-0-495-09632-0
ISBN-10: 0-495-09632-6

Thomson Higher Education
25 Thomson Place
Boston, MA
02210

For more information about our products, contact us at:
Thomson Learning Academic Resource Center
1-800-423-0563
For permission to use material from this text or product, submit a request online at
http://www.thomsonrights.com.
Any additional questions about permissions can be submitted by e-mail to
thomsonrights@thomson.com.

of the candidates, the parties, and the American people. As with its previous editions, *The Road to the White House 2008* discusses the following:

- Why particular strategies are being adopted
- Why certain tactics are utilized (and others are not)
- Whether these strategies and tactics are likely to achieve the desired results and at what cost
- Why particular appeals are made, to whom, and with what impact
- How the candidates try to influence the news media
- How the news media try to cover the campaign and break through the imagery and sound bites that the candidates and their handlers present
- Why the election turns out the way it does
- What the election augurs for the direction of public policy and the new administration's ability to govern

OUTLINE

The book is organized into four parts. Part I discusses the arena in which presidential elections occur. Its three chapters examine the electoral system, campaign finance, and the political environment. Chapter 1 provides a historical overview of nominations as well as elections with a special section devoted to the Florida vote controversy in 2000 and its consequences for future presidential elections. Chapter 2 examines recent developments in campaign finance, particularly the explosion of revenues and expenditures, the latest financial reform legislation, the Bipartisan Campaign Reform Act of 2002 (BCRA) and its impact, and the threat to the public funding posed by that legislation, the ability of candidates to raise huge amounts of private funds, and public indifference to the privatization of campaign finance. The chapter will also discuss the ways in which the BCRA was circumvented in 2004 and the reaction to that circumvention by the parties, the courts, and the commission overseeing federal elections. In the third chapter, continuities and changes in the political environment serve as the principal focus and provide a perspective on how the environment in which the elections occur affects the turnout of voters, the attitudes of the electorate, and the composition of partisan electoral coalitions.

Part II describes and analyzes the presidential nomination process from its early beginning through the national nominating conventions. Chapter 4 discusses the reforms that the parties have made in the way they select their standard-bearers, the legal issues that have arisen from these reforms, and the impact the reforms have had on the electorate, the parties, and the candidates. Chapter 5 continues this discussion through the competitive stage of the caucuses and primaries until the nominee is effectively determined. This chapter pays particular attention to the strategies the candidates adopt and the hurdles they must overcome, illustrating these strategies with case studies from recent nomination campaigns. Chapter 6 describes the period after the nominees have been effectively determined through the conventions that officially anoint them and launch their general election campaigns. It describes how the candidates attempt to heal divisions within the party; improve their leadership image, which may have been damaged during the nomination process; and begin to challenge their partisan opposition in the general election.

Part III examines the presidential campaign itself. Chapter 7 details the organization, strategy, and tactics of the candidates and assesses the new technologies used to identify voters, target appeals to them, and measure the effect of these appeals as the election progresses. Chapter 8 turns to the news media: how the press covers the campaign and how the candidates try to affect the coverage they receive as well as counter that coverage with paid advertising, scripted public performances, and participation in the presidential debates. The chapter evaluates the impact that media-driven forces can have on the voting behavior of the electorate.

Part IV of the book looks at the election and beyond. Chapter 9 discusses and evaluates the vote: What does it mean? Is there a mandate? How do the results affect the president's ability to govern? Chapter 10 considers problems in the electoral system and possible reforms to alleviate these problems. It examines some of the major difficulties that have affected the political system from party rules to finance issues to media coverage. The chapter also looks at proposals being discussed for improving the electoral system, making it more equitable to the citizenry, more responsive to popular choice, less prone to human error and fraud, and more likely to guide those in government and facilitate their policy making responsibilities.

PURPOSE

Elections link the people with their public officials, a vital component of a functioning democracy. However, that link is far from perfect. Voting is individualized, yet governing is a collective undertaking. Everyone does not participate in elections, but government makes rules for all the people. Presidential candidates regularly over promise and under deliver. They create unrealistic expectations that are impossible to achieve, certainly not by themselves in a system of shared powers and divided government. People can become disillusioned, apathetic, and cynical as a consequence.

How can we improve elections? How can we encourage more of the citizenry to participate? How can we persuade the most qualified people to run? How can we level the electoral playing field? How can we ensure that the mood of the voters will be reflected in the results of the election and that government officials, political reporters, and the general public will accurately interpret those results? In other words, how can we make sure that elections achieve their principal goals: to select the most qualified people, to provide them with a blueprint for governing, and to hold them individually and collectively accountable for their decisions and actions in government?

Without information on how the system works, that is, whether it is functioning properly and meeting its objectives, we can do none of the above. We cannot cajole the citizenry to meet their civic responsibilities and vote; we cannot recruit the best and the brightest to run; we cannot improve the people–government–public policy connection for which elections are the critical link. In the case of presidential politics, ignorance is definitely not bliss, nor is the norm always or usually the ideal.

The road to the White House is long and arduous. In fact, it has become more difficult to travel than in the past. Yet, surprisingly, given all the criticism, there continue to be many would-be travelers. Evaluating their journey is essential to rendering an intelligent judgment on Election Day. However, more is at stake than simply choosing the occupant of the Oval Office. The system itself is on trial in every presidential election. That is why it is so important to understand and appreciate the intricacies of the process and participate in it. Only an informed and active citizenry can determine whether the nation is being well served by the way we go about choosing our president and have some say in determining who that president will be.

ACKNOWLEDGEMENTS

Few books are written alone, and this one was no exception. For the 2008 edition, I was fortunate to have an excellent editorial and publishing team at Thomson/Wadsworth: Carolyn Merrill, Executive Editor; Joshua Allen, Senior Project Manager; and Charu Khanna, Copy Editor and Project Coordinator.

I would also like to express my thanks to the political scientists who have reviewed one or more of the eight editions of this book: John Bruce, University of Mississippi; Richard L. Cole, University of Texas at Arlington; Anthony Corrado Jr., Colby College; Stephen C. Craig, University of Florida at Gainesville; James W. Davis, Washington University; Gordon Friedman, Southwest Missouri State University; Jay S. Goodman, Wheaton College; Anne Griffin, the Cooper Union; Marjorie Randon Hershey, Indiana University; Hugh L. LeBlanc, George Washington University; Kuo-Wei Lee, Pan-American University; Robert T. Nakamura, State University of New York at Albany; Richard G. Niemi, University of Rochester; Diana Owen, Georgetown University; Charles Prysby, the University of North Carolina at Greensboro; Michael Robinson, Georgetown University; Lester Seligman, University of Illinois; Earl Shaw, Northern Arizona University; John W. Sloan, University of Houston; Priscilla Southwell, University of Oregon at Eugene; William H. Steward, University of Alabama; Edward J. Weissman, Washington College; and Clyde Wilcox, Georgetown University.

Finally, everyone makes personal sacrifices in writing a book. I want to thank my wife, Cheryl, for her patience and understanding and for relieving me on most Saturday mornings to continue my work on the book. I also want to thank my sons, Jared and Jeremy, who respectively allowed West Point and the U.S. Army, and *American Idol* and World Wide Wrestling to fill their lives while I wrote.

Stephen J. Wayne
Georgetown University

ABOUT THE AUTHOR

Stephen J. Wayne is a Professor of Government at Georgetown University. A Washington-based expert on the American presidency, he has authored or edited 10 books, several in multiple editions, and more than 100 articles, chapters, and book reviews. In addition to *The Road to the White House*, he has coauthored *Presidential Leadership* (with George Edwards) and *Conflict and Consensus in American Politics of American Democracy* (with G. Calvin Mackenzie and Richard L. Cole), all published by Thomson/Wadsworth. His most recent books include *Is This Any Way to Run a Democratic Election?*, *Is This Any Way to Run a Democratic Government?*, and *The Election of the Century and What It Tells Us about the Future of American Politics* (with Clyde Wilcox).

A much-quoted source for journalists covering the White House, he frequently appears on television and radio news programs and consults for television documentaries. He has testified before Congress on presidential elections, appeared before both Democratic and Republican advisory committees on the presidential nomination process, directed a presidential transition project for the National Academy of Public Administration, and participated in the 2000 White House transition project conducted by the Presidency Research Group. Professor Wayne lectures widely throughout the United States and abroad on the contemporary presidency and presidential elections.

CONTENTS

THE ELECTORAL ARENA

I CHAPTER | PRESIDENTIAL SELECTION: A HISTORICAL OVERVIEW

INTRODUCTION

The road to the White House is long, circuitous, and bumpy. It contains numerous hazards and potential dead ends. Those who choose to traverse it— and there are many who do so—need considerable skill, perseverance, and luck to be successful. They also need substantial amounts of time, money, and effort. For most candidates, there is no such thing as a free or easy ride to the presidency.

The framers of the Constitution worked for several months on the presidential selection system, and their plan has since undergone a number of constitutional, statutory, and precedent-setting changes. Modified by the development of parties, the expansion of suffrage, the growth of the media, and the revolution in contemporary communications technology, the electoral system has become more open and more participatory but also more contentious, more complex, and much more expensive. It has "turned off" many people who, for a variety of reasons, have chosen not to participate.

This chapter is about that system: why it was created; what it was supposed to do; the compromises that were incorporated in the original plan; its initial operation and the changes that have subsequently affected it; the groups that have benefited from these changes; and the overall effect on the parties, the electorate, and American democracy.

In addressing these questions, I have organized the chapter into four sections. The first discusses the creation of the presidential election process. It explores the motives and intentions of the delegates at Philadelphia and describes the procedures for selecting the president within the context of the constitutional and political issues of that day.

The second section examines the development of nominating systems. It explores the three principal methods that have been used to nominate presidential candidates: partisan congressional caucuses, brokered national conventions, and state primaries and caucuses. It also describes the political forces that helped to shape these modes of nomination and, in the case of the first two, destroyed them.

The third section discusses presidential elections. It focuses on the most controversial ones, those determined by the House of Representatives (1800 and 1824), influenced by Congress (1876), and decided by the Supreme Court (2000). The chapter also examines elections in the twentieth and twenty-first centuries in which the shift of a relatively small number of votes could have changed the outcome (1960, 1968, 1976, and 2004). In doing so, this section highlights the strengths and weaknesses of the Electoral College and assesses its consistency with the principles of a democratic electoral process.

The final section of the chapter examines the current operation of the electoral system. It describes its geographic and demographic biases and how they affect the national character of the presidential elections. The section also discusses the Electoral College's major party orientation and its adverse impact on third-party candidacies.

THE CREATION OF THE ELECTORAL COLLEGE

Of the many issues facing the delegates at the Constitutional Convention of 1787 in Philadelphia, the selection of the president was one of the toughest. Seven times during the course of the convention, the method for choosing the executive was altered.

The framers' difficulty in designing electoral provisions for the president stemmed from their need to guarantee the institution's independence and, at the same time, create a technically sound, politically effective mechanism that would be consistent with a republican form of government, a representative government based on consent, but not a direct democracy in which everyone had an opportunity to participate in the formulation of public policy. They wanted an electoral system that would choose the most qualified person but not necessarily the most popular. There seemed to be no precise model to follow; heredity was out of the question, and a direct popular vote was viewed as impractical and undesirable.

Three methods of election had been proposed. The Virginia Plan, a series of resolutions designed by James Madison and introduced by Governor Edmund Randolph of Virginia, provided for legislative selection. Eight states chose their governors in this fashion at the time. Having Congress choose the president would be practical and politically expedient. Moreover, members of Congress could be expected to exercise a considered judgment. Making a reasoned, unemotional choice was important to the delegates at Philadelphia, since many of them did not consider the average citizen capable of doing so.

The difficulty with legislative selection was the threat it posed to the institution of the presidency. How could the executive's independence be preserved if the election of the president hinged on popularity with Congress, and reelection depended on the legislature's appraisal of the president's performance in office? Only if the president were to serve a long term and not be eligible for reelection, it was thought, could the institution's independence be protected so long as Congress was the electoral body. But ineligibility also posed problems, as it provided little incentive for the president to perform well and denied the country the possibility of reelecting a person whose experience and success in office demonstrated qualifications that were superior to others.

Reflecting on these concerns, Gouverneur Morris urged the removal of the ineligibility clause on the grounds that it tended to destroy the great motive to good behavior, the hope of being rewarded by a reappointment.[1] A majority of the states agreed. Once the ineligibility clause was deleted, however, the term of office had to be shortened to prevent what the framers feared might become unlimited tenure, or in the words of Thomas Jefferson, "an elective monarchy." With a shorter term of office and permanent reeligibility, legislative selection was not nearly as desirable because it could make the president beholden to the legislature.

Moreover, there was still the issue of whether the Congress would vote as one body or as two institutions. The large states favored a joint vote; the small states wanted separate votes by the House and Senate.

Popular election did not generate a great deal of enthusiasm. It was twice rejected in the convention by overwhelming votes. Most of the delegates felt that a direct vote by the people was neither feasible nor wise.[2] Lacking confidence in the public's ability to choose the best qualified candidate, many delegates also believed that the size of the country and the relatively primitive state of its communications and transportation in the eighteenth century precluded a national campaign and election. The geographic expanse was simply too large to allow for proper supervision and control of the election. Sectional distrust and rivalry also contributed to the difficulty of holding a national election.

A third option, indirect election in which popular sentiment could be expressed but would not dictate the outcome, was proposed by James Wilson after he failed to generate support for a direct popular vote. Luther Martin, Gouverneur Morris, and Alexander Hamilton also suggested an indirect popular election through intermediaries. It was not until the debate over legislative selection divided and eventually deadlocked the delegates, however, that election by electors was seriously considered. Proposed initially as a compromise that incorporated previous convention agreements by a Committee on Unfinished Business, the Electoral College design was viewed as acceptable by weary delegates eager to return home and get the Constitution ratified.

The debate over the Electoral College was short and to the point. Viewed as a safe, workable solution to the election dilemma, it was deemed consistent with the constitutional and political features of the new government and resistant to the kind of cabal and corruption that a popular vote might permit. How the electors were to be selected was left to the states to determine. To ensure their independence, the electors could not simultaneously hold a federal government position.

The number of electors was to equal the number of senators and representatives from each state. At a designated time, they would meet, vote, and send the results to Congress, where they would be announced to a joint session by the president of the Senate, the vice president. Each elector had two votes since a president and vice president were to be selected separately. The only limitations on voting were that the electors could not cast both their ballots for inhabitants of their own states[3] nor designate which of the candidates they preferred to be president and which one vice president.[4]

Under the initial plan, the person who received a majority of votes cast by the Electoral College was elected president, and the one with the second highest total, vice president. In the event that no one received a majority, the House of Representatives would choose from among the five candidates with the most electoral votes, with each state delegation casting one vote. If two or more individuals were tied for second, then the Senate would select one as vice president. Both of these provisions were subsequently modified by the Twelfth Amendment to the Constitution.

The electoral system was a dual compromise that incorporated provisions of the Connecticut and North-South compromises. Both dealt with representation. The first provided for one legislative body to be based on population (the House of Representatives) and one in which the states were equally represented (the Senate); the other compromise allowed three-fifth of the slave population to be counted in the determination of a state's popular representation. Both compromises protected slave owners in the South by making it difficult for the representatives of the more populous North to determine public policy on their own.

Designating the number of electors to be equal to a state's congressional delegation gave the larger states an advantage in the initial voting for president; balloting by states in the House, if the Electoral College was not decisive, benefited the smaller states. It was anticipated that this two-step process would occur most of the time since there would probably not be a consensus national leader other than George Washington. In effect, the large states would nominate, much like the state primaries and caucuses do today, and the small states would exercise equal influence in the final election.[5]

The other compromise between the proponents of a federal system and those who favored a more centralized, national government allowed state legislatures to establish the procedures for choosing electors but had a national legislative body, the House of Representatives, decide among the candidates if there was no Electoral College majority. Finally, limiting the vote to the electors was intended to reduce intrigue, fraud, and cabal, fears that were expressed about the undesirability of state-based popular voting.

THE DEVELOPMENT OF NOMINATING SYSTEMS

Although the Constitution prescribed a system for electing a president, it made no reference to the nomination of candidates. Political parties had not emerged prior to the Constitutional Convention. Factions existed, and the framers of the Constitution were concerned about them, but the development of a party system was not anticipated. Rather, it was assumed that electors, whose interests were not tied to the national government, would make an independent judgment and hopefully would choose the person they felt was best suited for the job.

In the first two elections, the system worked as intended. George Washington was the unanimous choice of the electors. There was, however, no consensus on the vice president. The eventual winner, John Adams, benefited from some informal lobbying by prominent individuals prior to the vote.[6]

A more organized effort to agree on candidates for the presidency and vice presidency was undertaken in 1792. Partisan alliances were beginning to develop in Congress. Members of the two principal groups, the Federalists and the Anti-Federalists, met separately to recommend individuals. The Federalists chose Vice President John Adams; the Anti-Federalists picked Governor George Clinton of New York.

With political parties evolving during the 1790s, the selection of electors quickly became a partisan contest. In 1792 and 1796, a majority of the state legislatures chose them directly. Thus, the political group that controlled the legislature also controlled the selection of electors. Appointed for their political views, electors were expected to exercise a partisan judgment. When in 1796 a Pennsylvania elector did not do so, he was accused of faithless behavior. Wrote one critic in a Philadelphia newspaper: "What, do I chuse Samuel Miles to determine for me whether John Adams or Thomas Jefferson shall be President? No! I chuse him to act, not to think."[7]

Washington's decision not to serve a third term forced Federalist and Anti-Federalist members of Congress to recommend the candidates in 1796. Meeting separately, party leaders agreed among themselves on the tickets. The Federalists urged their electors to support John Adams and Thomas Pinckney, while the Anti-Federalists (or Democratic-Republicans, as they began to be called) suggested Thomas Jefferson and Aaron Burr.

Since it was not possible to specify presidential and vice presidential choices on the ballot, Federalist electors, primarily from New England, decided to withhold votes from Pinckney (of South Carolina) to make certain that he did not receive the same number as Adams (of Massachusetts). This strategy enabled Jefferson with sixty-eight votes to finish ahead of Pinckney with fifty-nine, but behind Adams, who had seventy-one. Four years of partisan differences followed between a president who, though he disclaimed a political affiliation, clearly favored the Federalists in appointments, ideology, and policy, and a vice president who was the acknowledged leader of the opposition party.

PARTISAN CONGRESSIONAL CAUCUSES

Beginning in 1800, partisan caucuses, composed of members of Congress, met for the purpose of recommending their party's nominees. The Democratic-Republicans continued to choose candidates in this manner until 1824; the Federalists did so only until 1808. In the final two presidential elections in which the Federalists ran candidates, 1812 and 1816, top party leaders, meeting in secret, decided on the nominees.[8]

"King Caucus," as the partisan congressional caucuses were called, violated the spirit of the Constitution. It effectively provided for members of Congress to pick the nominees. After the decline of the Federalists, the nominees of the Democratic-Republicans, or simply Republicans as they became known, were, in fact, assured of victory—a product of the dominance of that party.

There were competing candidates within the Republican caucus, however. In 1808, Madison prevailed over James Monroe and George Clinton. In 1816, Monroe overcame a strong challenge from William Crawford. In both cases, the electors united behind the successful nominee. In 1820, however, they did not. Disparate elements within the party selected their own candidates.

Although the caucus was the principal mode of candidate selection during the first part of the nineteenth century, it was never formally institutionalized. How the meetings were called, who called them, and when they were held varied from election to election, as did attendance. A sizable number of representatives chose not to participate at all. Some stayed away on principle; others did so because of the particular choices they would have to make. In 1816, less than half of the Republican members of Congress were at their party's caucus. In 1820, only 20 percent attended, and the caucus had to adjourn without formally supporting President Monroe and Vice President Daniel D. Tompkins for reelection. In 1824, almost three-fourths of the members boycotted the session.

The 1824 caucus did nominate candidates. But with representatives from only four states constituting two-thirds of those attending, the nominee, William Crawford, failed to receive unified party support. Other candidates were nominated by state legislatures and conventions, and the electoral vote was divided. Since no candidate obtained a majority, the House of Representatives had to make the final decision. John Quincy Adams was selected on the first ballot. He received the votes of thirteen of the twenty-four state delegations.

The caucus was never resumed. In the end, it was a victim of the Federalist Party's decline as a viable political force, the decentralization of political power, and Andrew Jackson's stern opposition to this method of nomination. As the Republican Party grew from being the majority to the only party, factions developed within it, the two principal ones being the National Republicans and the Democratic Republicans. In the absence of a strong opposition, there was little to hold these factions together. By 1830, they had split into two separate groups, one supporting and one opposing President Jackson.

Political leadership was changing as well. A relatively small number of individuals had dominated national politics for the first three decades following the ratification of the Constitution. Their common experience in the Revolutionary War, the Constitutional Convention, and the early government produced personal contacts, political influence, and public respect that contributed to their ability to agree on candidates and to generate public support for them.[9]

Those who followed them in office had neither the tradition nor the national orientation in which to affect the presidential selection process nor the national recognition to build support across the country for their candidates. Most of this new generation of political leaders owed their prominence and political influence to states and regions, and their loyalties reflected these bases of support.

The growth of party organizations at the state and local level affected the nomination system. In 1820 and 1824, it evolved into a decentralized mode of selection with state legislatures, caucuses, and conventions nominating their own candidates. Support was also mobilized on regional levels.

Whereas the congressional caucus had become unrepresentative, state-based nominations suffered from precisely the opposite problem. They were too sensitive to sectional interests and produced too many candidates. Unifying diverse elements behind a single national ticket proved extremely difficult, although Jackson was successful in doing so in 1828. Nonetheless, a system that was more broadly based than the old caucus and could provide a more decisive and mobilizing mechanism was needed. National nominating conventions filled the void.

NATIONAL NOMINATING CONVENTIONS

The first such convention was held in 1831 by the Anti-Masons. A small but relatively active third party, it had virtually no congressional representation. Unable to utilize a caucus, the party turned instead to a general meeting, which was held in a saloon in Baltimore, with 116 delegates from thirteen states attending. These delegates decided on the nominees as well as on an address to the people that contained the party's position on the dominant issues of the day.

Three months later, a second convention was held in the same saloon by opponents of President Jackson. The National Republicans (or Whigs, as they later became known) also nominated candidates and agreed on a platform critical of the Jackson administration.

The following year, the Democratic-Republicans (or Democrats, as they were later called) also met in Baltimore. The impetus for their convention was

Jackson's desire to demonstrate popular support for his presidency as well as to ensure the selection of Martin Van Buren as his running mate. In 1836, Jackson resorted to another convention—this time to handpick Van Buren as his successor.

The Whigs did not hold a convention in 1836. Believing that they would have more success in the House of Representatives than in the nation as a whole, they ran three regional candidates, nominated by the states, who competed against Van Buren in their areas of strength. The plan, however, failed to deny Van Buren an electoral majority. He ended up with 170 votes compared with a total of 124 for the other principal contenders.

Thereafter, the Democrats and their opponents, first the Whigs and then their Republican successors, held nominating conventions to select their candidates. The early conventions were informal and rowdy by contemporary standards, but they also set the precedents for later meetings.

The delegates decided on the procedures for conducting the convention, developed policy statements (addresses to the people), and chose nominees. Rules for apportioning the number of delegates were established before the meetings were held. Generally speaking, states were accorded as many votes as their congressional representation merited, regardless of the number of actual participants. The way in which the delegates were chosen, however, was left up to the states. Local and state conventions, caucuses, or even committees chose the delegates.

Public participation was minimal. Party leaders designated the delegates and made the deals. In time, it became clear that successful candidates owed their selection to the heads of the powerful state organizations, not to their own political prominence and organizational support. But the price they had to pay, when calculated in terms of patronage and other political payoffs, was often quite high.

Nineteenth-century conventions served a number of purposes. They provided a forum for party leaders, particularly at the state level. They constituted a mechanism by which agreements could be negotiated and support mobilized. By brokering interests, conventions helped unite the disparate elements within a party, thereby converting an organization of state parties into a national coalition for the purpose of conducting a presidential campaign.

Much of the bartering was conducted behind closed doors. Actions on the convention floor often had little to do with the wheeling and dealing that occurred in the smaller "smoke-filled" rooms. Since there was little public preconvention activity, many ballots were often necessary to reach the number that was required to win the party's nomination, usually two-thirds of the delegates.

The nominating system buttressed the position of individual state party leaders, but it did so at the expense of rank-and-file participation. The influence of the state leaders depended on their ability to deliver votes, which in turn required that the delegates not exercise independent judgment. To guarantee their loyalty, the bosses controlled their selection.

POPULAR PRIMARIES AND CAUCUSES

Demands for reform began to be heard at the beginning of the twentieth century. The Progressive movement, led by Robert La Follette of Wisconsin and Hiram Johnson of California, aimed to break the power of state bosses and their machines through the direct election of convention delegates or, alternatively, through the expression of a popular choice by the electorate.

Florida became the first state to provide its political parties with such an option. In 1904, the Democrats took advantage of it and held a statewide vote for convention delegates. One year later, Wisconsin enacted a law for the direct election of delegates to nominating conventions. Others followed suit. By 1912, fifteen states provided for some type of primary election. Oregon was the first to permit a preference vote for the candidates themselves.

The year 1912 was also the first in which a candidate sought to use primaries as a way to obtain the nomination. With almost 42 percent of the Republican delegates selected in primaries, former President Theodore Roosevelt challenged incumbent William Howard Taft. Roosevelt won nine primaries to Taft's one, yet lost the nomination. (See Table 1.1.) Taft's support among regular party leaders who delivered their delegations and controlled the convention was sufficient to win renomination. He received one-third of his support from southern delegations, although the Republican Party had won only a small percentage of the southern vote in the previous election.

Partially in reaction to the unrepresentative, "boss-dominated" convention of 1912, additional states adopted primaries. By 1916, more than half of them held a Republican or Democratic contest. Although a majority of the delegates in that year were chosen by some type of primary, most of them were not bound to support specific candidates. As a consequence, the primary vote did not control the outcome of the conventions.

The movement toward popular participation was short-lived, however. Following World War I, the number of primaries declined. State party leaders, who saw primaries as a threat to their own influence, argued against them on three grounds: they were expensive; they did not attract many voters; and major candidates tended to avoid them. Moreover, primaries frequently encouraged factionalism, thereby weakening a party's organization.

In response to this criticism, the reformers who supported primaries could not claim that their principal goal, rank-and-file control over the selection of party nominees, had been achieved. Public involvement was disappointing. Primaries rarely attracted more than 50 percent of those who voted in the general election, and usually much less. The minority party, in particular, suffered from low turnout for an obvious reason—its candidates stood little chance of winning the general election. In some states, rank-and-file influence was further diluted by the participation of independents.

As a consequence of these factors, some states that had enacted new primary laws reverted to their former method of selection. Others made their primaries advisory rather than mandatory. Fewer convention delegates were elected in them. By 1936, only fourteen states held Democratic primaries, and

TABLE 1.1 | THE NUMBER OF PRESIDENTIAL PRIMARIES AND PERCENTAGE OF CONVENTION DELEGATES FROM PRIMARY STATES, BY PARTY, 1912–2004

Year	Democratic		Republican	
	Number of State Primaries	Percentage of Delegates from Primary States	Number of State Primaries	Percentage of Delegates from Primary States
1912	12	32.9%	13	41.7%
1916	20	53.5	20	58.9
1920	16	44.6	20	57.8
1924	14	35.5	17	45.3
1928	16	42.2	15	44.9
1932	16	40.0	14	37.7
1936	14	36.5	12	37.5
1940	13	35.8	13	38.8
1944	14	36.7	13	38.7
1948	14	36.3	12	36.0
1952	16	38.7	13	39.0
1956	19	42.7	19	44.8
1960	16	38.3	15	38.6
1964	16	45.7	16	45.6
1968	15	40.2	15	38.1
1972	21	65.3	20	56.8
1976	27	76.0	26	71.0
1980	34	71.8	34	76.0
1984	29	52.4	25	71.0
1988	36	66.6	36	76.9
2004	38	83.2	27[a]	56.9

[a]Five Republican primaries with a total of 309 delegates were cancelled because only George W. Bush qualified as a candidate.

Source: Harold W. Stanley and Richard G. Niemi, *Vital Statistics on American Politics, 2005–2006.* Washington D.C.: Congressional Quarterly, 2006, Table 1–23, p. 66.

twelve held Republican ones. Less than 40 percent of the delegates to each convention that year were chosen in this manner. For the next twenty years, the number of primaries and the percentage of delegates hovered around this level.

Theodore Roosevelt's failure in 1912 and the decline in primaries thereafter made them at best an auxiliary route to the nomination. Although some presidential aspirants became embroiled in primaries, none who depended on them won. In 1920, a spirited contest between three Republicans (General Leonard Wood, Governor Frank Lowden of Illinois, and Senator Hiram Johnson) failed to produce a convention majority for any of these candidates and resulted in party leaders choosing Warren Harding as the standard-bearer. Similarly, in 1952, Senator Estes Kefauver, who chaired the highly publicized and televised Senate hearings on organized crime, entered thirteen of seventeen presidential primaries, won twelve of them, and became the most popular Democratic contender, but failed to win his party's nomination.

The reason Kefauver could not parlay his primary victories into a convention victory was that a majority of the delegates were not selected in primaries. Of those who were, many were chosen separately from the presidential preference vote. Kefauver did not contest these separate delegate elections. As a consequence, he obtained only 50 percent of the delegates in states in which he actually won the presidential preference vote. Moreover, the fact that most of his wins occurred against little or no opposition undercut Kefauver's claim to being the most popular and electable Democrat. He had avoided primaries in four states in which he feared that he might either lose or do poorly.

Not only were primaries not considered to be an essential road to the nomination, but running in too many of them was interpreted as a sign of weakness, not strength. It indicated a lack of national recognition, a failure to obtain the support of party leaders, or both. For these reasons, leading candidates tended to choose their primaries carefully, and the primaries, in turn, tended to reinforce the position of the leading candidates.

Those who entered primaries did so mainly to test their popularity rather than to win convention votes. Dwight D. Eisenhower in 1952, John F. Kennedy in 1960, and Richard M. Nixon in 1968 had to demonstrate that being a general, a Catholic, or a once-defeated presidential candidate would not be fatal to their chances. In other words, they needed to prove they could win the general election if nominated by their party.

With the possible exception of John Kennedy's victories in West Virginia and Wisconsin, primaries were neither crucial nor decisive for winning the nomination until the 1970s. When there was a provisional consensus within the party, primaries helped confirm it; when there was not, primaries could not produce it.[10] In short, they had little to do with whether the party was unified or divided at the time of the convention.

Primary results tended to be self-fulfilling in the sense that they confirmed the front-runner's status. Between 1936 and 1968, the preconvention leader, the candidate who was ahead in the Gallup Poll before the first primary, won the nomination seventeen out of nineteen times. The only exceptions were Thomas E. Dewey in 1940, defeated by Wendell Willkie, and Kefauver who lost his race for the nomination to Adlai Stevenson in 1952. Willkie, however, had become the leader in public opinion by the time the Republican convention met. Even when leading candidates lost a primary, they had time to recoup. Dewey and Stevenson, defeated in early primaries in 1948 and 1956, respectively, went on to reestablish their credibility as front-runners by winning later primaries.

This situation in which the primaries were not the essential route to the nomination changed dramatically after 1968. Largely as a consequence of the tumultuous Democratic convention of that year, in which the party's nominees and platform were allegedly dictated by party "bosses," demands for a larger voice for rank-and-file partisans increased. In reaction to these demands, the Democratic Party began to look into the matter of delegate selection. The party enacted a series of reforms designed to ensure broader representation at its convention. To avoid challenges to their delegations, a number of states that had used caucus and convention systems changed to primaries. As Table 1.1 indicates, the number of primaries began to increase as did the percentage of convention delegates chosen from them.

New finance laws, which provided for government subsidies for pre-convention campaigning, and increased media coverage, particularly by television, also added to the incentive to enter primaries. By 1972, primaries had become decisive. In that year, Senator Edmund Muskie, the leading Democratic contender at the beginning of the process, was forced to withdraw after doing poorly in the early contests. In 1976, President Gerald Ford came close to being the first incumbent president since Chester A. Arthur in 1884 to be denied his party's nomination because of a primary challenge by Ronald Reagan. In 1980, President Jimmy Carter was also challenged for renomination by Senator Edward Kennedy, as was George H.W. Bush by Pat Buchanan in 1992. Bill Clinton and George W. Bush were not challenged for renomination, but nonetheless, both raised millions to ensure that a credible candidate would not oppose them.

Since the 1970s, primaries have revolutionized the presidential nomination process. They have been used to build popularity rather than simply reflect it. Challengers can no longer hope to succeed without entering them; incumbents can no longer ignore them.

The impact of primaries has been significant, affecting the strategies and tactics of the candidates, the composition and behavior of the convention delegates, and the decision-making process at the national conventions. The contests for the nomination have shifted power within the parties. They have enlarged the selection zone of potential nominees. They have also made governing more difficult. Each of these developments will be discussed in subsequent chapters.

THE EVOLUTION OF THE GENERAL ELECTION

The general election has changed as well. The Electoral College no longer operates in the manner in which it was designed. It now has a partisan coloration. There is greater opportunity for the general public to participate, but the campaign is not geared to obtaining the most popular votes. Although the system bears a resemblance to its past form, it has become more subject to democratic influences but continues to contain many electoral biases.

The electoral system for president and vice president was one of the few innovative features of the Constitution. It had no immediate precedent, although it bore some relationship to the way the state of Maryland selected its senators. In essence, it was designed by the framers, not synthesized from British and American experience, and it is one aspect of the constitutional system that has rarely worked as intended.

Initially, the method by which the states chose their electors varied. Some provided for direct election in a statewide vote. Others had the legislatures do the choosing. Two states used a combination of popular and legislative selection.

As political parties emerged at the beginning of the nineteenth century, state legislatures maneuvered the selection process to benefit the party in power. This maneuvering resulted in the selection of more cohesive groups of electors who shared similar partisan views. Gradually, the trend evolved into a winner-take-all system, with most electors chosen on a statewide basis by popular vote. South Carolina was the last state to move to popular selection, doing so only after the Civil War.

PARTISAN ELECTORS

The development of the party system changed the character of the Electoral College. Only in the first two elections, when Washington was the unanimous choice, did the electors exercise a nonpartisan and presumably independent judgment. Within ten years from the time the federal government began to operate, electors quickly became the captives of their party and were expected to vote for its candidates. The outcome of the election of 1800 vividly illustrates this new pattern of partisan voting.

The Federalist Party supported President John Adams of Massachusetts and Charles C. Pinckney of South Carolina. Democratic-Republicans, who had emerged to oppose the Federalists' policies, backed Thomas Jefferson of Virginia and Aaron Burr of New York. The Democratic-Republican candidates won, but, unexpectedly, Jefferson and Burr received the same number of votes. All electors who had cast ballots for Jefferson also cast them for Burr. Since it was not possible in those days to differentiate the candidates for the presidency and vice presidency on the ballot, the results had to be considered a tie, though Jefferson was clearly his party's choice for president. Under the terms of the Constitution, the House of Representatives, voting by state, had to choose the winner.

CONGRESSIONAL DECISIONS

On February 11, 1801, after the results of the Electoral College vote were announced by the vice president, who happened to be Jefferson, a Federalist controlled House convened to resolve the dilemma. Since the winners of the 1800 election did not take office until March 4, 1801, representatives from a "lame-duck" Congress would have to choose the next president.[11] A majority of Federalists supported Burr, whom they regarded as the more pragmatic politician, a person with whom they could deal. Jefferson, on the other hand, was perceived as a dangerous, uncompromising radical by many Federalists. Alexander Hamilton, however, was outspoken in his opposition to Burr, a political rival from New York, whom Hamilton regarded as "the most unfit man in the United States for the office of President."[12]

On the first ballot taken on February 11, Burr received a majority of the total votes, but Jefferson won the support of more state delegations.[13] Eight states voted for Jefferson, six backed Burr, and two were evenly divided. This vote left Jefferson one short of the needed majority. The House took nineteen ballots on its first day of deliberations, and a total of thirty-six before it finally elected Jefferson. Had Burr promised to be a Federalist president, it is conceivable that he could have won.

The first amendment to reform voting procedures in the Electoral College was enacted by the new Congress, controlled by Jefferson's party, in 1803. It was accepted by three-fourths of the states in 1804. This amendment to the Constitution, the twelfth, provided for separate voting for president and vice president. It also refined the selection procedures in the event that the president or vice president did not receive a majority of the electoral vote. The House of Representatives, still voting by state delegation, was to choose from among the three presidential candidates with the most electoral votes, and the Senate, voting by individual Senators, was to choose from the top two vice presidential candidates. If the House could not make a decision by March 4, the amendment provided for the new vice president to assume the presidency until such time as the House could render a judgment.

The next nondecisive presidential vote did not occur until 1824. That year, four people received electoral votes for president: Andrew Jackson (ninety-nine votes), John Quincy Adams (eighty-four), William Crawford (forty-one), and Henry Clay (thirty-seven). According to the Twelfth Amendment, the House of Representatives had to decide from among the top three, since no one had a majority. Eliminated from the contest was Henry Clay, who happened to be Speaker of the House. Clay threw his support to Adams, who won. It was alleged that Clay did so in exchange for appointment as secretary of state, a charge that Clay vigorously denied. After Adams became president, however, he nominated Clay for secretary of state, a position Clay readily accepted.[14]

Jackson was the winner of the popular vote in 1824. In eighteen of the twenty-four states that chose electors by popular vote that year, he received 192,933 votes compared with 115,696 for Adams, 47,136 for Clay, and 46,979 for Crawford. Adams, however, had the backing of more state delegations. A Massachusetts resident, he enjoyed the support of the six New England states, and with Clay's help, the representatives of six others backed his candidacy. The votes of thirteen states, however, were needed for a majority. New York seemed to be the pivotal state and Stephen Van Rensselaer, a Revolutionary War general, the swing representative. On the morning of the vote, Speaker Clay and Representative Daniel Webster tried to persuade Van Rensselaer to vote for Adams. It was said that they were unsuccessful.[15] As the voting began, Van Rensselaer bowed his head as if in prayer. On the floor he saw a piece of paper with "Adams" written on it. Interpreting this as a sign from the Almighty, he dropped the paper in the box. New York went for Adams by 1 vote, providing him with the barest majority.[16]

Jackson, outraged at the turn of events, urged the abolition of the Electoral College. His claim of a popular mandate, however, was open to question. The most populous state at the time, New York, did not permit its electorate to participate in the selection of electors. Rather, the New York state legislature made the decision. Moreover, in three of the states in which Jackson won the electoral vote but lost in the House of Representatives, he had fewer popular votes than Adams.[17]

Opposition to the system mounted, however, and a gradual democratization of the process occurred. More states began to choose their electors directly by popular vote. In 1800, ten of the fifteen used legislative selection. By 1832, only South Carolina retained this practice.

The trend was also toward statewide election of an entire slate of electors. States that had chosen their electors within legislative districts converted to a winner-take-all system to maximize their voting power in the Electoral College. This change, in turn, created the possibility that there could be a disparity between the popular and electoral vote. A candidate could be elected by winning the popular vote in the big states but losing most of the small states or vice versa.

The next disputed election did not occur until 1876. In that election, Democrat Samuel J. Tilden received the most votes. He had 250,000 more popular votes and 19 more electoral votes than his Republican rival, Rutherford B. Hayes. Nonetheless, Tilden fell 1 vote short of a majority in the Electoral College. Twenty electoral votes were in dispute. Dual election returns were received from Florida (4 votes), Louisiana (8 votes), and South Carolina (7 votes). Charges of fraud and voting irregularities were made by both parties. The Republicans, who controlled the three state legislatures, contended that Democrats had forcibly prevented newly freed slaves from voting. The Democrats, on the other hand, alleged that many nonresidents participated as did people who were not registered to vote. The other disputed electoral vote occurred in the state of Oregon. One Republican elector was challenged on the grounds that he held another federal position (assistant postmaster) at the time he was chosen and thus was ineligible to be an elector.

Three days before the Electoral College vote was to be officially counted, Congress established a commission to examine and try to resolve the dispute. The electoral commission was to consist of fifteen members: ten from Congress (five Republicans and five Democrats) and five from the Supreme Court. Four of the Supreme Court justices were designated by the act (two Republicans and two Democrats), and they were to choose a fifth justice. David Davis, a political independent, was expected to be selected, but on the day the commission was created, Davis was appointed by the Illinois legislature to the U.S. Senate. The Supreme Court justices then picked Joseph Bradley, an independent Republican from New Jersey. Bradley sided with his party on every issue. By a strictly partisan vote, the commission validated the credentials of all the Republican electors, thereby giving Hayes a one-vote margin of victory in the Electoral College.[18]

Prior to the election of 2000, the only other one in which the winner of the popular vote was beaten in an undisputed Electoral College vote occurred in 1888. Democrat Grover Cleveland had a plurality of 95,096 popular votes, but only 168 electoral votes compared with 233 for Republican Benjamin Harrison. Cleveland's losses in Indiana by about 3,000 votes and New York by about 15,000 led to his defeat.

JUDICIAL DETERMINATION

The 2000 election was different. Not only was the popular vote very close, but the electoral vote was close as well. Al Gore was ahead in twenty states plus the District of Columbia, which had a total of 267 electoral votes. George W. Bush led in twenty-nine states with a total of 238 electoral votes. One state, Florida, was in dispute. Out of more than 5.9 million votes cast in that state, 537 votes separated the two candidates. Both sides alleged procedural irregularities, voter eligibility issues, and ballot counting errors.

The Issues in the 2000 Florida Vote

Four legal issues marred the Florida election: voter confusion over the design of the ballot in one county, disagreement over eligible voters and absentee ballots in several others, tabulation problems in counties that used punch-card ballots, and the date when the official results had to be certified by the secretary of state.

Voter confusion stemmed from a "butterfly ballot" used in Palm Beach County where many retirees live. Designed by a Democratic campaign official, the ballot was intended to help senior citizens read the names of the candidates more clearly by using larger type. To fit all the names on a single punch card, however, two columns had to be used with the punch holes for voting, or "chads" as they are called, between them. Although Democrats Al Gore and Joe Lieberman were listed second on the left-hand column, their chad was positioned third, after the chad of the candidates on the right-hand column, Pat Buchanan and Ezola Foster of the Reform Party. (See Figure 1.1.) Some voters, who claimed that they intended to vote for the Democratic candidates, punched out the second rather than the third chad, which registered as a vote for Buchanan. Others, in confusion, pushed out both the second and third chads, automatically voiding their ballots.[19]

Aggrieved Democrats in the county immediately filed a lawsuit to contest the election and demand a new vote. A Florida state court, however, rejected their request, effectively terminating the revote option.

A second issue concerned ballots that were not properly included in the machine count. Many counties in Florida still used a punch-card system of voting in which chads, a small perforated box on the card, must be removed with a specially designed instrument for the vote to be properly cast. The holes

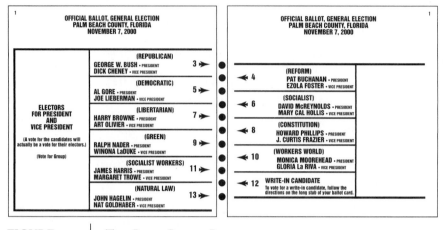

FIGURE 1.1   THE PALM BEACH BALLOT

Source: WPBF Eyewitness News 25, West Palm Beach, FL.

in the card are then tabulated by a machine. However, if a chad is not completely removed, the vote may not be counted. The Gore campaign alleged that thousands of presidential votes in three Democratic counties—Miami-Dade, Broward, and Palm Beach—were not counted because part or all of a chad was still attached to the ballot. In other words, voters had not completely punched through the card. Democrats appealed to county officials for a hand count of these ballots.

One county, Palm Beach, began such a count; another, Miami-Dade, initiated a sample count to see whether a hand count was merited; the third, Broward, initially chose not to recount at all. Gore's representatives put pressure on the reluctant counties to proceed with a hand count of these uncounted ballots while Bush's attorneys went to federal court to stop it, arguing that a selective hand count in some counties was unfair to people in other counties.

Before the courts had rendered a judgment, however, Florida's secretary of state, a Republican appointee, certified the original county vote as the official one to which only absentee ballots, postmarked no later than election day and received by the counties within one week of the election, could be added. The secretary of state's certification prompted Gore's legal team to go to state court to force the secretary to accept hand-counted votes and an amended vote total submitted after the certification.

A Florida circuit court ruled that the secretary had discretion to accept or reject additional vote counts submitted by counties as long as she did not exercise that discretion arbitrarily. The secretary then asked the counties to justify why they wished to amend their original submission with an additional hand count of some votes. After they did so, however, she rejected their arguments, thereby forcing Gore's attorneys to take the entire matter to the Florida Supreme Court.

In an extraordinary session, televised across the country, lawyers for both sides debated the hand count and vote deadline issues within the context of state and federal law and the U.S. Constitution. The Gore side claimed that the only way to ensure a "full, fair, and accurate" vote that represented the will of the Florida electorate would be to tabulate the disputed ballots by hand. But Bush's legal counsel contended that a hand count was blatantly unfair to those who had voted in accordance with the established rules and procedures of the state. Besides, they contended, extending the deadline for certified results violated an 1887 federal law that requires states to choose their electors by laws that are enacted *prior* to Election Day.

The Florida Supreme Court, consisting of eight judges, all but one of whom were appointed by Democratic governors, sided with Gore and proceeded to give the counties an additional six days to submit a revised vote that included hand-counted ballots. Bush's lawyers appealed the Florida Supreme Court's decision to the U.S. Supreme Court.

What followed was a frantic hand count in two counties while a third, Miami-Dade, decided not to go ahead with one, in part because officials believed that they could not do so within the time frame established by the court.[20]

Meanwhile, in another part of the state, Democrats filed suit to exclude all absentee ballots from certain counties because Republicans had been given an opportunity to add required voter registration numbers to the forms, omitted erroneously by a glitch in the software program that printed the request forms. Democrats had not been given a chance to add the numbers. However, a circuit judge ruled against the Democrats' claim.

On Monday, December 4, nearly a month after the presidential election, the U.S. Supreme Court vacated the Florida Supreme Court's verdict that had extended the deadline for hand-counted ballots in the three Florida counties on the grounds that its legal basis for this decision was unclear. The Court remanded the case back to the Florida Supreme Court for clarification and judgment.

Later in the day, a Florida state court judge dismissed Gore's claims for an additional hand count of thousands of ballots from Palm Beach and Miami-Dade counties that had registered no presidential preference as well as the hand-counted ballots that had been submitted after the court-imposed deadline.[21] The judge also refused to overturn the certification of Florida's electoral vote for Bush. In a last-ditch effort to salvage a Florida victory, Gore appealed this state court judgment to the Florida Supreme Court.

Thus, the state supreme court was faced with two issues: One concerned its decision, and the legal basis on which it was predicated, for extending the state certification deadline for those counties that chose to submit an amended vote based on disputed hand-counted ballots; the other was Gore's appeal to overturn the lower court's decision that additional hand counts and time to certify results were not merited. The Supreme Court of Florida again sided with Gore, ordering an immediate recount of ballots that had not been included in the machine tabulation in *all* Florida counties. Bush's lawyers immediately appealed that decision to the U.S. Supreme Court.

The final legal maneuvering ended in the U.S. Supreme Court. After agreeing to hear the appeal, the Court stopped the recount of the disputed ballots, pending its judgment on the matter. On December 11, 2000, one day before Florida law required the designation of its electors, the Court heard oral arguments in *Bush v. Gore*. Its decision, announced the next evening, reversed the Florida Supreme Court's judgment that ordered the hand count to be resumed. The Supreme Court stated that the absence of a single standard to be used throughout the state by election officials violated the Fourteenth Amendment, which requires states to provide all their residents with equal protection under the laws. A majority of the U.S. Supreme Court went on to conclude that there was not sufficient time, given the state legislature's intent to designate Florida's electors by December 12, to establish such a standard. Hence, the certified vote that had Bush leading by 537 was final.

Four justices dissented from the finding that time had run out on the Florida Supreme Court. Two of these justices believed that the deadline for the designation of electors specified by U.S. law, the first Monday following the second Wednesday in December, the 18th in 2000, took precedence over the state legislature's date of December 12th and thus provided sufficient time for the state Supreme Court to establish a single statewide standard for recounting the votes. The two other dissenters felt that the Florida Supreme Court had acted properly, that the vote count was legal, and that it should not have been halted by the U.S. Supreme Court.

The Consequences of the Florida Voting Controversy
The Supreme Court had decided in favor of Bush. Gore had no viable options; he had exhausted all of his legal remedies. On December 13, 2000, he conceded the election even though he was the popular vote winner. Bush began his transition to the presidency.

But the election had more consequences than who was to be the president. Despite the strong emotions, largely along partisan lines, that the controversy engendered, the electoral system survived the challenge. Bush's victory was greeted with a mixed public reaction. According to a Gallup Poll conducted in December 2000, almost half the population believed that he won the election fair and square compared to 18 percent who thought he had stolen it and 32 percent who said that he won it on a technicality.[22]

Even in light of the Florida controversy, a majority of people still believed the electoral system to be fair, although they also believed it needed a major or complete overhaul. One year later, people voiced more support for the equity of the system and less desire to overhaul it.[23] In the aftermath of his first few weeks in office, President Bush received a positive job approval rating from 57 percent of the population despite the Florida debacle.

Election law changes occurred on both state and national levels. Florida enacted electoral reforms in the aftermath of the election to prevent a repetition of the problems that occurred in 2000. Its new law provided more training for election workers, more accurate registration records, and provisional voting for those who claimed to be registered but whose names did not appear on county and precinct voting lists. The state also allocated money for counties to replace their antiquated punch-card machines with more updated scanning equipment and voting machines.

National electoral reforms, along the lines of the Florida law, were also passed by Congress in 2002. The Help America Vote Act provided almost $4 billion in federal funds to the states to consolidate and computerize their voter registration lists by January 2006, a goal which nineteen states failed to meet. The money was also intended to buy more modern, touch screen voting machines and make voting places more accessible to the disabled and ballots more understandable to non-English speakers. The law required states to allow provisional voting for people who believe that they were properly registered but who were not listed as registered at the precinct at which they voted.

Although registration problems, late absentee ballots, and long lines to vote were still apparent in the 2004 election, no controversy of the magnitude of the 2000 Florida election marred the outcome. President Bush was reelected by a margin of 3.5 million popular votes and 35 more electoral votes. However, the shift of about 117,000 votes in Ohio, out of 5.6 million cast in that state, would have changed the outcome of the election in the Electoral College and resulted in a victory for Democrat John Kerry. Similarly, if 20,417 voters in Iowa, New Mexico, and Nevada changed their presidential vote from Republican to Democratic, Bush would not have had an Electoral College majority, and the House of Representatives, controlled by the Republicans, would have had to choose the president.

OTHER CLOSE ELECTIONS

There have been other close elections in which the vote choice of a relatively small number of people would have altered the results. In 1860, a shift of 25,000 in New York from Abraham Lincoln to Stephen Douglas would have denied Lincoln a majority in the Electoral College. A change of less than 30,000 in three states in 1892 would have given Benjamin Harrison another victory over Cleveland. In 1916, Charles Evans Hughes needed only 3,807 more votes in California to have beaten Woodrow Wilson. Similarly, Thomas E. Dewey could have denied Harry S Truman a majority in the Electoral College with 12,487 more California votes in 1948. A change in the votes of less than 9,000 people in Illinois and Missouri in 1960 would have meant that John F. Kennedy would have lacked an Electoral College majority. In 1968, a shift of only 55,000 votes from Richard M. Nixon to Hubert H. Humphrey in three states would have thrown the election into the House of Representatives, which at that time was controlled by the Democrats. In 1976, a shift of only 3,687 in Hawaii and 5,559 in Ohio would have cost Jimmy Carter the election.[24]

Not only could the results of these elections have been affected by very small shifts in voter preferences, but in 1948, 1960, 1968, and 1992, there was the added possibility that the Electoral College vote would not be decisive. In each of these elections, third-party or independent candidates threatened to secure enough votes to prevent either majority party candidate from gaining a majority. In 1948, Henry Wallace (Progressive Party) and Strom Thurman (States' Rights Party) received almost 5 percent of the total popular vote, and Thurmond won 39 electoral votes. In 1960, fourteen unpledged electors were chosen in Alabama and Mississippi. In 1968, George Wallace of Alabama, running on the American Independent Party label, received almost 10 million popular votes and 46 electoral votes, while in 1992, H. Ross Perot received 19.7 million popular votes (almost 19 percent of the total) but none in the Electoral College. Four years later, he got 8.1 million popular votes but again, no electoral votes. Ralph Nader received less than 3 percent of the popular vote in 2000, but his 97,488 votes in Florida undoubtedly cost Gore that state and an overall election victory.

It is clear that close competition between the two major parties combined with a strong third party or independent candidate provides the Electoral College with its most difficult test.

THE POLITICS OF ELECTORAL COLLEGE VOTING

The presidential campaign and election is shaped by the Electoral College. The strategies the candidates pursue, the resources they utilize, and the states in which they place their major efforts are all calculated on the basis of Electoral College politics, not the popular vote.

The Electoral College is not neutral. No system of election can be. The way votes are aggregated does make a difference. It benefits some of the electorate at the expense of others. The Electoral College usually works to the advantage of the candidate who wins the most popular votes. More often than not, it tends to exaggerate that candidate's margin of victory. Bill Clinton received only 43 percent of the popular vote in 1992 but 69 percent of the electoral vote; in 1996, he received 49 percent of the popular vote, 54.6 percent of the two-party vote, and 70.4 percent of the electoral vote. Similarly in 1968, Richard Nixon won only 43.4 percent of the popular vote but 56 percent of the electoral vote. In 1980, Ronald Reagan received 51 percent of the popular vote but a whopping 91 percent of the electoral vote. Even in the very close elections of 2000 and 2004, Bush received a higher percentage of the electoral vote, 50.4 (2000) and 53.2 (2004), than the popular vote, 48 (2000) and 50.7 (2004).

Why does the Electoral College usually enhance the margin of the popular vote winner? The reason has to do with the winner-take-all system of voting that has developed in most states. In almost every instance, the presidential and vice presidential candidates who receive a plurality of the popular vote within the state get all its electoral votes.[25] This translates into a larger percentage of the Electoral College vote than it would with a direct popular vote.[26] According to one study of presidential elections from 1924 to 1992, the plurality winner who received more than 53.5 percent of the two-party vote received over 75 percent of the electoral vote.[27]

Advocates of the system see this enlarged Electoral College vote as an advantage for the new or reelected president. They claim that it increases the president's mandate for governing as well as the coalition of supporters on whom the president can depend. Most states also perceive a benefit from casting their votes as a unit. They believe that it enhances their political clout. In 2004, voters in Colorado soundly defeated a constitutional amendment that would have allocated their state's electoral vote in proportion to the popular vote that the candidates received. Such an amendment would have decreased that state's importance to the candidates and the state's impact on the Electoral College vote.

The large states, theoretically, gain more influence in the Electoral College by winner-take-all voting. The very smallest states do so as well because they receive a minimum of three electoral votes regardless of the size of their population. As a consequence, their citizens have greater voting power than they would have in a direct election system. To illustrate, if Wyoming's population of approximately 506,529 in 2004 were divided by its three electoral votes, there would be one elector for every 168,843 people. Dividing California's estimated 2004 population of 35,893,799 by its fifty-five electoral votes yields one elector for every 653,615 persons.[28] Medium-sized states are comparatively disadvantaged.[29]

But the advantage that the largest and smallest states reap from the current Electoral College system pales by comparison to the benefit that the most competitive states receive regardless of size. Since the advent of frequent public opinion polling during the election period, candidates have tended to concentrate their time, efforts, and resources in those states that seemed to be up-for-grabs— at least, according to the polls. Noncompetitive states, large or small, see little of the presidential campaign. The candidates rarely visit them; they spend little, if any, money in them; run few, if any, political advertisements in their major media markets; and mount little, if any, grass-roots efforts. They are essentially ignored because their Electoral College vote is predictable.

And the number of competitive states at the presidential level has been declining. In 1960, about half the states were deemed competitive; either of the major party candidates had a realistic chance to win them; in 2000 and 2004, only about one-third of the states were seen as competitive at the beginning of the general election campaign and less than one-fifth at the end. In short, the one national election in the United States has been reduced to a contest fought in a decreasing number of states.

Not only does the Electoral College in practice give disproportionate influence to the most competitive states, but it also advantages the groups that live in them. Many of the larger battleground states are located in the Midwest and the smaller ones in the Southwest. Minorities, such as African Americans, Hispanics, Asian Americans, and Native Americans, are less well represented in the large, more competitive Midwestern states. Thus the Electoral College also contains a *de facto* racial and ethnic bias, which may be reflected in the public policy initiatives of the winning candidate and party.

The Electoral College also benefits the two major parties at the expense of third parties and independent candidates.[30] The reason it does so is that the winner-take-all system of voting by states when combined with the need for a majority of the total electoral vote makes it difficult for third parties to accumulate enough votes to win an election. To have any effect, minor party candidates must have support that is geographically concentrated, as Strom Thurmond's was in 1948 and George Wallace's in 1968, rather than more broadly distributed across the country, as Henry Wallace's was in 1948, H. Ross Perot's in 1992 and 1996, and Ralph Nader's in 2000.

Given the limitations on third parties, their most realistic electoral objectives would seem to be to defeat one of the major contenders rather than to elect their own candidate. In 1912, Theodore Roosevelt's Bull Moose campaign split the Republican Party, thereby aiding the Democratic Party candidate, Woodrow Wilson. More recently, Ralph Nader's vote, though small, hurt Gore more than Bush and cost the Democrats a victory in Florida. In other elections, third parties may have dipped into the major two-party vote but do not appear to have changed the outcome of elections.

Which of the major parties is advantaged by the Electoral College has been much debated. The conventional wisdom holds that the Republicans are advantaged more than the Democrats. Since 1968, their candidates have won seven of the last ten presidential elections. The Republicans can rely on the support of more noncompetitive states, particularly those in the Rocky Mountain region and the South.[31] The Democrats' principal support comes from the states in the Northeast and on the Pacific Coast. However, the closeness of the last two elections and the relative parity between the major parties today suggests that either one could win a majority in the Electoral College if they nominate a candidate with broad national appeal.

SUMMARY

The quest for the presidency has been and continues to be influenced by the system designed in Philadelphia in 1787. The objectives of that system were to protect the independence of the institution, to ensure the selection of a well-qualified, national candidate, and to do so in a way that was politically expedient and technologically feasible, given the state of communications and transportation in 1787. The Electoral College was also thought to be consistent with the tenets of a republican form of government.

Although many of the objectives remain the same, the system has changed significantly over the years. Of all the factors that have influenced these changes, none has been more important than the advent of political parties. Their development created an additional first step in the process, the nomination, which has influenced the selection and behavior of electors ever since.

The nomination process is necessary to the parties, whose principal interest is to get their candidates elected. At first, members of Congress, meeting in partisan caucuses, decided on the nominees. On the basis of common friendships and shared perspectives, they reached a consensus and then used their influence to mobilize support for the agreed-upon candidates. In effect, the ad hoc system that developed provided for legislative selection of the president in violation of the letter and spirit of the Constitution.

The caucus method broke down with the weakening of the parties, the demise of the Federalists, and the factionalization of the Republicans. It was never restored. In its place, a more decentralized mode of selection reflective of the increasing sectional composition of the parties emerged.

The new nomination process, controlled by state leaders, operated within the framework of a brokered national convention. There was little rank-and-file participation. Demands for greater public participation eventually opened up the nomination process, thereby reducing the influence of state leaders and decreasing the dependence of presidential candidates on them. Power eventually shifted from the political leaders to the candidates themselves with party partisans making the final judgment.

Similar trends, rooted in the development of parties and the expansion of suffrage, affected the way in which the electors were selected and how they voted. Instead of being chosen on the basis of their personal qualifications, electors were selected on the basis of their partisan loyalties; instead of being elected as individuals, they were chosen as part of a partisan slate; instead of exercising independent judgment, the electors became agents of their party. The inevitable soon happened: bloc voting by electors in states.

The desire of the populace for greater participation in the presidential election process also had an effect. It accelerated the movement of the popular election of the electors with the result that the electoral vote tended to reflect, even exaggerate, the popular vote. There have been only four times in U.S. history in which the plurality winner was not elected: 1824, 1876, 1888, and 2000.

In the presidential election of 2000, the electoral system was put to a severe test. Although allegations of voter intimidation, inaccurate registration lists, machine malfunctions, and tabulation disputes have characterized elections in the past and occasionally become issues as in 1960, they rarely affected the overall result. In 2000, they did by focusing attention on the popular vote of one state, Florida, which ultimately determined the winner of the election.

The 2000 election and the one following it have brought into focus a multitude of issues that critically address the fairness and adequacy of the Electoral College as a national voting system. Critics alleged that it is undemocratic, unequal, and unwise. It advantages the most competitive states. The presidential candidates spend the vast amount of their time and resources in these states; they virtually ignore the rest of the country, thereby raising the issue of whether the presidential election is truly a national election.

In summary, the electoral system works, but it does so imperfectly. It permits a partisan choice but has not generally facilitated partisan

accountability or responsible party governance. It provides greater opportunities for public participation in the nomination and election processes but
has not usually resulted in a broad cross-section of partisans contributing
money, working, or even voting in their party's primaries, nor has it encouraged all segments of the electorate to get involved and to vote in the general
election. In recent elections, the winning candidate has usually only received a
plurality of the vote. George W. Bush's 50.73 percent in 2004 was the first
majority vote a presidential candidate received since 1988. Considering that a
substantial portion of the voting-age population do not vote, and the popular
vote has been closely divided in recent elections, the winner cannot usually
claim the support of more than one out of three or four adults, hardly the
mandate we might expect or desire in a democracy, nor one that is usually
sufficient for governing effectively.

 WHERE ON THE WEB?

General Sites

- 270towin.com
  www.270towin.com

  Contains an interactive electoral map for current and past presidential
  elections.

- Atlas of Presidential Elections
  www.uselectionatlas.org

  Presents information on contemporary and past presidential elections,
  including comprehensive results broken down by states and counties.

- C-SPAN: Road to the White House 2008
  www.cspan.org

  Provides up-to-date information about the campaign.

- Center or Voting and Democracy
  www.fairvote.org

  An organization that promotes democratic reforms for the electoral
  process such as the direct election of the president.

- Democracy in Action
  www.P2008.org

  A site maintained by Eric M. Appleman under the sponsorship of the
  Graduate School in Campaign Management of the George Washington
  University. It has a wealth of up-to-date information on the 2008 pre-
  sidential campaign with links to other sources.

- Google
  www.google.com

  Comprehensive search engine.

- National Popular Vote
  www.NationalPopularVote.com

An organization that has proposed an interstate compact in which states would agree to cast their electoral voters for the national popular vote winner.

- **Political Web Info**
  www.politicalweb.Info
  Contains information that identifies features on the candidates' Web sites.

- **Politics 1**
  www.politics1.com
  An online guide to current politics with links to other relevant sites for the 2008 campaign.

- **Yahoo**
  www.yahoo.com
  A comprehensive link for campaign news and information.

Government Sources

- **Electoral Assistance Commission**
  www.eac.gov
  The commission set up by Congress in the 2002 Help America Vote Act to facilitate voter registration and voting procedures in U.S. elections. It publishes the official results.

- **Federal Election Commission**
  www.fec.gov
  This commission collects and disseminates data on election turnout, voting, and most importantly, candidate, party, and nonparty group revenues and expenditures.

- **National Archives and Records Administration; Office of the Federal Register**
  www.archives.gov/federal_register/electoral_college
  Provides access to federal laws and presidential documents as well as statistics on past presidential elections and information on the Electoral College.

- **The White House**
  www.whitehouse.gov
  Provides information on the activities of the president and vice president: what they say, who they meet, and their positions on current issues.

EXERCISES

1. Prior to the completion of the 2008 nomination process, obtain the most recent schedule of primaries and caucuses for the selection of delegates to the Democratic and Republican national nominating conventions of that year. You can do this on most major news networks' Web sites or at the Election Assistance Commission or the Federal Election Commission. Try to figure out which of the declared and undeclared candidates for each party's nomination is most and least advantaged by this schedule. Then predict which of the candidates will be the popular vote winner in the individual primaries and caucuses.

2. Get up-to-speed on the Electoral College by accessing and reviewing the material on the Electoral College at the National Archives and Records Administration site, (www.archives.gov/federal-register/electoral-college). Use the links available at this site to find out how the electors in your state are selected and the dates and procedures by which they will vote in 2008.

3. Access the Web site www.270towin.com. Look at the Electoral College maps for the 2000 and 2004 elections, and explain how they differ. Then construct a winning Electoral College strategy for the Democratic or Republican candidate you prefer in 2008. Focus on the likely swing states in your analysis. Why do you think these states may go Democratic or Republican in 2008?

SELECTED READINGS

Abbot, David W., and James P. Levine. *Wrong Winner: The Coming Debacle in the Electoral College*. New York: Praeger, 1991.

Amar, Vikram David. "The 2004 Presidential Election and the Electoral College: How the Results Debunk Some Defenses of the Current System," (Nov. 12, 2004). http://www.writ.news.findlaw.com/amar/20041112.html.

Bennett, Robert W. *Taming the Electoral College*. Stanford, C.A.: Stanford University Press, 2006.

Berns, Walter. "Third Party Candidates Face a High Hurdle in the Electoral College." *American Enterprise* (Jan./Feb. 1996): 48–49.

Best, Judith. "Presidential Selection: Complex Problems and Simple Solutions." *The Political Science Quarterly*, 119 (Spring 2004): 39–59.

Brunell, Thomas, and Bernard Grofman, "The 1992 and 1996 Presidential Elections: Whatever Happened to the Republican Electoral College Lock?" *Presidential Studies Quarterly* (Winter 1997): 134–138.

Destler, I. M. "The Myth of the Electoral College Lock." *PS* (September 1996): 189–193.

Edwards, George C. III. *Why the Electoral College is Bad for America*. New Haven: Yale University Press, 2004.

FairVote. *Presidential Election Inequality: The Electoral College in the Twenty-First Century*. Takoma Park, M. D.: Center for Voting and Democracy, 2006.

Fortier, John C. ed. *After the People Vote: A Guide to the Electoral College*. Washington, D.C.: The AEI Press, 2004.

Longley, Lawrence D., and James D. Dana Jr. "The Biases of the Electoral College in the 1990s." *Polity*, 25 (Fall 1992): 123–145.

Rakove, Jack. "Presidential Selection: Electoral Fallacies." *The Political Science Quarterly*, 119 (Spring 2004): 21–38.

Schumaker, Paul D., and Burdett A. Loomis, eds. *Choosing a President*. New York: Chatham House, 2002.

Troy, Gil. *See How They Ran: The Changing Role of the Presidential Candidate*. New York: Free Press, 1991.

U.S. Senate Committee on the Judiciary. *The Electoral College and Direct Election of the President*. Hearings, 102nd Cong., 2nd sess, July 22, 1992. Washington, D.C.: Government Printing Office, 1992.

———. *Direct Popular Election of the President and Vice President of the United States*. Hearings. 95th Cong., 1st sess. Washington, D.C.: Government Printing Office, 1979.

NOTES

1. Gouverneur Morris, *Records of the Federal Convention,* ed. Max Farrand (New Haven, C.T.: Yale University Press, 1921), pp. 2, 33.

2. The first proposal for direct election was introduced in a very timid fashion by James Wilson, delegate from Pennsylvania. James Madison's *Journal* describes Wilson's presentation as follows: "Mr. Wilson said he was almost unwilling to declare the mode which he wished to take place, being apprehensive that it might appear chimerical. He would say however at least that in theory he was for an election by the people; Experience, particularly in N. York & Massts, shewed that an election of the first magistrate by the people at large, was both convenient & successful mode." Farrand *Records of the Federal Convention,* vol. I, p. 68.

3. This provision was intended to decrease parochialism and facilitate the selection of a national candidate. It forced Dick Cheney, George W. Bush's choice to be his vice presidential running mate in 2000, to move his official residence from Texas to Wyoming so that Texas' electors could vote for the entire Republican ticket if Bush and Cheney won the popular vote in that state.

4. So great was the sectional rivalry, so competitive the states, so limited the number of people with national reputations, that it was feared electors would tend to vote primarily for people from their own states. To prevent the same states, particularly the largest ones, from exercising undue influence in the selection of both the president and vice president, this provision was included.

5. George Mason declared, "Nineteen times out of twenty, the President would be chosen by the Senate." Farrand, *Records of the Federal Convention,* vol. II, 500. The original proposal of the Committee on Unfinished Business was that the Senate should select the president. The delegates substituted the House of Representatives, fearing that the Senate was too powerful with its appointment and treaty-making powers. The principle of equal state representation was retained. Choosing the president is the only occasion on which the House of Representatives votes by state.

6. Thomas R. Marshall, *Presidential Nominations in a Reform Age* (New York: Praeger, 1981), p. 19.

7. Neal R. Peirce and Lawrence D. Longley, *The People's President* (New Haven, C.T.: Yale University Press, 1981), p. 36.

8. Marshall *Presidential Nominations,* p. 20.

9. Ibid., p. 21.

10. Louis Maisel and Gerald J. Lieberman, "The Impact of Electoral Rules on Primary Elections: The Democratic Presidential Primaries in 1976," in *The Impact of the Electoral Process,* ed. Louis Maisel and Joseph Cooper (Beverly Hills, C.A.: Sage, 1977), p. 68.

11. Until the passage of the Twentieth Amendment, which made January 3 the date when members of Congress took their oaths of office and convened, it was the second session of the preelection Congress that met after the election.

12. Lucius Wilmerding, *The Electoral College* (New Brunswick, N.J.: Rutgers University Press, 1953), p. 32.

13. There were 106 members of the House (58 Federalists and 48 Republicans). On the first ballot, the vote of those present was for Burr, pp. 53–51.

14. In those days, being secretary of state was considered a stepping-stone to the presidency. With the exception of Washington and John Adams, all the people who became president prior to Andrew Jackson had first held appointment as secretary of state.

15. Peirce and Longley, *People's President*, p. 51.

16. Marquis James, *The Life of Andrew Jackson* (Indianapolis: Bobbs-Merrill, 1938), p. 439.

17. He captured the majority of electoral votes in two of these states because the electors were chosen on a district rather than statewide basis. William R. Keech, "Background Paper," in *Winner Take All: Report of the Twentieth Century Fund Task Force on Reform of the Presidential Election Process* (New York: Holmes & Meier, 1978), p. 50.

18. The act that created the commission specified that its decision would be final unless overturned by both houses of Congress. The House of Representatives, controlled by the Democrats, opposed every one of the commission's findings. The Republican Senate, however, concurred. A Democratic filibuster in the Senate was averted by Hayes's promise of concessions to the South, including the withdrawal of federal troops. Tilden could have challenged the findings in court but chose not to do so.

19. The vote tabulated in this county provided some evidence of the confusion. Buchanan's vote was larger in Palm Beach than in any other Florida county. Palm Beach has a large, elderly Jewish population unlikely to have supported Buchanan. Moreover, Palm Beach had a larger percentage of ballots in which no presidential vote was recorded than all but two of the other sixty-seven counties in the state.

20. At the time of the court-imposed deadline, only one county, Broward, had submitted a recount that moved Gore to within 537 votes of Bush. Palm Beach County was unable to get its votes in by the 5:00 PM deadline. That county submitted its revised tabulation several hours later, too late to be included in the revised state vote count. Still trailing his Republican opponent, Gore went back to state court to seek a court order forcing an immediate hand count in Miami-Dade, but a Florida appeals court refused to do so as did the state supreme court. These refusals prompted Gore to return to state court to ask for a court order to count the disputed ballots in Miami-Dade and include the revised vote totals from Palm Beach that had been completed after the deadline.

21. The judge held that Gore's attorneys had not provided statistical evidence to demonstrate the *probability,* not a mere *possibility,* that the results of the Florida election would be different if a hand count were to occur and be included in the vote totals.

22. David W. Moore, "One Year after Election, Controversy over Winner Appears Less Serious," Gallup Poll, (Nov. 6, 2001). www.gallup.com.

23. Ibid.

24. Richard M. Scammon and Alice V. McGillivray, *America Votes 12,* (Washington D.C.: Congressional Quarterly, 1977), p. 15.

25. Theoretically, two states, Maine and Nebraska, will not always vote as a bloc because they do not select all their electors on an at-large basis. Two are chosen at large, and the remaining ones are elected in each of the states' congressional districts. Since these states have enacted their laws for selecting electors, however, they have cast all their electoral votes for the same candidate.

26. Thomas Brunell and Bernard Grofman, "The 1992 and 1996 Presidential Elections: Whatever Happened to the Republican Electoral College Lock?" *Presidential Studies Quarterly* (Winter 1997): pp. 134–138.

27. I. M. Destler, "The Myth of the Electoral Lock," *PS* (Sept. 1996): p. 491.

28. The 2004 population estimates are based on 2000 census by the Census Bureau. www.factfinder.census.gov.

29. Lawrence D. Longley and James D. Dana, "The Biases of the Electoral College in the 1990s," *Polity,* 25 (Fall 1992), p. 134. There are two other, less obvious, biases in the Electoral College. The distribution of electoral votes is calculated on the basis of the census, which occurs every ten years. Thus, the college does not mirror population shifts within this period. Nor does it take into account the number of people who actually cast ballots. It is a state's population, not its turnout, that determines the number of electoral votes it receives, over and above the automatic three.

30. James C. Garand and T. Wayne Parent, "Representation, Swing, and Bias in U.S. Presidential Elections, 1872–1988," *American Journal of Political Science* 35 (Nov. 1991): pp. 1024, 1029.

31. John E. Berthoud, "The Electoral Lock Thesis: The Weighting Bias Component," *PS* (June 1997): pp. 189–193.

2 CHAPTER | CAMPAIGN FINANCE

INTRODUCTION

Running for president is very expensive. In the 2003–2004 election cycle, over $4 billion was spent on federal elections, a 30 percent increase over the 2000 presidential and congressional elections.[1] Of that amount, approximately $1 billion was expended on the presidential campaign. The parties spent or distributed over $1.4 billion, with political interest groups accounting for the balance.[2]

The magnitude of these expenditures poses serious problems for presidential candidates, who must raise considerable sums during the preconvention struggle, closely watch their expenses, make important allocation decisions, and conform to the intricacies of finance laws during both the nomination and general election campaigns. In addition, the candidates must coordinate their financial activities with party leaders who must also solicit, distribute, and spend millions on behalf of their candidates for national office. Moreover, such large expenditures raise important issues for a democratic selection process. This chapter explores some of these problems and those issues.

The chapter is organized into five sections. The first details the costs of presidential campaigns, paying particular attention to the increase in expenditures since 1960. The next section looks at the sources of support and the questions that arise from the connection between candidates and donors.

Should people's right to use their own money take precedence over the governmental ability to limit the size of contributions to level the playing field? Congressional attempts to set donation limits to federal elections, require disclosure, control spending, and subsidize elections are discussed in the third section. The fourth section examines the impact of campaign finance laws on revenues and expenditures in presidential campaigns and on the party system. In the final section, the relationship between campaign spending and electoral success is explored. Can money buy elections? Have the big spenders been the big winners?

THE COSTS OF CAMPAIGNING

Candidates have always spent money in their quest for the presidency, but it was not until they started personal campaigning across the country that these costs began to increase sharply.

A BRIEF OVERVIEW OF EXPENDITURES IN AMERICAN ELECTIONS

When electioneering was conducted within a highly partisan press environment before the Civil War, there were few expenses other than for the occasional biography and campaign pamphlet printed by the party and sold to the public at less than cost. With the advent of more active public campaigning toward the middle of the nineteenth century, candidate organizations turned to buttons, billboards, banners, and pictures to symbolize and illustrate their campaigns. By the beginning of the twentieth century, the cost of this type of advertising in each election exceeded $150,000, a lot of money then but a minuscule amount by contemporary standards.[3]

In 1924, radio was employed for the first time in presidential campaigns. The Republicans spent approximately $120,000 that year, whereas the Democrats spent only $40,000.[4] Four years later, however, the two parties together spent more than $1 million. Radio expenses continued to equal or exceed a million dollars per election for the next twenty years.[5]

Television emerged as a vehicle for presidential campaigning in 1952. Both national party conventions were broadcast on television as well as radio. Although there were only 19 million television sets in the United States at that time, almost one-third of Americans were regular television viewers.

The number of households with television sets rose dramatically over the next four years. By 1956, an estimated 71 percent had television, and by 1968, the figure was close to 95 percent; today it exceeds 99 percent, with most homes having two or more sets. Cable and satellite subscribers have increased to over 70 percent of the television viewing audience.[6]

The first commercials for presidential candidates appeared in 1952. They became regular fare thereafter, contributing substantially to campaign costs. Film biographies, interview shows, political rallies, town meetings, and election eve telethons have all been seen with increasing frequency.

In 1948, no money was spent on television by either party's candidate. Twenty years later, $13 million was expended for television advertising, approximately one-fourth of the total cost of the campaign.

CONTEMPORARY CAMPAIGN COSTS

The advent of the electronic campaign following World War II was the principal reason campaign costs skyrocketed. In 1960, John Kennedy and Richard Nixon each spent a hundred times the amount Lincoln had spent 100 years earlier. In the 12 years following the 1960 general election, expenditures increased from about $20 million to over $90 million, an increase that far outstripped the inflation rate during that period. Table 2.1 lists the costs of the major party candidates in presidential elections from 1860 to 1972, the last general election in which campaign spending by major party candidates was unrestricted.

TABLE 2.1 | COSTS OF PRESIDENTIAL GENERAL ELECTIONS, MAJOR PARTY CANDIDATES, 1860–1972

Year	Democrats		Republicans	
1860	Stephen Douglas	$ 50,000	Abraham Lincoln*	$ 100,000
1864	George McClellan	50,000	Abraham Lincoln*	125,000
1868	Horatio Seymour	75,000	Ulysses Grant*	150,000
1872	Horace Greeley	50,000	Ulysses Grant*	250,000
1876	Samuel Tilden	900,000	Rutherford Hayes*	950,000
1880	Winfield Hancock	335,000	James Garfield*	1,100,000
1884	Grover Cleveland*	1,400,000	James Blaine	1,300,000
1888	Grover Cleveland	855,000	Benjamin Harrison*	1,350,000
1892	Grover Cleveland*	2,350,000	Benjamin Harrison	1,700,000
1896	William Jennings Bryan	675,000	William McKinley*	3,350,000
1900	William Jennings Bryan	425,000	William McKinley*	3,000,000
1904	Alton Parker	700,000	Theodore Roosevelt*	2,096,000
1908	William Jennings Bryan	629,341	William Taft*	1,655,518
1912	Woodrow Wilson*	1,134,848	William Taft	1,071,549
1916	Woodrow Wilson*	2,284,950	Charles Evans Hughes	2,441,565
1920	James Cox	1,470,371	Warren Harding*	5,417,501
1924	John Davis	1,108,836	Calvin Coolidge*	4,020,478
1928	Alfred Smith	5,342,350	Herbert Hoover*	6,256,111
1932	Franklin Roosevelt*	2,245,975	Herbert Hoover	2,900,052

(*continued*)

Year	Democrats		Republicans	
1936	Franklin Roosevelt*	5,194,751	Alfred Landon	8,892,972
1940	Franklin Roosevelt*	2,783,654	Wendell Willkie	3,451,310
1944	Franklin Roosevelt*	2,169,077	Thomas Dewey	2,828,652
1948	Harry Truman*	2,736,334	Thomas Dewey	2,127,296
1952	Adlai Stevenson	5,032,926	Dwight Eisenhower*	6,608,623
1956	Adlai Stevenson	5,106,651	Dwight Eisenhower*	7,778,702
1960	John Kennedy*	9,797,000	Richard Nixon	10,128,000
1964	Lyndon Johnson*	8,757,000	Barry Goldwater	16,026,000
1968†	Hubert Humphrey	11,594,000	Richard Nixon*	25,042,000
1972	George McGovern	30,000,000	Richard Nixon*	61,400,000

*Indicates winner.

†George Wallace spent an estimated $7 million as the candidate of the American Independent Party in 1968.

Source: Data based on *Financing Politics: Money, Elections, and Political Reform*, 3rd ed. By Herbert E. Alexander. Copyright 1984 by Congressional Quarterly.

Prenomination costs have risen even more rapidly than those in the general election as indicated in Table 2.2. Until the 1960s, large expenditures were the exception, not the rule, for gaining the party's nomination. General Leonard Wood spent an estimated $2 million in an unsuccessful quest to head the Republican ticket in 1920. The contest between General Dwight D. Eisenhower and Senator Robert A. Taft in 1952 cost about $5 million, a total that was not exceeded until 1964, when Nelson Rockefeller and Barry Goldwater together spent approximately twice that amount.

Since 1968, preconvention expenditures have generally exceeded those in the general election. The increasing numbers of primaries, caucuses, and candidates, combined with the willingness of several recent hopefuls to forego federal matching grants entirely and the expenditure limits that go with them, have been largely responsible for the rise.

In the 1950s, the preconvention contests were optional; since the 1970s, they have been mandatory. Even incumbent presidents have to enter them, and they spend money even when they are not challenged. In 1984, the Reagan campaign committee spent almost $28 million during the nomination period, much of it on voter registration drives for the general election; in 1992, George H. W. Bush spent over $27 million in defeating Pat Buchanan, a conservative newspaper columnist who had not previously sought public office. In 1996, Bill Clinton spent almost $35 million running unopposed for the Democratic nomination; eight years later, George W. Bush spent over $250 million running unopposed. In 2004, the candidates for their party's nomination raised and spent close to $660 million in addition to the millions spent by the parties, nonparty groups, and individuals.[7]

TABLE 2.2 | COSTS OF PRESIDENTIAL NOMINATIONS, 1964–2004 (IN MILLIONS OF DOLLARS)

| Year | Expenditures | |
	Democrats	Republicans
1964	(uncontested)	$10.0
1968	$25.0	20.0
1972	33.1	*
1976	40.7	26.1
1980	41.7	86.1
1984	107.7	28.0
1988	94.0	114.6
1992	66.0†	51.0
1996	41.8	182.0
2000	95.8	247.2
2004	389.7	268.9

*During a primary in which Richard M. Nixon's renomination was virtually assured, Representative John M. Ashbrook spent $740,000 and Representative Paul N. McCloskey spent $550,000 in challenging Nixon.

†Estimates based on Alexander and Corrado, *Financing the 1992 Elections*, Tables 2.1 and 2.4.

Sources: 1964–1972, Herbert E. Alexander, *Financing Politics* (Washington, D.C.: Congressional Quarterly, 1976), 45–47, Copyright © 1984 by Congressional Quarterly, Inc. Reprinted with permission of the publisher; 1976–1984, Federal Election Commission, "Reports on Financial Activity, 1987–88," *Presidential Pre-Nomination Campaigns* (August 1989), Table A.7, 10; Herbert E. Alexander, "Financing the Presidential Elections" (paper presented at the Institute for Political Studies in Tokyo, Japan, September 8–10, 1989), 4, 10; 1988–1992, Herbert E. Alexander, and Anthony Corrado, *Financing the 1992 Elections* (Armonk, N.Y.: Sharpe , 1995), Copyright © 1995 by M. E. Sharpe, Inc. Reprinted with permission of the publisher; 1996–2004, updated by author from data published by the Federal Election Commission, "Presidential Campaign Disbursements" (inception through July 31, of the 1996 and 2000 election years and December 31, 2004). (www.fec.gov)

Why is it so expensive to run for a presidential nomination, much less in the general election? The answer is that it costs money to raise money, to hire a staff, and to travel around the country. Designing and airing advertisements, conducting public opinion polls, and setting up an interactive Web site are also costly operations. Add to these office and equipment rentals, event organizers and advance teams, media consultants, grassroots organizers, researchers and speechwriters, a press operation, and the professional lawyers, accountants, policy advisers, and the money never seems to be enough.

Moreover, candidates are now forced to campaign simultaneously in several states for several months before those states' primaries and caucuses are held. To do so, they need to use the electronic media, radio, and television, which is also costly. By 2000, television expenses for the presidential race alone exceeded $205 million and $578 million when the congressional elections were included; in 2004, they exceeded $600 million just for the presidential contest.[8]

THE PROBLEMS WITH LARGE EXPENDITURES

Three major issues arise from the high costs of contemporary elections. One pertains to the donors. Who gives, how much, and what do they get for their money? A second relates to the costs. Are they too high, and can they be controlled without impinging on First Amendment freedoms? The third concerns the impact of spending on the election. To what extent does access to large amounts of money improve a candidate's chances of winning? The next section turns to the first of these issues, that of private sources of financial support and the attempts by government to regulate them.

THE SOURCES OF SUPPORT

Throughout most of U.S. electoral history, parties and candidates have depended on large contributions. In the midst of the industrial boom at the end of the nineteenth century, the Republicans were able to count on the support of the Astors, Harrimans, and Vanderbilts; while the Democrats looked to financier August Belmont (American representative of the Rothschild banking interests) and inventor and industrialist, Cyrus McCormick. Corporations, banks, and life insurance companies soon became prime targets of party fund-raisers. The most notorious and probably most adroit fund-raiser of this period was Mark Hanna. A leading official of the Republican Party, Hanna owed most of his influence to his ability to obtain substantial political contributions. He set quotas, personally assessing the amount that businesses and corporations should give. In 1896, and again in 1900, he was able to obtain contributions of $250,000 from Standard Oil. Theodore Roosevelt personally ordered the return of some of the Standard Oil money in 1904 but accepted large gifts from magnates E. H. Harriman and Henry C. Frick. Roosevelt's trust-busting activities during his presidency led Frick to remark, "We bought the son of a bitch and then he did not stay bought."[9]

Sizable private gifts remained the principal source of party and candidate support until the mid-1970s. In 1972, Richard Nixon and George McGovern raised an estimated $27 million from fewer than two hundred individual contributors.[10] In general, the Republicans benefited more than the Democrats from wealthy contributors, known in the campaign vernacular as "fat cats." Only in 1964 was a Democrat, incumbent president Lyndon B. Johnson who enjoyed a large lead in the pre-election polls, able to raise more money from large donors than his Republican opponent, Barry Goldwater, although Bill Clinton and John Kerry came close to doing so in 1996 and 2004 respectively.

The reluctance of regular Republican contributors to support the Goldwater candidacy forced his organization to appeal to thousands of potential supporters through direct mail. The success of this effort, raising $5.8 million from approximately 651,000 people, showed the potential of a popular appeal for funds and shattered what had been an unwritten "rule" of politics that money could not be raised by a letter sent through the mail. In 1968, Alabama Governor George Wallace, running as a third-party candidate, solicited the bulk of his funds in this fashion as have other lesser-known candidates since then.

Despite the use of mass mailings and party telethons to broaden the base of political contributors in the 1960s, dependence on large donors continued. In 1964, more than $2 million was raised in contributions of $10,000 or more. Eight years later, approximately $51 million was collected in gifts of this size or larger. Some gifts were in the million-dollar range.

The magnitude of these contributions, combined with the heavy-handed tactics of the Nixon fund-raisers in 1971–1972, brought into sharp focus the difficulty of maintaining a democratic selection process that was dependent on private funding.[11] Reliance on large contributors who did not want to be identified, the inequality of funding between parties and candidates, and the high cost of campaigning, especially in the mass media, all raised serious questions: Were there assumptions implicit in giving and receiving? Could elected officials be responsive to individual benefactors and to the general public at the same time? Was the need to obtain large contributors and keep them "happy" consistent with the tenets of a democratic society that all people have equal influence on the selection of and access to public officials? Did the high cost of campaigning, in and of itself, eliminate otherwise qualified candidates from running? Were certain political parties, interest groups, or individuals consistently advantaged or disadvantaged by the distribution of funding? Had the presidency become an office that only the wealthy could afford or that only those with wealthy supporters could seek?

THE HISTORY OF CAMPAIGN FINANCE LEGISLATION

Reacting to these issues, Congress in the 1970s enacted far-reaching legislation designed to reduce dependence on major donors that contribute large amounts of money, bring donors out in the open, discourage illegal contributions, broaden the base of public support, and control escalating costs at the presidential level. Additionally, the Democratic Congress that passed these laws wanted to equalize the funds available to the Republican and Democratic nominees. Finally, the legislation was designed to buttress the two-party system, making it more difficult for minor candidates to challenge the major parties' nominees for elective office successfully.

REGULATION, DISCLOSURE, AND PUBLIC FINANCING

The Federal Election Campaign Act (FECA), enacted in 1971, set ceilings on the amount of money presidential and vice presidential candidates and their families could contribute to their own campaigns.[12] It allowed unions and corporations, which had been prohibited from contributing, to form political action committees (PACs), consisting of their members, employees, and stockholders, to solicit voluntary contributions to be given to candidates or parties or to fund the group's election activities. The FECA also established procedures for public disclosure of contributions over a certain amount.

A second statute, the Revenue Act of 1971, created tax credits and deductions to encourage private contributions. It also provided for public funding by creating a presidential election campaign fund. Financed by an income tax check-off provision, the fund initially allowed taxpayers to designate one dollar of their federal income taxes to a special presidential election account.

These laws began a period of federal government regulation of national elections that has continued into the twenty-first century. The history of that regulation is a history of good intentions built on political compromise but marred by unintended consequences of the legislation and its implementation as candidates, parties, and nonparty groups have circumvented the letter and spirit of the law to gain electoral advantage.

Partisan compromises in the enactment of campaign finance legislation were evident from the outset. Although the original funding provision was enacted in 1971, it did not go into effect until the 1976 presidential election. Most Republicans, including President Nixon, opposed the policy of government financial support and regulation. In addition to conflicting with their general ideological belief that the national government's role in the conduct of elections be limited, the legislation offset their party's traditional fund-raising advantage. President Nixon was persuaded to sign the public-funding bill, however, after Democrats agreed to delay the effective start of the bill until after his likely reelection.[13]

The 1972 election was marked by heavy-handed fund-raising tactics. The Nixon campaign in that election cycle raised more money than in any other previous presidential campaign. In addition to aggressive solicitation, the expenditures of the Nixon reelection effort also became an issue, albeit after the election. Investigative reporting by the *Washington Post* and hearings conducted by a Senate committee revealed that the Committee to Reelect the President, referred to by Nixon's opponents as CREEP, had spent some of its funds on "dirty tricks" and other unethical and illegal activities, such as the break-in at the Democratic National Committee's headquarters at the Watergate office building. These revelations aroused public ire and created the incentive for a Democratic Congress to enact new and even more stringent legislation.

In 1974, the FECA was amended to include public disclosure provisions, contribution ceilings for individuals and groups, spending limits for the campaigns, federal subsidies for major party candidates in the nomination process, and complete funding for them in the general election. The law also restricted the amount candidates could contribute to their own campaign and the amount that others could spend independently on their behalf. Finally, it established a six-person commission, the Federal Election Commission (FEC), to implement and enforce the law.

The 1974 amendments were highly controversial. Critics immediately charged a federal giveaway, a raid on the treasury. Opponents of the legislation also argued that the limits on contributions and spending violated the constitutionally guaranteed right to freedom of speech, that the funding provisions unfairly discriminated against third-party and independent candidates, and that Congress' appointment of some of the commissioners violated the separation of powers.

In the landmark decision of *Buckley v. Valeo,* 424 U.S. 1 (1976), the Supreme Court upheld the right of Congress to regulate campaign contributions and expenditures but negated the overall limits on spending by individuals and non-party groups and the appointment by Congress of four of the six election commissioners. The majority opinion in that case contended that by placing restrictions on the amount of money a person or organization could spend during a campaign, the law directly and substantially restrained freedom of speech, a freedom protected by the First Amendment to the Constitution.

The Supreme Court did allow limits on contributions to candidates' campaigns, however, and limits on expenditures of those candidates who accepted public funds but not those who refused these funds. By holding that contributions to and expenditures of presidential candidates could be limited, the justices acknowledged that large, often secret, contributions and rapidly increasingly expenditures did pose problems for a democracy, problems that Congress could address.

The Court's decision required that the election law be amended once again. It took Congress several months to do so. In the spring of 1976, during the presidential primaries of that year, amendments were enacted that continued public funding of the presidential nomination and election campaigns, based on a figure of $10 million in 1974 to be adjusted for inflation, but did so on a voluntary basis. Candidates did not have to accept government funds, but if they did, they were limited in how much they and others could contribute to their own campaigns and how much those campaigns could spend. The FEC was reconstituted with all six members to be nominated by the president and appointed subject to the advice and consent of the Senate. The law required that three commissioners be Democrats and three be Republicans to ensure that the Commission would be fair to both major parties.

ADJUSTING THE FEDERAL ELECTION CAMPAIGN ACT

With limited amounts of money available, the candidates opted to spend most of it on television advertising. Gone were the buttons, bumper stickers, and other election paraphernalia that had characterized previous campaigns. Fewer resources were directed toward grassroots organizing. Turnout fell. The national parties lost influence. Congress was concerned.

In 1979, additional amendments to the FECA were enacted to rectify these problems. To encourage voluntary activities and higher voter turnout, the amendments allowed party committees at the national, state, and local levels to raise and spend unlimited amounts of money for party-building activities such as on registration and getting out the vote. Known as the *soft money* provision, this amendment, as interpreted by the FEC, created a gigantic loophole in the law.[14] It permitted, even encouraged, the major parties to solicit large contributions and distribute the money to their state and local affiliates as they saw fit. Pandora's Box had been opened, although it took another decade and a half to exploit it completely.[15]

Later amendments to the FECA increased the base grant for nominating conventions of the major parties to $3 million in 1979 and $4 million in 1984.

It was not until 1993 that the law was amended again to increase the amount of money in the fund used to subsidize candidates for their party's presidential nomination and provide general election grants. Congress' failure to tie the amount of money taxpayers could designate for the fund to inflation, the decline in the percentage of taxpayers making such a designation, and the increasing number of candidates vying for party nominations all contributed to a shortfall that was expected to only get worse in the years ahead.

To rectify the problem, Congress increased the income tax checkoff from $1 to $3, a little less than the cost-of-living adjustment since the provision originally went into effect. However, the portion of taxpayers designating a payment to the fund had fallen significantly from its high of 28.7 percent in 1980. At the beginning of the twenty-first century, only about 10-11 percent of taxpayers were contributing to the election fund on a regular basis.[16]

A new problem of a very different magnitude emerged in 1996—the exploitation of the soft money loophole to circumvent the law's intended contribution and expenditure limits. This exploitation resulted from a very creative interpretation of the 1979 amendments by President Clinton's political advisers, the major parties, subsequently by the FEC, and finally, the courts. Here's what happened.

In 1995, Clinton and his advisers began planning for the president's reelection campaign. Their strategy was to position Clinton as a centrist by airing a series of advertisements that touted his record and favorably contrasted it with that of the congressional Republicans. The ad campaign was costly. After $2 million was spent by the president's reelection committee in the summer of 1995, the president's advisers feared that there would not be sufficient funds left to handle a challenge for the Democratic nomination if one developed and also respond to a strong Republican opponent prior to the nominating conventions.

They resolved this dilemma by turning to the "soft money" loophole created by the 1979 amendment. Since the commercials that the Clinton administration aired were policy-oriented and did not specifically and directly urge the president's reelection, the president's advisers argued that the Democratic Party could pay for the ads with soft money, which the president would help raise. Lawyers for the party agreed.

What followed was a frantic, no-holds-barred, fund-raising effort in which the president and the vice president actively participated. Inducements to contribute included dinners with the president and vice president at expensive

Washington hotels, sleepovers in the Lincoln bedroom in the White House, state dinners with world leaders, rounds of golf with Clinton, trips on Air Force One, VIP treatment at Democratic Party functions such as its 1996 nominating convention, even invitations to join the commerce secretary on official U.S. trade missions abroad.

Naturally, Republicans were outraged by these activities, particularly the use of public office for partisan purposes. Their party officials and elected leadership protested, and congressional investigations followed but to no avail. In the end, the Republicans resorted to the same tactics as the Democrats, using their control of Congress as leverage to raise their own soft money. They eventually netted more of it than did the Democrats.

The soft-money issue reemerged during the 2000 nomination campaign. Republican candidate John McCain and Democrat Bill Bradley promised, if elected, to support a ban on soft money. Although neither candidate's bid for their party's nomination was successful, the campaign finance issue remained salient; it put candidates Bush and Gore on the defensive and led to cries for reform. In April 2001, the Senate enacted the Bipartisan Campaign Reform Act (BCRA), also known by the name of its sponsors as the McCain–Feingold bill, to close the soft money loophole. The legislation also restricted the use of the principal instrument by which nonparty, advocacy groups had tried to affect the election's outcome—issue advocacy advertising. Nine months later, the House of Representatives followed suit, and in March 2002, the legislation became law. Table 2.3 lists the major contribution limits of the new law as adjusted for inflation for the years 2007–2008.

THE BIPARTISAN CAMPAIGN REFORM ACT AND ITS IMPACT

The BCRA banned the national party committees from raising soft money, but to compensate, the new law also raised individual and overall federal contribution limits to candidates and parties and restricted the use of issue advocacy ads, in which candidates were cited by name, to periods that exceeded thirty days before a primary and sixty days before the general election. Exemptions, however, remained for tax-exempt organizations.

Opponents of the law immediately questioned its constitutionality. Such disparate groups as the National Rifle Association, the American Civil Liberties Union, and the Christian Coalition argued that the ban on issue advocacy advertising in the final days of the campaign violated the First Amendment's protection of freedom of speech and freedom of the press. The Republican National Committee claimed that the prohibition on soft money violated the state parties' right to raise money to organize and mobilize voters in all elections in which state representatives were selected, while groups representing poorer Americans contended that the increase in amount of money that could be contributed by individual donors under the new law violated the rights of less wealthy people under the Fifth Amendment's equal protection clause. In contrast, the bill's sponsors, the FEC, Common Cause and other public interest groups, and twenty-one state attorneys general supported the law.

TABLE 2.3 | CONTRIBUTION LIMITS FOR 2007–2008

	To Each Candidate or Candidate Committee Per Election	To National Party Committee Per Calendar Year	To State, District & Local Party Committee Per Calendar Year	To Any Other Political Committee Per Calendar Year[1]	Special Limits
Individual may give	$2,300*	$28,500*	$10,000 (combined limit)	$5,000	$108,200* overall biennial limit: • $42,700* to all candidates • $65,500* to all PACs and parties[2]
National Party Committee may give	$5,000	No limit	No limit	$5,000	$39,900* to Senate candidate per campaign[3]
State, District & Local Party Committee may give	$5,000 (combined limit)	No limit	No limit	$5,000 (combined limit)	No limit
PAC (multicandidate)[4] may give	$5,000	$15,000	$5,000 (combined limit)	$5,000	No limit
PAC (not multicandidate) may give	$2,300*	$28,500*	$10,000 (combined limit)	$5,000	No limit
Authorized Campaign Committee may give	$2,000[5]	No limit	No limit	$5,000	No limit

*These contribution limits are indexed for inflation.

[1] A contribution remarked for a candidate through a political committee counts against the original contributor's limit for that candidate. In certain circumstance, the contribution may also count against the contributor's limit to the PAC. 11 CFR 110.6. See also 11 CFR 110.1(h).

[2] No more than $42,700 of this amount may be contributed to state and local party committees and PACs.

[3] This limit is shared by the national committee and the national Senate campaign committee.

[4] A multicandidate committee is a political committee with more than 50 contributors which has been registered for at least 6 months and with the exception of state party committees has made contributions to 5 or more candidates for federal office 11 CFR 100.5(c)(3).

[5] A federal candidate's authorized committee(s) may contribute no more than $2,000 per election to another federal candidate's authorized committee(s). 11 CFR 102.12(c)(2).

Source: Federal Election Commission, "Contribution Limits for 2007–2008," January 23, 2007. (www.fec.gov/pages/brochures/contrib.shtml#Chart)

Anticipating a constitutional challenge, the drafters of the legislation included a provision for a quick judicial review. In early 2003, a three-judge federal panel heard the case and decided in May of that year that the soft money provision was constitutional but the limits placed on issue advocacy were not. The judges, however, stayed their decision pending an appeal to the Supreme Court, which promptly heard the case. On December 10, 2003, as the Democratic nomination campaign was underway, the Court issued its decision in the case of *McConnell v. FEC*, 540 U.S.93 (2003).

By a 5 to 4 vote, the justices upheld most of the provisions of the BCRA, including the ban on soft money solicitation by the national parties and the limits placed on issue advocacy ads that identified specific candidates in the closing month of primaries and sixty days or less in the general election.[17] It was left to the FEC to regulate its enforcement.[18]

The FEC issued a series of regulations, some of which were very contentious.[19] New legal challenges to these regulations immediately ensued. In the end, the courts invalidated a number of the FEC's regulations. One of the most controversial involved "nonpolitical" organizations, which the FEC had indicated were not subject to the soft money restrictions. But how was nonpolitical to be defined? Did it mean that the group could not engage in political activities, or that most of its expenditures could not be devoted to electioneering, or that its primary purpose could not be to elect a specific candidate?

The question was more than a theoretical one. It had very practical and immediate consequences. The reason is that Democrats, fearing that the prohibition on soft money would place their party at a competitive disadvantage, had turned to nonprofit, nonpartisan groups to raise unlimited amounts of money and spend it on election-related activities.[20] Sponsors of the BCRA and their supporters urged the FEC to regulate these groups in accordance with the intent of the law to prohibit soft money in national elections. Republicans who had previously opposed the law also urged the FEC to issue new regulations that prohibited nonparty groups from engaging in these activities. However, the Commission voted 4 to 2 not to do so. (See Box 2.3, "Soft Money Subterfuge in 2004," later in this chapter for an extended discussion of these groups and their activities during the 2003–2004 election cycle.)

After the election, and with prodding from a federal judge, the commission said that it would regulate these groups on an ad hoc basis rather than prescribing general rules for all of them. It fined four of the groups, two Democratic and two Republican, a total of $1.38 million for not registering with the FEC as a political organization and for accepting contributions that exceeded the legal amount.[21] Since the groups raised millions, the fines were considered minimal—the cost of doing business. Fines of this magnitude are not expected to deter similar groups from large-scale fund-raising in the 2007–2008 election cycle.

Although the Supreme Court upheld the Congress' right to prohibit advocacy ads in which candidates are identified by name in the final days before the election, the issue came up again in 2006 after a pro-life group in Wisconsin sued the FEC for ruling that the group's advocacy ads violated the sixty-day rule. During the fall of 2006, the pro-life group had urged people to write to their Senators opposing the confirmation delay of several of President Bush's judicial nominations. Mentioned in the ad were the names of the state's two Senators, Russell Feingold and Herbert Kolh, but not their voting records on nomination or abortion-related issues. Feingold was running for reelection in that year. A three-judge federal court reversed the FEC's ruling on the grounds that the group's freedom of speech was violated. In 2007, the Supreme Court agreed to review the lower court ruling.[22]

The BCRA thus achieved only some of its intended goals. It encouraged the major parties to improve their fund-raising operations, and to do so by soliciting contributions that fell within the federal limits. In fact, the Republicans and Democrats actually raised more money in the 2003–2004 election cycle without soft money than they had in previous cycles with it, and they continued this record fund-raising pace for the 2006 midterm and the 2008 presidential election.[23] The number of small donors, those who contributed $200 or less, also increased—another goal of the legislation. Nonetheless, soft money found its way back into the election process, undermining a principal objective of the legislation.

REVENUE: WHERE DOES THE MONEY COME FROM?

The new law has had a significant impact on the base of contributors, the modes of solicitation, and the objects of spending in the 2004 presidential election. This section of the chapter explains how the legislation has affected donors, donations, and the overall revenues that candidates, parties, and nonparty groups receive.

INDIVIDUAL CONTRIBUTORS

One of the most important objectives of the BCRA as well as its predecessor, the FECA, was to reduce the influence that a small number of major contributors had on the presidential nomination and election. To a limited extent, both laws have achieved this goal. No longer can candidates depend on a few wealthy friends to finance their quest for their party's nomination. Since 2002, the limit on individual donors ($2,000 per candidate plus inflation, per election—$2,300 in 2007–2008), the $250 ceiling on matching grants, and the eligibility requirements for federal funds have made the solicitation of a large number of small contributors absolutely essential.

The costs of contemporary campaigns and the decline in the purchasing power of the dollar—it is less than one-third of what it was in 1976—have forced candidates to appeal to more donors than they did before the FECA went into effect, although they have also become increasingly dependent on contributors who give the maximum amount. In 2000, George W. Bush received about two-thirds of his funds from donors who "maxed out" at $1,000; in 2004, he received less than half (43 percent) from those who gave the maximum which the BCRA permitted. In the past two presidential elections, the Democratic candidates received even less from donors who gave the maximum amount. Bradley and Gore averaged 64 percent in 2000, much more than the 23 percent Kerry received from the donors who maxed out in 2004.[24]

In addition to gifts from individuals, the largest single source of revenues, candidates have found other ways to supplement their campaign funds. They can provide some of their own money. There is no restriction on the amount of personal funds that can be spent in the years prior to the election cycle. At the point of candidacy, a $50,000 personal contribution limit is imposed if a candidate accepts federal funds. There are no personal limits for candidates who do not accept federal funds. Thus, in 1992, H. Ross Perot was able to spend over $63 million of his own money on his campaign in lieu of taking government funds. He chose to accept federal funds in 1996, thus limiting his private contribution to $50,000. However, Perot ended up spending more than $8 million of his money to secure the Reform Party's 1996 nomination, fund its nominating conventions, and get the party on the ballot in all fifty states. Of the major party candidates, the single largest personal contributor to his own campaign has been Republican Steve Forbes, who spent close to $38 million of his own fortune in 1996 and more than $48 million in 2000 on his unsuccessful attempts to win the Republican nomination.

Borrowing money is also allowed. The law permits candidates to obtain loans (if they can), provided that the terms of payment are clear and that the money is lent in accordance with regular business practices. Kerry mortgaged his Boston house for $6.4 million to help pay campaign expenses in November 2003. His campaign's success enabled him to pay off his loan from contributions he received in 2004. Losing candidates are usually not as fortunate. They often need the help from the winner to help them pay their campaign debts.

Funds raised but not spent by candidates in their campaigns for other federal offices can be used in their quest for the presidential nomination. John McCain transferred $2 million from his Senate account to fund the initial stages of his 2000 campaign for the Republican nomination. Democratic hopefuls did the same for the 2004 nominations. Kerry and Gephardt transferred $2.9 and $2.6 million respectively from their congressional campaign war chests in 2003.[25]

The ability to tap funds raised in other federal campaigns encourages potential candidates in the House and Senate to raise as much money as they can prior to an anticipated bid for their party's presidential nomination. Thus in her campaign to win reelection in 2006, Senator Hillary Rodham Clinton raised $11 million more than she spent, putting her in a strong financial position to begin her quest for the 2008 Democratic presidential nomination. Other Democrats also transferred money from their Senate to presidential accounts in 2003: Joe Biden ($3.6 million) and Chris Dodd ($4.9 million).[26]

Although cash contributions are restricted, voluntary goods and services are not. Artists and musicians, in particular, can generate considerable revenue for candidates by offering their time and talent. Concerts, and to a lesser extent, art sales, have become excellent sources of revenue. In fact, $2,000-a-plate dinners have become a particularly popular way to bring in large amounts of money early in the nomination process. Incumbents who run for reelection have used their fund-raising prowess to benefit themselves, other partisans, and their party in this manner.

Nonparty Groups

Although election law prohibits corporations and labor unions from making direct contributions to political candidates, it does allow their employees, stockholders, or executives to form Political Action Committees (PACs) and fund them with their voluntary contributions. These groups can affect federal elections in general and the presidential election process in particular by endorsing a candidate, by contributing up to $5,000 to that candidate's campaign, by spending an unlimited amount of money independently for or against a candidate, and by internal communications with their members and sympathizers.

The Federal Election Commission has designated six categories of PACS: corporate, labor, trade/membership/health, nonconnected (not attached to an economic association), cooperative, and corporations without stock. The latter two are the smallest in number and spend the least amount. Corporate PACs are the most numerous and well endowed followed by nonconnected PACs, trade/membership/health, and labor.

With a $5,000 limit on contributions, PACs help presidential candidates more by the dollars they spend on them than by the money they give to them. Republican candidates have generally received more money from PACs than have Democrats, but still PAC contributions represent only a small fraction of the funds they raise. In 2004, a total of $3.5 million was given to candidates seeking the nomination, $2.9 million to Bush, and $600,000 to his Democratic opponents in PAC money.[27]

In the prenomination period before candidates officially declare their candidacy and well before the primaries and caucuses are scheduled, candidates establish Leadership PACs to fund their preprimary activities. They use these PACs to pay staff, travel, and contributions to other campaigns during the midterm election cycle. Leadership PACs have also become mechanisms for identifying and tapping potential donors, not once but continually until the limit for individual contributions is reached. Candidates also set up advocacy PACs to promote their issues and policy positions.

Prior to the 2007–2008 election cycle, seven Republicans and ten Democrats who were contemplating running for their party's nomination had set up one or both of these types of Leadership PACs. In 2006, the seven Republican PACs contributed $1.3 million to other Republican candidates, while the ten Democratic PACs gave $2.2 million to Democratic candidates.[28]

Government Funds

In addition to individuals and nonparty groups, a third source of money is the government matching grants for the nomination and grants for the national party conventions and the general election. Table 2.4 shows the government funds distributed by the Treasury since 1976.

TABLE 2.4 | GOVERNMENT FUNDING OF THE NOMINATION PROCESS, 1976–2004

Year	Matching Funds	Convention Grants	General Election	Total
1976	$24.8	$4.1	$43.6	$73.6
1980	31.3	8.8	63.1	103.3
1984	36.5	16.1	80.8	133.5
1988	67.5	18.4	92.2	178.2
1992	42.9	22.1	110.5	175.4
1996	58.5*	24.7	152.7	236.0
2000	62.3	29.5	147.7	239.5
2004	28.4	29.8	149.2	207.5

*In 1996, H. Ross Perot received partial general election funding as a third party candidate as did Pat Buchanan in 2000.

Source: Federal Election Commission, "Public Funds in Presidential Campaigns." (www.fec.gov/press/press2005/20050203pressum/fundhistory.pdf)

Matching Funds

Here's how matching grants work. Eligible federal candidates who receive individual contributions up to $250 in the election year or the year before can match those contributions by an equal amount from the federal election fund, not to exceed $250 per contribution. These funds, however, are only distributed in the calendar year of the election. To be eligible, candidates must raise $5,000 in twenty states in contributions of $250 or less, a total of $100,000.

Remaining eligible for matching funds is harder than simply qualifying for them. To remain eligible, candidates must receive at least 10 percent of the vote in two consecutive primaries in which they are entered. If they are entered in more than one primary on a given day, they need to win 10 percent in only one of them. Failing to receive this percentage negates their eligibility for federal funds until such time as they receive at least 20 percent of the vote in a subsequent primary.[29]

The 10 percent rule helps front-runners and hurts lesser-known candidates. Twice during the 1984 campaign, Democrat Jesse Jackson lost his eligibility for matching funds, only to regain it later. Similarly in 2004, Al Sharpton and Dennis Kucinich lost their eligibility early in the process and thus could not benefit from the multiplier effect that federal funds provide. The only strategy for a candidate who is fearful of falling short of the required percentage is not to enter a primary, a risky practice for nonfront-runners early in the process, which contributes to the perception that they cannot win.

Minor party candidates may also receive matching funds if they seek their party's nomination. In 2004, Ralph Nader received almost $900,000 in matching funds.

Although the matching fund provision provides opportunities for candidates who begin with less funding, it has not substantially reduced the advantage that nationally recognized candidates have in the private solicitation process. Moreover, the provision encourages all candidates to begin their fund-raising well before the election to qualify as soon as possible and have money available upfront.

The catch is that candidates who accept matching funds have to abide by individual state and overall spending limits. In 2004, the state limits ranged from about $730,000 in the smallest states to almost $15 million for California; in 2008, they are expected to be about $820,000 in the smallest states to almost $18 million in California. The total spending limit, excluding fund-raising and compliance costs, was $37.3 million; in 2008, it will be a little more than $41 million.[30] Theoretically, if candidates qualified, they could receive up to half this limit in matching funds ($18.65 million for 2004).

Additionally, candidates can raise up to 20 percent of their nomination spending total for fund-raising ($7.5 million in 2004 and about $8.2 million in 2008) and 15 percent for legal and compliance costs ($5.6 million in 2004 and about $6.2 million in 2008). Thus the overall total for 2004 was $50.4 million; in 2008 it should be around $56 million.

Although $50 million may seem like a lot of money, it actually is not for multistate caucuses and primaries plus the extended period that bridges the end of the contested phase of the nomination to the national party conventions. The spending limits put federally funded candidates at a disadvantage when competing against privately funded candidates who can raise and spend more. Take the case of John McCain in his quest for the 2000 Republican presidential nomination. McCain was approaching the overall funding limit when the 2000 Republican nomination was effectively decided. Had he chosen to stay in the race and compete in the later primaries, he would have quickly reached the maximum amount that he could have spent under the law. Moreover, had he won the nomination, he would have had no money to spend until the Republican convention, no money to enhance his image, which may have been tarnished during the caucuses and primaries; no money to tell his life story, defining himself before his opponents defined him; and no money to respond to negative assertions or claims that the other party or its nominees made about him prior to the official start of the presidential campaign. It was these reasons that prompted George W. Bush in 2000 and 2004 and Howard Dean and John Kerry in 2004 not to accept federal funds in their quest for their party's nomination, and will prompt most candidates not to do so in 2008 unless they are unable to raise sufficient funds from private sources.

Moreover, since government matching funds are not indexed to inflation as contributions have become, they constitute a decreasing proportion of the total revenues candidates receive. Thus, they will become less important in 2008 and future campaigns unless the law is changed, the grant is indexed to inflation, and the spending limits are increased. (See Box 2.1 "The Costs

| BOX 2.1 | THE COSTS AND BENEFITS OF FEDERAL FUNDS |

Federal funds come with strings attached. Over the years, these strings have become tighter constraints on the candidates. They explain why Bush, Kerry, and Dean decided not to accept matching funds in 2004, although Bush and Kerry did take the general election grant. They did so in part because it was expected of them; it eliminated the burdens of fund-raising during the campaign; and it provided a known amount of upfront money with which to plan and implement a campaign strategy.

Taking government funds creates an impression that a candidate is willing to play by the same rules as everyone else. Conversely, it downplays the perception that money "buys" elections; that the wealthy candidates are always advantaged. For the Republicans, it also works against the Democratic stereotype of them as the party of the rich.

Federal funds also reduce the time and effort that candidates need to devote to fund-raising activities, an original intent of the FECA. With the nominating conventions scheduled later and later, the general election period for spending the funds has been condensed. Not only does the shorter period stretch the funds provided by the government, but it also would make fund-raising during this period more arduous because it would take away time from campaigning. However, money can be raised for the presidential election during the nomination period as long as it is specifically designated for the general election. If a candidate raises money for the general election in this manner and does not win the party's nomination, then that candidate must return the general election funds to the donors. Presidential candidates who raise money are always competing with their partisan brethren for a finite amount from partisan supporters.

Presidential candidates are expected to raise funds from private contributions before, during, and after the caucuses and primaries. They can also use money left over from

---

and Benefits of Federal Funds.") Table 2.5 lists the revenues of the major party candidates in their quest for their party's 2004 presidential nomination.

Convention and Election Grants
Federal funding also extends to the major parties for their national nominating conventions. The convention grant in 2004 was $14.6 million for the major parties and $2.5 for the Reform Party. In 2008, it is expected to be about $16 million for the major parties.

Parties may also seek convention funding from the cities and states in which the event occurs as well as goods and services from the private sector. These supplements can be substantial. In 2000, the Democratic and Republican national committees received $161 million with about $56 million from private sources, mostly companies. In 2004, the private sector contributed $139 million with an additional $142.5 million coming from the host cities of Boston ($56.8 million) and New York ($85.7 million).[31]

Once the major party candidates have been officially nominated, they are eligible for a direct grant. In 2004, $74.6 million was given to the Republican and Democratic candidates; in 2008, it expected to be around $82 million. The actual dollar amount is calculated in the election year by the FEC on the basis of the rate of inflation.

previous federal campaigns to jump-start their race. Moreover, they can begin their quest for contributions the year before the election and have time to develop donor lists and turn to their contributor base several times over the course of the nomination cycle.

Early fund-raising enables candidates to hire staff, design and target advertising, develop an Internet operation with a Web site, and do polling and conduct focus groups. An added bonus is that they can give their leftover funds to party committees to use in the general election. In 2004, John Kerry gave over $40 million back to the Democratic Party, and George W. Bush gave about $30 million to the Republican National Committee and its two congressional campaign committees.[32]

Candidates who can amass a large war chest on their own, such as Hillary Rodham Clinton, Barack Obama, and Mitt Romney in 2007–2008 are disadvantaged by accepting federal funds. If they decide only to accept private contributions, they can continue to raise and spend money up to the day they receive their party's nomination.

George W. Bush's prodigious fund-raising in 2000 and 2004 as well as Kerry's fund-raising in 2004 suggest that presidential candidates in the future will not accept matching grants if they have the potential to raise large amounts of money on their own. (See Box 2.2.) They may not even accept the federal grant for the general election if they believe that they can raise more money than they would receive from federal funds. Hillary Rodham Clinton was the first candidate in the 2007–2008 election cycle to say that she would not accept federal funds during the nomination period, and if she was nominated, during the general election. Barack Obama and John McCain said that they would do so in the general election but only if their opponents did so as well. Lesser-known candidates who are not independently wealthy may have no other viable option than accepting the largess of the federal government with all the strings attached.

If candidates accept federal funds, they must limit their campaign expenditures in the general election to the amount of the grant. To comply with the law, they cannot accept private contributions except those designated for a special account to cover legal fees, accounting, and compliance costs (GELAC accounts). In 2004, the major party candidates collected $21 million for these general election-related costs; Bush collected $12.2 million, and Kerry $8.9 million.[33]

Minor party candidates may receive private contributions and also are eligible for federal funds in amounts equal to the proportion of the vote they receive, provided it is at least 5 percent of the total. Had Perot accepted federal funds in 1992, he would have received $25.96 million, 47 percent of the amount the major party candidates were given; however, he would have received it after the election was over. Automatically eligible for federal funds in 1996 because of the size of the vote he received in 1992, Perot got $29 million; in 2000, the Reform Party nominee, Pat Buchanan, was eligible for $12.6 million from the campaign fund, but the small vote he received in that election has made the Reform Party ineligible for federal funds thereafter. Green Party candidate Ralph Nader did not receive sufficient votes in 2000 or 2004 to qualify the party that nominated him for federal funding (Green in 2000 and Reform in 2004).

TABLE 2.5 | PRENOMINATION REVENUES OF MAJOR PARTY CANDIDATES IN 2004 (THROUGH DECEMBER 31, 2004) IN MILLIONS

Candidate	Federal Matching Funds	Individual Contributions	Other Funds: PAC and Other Committee Contributions, Transfers, Loans	Campaign Total
Democratic				
Clark	$7.6	17.3	.2	25.1
Dean	0	51.1	0	51.1
Edwards	6.6	21.6	1.0	29.2
Gephardt	4.1	14.3	2.8	21.2
Kerry	0	215.3	19.2	234.5
Kucinich	3.1	8.0	Less than .1	11.1
LaRouche	1.5	8.2	.1	9.8
Lieberman	4.3	14.1	Less than .1	18.4
Braun	0	.5	Less than .1	.5
Sharpton	0	.5	Less than .1	.5
Total	$27.2	350.9	23.6	401.7
Other				
Nader	.9	1.5	Less than .1	2.4
Republican				
Bush	0	258.8	9.4	268.2
Grand Total	28.1	611.4	34.3	673.8

Source: Federal Election Commission, "Presidential Pre-Nomination Campaign Receipts through December 31, 2004." Press Release, February 3, 2005. (www.fec.gov/press/press2005/20050203pressum/presrec2004full.pdf)

EXPENDITURES

Additional sources of revenue are necessary because campaign costs keep rising with more candidates seeking their party's nomination and with greater use of advanced communications technology and mass media to reach the electorate and the grassroots organizations necessary to turn them out to vote. In most election cycles, these increased costs have exceeded the rate of inflation, requiring greater efforts at fund-raising by the candidates.

The crunch in expenditures represents the greatest problem at the beginning of the nomination process. The need to gain recognition, get a boost, or maintain a lead prompts candidates to spend much of their money early, well before the first contest is held.

BOX 2.2	THE MONEY RACE FOR THE 2004 NOMINATION

The Democrats The money race for the 2004 presidential election began more than two years before the nomination when Democratic candidates began to map their initial strategies and assemble their fund-raising teams. They did not start equally. Some of them had campaign funds left over from previous contests that they could use in their presidential quest: John Kerry transferred $2.9 million, Richard Gephardt $2.6 million, and John Edwards about $2 million.[34]

Some Democrats set up Leadership PACs; some had created nonfederal soft money PACs in the 2000–2001 election cycle, the last one in which they were allowed to do so. Edwards' New American Optimists PAC raised $3 million, and his nonfederal, soft money PAC raised $4.6 million; Gephardt's Effective Government Committee took in $1.5, while his soft money PAC raised $1.4 million; Kerry's Citizen Soldier Fund raised $1 million, and his soft money PAC raised $1.4 million; Joe Lieberman had a Leadership PAC that raised $1.7 million.[35]

The front-loaded and compressed Democratic calendar of caucuses and primaries now requires candidates to raise money earlier and earlier. They do so for several reasons. Upfront money is viewed as a sign of candidate viability by the news media, political pros, and especially by donors who want to give to a winner. Money begets money. It enhances a candidate's fund-raising potential. Having a large war chest early also gives candidates more flexibility in where and how to campaign.

Being perceived as a front-runner is advantageous in the money race. John Kerry benefited from this perception at the beginning of the 2003–2004 election cycle, raising $7 million in the first quarter of 2003. The big surprise, however, was John Edwards who outdid Kerry by raising $7.4 million. Edwards' early success was the big news because it was unexpected; Kerry's was not.

The rest of the Democrats with less initial recognition raised much less. Former governor of Vermont, Howard Dean, was one of the lesser-known candidates who found an issue, the war in Iraq, and an instrument to exploit it, the Internet. With the exception of Dennis Kucinich, all the Democratic contenders were members of Congress who had voted in favor of a resolution authorizing the president to use force, if necessary, against Iraq. Dean (and the other minor Democratic candidates) stood alone in their opposition to the war. As the news from Iraq worsened, Dean's outspoken denunciation of the president's foreign policy in general and the war in Iraq in particular, hit a responsive cord among Democratic activists who contributed money to his campaign.

The use of the Internet by the Dean campaign accelerated his fund-raising success. Moreover, the Internet greatly reduced the cost and time that a direct-mail, fund-raising campaign would have taken. In the words of Dean's campaign director, Joe Trippi: "On the Net, we were the first mover, and every day that no one tried to do anything to get in it meant it was another day we were getting closer to having that $200 that we thought we could get to."[36] A Web site with a blog for communication among Dean's supporters and officials of the campaign generated millions of dollars and thousands of volunteers; it took on the appearance of a spontaneous grassroots operation. The news media took notice.

During the summer and fall of 2003, the Dean campaign raised more than $30 million, much of it from small donors who gave $200 or less. In the previous six months, he had raised $10 million, most of it after May 1, 2003, the day that the president announced that the military phase of the war had been successfully completed. In total, almost 1 million people gave money to Dean.[37]

(continued)

BOX 2.2

THE MONEY RACE FOR THE 2004
NOMINATION *continued*

As the former Vermont governor was reaping the benefits of Democratic discontent with the war, the economy, and spiking gasoline prices, other Democratic candidates were struggling to compete in the money race. Not only were they hurt by their initial support of the war but also by the emergence of a new candidate, former General Wesley Clark, who had stronger national security credentials than did the other Democrats. Clark's belated candidacy sparked an initial burst of contributions from Democrats eager to defeat Bush. Clark raised almost $17 million, much of it on his Web site.

With the Iowa caucus and New Hampshire primary rapidly approaching, the Democrats began to adopt strategies dictated in part by their financial positions. Senator Bob Graham (Florida) dropped out; Representative Gephardt (Missouri) turned to his labor supporters and neighboring Iowa as a make or break state; Senator Lieberman (Connecticut) decided to forego Iowa entirely and literally moved to New Hampshire for several months, renting an apartment for he and his wife. General Clark looked past the early contests to the southern primaries that would be held later. He hoped his military background and Arkansas birthplace might give him an edge in those states; Senator Edwards continued to focus on Iowa, articulating a positive, upbeat message that distinguished his candidacy from the negative campaigns of Gephardt and Dean. And all of these Democrats looked forward to January 2004 when they would receive their matching grants from the federal treasury, funds they needed to keep their campaigns alive.

Dean's fund-raising advantage also shaped his initial strategy. He decided to put everything he had into Iowa and New Hampshire with the hope of knocking out the other contenders and being the only Democratic candidate left standing after these early contests. To pursue such a strategy, Dean had to maintain his momentum from the summer and fall, move his volunteers en mass first to Iowa and then New Hampshire, and spend more than his rivals on the ground and on the air. Not wanting to be restricted by the federal limits imposed on candidates who accepted federal funds, Dean announced that he would forego these funds, thereby freeing up his campaign to spend whatever they believed was necessary to win. In December 2003 when he made this decision, Dean had the largest war chest of all the Democrats, about $40 million.

In late November, rival John Kerry had practically run out of funds. Had he accepted matching grants, he would be limited in what he could spend and most importantly, what he could give or lend his own campaign. After Dean's announcement, Kerry also decided to forego government funds. He then dug into his own family wealth to lend his campaign the money it needed to match Dean's effort and stay afloat: $850,000 in mid December and an additional $6.4 million in December and January.[38]

The gamble for Kerry paid off. Not only was he able to mount an effective campaign in Iowa, building on the boost he received from veterans, including the man whose life he had saved in Vietnam, but he also put himself in a position to raise additional funds if he was successful. Money started flowing into his campaign after his surprising victory in Iowa. With no limits placed on spending it, Kerry was able to keep up a heavy media effort in New Hampshire to buttress an already large grassroots operation. Success in New Hampshire led to more money and greater opportunities in other states. Kerry was on his way to capturing the Democratic nomination.

With the exception of Clark, most of the other candidates had spent almost all of what they had raised in 2003 and were down to the last of their matching grants at the beginning of 2004. Without substantial wins, they couldn't raise additional money; without additional money, they could not mount effective campaigns. Only Kerry, and Edwards for a short time, were in a position to do so.

Even after his victories in the early contests, Kerry's fund-raising was far from over. He had spent $39.1 million by the end of February, less than Dean but more than the others. In March, he spent only $14.5 million, enough to sew up the Democratic nomination but not enough to counter the Bush campaign in the months that followed. Once Kerry had effectively secured the Democratic nomination by early March, he had to begin raising money again, lots of it, not only to pay off his campaign debt to himself, but also to be in a position to counter Bush and the Republicans in the period leading up to the national nominating conventions in the summer. In the end, Kerry raised $234.5 million—almost $1 million a day after he became the preordained Democratic nominee.

The Republicans George W. Bush's fund-raising strategy was straightforward and similar to his successful operation in 2000. Not having to worry about a challenger, Bush desired to raise enough money to respond to any potent criticism voiced by the Democratic candidates, define his eventual challenger as he wanted him defined, and lay the foundation for his reelection campaign. Bush's finance people did not see their fund-raising task as particularly difficult. It hadn't been difficult for Bush in 2000. With the individual contribution limits doubled and party contributions increased, with a network of donors and fund-raisers in place, and with the president remaining very popular among Republicans, the Bush reelection team was extremely confident that the campaign could raise as much money as needed to win. The campaign began with $671,000 left over from the 2000 election.

Bush's fund-raising effort commenced in the summer of 2003 after the military phase of the war in Iraq had been completed. The initial focus was on the large donors. Throughout the summer and into the fall, the reelection committee held a series of fund-raisers in which the president, First Lady, and/or vice president spoke and chattered with donors. Millions of dollars were raised at these events.

In addition, the president's principal bundlers, the people who raised the largest amounts, went into action. Mavericks, fund-raisers under the age of forty, promised to raise $50,000 each; Pioneers, many of whom helped Bush 2000, pledged to raise at least $100,000, while the Rangers, the best connected and most successful solicitors, set $200,000 or more as their goal. A new category of Super Rangers was also established, people who raised at least $200,000 for Bush and $300,000 for the Republican National Committee. By the time of the Republican National Convention in late August, 2004, these groups of bundlers had raised almost $77 million for the president's reelection efforts and millions more for the national party's campaign.[39]

To appreciate how successful the Bush reelection committee was in raising money, the Bush team had received $132.7 million compared to $139 for all the Democrats combined by the end of 2003. But the campaign had spent only $33.6 million, while the Democrats had been forced to spend most of the money they raised. The president's fund-raising continued as the Democratic primaries got underway. By March 31, 2004, over $181 million had been collected in the Bush war chest. Activities were then scaled back; major events at which the president and vice president appeared were concluded,

(continued)

THE MONEY RACE FOR THE 2004
NOMINATION *continued*

but money still kept pouring in. By the end of May, $213 million had been raised; the total figure for the nomination period was close to $259 million.

Most of Bush's contributions came from large donors: 56 percent from those who gave $1,000 or more; 43 percent by those who gave the maximum $2,000. The small contributors, people who gave $200 or less, accounted for 30 percent of the total contributions. Kerry, in contrast, received 34 percent from the smallest donors ($200 or less) and 23 percent from the largest $2,000.[40]

Having so much money so early in the process gave Bush and the Republicans an advantage. They could begin their campaign just as soon as the Democrats completed the contested stage of their nomination process. Kerry had spent most of what was in his war chest. Although he could and did raise more money, it took him time to do so. Thus, the Democrats had to depend on nonparty groups, with whom they could not coordinate activities, to mount a campaign from early March until mid May while the president's reelection campaign could spend money as it saw fit. The Republicans were also helped financially by holding their convention at the end of August. They had five less weeks than the Democrats over which to distribute public funds from their general election grant.

In the end, both sides spent about the same amount, but the strategic financial advantages gave the Republicans more control over their spending. Those advantages may have made the difference in the close presidential election.

Independent Ralph Nader   Ralph Nader raised less money in 2004 ($3.4 million) than in 2000 ($5.1 million) when he was the Green Party's presidential nominee. He was forced to spend most of his 2004 funds on gaining ballot access. Democrats successfully challenged his petitions in several of the key battleground states, including Ohio, Pennsylvania, and Oregon. As a result, Nader competed in only thirty-four states, nine less than in 2000. He had only about $1 million left to spend on his actual presidential campaign.

CAMPAIGN SPENDING STRATEGIES

For most candidates, the most important caucuses and primaries are the first ones in Iowa and New Hampshire, two relatively small states with low spending limits. The desire to be free of these limits has led three Republican aspirants, John Connally (1980), Steve Forbes (1996 and 2000), and George W. Bush (2000 and 2004), and two Democrats, Howard Dean and John Kerry (2004), to reject matching funds.

It has become common practice for campaign workers to commute to the early states from neighboring ones, thus allowing the campaign to allocate only a portion of its expenses to the state in which the early contest will be held. Another tactic is to use national phone banks to canvas voters within these states. Television ads, particularly those directed at New Hampshire, are aired on Boston television, where 85 percent of the cost can be applied to the Massachusetts limit.[41]

As the campaign progresses, candidates do bump up against the total spending ceiling, but since the contests have been effectively settled fairly early in

TABLE 2.6 | PRESIDENTIAL SPENDING LIMITS AND COLAS (COST OF LIVING ADJUSTMENTS) FOR THE DEMOCRATIC AND REPUBLICAN PARTIES, 1976–2008 (IN MILLIONS)

	1974	1976	1980	1984	1988	1992	1996	2000	2004	2008*
Primary election limit[†]	$10	$10.9	$14.7	$20.2	$23.1	$27.6	$31.0	$33.8	$37.3	$41.0
General election limit[‡]	20	21.8	29.4	40.4	46.1	55.2	61.8	67.6	74.6	82.0
Party convention limit[§]	2	2.2	4.4	8.1	9.2	11.0	12.4	13.5	14.6	16.2
Party general election limit	–	3.2	4.6	6.9	8.3	10.3	11.6	13.7	14.8	16.4

*2008 figures are estimated based on the announced increase in individual contributions.

[†]Primary candidates receiving matching funds must comply with two types of spending limits: a national limit (listed in this table) and a separate limit for each state. The state limit is $200,000 or 164 multiplied by the state's voting-age population, whichever is greater. (Both amounts are adjusted for increases in the cost of living.)

[‡]Legal and accounting expenses to comply with the law are exempt from this limit. These funds may be raised through private contributions.

[§]This limit has been raised twice by legislation: once in 1979 and once in 1984.

Source: Federal Election Commission, *Annual Report, 1984* (June 1, 1985), 8–9, updated by the author with data supplied by the Federal Election Commission.

the calendar year, the overall limits have not been as much of a problem as the individual state limits in Iowa and New Hampshire. As noted previously, the overall limits would have been a problem for McCain, however, had he stayed in the 2000 race for the Republican nomination after the first Tuesday in March; they quickly would have become one for Gore and Bradley as well had the 2000 Democratic contest continued. They were also a problem for Dole in 1996 but only after he had effectively secured the Republican nomination. Table 2.6 lists the limits since the Federal Election Campaign Act went into effect.

SUPPLEMENTARY CAMPAIGNS

In addition to the campaign run by the presidential candidates' organizations, party and nonparty groups are also involved in presidential elections; sometimes they are involved independently and sometimes in coordination with the presidential candidates.

The Major Parties
The national party organizations tend to remain on the sidelines during the primaries and caucuses until their nomination contests have been decided. They

TABLE 2.7 | NATIONAL PARTY REVENUES IN RECENT PRESIDENTIAL
ELECTIONS (IN MILLIONS)

	1991–1992	1995–1996	1999–2000	2003–2004
Democrats	$163.3	221.6	275.2	683.8 (84%)*
Republicans	$264.9	416.5	465.8	784.8 (78%)*

*Indicates the percentage of the funds from individual donors.

Source: Federal Election Commission, "National Party Federal Financial Activity Through the 2004 Election Cycle," Press Release March 2, 2005. (Corrected March 14, 2005.) (www.fec.gov/press/press2005/20050302 party/Parety2004final)

do not make direct financial contributions to the various people seeking their nomination, but they can and do help their potential nominee once a winner has emerged from the process.

To do this, they need money, lots of it. Despite the prohibition placed on soft money solicitation beginning in 2002, national party committees raised record amounts during the 2003–2004 election cycle. Table 2.7 lists the amount they raised in the past four presidential elections.

In 2004, the Democrats and Republicans raised more hard money by taking advantage of the polarized climate and divided electorate, exploiting the strong feelings for and against the war in Iraq and the Bush administration, and investing in computerized databases and technologies that facilitated the identification and targeting of large numbers of potential contributors. Additionally, they benefited from increased contribution limits that were established in the BCRA.

Each party set up a special program designed to encourage its most well-connected fund-raisers to obtain large gifts and bundle smaller ones. By the end of the election cycle, the Democrats could point to 17 "Trustees" who raised $250,000 for their party and 188 "Patriots" who solicited donations that totaled $100,000 or more; the Republicans had 104 "Super Rangers" who raised $300,000 each for the GOP as well as $200,000 for the Bush campaign.[42]

The major parties' successes in fund-raising gave them more money to spend on the presidential election, and the BCRA gave them more ways to spend it. The Supreme Court's decision in *Colorado Republican Federal Campaign Committee v. Federal Election Commission*, 518 U.S.604 (1996), voided a regulation by the FEC that prohibited parties from spending independently on the presidential contest if they also engaged in a coordinated campaign with their presidential candidate. Thus, in addition to the $16.25 million that the parties were permitted to spend in coordination with their presidential campaign, in 2004, they also spent millions more independently. The Democrats spent $120 million independently, most of it in opposition to Bush. Republicans spent much less independently, $18.3 million, but the National Campaign Committee also shared advertising expenses with the Bush campaign by airing commercials that contained a generic party appeal (for which they paid)

TABLE 2.8 | PAC CONTRIBUTIONS AND EXPENDITURES FOR 2003–2004 FEDERAL ELECTIONS (IN MILLIONS)

Type	Contributions		Partisan Division		Money Spent	
	Pres.	Total (to all federal candidates)	Dem.	Rep	For	Against
Corporate	$1.6	115.6	37.1	76.6	.2	–
Labor	.2	52.1	45.4	6.6	19.5	1.3
Trade*	.4	83.2	30.3	52.9	14.5	3.5
Nonconnected	.7	52.5	18.5	33.9	14.1	4.0
Cooperative	*	2.9	1.4	1.4	*	0
Corporations Without Stock	*	4.1	1.6	2.6	*	*

*less than 1 percent

Source: Federal Election Commission, "PAC Activity Increases for 2004 Elections," April 13, 2005. (www.fed.gov/press/press2005/20050412pac/PACFinal)

as well as a specific pro-Bush and/or anti-Kerry message (paid for by the Bush campaign). In this coordinated advertising effort, the GOP spent a total of $45.8 million.

Nonparty Groups

In addition to party spending, there is also spending by nonparty groups. The election law defines and legitimizes these groups. It permits them to get involved in the electoral process by contributing a limited amount of money to federal candidates, communicating in an unrestricted manner with their members, and mounting public appeals that are only constrained thirty days or less before a primary or caucus and sixty days or less before the general election.

During the 2003–2004 election cycle, political action committees raised $915.7 million and spent $842.9 million, an increase of 28 percent from the previous presidential election cycle.[43] Corporate and Trade PACs raised and spent the most with the majority of funds going to Republican candidates; Labor groups gave overwhelmingly to the Democrats. Table 2.8 lists PAC contributions and expenditures reported to the FEC for 2004 for their federal accounts, for example, contributions in which the limits were applicable.

But the big PAC news in 2004 was not their adherence to the individual contribution limits prescribed by the BCRA but how some groups, referred to as 527s and 501c, circumvented those limits by raising large amounts of money from a relatively few wealthy donors. (See Box 2.3 "Soft Money Subterfuge in 2004.")

The other major shift in nonparty group activities in 2004 was also related to BCRA. The thirty- and sixty-day-limits placed on advertising that mentioned

BOX 2.3 | SOFT MONEY SUBTERFUGE IN 2004

Although some nonparty groups had organized themselves before the 2004 presidential election as nonpartisan, nonprofit, advocacy groups under section 527 of the Internal Revenue Service code, they had not played a major role in the presidential election campaign.[44] The reason that they did not do so is that political parties did not need or want such groups to solicit soft money; they wanted to do so themselves. The enactment of the BCRA, however, changed the situation and created incentives for nonparty groups to appeal to the large donors who could no longer give unlimited contributions to the national parties.

The Democrats were especially fearful that the BCRA would hurt them more than the Republicans, in part because they had been more dependent on soft money donations than the Republicans. Moreover, George W. Bush had been an extraordinarily successful fund-raiser and would be in an even better position to raise even more because he was the incumbent, and his contributors could give twice as much ($2,000) as they had in the past. It also seemed likely to the Democrats that all their candidates for their party's nomination, with the possible exception of Kerry, would need to accept federal matching funds and thereby would have to abide by the individual state and overall nomination limits. Democratic leaders assumed that their winning nominee would be battered and broke by mid March, the point in the nomination calendar when a candidate would probably emerge from the pack with a large enough lead to be designated as the all-but-certain nominee.

What could the party do about this problem? How could it help its nominee as it had done for Gore during a similar period prior to the party's national convention if it lacked sufficient funds to run a generic campaign? These problems prompted Terry McAuliffe, Chair of the Democratic National Committee, to create a task force of party officials and Democratic-leaning campaign consultants to look into the potential financial disaster that loomed ahead for the Democrats and suggest ways of overcoming it. The task force's suggestion was to set up more active 527 organizations that could raise soft money from the party's traditional big donors. Such groups are permitted to engage in political activities, including issue advocacy and get-out-the-vote campaigns, but they are not subject to the federal contribution limits unless they constitute a political party or political action committee. The 527 groups also are prohibited from coordinating their political activities with the candidates or their parties. They can, however, coordinate among themselves, and most did in 2004.

Beginning in the spring of 2003, stealth Democratic groups began to organize and raise money, helped in large part by millions of dollars in "seed money" given to them by financier George Soros and insurance magnate, Peter Lewis.[45] (See Table 2.9.) They also hired political operatives and campaign consultants who possessed knowledge of previous Democratic Party campaigns. In one case, two of the largest, democratically oriented 527s, Americans Coming Together and the Media Fund, used the same consulting firm to run their public communications, a firm headed by the former director of the Kerry campaign, Jim Jordan. Moreover, the groups' offices were housed in the same building on Capitol Hill.

The 527s went into action after the Democratic nomination was settled and the Bush campaign started running anti-Kerry ads in early March. For most of that month and the one that followed, these groups took up the slack in the campaign. As Kerry was busy raising money, the 527s were spending it on his behalf.[46]

TABLE 2.9 | THE TOP 527 GROUPS IN THE 2003–2004 ELECTION CYCLE

Democratic-Oriented	Amt. Raised (in Millions)	Republican-Oriented	Amt. Raised (in Millions)
America Coming Together	$79.8	Progress for America Voter Fund	44.9
Joint Victory Camp.2004	71.8	Swift Boat Veterans for Truth	17.0
The Media Fund	59.4	College Republican National Com.	12.8
		Club for Growth	10.6
Service Employees International Union, Political Education and Action Fund	48.4	National Assn. of Realtors, 527 Fund	3.0
American Federation of State, County, & Municipal Employees, Sp. Acct.	25.5	November Fund	3.2
Moveon.Org Voter Fund	13.0	Republican Leadership Coalition	1.3
New Democratic Network	12.7	California Republican National Convention Delegation, 2004 Acct.	1.6
Citizens for a Strong Senate	10.8	Nat'l Federation of Republican Women	1.4
Sierra Club Voter Education Fund	8.7		
Emily's List	7.7		

*Many of these groups also had federal accounts in which contributions were limited to those prescribed in the BCRA of 2002.

Source: "527 Committee Activity, 2004" the Center for Responsive Politics. (www.opensecrets.org/527s/527 cmtes.asp?level=C&cycle=2004, accessed November 1, 2006)

Naturally, Republicans were furious at this attempt to skirt the new law. They appealed to the Federal Election Commission to ban large-scale solicitations by these groups. A majority of the commissioners, however, did not want to touch this new and explosive political issue during the campaign and decided not to regulate this activity at that time, a decision later affirmed by the FEC after the election.[47]

The FEC's decision not to intervene left the Republicans no option but to establish their own 527s. In doing so, they followed the Democratic pattern of raising money from wealthy contributors and having their 527 groups hire people with knowledge of

(continued)

| BOX 2.3 | SOFT MONEY SUBTERFUGE IN 2004 *continued* |

Republican Party campaigns to spend it most effectively. Because the Bush campaign was dominating the airwaves in the key battleground states, most of the GOP groups waited until after the Democratic Convention to go into action.

Combined, the 527s raised $424 million during the 2003–2004 election cycle, considerably less than the amount of soft money the parties had received in the previous presidential and congressional elections. Almost 70 percent of the money that these groups solicited came from donors of $1 million or more. Interestingly, the 527 donors were not, by and large, the same individuals and groups that contributed most of the soft money two or four years earlier.[48] Table 2.9 lists the major Democratic and Republican-oriented 527s and the amount of money that these expenses received in the 2003–2004 election period; Table 2.10 indicates their major contributors and the amount of soft money these contributors gave. (For a discussion of the 527s, their advertising, and their impact in the general election, see pages 284–286.)

Even though 527 groups may accept unlimited campaign contributions, they still have to disclose the names of their contributors and the amount they gave. This disclosure provision, enacted by Congress in 2003, prompted the use of still another part of the Internal Revenue code, section 501c, to skirt the reporting provision entirely. The so-called 501c groups have less restrictive reporting requirements than 527s. They do not have to make their donors names and the size of their contributions public. Moreover, their campaign expenditures are tax deductible as long as they do not exceed 50 percent of the group's annual budget. The only requirement that 501c groups have is to make their annual tax returns public.

Although 501c groups cannot engage in express advocacy, they can discuss controversial issues and emphasize the positions the candidates have taken on them. Thus, they can bring issues to public attention that the presidential candidates and their parties might be unwilling to do, and in some cases, might not even want them to do. They can also engage in voter mobilization efforts.[49] Examples of 501c groups that were involved

---

candidates by name encouraged these groups as well as the parties to spend more money on grassroots organizing in the final days of the campaign and less on television advertising. This shift coincided with the mobilization efforts of the candidates and the parties to maximize their base vote. Thus, nonparty groups contributed to the higher turnout in 2004, as they will probably also do in 2008.

PATTERNS OF CAMPAIGN EXPENDITURES

Despite the increase in the amount of money spent on grassroots efforts, the bulk of expenditures were still devoted to the design, production, and airing of political commercials. About 70 percent of the Bush campaign budget and 66 percent of Kerry's went into advertising.[50] Candidate and nonparty groups devoted the bulk of their spending to media-related campaigning. Party expenditures were more evenly divided among fund-raising, political ads, polling, and grassroots turnout activities with the Republicans devoting a

TABLE 2.10 | THE BIG CONTRIBUTORS TO THE 527S IN THE 2003–2004
ELECTION CYCLE

Contributor	Business	Amount Given to 527s (in Millions)
George Soros	Finance	$ 24.0
Peter Lewis	Insurance	22.5
Stephen Bing	Entertainment	13.9
Sandler, Herb & Marion	Finance	13.0
Bob Perry	Construction	8.0
Dawn Arnall	Finance	5.0
Alex Spanos		5.0
Ted Waitt		5.0
T. Boone Pickens	Finance	4.6
Jerry Perenchio		4.0

Source: Steve Weissman, and Ruth Hazssan, "BCRA and the 527 Groups," in Michael J. Malbin, ed. *The Election after Reform: Money, Politics and the Bipartisan Campaign Reform Act*, Lanham, MD. Rowman and Littlefield, 2006: 94.

in the most recent presidential election include the National Rifle Association with a budget in the millions and the Sierra Club, which also had a regular PAC and a 527 in addition to a 501c PAC. The top ten groups with nonfederal accounts listed in terms of the amount of money they raised are listed in Table 2.9.

larger percentage of their funds to identifying, contacting, and turning out voters than the Democrats. Table 2.11 indicates the distribution of expenditures by candidates, parties, and nonparty groups in the 2003–2004 election cycle.

FINANCIAL ILLEGALITIES AND IMPROPRIETIES

The complexity of the federal laws governing elections, the desire of parties and nonparty groups to skirt the restrictions imposed on them whenever possible, and the thin line between illegal coordination and legal cooperation has led to charges and counter charges of campaign violations and illegal activities during and after elections.

In 1996, the FEC charged that the Christian Coalition violated the law by coordinating its nonpartisan advocacy advertising with the Republican Party and its candidates, but a federal court dismissed the charges. The Republicans made similar accusations against organized labor in 1996 when union dues financed a $35 million campaign in seventy-five key congressional districts

TABLE 2.11 | CAMPAIGN EXPENDITURES IN 2004: WHO AND ON WHAT?

	Republicans			Democrats		
	RNC	Bush Campaign	527s	DNC	Kerry Campaign	527s
Total Amount Spent (Millions)	$322.6	328.7	57.8	337.2	320.4	177.8
Expenses (percentages)						
Administrative	40%	17	12	14	8	10
Fund-raising	21	13	2	18	27	38
Media	20	54	81	45	45	27
Grassroots campaigning	18	7	5	20	7	21
Other	1	9	0	3	13	4

Source: "The Costliest Campaign," *Washington Post*, December 30, 2004, A7.

primarily for Democratic candidates. In 2004, Benjamin Ginsberg, attorney for the Republican National Committee, also advised a Republican-oriented 527 group on campaign finance law. When his nonparty, consultative role became public, Ginsberg was forced to sever his tie to the 527 group because of the noncoordination restriction placed on nonparty groups with the parties and candidates.

Throughout the years, there have been numerous other allegations about illegal campaign finance activities. Republicans claimed that a Democratic Party fund-raiser in a Buddhist temple in Los Angeles in 2000, one in which Vice President Gore participated, violated the law because of religious institutions' nonpartisan status as tax-exempt organizations precluded their use for partisan political purposes. Questions were also raised about the $5,000 contributions from monks who had taken vows of poverty and thus probably did not have much, if any, personal wealth to donate. None of the monks were prosecuted, however. The Democrats returned the money, but the accusation plagued the campaign.[51]

Short of illegalities, the need for money has led candidates to take funds from questionable sources and to reward those who can raise the most money. In 1996, the Clinton-Gore campaign and the Democratic Party were forced to return thousands of dollars donated by people with criminal ties and records and foreign nationals who are not permitted by law to contribute to U.S. federal elections. In 2006, President Bush returned $6,000 his campaign received directly from lobbyist Jack Abramoff, his wife, and a friend after

Abramoff admitted his guilt in business transactions, lobbying activities, and tax evasion.[52]

The use of government facilities for rewarding private contributors has also raised concerns. The White House served as a backdrop during the Clinton years; Vice President Cheney held a large fund-raising event on the grounds of his official residence at the Naval Observatory. It has become common practice for recent presidents to schedule public events before fund-raising activities in the same cities so that taxpayers will pick up the tab for the bulk of the president's travel expenses, and the press can report on what the presidents said and did during the public phase of their travels.

A related issue is the special treatment that major contributors and fund-raisers receive. The Center for Responsive Politics, which charts the money flow and special treatment, reported that 40 percent of George W. Bush's Pioneers ($100,000+ fundraisers) in his 2000 campaign ended up on a presidential transition task force or with a government job during Bush's first term. Twenty-three became ambassadors, three cabinet secretaries, thirty-seven were on the teams that recommended people for federal appointments, people who would be in a position to return favors later to their benefactors. Why would these benefactors need favors? The short answer is that 25 percent of Bush's Pioneers were employed as lobbyists.[53]

George W. Bush, of course, is not the first and will not be the last president to appoint campaign staff, financial supporters, and party workers to executive branch positions. The spoils system has deep roots in American politics that extend back to the beginnings of the party system in the Jefferson administration. The conundrum for a democratic election process, however, remains the same. Is it fair that those with the greater resources—money, expertise, and time—exercise more influence than others over the course of the election? Is it fair that money "buys" access in some cases and appears to have bought votes as the activities of lobbyist Jack Abramoff and some members of Congress suggest?[54]

MONEY AND ELECTORAL SUCCESS

The relationship between money and electoral success has spurred considerable debate in recent years and generated much anger by those who believe unequal resources undermine the democratic character of the U.S. electoral process. Is the conventional wisdom correct? Do those with more money have an advantage? Do they usually win? The simple answer is usually yes, but the longer answer is more complicated. First, who has or gets the money? Second, what difference does the money make in the election?

Two types of candidates tend to have disproportionate resources at their disposal: those who are personally wealthy and those who are well-known and well-connected public figures. Money can buy recognition as it did for Ross Perot in 1992 and 1996 and Steve Forbes in 1996; it gave them a chance that they would not otherwise have had. But obviously, money cannot, in and of itself, buy an electoral victory as both Perot and Forbes found out. Similarly, frontrunners, such as Bill Clinton and Robert Dole in 1996, Al Gore and George W. Bush in 2000, and Bush and John Kerry, once he won in Iowa and New Hampshire in 2004, can raise more money because they are perceived as likely to win the nomination, and that money in turn contributes to their likelihood for success.

Theoretically, campaign spending should have a greater impact on the nomination process than on the general election and at the beginning of the process rather than at the end. According to political scientists Michael Robinson, Clyde Wilcox, and Paul Marshall, money matters most when the candidates are least known to the voters, when they do not receive a lot of news coverage, and when paid advertising, which, of course, is expensive, can bring recognition and enhance images.[55]

As the nomination process progresses and candidates become more easily recognized by the public, the expenditure of funds is not as critical to electoral success. What money buys initially are name recognition, organizational support, and campaign consultants; what it buys over the course of the campaign are advertising and a turn-out-the-vote operation.

Have the candidates with the largest bankrolls generally been victorious in the general election? The answer again seems to be yes, although as in the nomination process, it is difficult to determine precisely whether money contributed to victory or simply flowed to the likely winner.

Between 1860 and 1972, the winner outspent the loser twenty-one out of twenty-nine times. Republican candidates have spent more than their Democratic opponents in twenty-five out of twenty-nine elections during this period. The four times they did not, the Democrats won.

The correlation between money and electoral success has continued in the contemporary period even though the major party candidates are offered the same amount of money from the federal treasury for the general election if they choose to accept it. Independent spending can make a difference. In the 1980s, considerably more was spent on behalf of Republican nominees than for their Democratic opponents, and the GOP won each presidential election during this period. In the 1990s, the Democrats benefited from substantial expenditures by organized labor and the impact of the Perot campaign, although their total spending was still less than the Republicans'. George W. Bush was the financial as well as electoral victor in 2000; in 2004, however, the amount of money each side had was about equal and the results of the vote were very close. In Congress, however, the big spenders won 95.6 of the House races and 91 percent of those in the Senate in 2004.[56]

What do all these trends suggest? The pattern of greater spending and electoral victories indicates that money contributes to success, but potential success also attracts money. Having more funds is an advantage, but it does not explain all outcomes. The fact that heavily favored incumbent Richard Nixon outspent rival George McGovern more than 2 to 1 in 1972 does not explain McGovern's huge defeat, although it probably portended it. On the other hand, Hubert Humphrey's much narrower defeat by Nixon four years earlier was partially influenced by Humphrey spending less than $12 million, compared with more than $25 million spent by Nixon. The closer the election, the more the disparity in funds can make a difference.

SUMMARY

Campaign finance became an important aspect of presidential elections by the end of the nineteenth and the beginning of the twentieth centuries. In recent years, however, it has become even more important as campaign costs have escalated and legal restrictions have limited large gifts to candidates and their political parties. Expanded use of high technology and multiple channels of communication to reach the voters have been partially responsible for the large increase in expenditures.

In the early- and mid-twentieth century, candidates of both major parties turned to large contributors for financial support. Their dependence on a relatively small number of large donors, combined with spiraling costs, created serious problems for a democratic selection process. The 1972 presidential election, with its high expenditures, "dirty tricks," and illegal campaign contributions, vividly illustrated these problems and generated public and congressional support for rectifying them.

In the 1970s, Congress enacted and amended the Federal Election Campaign Act to bring donors into the open, to limit the size of their contributions, and to provide government subsidies for the presidential election. These reforms were designed to make the presidential selection process less costly and more equitable. A Federal Election Commission was also established to monitor election activities, oversee compliance, and prosecute offenders.

But the legislation was only partially successful. It increased the importance of having a large base of contributors during the preconvention period but did not eliminate the impact of large donors on the parties' and candidates' efforts in the general election. For candidates who accepted federal funds, it limited the expenditures of individual campaigns in both the nomination process and general election but has not reduced the amount of money spent on presidential elections. It produced greater equity by limiting contributions and expenditures and by providing federal subsidies but has not evened the playing field among the candidates during the nomination stage, or until recently, between parties in the general election. It has given greater opportunities for candidates who lack national recognition, but it has not lessened the advantages that well-known and well-funded candidates still have. It has benefited major party candidates in the general election but also has contributed to their fractionalization during the nomination. It has reduced party leaders' control over the nomination process and over the conduct of the general election campaign, but it has also enhanced the strategic value of the national parties' fund-raising and grassroots organizing activities. It has encouraged the formation and involvement of nonparty groups, which supplement the campaign of the candidates and their parties but cannot coordinate their efforts with their candidates and their parties.

Finally, the law has contributed to public knowledge of campaign finance by placing contributions and expenditures on the public record. Although it has forced campaigns to engage in additional bookkeeping and reporting procedures, it has generated a wealth of data: who gives how much to whom and when? The laws have also made those data available to the press, electorate, and other political candidates. The reporting and publicizing of campaign contributions and expenditures has generated more media scrutiny, more public awareness, greater activity by citizen watchdog groups, and in the cases of possible violations, congressional investigations, and FEC sanctions.

The Bipartisan Campaign Reform Act, which banned soft money solicitation and distribution by the national parties, prohibited candidates from being named directly in issue advocacy ads thirty days or less before a primary and sixty days or less before the general election, and raised the individual and party contribution limits but has not eliminated the problems that prompted the legislation.

Although the major provisions of the new law have withstood most of their constitutional challenges, broadened the base of contributions, and reduced the influence of large donors on the parties, they have not lowered the costs of presidential elections nor the advantage that superior resources bring to the candidates. Nor has it changed public perceptions that money influences elections, that those who win are beholden to their big donors, that special interests wield more power than do average citizens, that the campaign finance system is unfair, and that politicians and their handlers will find way to get around any law that seeks to constrain their political advantage. The old adage, where there is a will, there is a way, continues to dominate thinking about campaign finance and adds incentives to the hunt for sufficient money to fund the next election.

WHERE ON THE WEB?

- **The Campaign Finance Institute**
  www.cfinst.org

  A nonprofit institute that collects and analyzes current information on campaign finance, reviews the impact of legislation on election giving and spending, and makes recommendations for legal reforms.

- **Center for Public Integrity**
  www.publicintegrity.org

  Evaluates public service, government accountability, and various ethical issues on democratic governance. Has also been concerned with campaign finance reform.

- **Center for Responsive Politics**
  www.opensecrets.org

  A nonpartisan, public interest group that is concerned with providing the public with information on the conduct of federal elections, particularly how money is raised and spent. Publishes alerts, press releases, and major studies on campaign finance.

- **Common Cause**
  www.commoncause.org

  Another public interest group that is concerned with large and unreported contributions and expenditures and has continually urged campaign finance reform.

- **Democracy 21**
  www.democracy21.org

  Still another public interest group interested in campaign finance reform, especially to reduce the influence of money on elections and government.

- **Federal Election Commission**
  www.fec.gov

  The first stop for any study of campaign finance, the FEC collects and disseminates data on contributions to and expenditures of candidates seeking federal office as well as money donated to and spent by parties, PACs, and other nonparty groups.

- **Political Money Line**
  www.politicalmoneyline.com

  A for-profit organization that tracks campaign revenues and expenses.

- **Public Campaign**
  www.publicampaign.org

  A public interest organization devoted to campaign reform to reduce the role of special interest money and large contributors in American politics.

Exercises

1. During the preelection period, see if you can identify the leadership PACs and other groups that potential candidates on the Republican and Democratic side have created for their 2008 campaign. You can find these groups on the Web site of the Center for Responsive Politics (www.opensecrets.org). Some of them are also listed on the "Where on the Web?" section in Chapter 5. Note how much money groups have raised, from whom, and how they have spent it.

2. Compile a running summary of revenue and expenditures as filed with the FEC (www.fec.gov) by candidates who have officially declared themselves for their party's 2008 presidential nomination. Does the differential in their war chests explain their respective campaign activities and/or their position in the public opinion polls?

3. Note the impact of the BCRA on the candidates, parties, and nonparty groups in the 2007–2008 election cycle. Are the same patterns evident during the 2004 nomination and election apparent in 2008 as well? Based on your answer, indicate whether you would or would not amend the BCRA? If you favor amending the law, what are the principal reforms that you would propose?

Selected Readings

Corrado, Anthony, Thomas E. Mann, and Trevor Potter. *Inside the Campaign Finance Battle: Court Testimony on the New Reforms.* Washington, D.C.: Brookings Institution, 2003.

Gais, Thomas. *Improper Influence: Campaign Finance Law, Political Interest Groups and the Problem of Equity*. Ann Arbor: University of Michigan Press, 1996.

Haynes, Audrey A., Paul-Henri Gurian, and Stephen Nichols. "The Role of Candidate Spending in Presidential Nomination Campaigns." *Journal of Politics* (Feb. 1997): 213–235.

Magleby, David B., Anthony Corrado, and Kelly D. Patterson. eds. *Financing the 2004 Elections*. Washington, D.C.: Brookings Institution, 2006.

Malbin, Michael J. ed. *The Election after Reform: Money, Politics and the Bipartisan Campaign Reform Act*. Lanham, M.D.: Rowman and Littlefield, 2006.

Wayne, Stephen J. "The 2000 Presidential Election: Traveling the Hard and Soft Roads to the White House," in *The Interest Group Connection: Electioneering, Lobbying, and Policymaking*, 2nd. ed., edited by Paul S. Herrnson, Ronald Shaiko, and Clyde Wilcox. Washington, D.C.: Congressional Quarterly, 2003.

NOTES

1. "'04 Elections Expected to Cost Nearly \$4 Billion," Center for Responsive Politics, Press Release, October 21, 2004. www.opensecrets.org/pressreleases/2004/04spending (accessed October 21, 2004); Kelly D. Patterson, "Spending in the 2004 Election," in David B. Magleby, Anthony Corrado, and Kelly D. Patterson, eds., *Financing the 2004 Election* (Washington, D.C.: Brookings, 2006), p. 69.

2. Patterson, "Spending in the 2004 Election," in Magleby, Corrado, and Patterson, *Financing the 2004 Election*, 60–70; "2004 Presidential Campaign Financial Activity Summarized," Federal Election Commission, February 3, 2005. www.fec.gov/press/press2005/20050203preseum (accessed March 1, 2005).

3. Herbert E. Alexander, "Making Sense about Dollars in the 1980 Presidential Campaigns," in *Money and Politics in the United States*, ed. Michael J. Malbin (Washington, D.C.: American Enterprise Institute/Chatham House, 1984), p. 24.

4. Edward W. Chester, *Radio, Television, and American Politics* (New York: Sheed & Ward, 1969), p. 21.

5. Herbert E. Alexander, *Financing Politics: Money, Elections, and Political Reform*, 3rd ed. (Washington D.C.: Congressional Quarterly, 1984), pp. 11–12.

6. *Statistical Abstract of the United States* (Washington D.C.: Bureau of the Census, 2006), p. 737.

7. "Party Financial Activity Summarized for the 2004 Election Cycle," Federal Election Commission, March 2, 2005 (corrected March 14, 2005). www.fec.gov/press/press2005/20050302party/Party2004final (accessed, June 26, 2005).

8. Craig B. Homan and Luke P. McLoughlin, *Buying Time 2000: Television Advertising in the 2000 Federal Elections* (New York: Brennan Center for Justice, 2001), pp. 39–40. Michael M. Franz, Joel Rivlin, and Kenneth Goldstein, "Much More of the Same: Television Advertising Pre- and Post-BCRA," in Michael J. Malbin, ed. *The Election after Reform: Money, Politics and the Bipartisan Campaign Reform Act* (Lanham, M.D.: Rowman and Littlefield, 2006), p. 142.

9. Jasper B. Shannon, *Money and Politics* (New York: Random House, 1959), p. 35.

10. Herbert E. Alexander and Brian Haggerty, *Financing the 1984 Election* (Lexington, M.A.: Lexington Books, 1987), p. 148.

11. In 1972, the chief fund-raiser for the Nixon campaign, Maurice Stans, and Richard Nixon's private attorney, Herbert Kalmbach, collected contributions, some of them illegal, on behalf of the president. They exerted strong pressure on corporate executives, despite the prohibition on corporate giving. Secret contributions totaling millions of dollars were received, and three special secured funds were established to give the White House and the Committee to Reelect the President (known as CREEP) maximum discretion in campaign expenditures. It was from these funds that the "dirty tricks" of the 1972 campaign and the Watergate burglary were financed.

12. The 1971 act also limited the amount that could be spent on media advertising, but that limit was eliminated in 1974.

13. There was also a short but critical delay in the effective date for the disclosure provision of the other 1971 campaign finance act. Signed by the president on February 14, 1972, it was scheduled to take effect in sixty days. This delay precipitated a frantic attempt by both parties to tap major donors who wanted to remain anonymous. During this period, the Republicans collected an estimated $20 million, much of it pledged beforehand, and some of it in forms that could not even be traced.

14. The FEC defined these activities broadly. It permitted parties to engage in a variety of public-oriented communications with one proviso. They could not expressly advocate the election of a specific candidate for federal office. Express advocacy included such words and expressions as "vote for," "support," and "elect." If these magic words were not included in the communication, then soft money could be used to pay for it.

15. It was not until 1992 that the FEC imposed reporting requirements on this soft money.

16. "Presidential Election Campaign Fund," Federal Election Commission, 2002. www.fec.gov/press/bkgnd/fund (accessed January 6, 2006).

17. The Court did strike down a provision of the law that prohibited minors from making contributions on the grounds that it violated their freedom of speech. It also held that a requirement that prevented the national parties from independent spending if they coordinated their campaign activities with their candidates was unconstitutional.

18. Even here there was controversy. The bill's sponsors objected to many of the regulations that the FEC issued, claiming that they undermined the objectives of the law. In September 2004 during the general election campaign, a district court sided with the critics of the FEC rules and voided many of them.

19. For an extended discussion of the FEC's rulings, see Anthony Corrado, "The Regulatory Environment: Uncertainty in the Wake of Change," in Magleby, Corrado, and Patterson, eds. *Financing the 2004 Election*, pp. 48–53.

20. The Supreme Court had defined political organizations in its *Buckley v. Valeo* decision as a group controlled by a candidate or created for the purpose of nominating or electing a specific candidate. The groups claimed that their primary

purpose was not the election of a specific candidate, so they did not have to file with the FEC nor were they subject to the soft money restrictions.

21. R. Jeffrey Smith, "FEC Fines 3 '527' Groups for Use of Large Donations in '04," *Washington Post*, (December 14, 2006), p. A5. "FEC to Collect $750,000 Civil Penalty from Progress for America Fund," FEC, February 28, 2007. www.fec.gov/press/press2007/20070228MUR.html.

22. Robert Barnes and Matthew Mosk, "High Court to Revisit Campaign Finance Law," *Washington Post*, (January 20, 2007), pp. A1, A8.

23. The congressional campaign committees of both parties, particularly in the Senate, did not do as well as the parties' national committees in raising funds. In 2003–2004, the congressional committees in the House received a total of $278.9 million in federal donations compared to $296.2 million in federal and nonfederal (soft money) contributions in 1999–2000. In the Senate, the differences were even greater, $167.7 million in 2003–2004 compared to $269.0 million in the previous presidential election cycle.

24. John C. Green, "Financing the 2004 Presidential Nomination Campaigns," in Magleby, Corrado, and Patterson, *Financing the 2004 Election*, pp. 104–105.

25. "Financing Presidential Elections," Campaign Finance Institute. www.cfinst.org/president (accessed April 2, 2007).

26. Ibid.

27. "2004 Presidential Campaign Financial Activity Summarized," Federal Election Commission, February 3, 2005.

28. Calculated from date complied by the Center for Responsive Politics. www.opensecrets.org/pacs/industry.asp?txt=Q03&cycle=2006.

29. The FEC sought to impose still another eligibility rule—how matching funds had been spent in the past. The commission denied matching funds to Lyndon LaRouche in 1992 on the grounds that his campaign had misused such funds in previous elections. LaRouche, who had been convicted and jailed for engaging in fraudulent fund-raising practices, appealed the FEC's decision and won.

30. "Presidential Spending Limts—If the Election Were Held in 2007," Federal Election Commission. www.fec.gov/pages/brochures/pubfund_limits_2007.shtml (accessed April 3, 2007).

31. "Financing Conventions," Campaign Finance Institute, 2004. www.cfinst.org/eguide/PartyConventions/financial/fundraisers_donors (accessed January 7, 2006).

32. John C. Green, "Financing the 2004 Presidential Nomination Campaigns," in Magleby, Corrado, and Patterson, *Financing the 2004 Election*, p. 119.

33. "2004 Presidential Campaign Financial Activity Summarized," Federal Election Commission, February 3, 2005. www.fec.gov/press/press2005/20050203pressum.

34. "Financing Presidential Elections," Campaign Finance Institute. www.cfinst.org/president (accessed April 2, 2007).

35. "Small Donors and Online Giving: A Study of Donors to the 2004 Presidential Campaigns," Institute for Politics, Democracy & the Internet in Collaboration with the Campaign Finance Institute.

36. *Campaign for President* ed. by The Institute of Politics, John F. Kennedy School of Government, Harvard University (Lanham, M.D.: Rowman and Littlefield, 2006), p. 67.

37. "Small Donors and Online Giving," p. 4.

38. Michael J. Malbin, "A Public Funding System in Jeopardy: Lessons from the Presidential Nomination Contest of 2004," in Malbin ed. *The Election after Reform: Money, Politics and the Bipartisan Campaign Reform* (Lanham, M.D.: Rowman and Littlefield, 2006), p. 237.

39. Green, "Financing the 2004 Presidential Nomination Campaigns," in Magleby, Corrado, and Patterson, *Financing the 2004 Election*, p. 104.

40. Ibid., pp. 104–105.

41. Beginning with the 1992 nomination process, the FEC took these practices into account by liberalizing its cost allocation policy. It permitted candidates to allocate expenses if they pertained to media, mailings, telephoning, polling, and overhead. Moreover, the commission allowed up to 50 percent of the expenses to be considered fund-raising and thus entirely exempt from the state spending limits.

42. Anthony Corrado, "Party Finance in the Wake of BCRA: An Overview," in Malbin, ed. *The Election after Reform*, pp. 22–24.

43. "PAC Activity Increases for 2004 Elections," Federal Election Commission, April 13, 2005. www.fec.gov/press/press2005/20050412pac/PACFinal2004.

44. The number 527 refers to the section of the IRS code (26 U.S.C. 527) that deals with organizations organized for the purpose of accepting contributions or making expenditures, or both, for the purpose of influencing the selection, nomination, election, or appointment of any individual to any federal, state, or local office.

45. Soros gave $24 million to Democratic-oriented 527 groups and also spent $4 million independently during the 2004 general election campaign. Anthony Corrado, "Financing the 2004 Presidential General Election" in Magleby, Corrado, and Patterson, *Financing the 2004 Election*, p. 141.

46. Steve Weissman and Ruth Hassan, "BCRA and the 527 Groups," in Malbin, ed. *The Election after Reform*, p. 151.

47. Thomas B. Edsall, "In Boost for Democrats, FEC Rejects Proposed Limits on Small Donors," *Washington Post*, (May 14, 2004), p. A9; Glen Justice, "F.E.C. Declines to Curb Independent Fund-Raisers," *New York Times*, (May 14, 2004), p. A16.

48. Robert G. Boatright, Michael J. Malbin, Mark J. Rozell, and Clyde Wilcox, "Interest Groups and Advocacy Organizations after BCRA," in Malbin, *The Election after Reform*, pp. 117–121.

49. Thomas B. Edsall and James V.Grimaldi, "New Routes for Money to Sway Voters," *Washington Post*, (September 27, 2004), pp. A1, A5. Legislation has been introduced in the 109th Congress to treat 501c groups as ordinary PACs subject to the restriction on contributions and the reporting requirements. Kristin Jensen and Michael Forsythe, "Congress May Push Donors to Unregulated US Political Group," *Bloomberg News Service*, (July 11, 2005).

50. Anthony Corrado, "Financing the 2004 Presidential General Election, in Magleby, Corrado, and Patterson, *Financing the 2004 Election*, p. 142.

51. Beaulieu of America, a large carpet manufacturer, was not as fortunate as the Buddhist monks. Accused of funneling $36,000 in illegal contributions to Lamar Alexander's 1996 presidential campaign, the company entered into a plea-bargaining agreement with the government in which it agreed to pay a $1 million fine and civil penalties to be determined by the FEC. Kevin Sack, "Campaign Finance Case Costs a Carpet Company $1 Million," *New York Times*, (December 2, 1998), p. A23.

52. Abramoff was also a successful Pioneer in Bush's 2004 campaign, who once bragged: "Everyone in town is trying to be a Pioneer or Ranger. So far I've raised about $120,000, and I haven't even really started to make calls." David Firestone, "Bush Loyalists Compete for Spots on the President's A-Team by Raising Record Money for 2004," *New York Times*, (July 21, 2003), p. A10. The money Abramoff raised was not returned or given to charity by the campaign.

53. Thomas B. Edsall, Sarah Cohen, and James V. Grimaldi, "The Bush Money Machine: Pioneers Fill War Chest, then Capitalize," *Washington Post*, (May 16, 2004), pp. A1, A15–A16. See also Committee on Responsive Politics, "George W. Bush," and "Embassy Row." (www.opensecrets.org/bush/index and www.opensecrets.org/bush/ambassadors/index.)

54. Abramoff provided members of Congress with dinners at his restaurant and sporting events at his box at the Verizon Center in Washington D.C., paid for foreign travel, directly or indirectly hired spouses of members and their aides— all for help on legislative matters on which he was representing clients with an interest in the legislation.

55. Michael Robinson, Clyde Wilcox, and Paul Marshall, "The Presidency: Not for Sale," *Public Opinion* II (March/April 1989), p. 51.

56. Gary C. Jacobson, "The Congress: The Structural Basis of Republican Success," in Michael Nelson, ed., *The Elections of 2004* (Washington, DC: Congressional Quarterly, 2005), p. 126.

THE POLITICAL
ENVIRONMENT

CHAPTER 3

INTRODUCTION

The nature of the electorate influences the content, images, and strategies of the campaign and affects the outcome of the election—an obvious conclusion to be sure, but one that is not always appreciated. Campaigns are not conducted in ignorance of the voters. Rather, they are calculated to appeal to the needs and desires, attitudes and opinions, and associations and interactions of the electorate.

Voters do not come to the election with completely open minds. They come with preexisting views. They do not see and hear the campaign in isolation. They observe it and absorb it as part of their daily lives. In other words, people's attitudes and associations affect their perceptions and influence their behavior. Preexisting views make it important for students of presidential elections to examine the formation of political attitudes and the patterns of social interaction.

Who votes and who does not? Why do people vote for certain candidates and not others? Do campaign appeals affect voting behavior? Are the responses of the electorate predictable? Political scientists have been interested in these questions for some time. Politicians have been interested in them for even longer.

A great deal of social science research and political savvy has gone into finding the answers to these questions. Spurred by the development of sophisticated survey techniques and methods of data analysis, political scientists, sociologists, and social psychologists have uncovered a wealth of information on how the public reacts and the electorate behaves during a campaign. They have examined correlations between demographic characteristics and voter turnout. They have explored psychological motivations, social influences, and political pressures that contribute to voting behavior. This chapter discusses some of their findings.

It is organized into three parts. The first looks at who votes. Describing the expansion of suffrage in the nineteenth and twentieth centuries, the section then turns to recent voting trends in the twentieth and twenty-first centuries. Turnout is influenced by personal feelings and beliefs, especially partisanship; social factors such as age, education, and group associations; and situational variables such as the state of the domestic and foreign affairs, the competitiveness of the election, the weather, and the efforts by parties and nonparty groups to get out the vote. Turnout is also affected by state and national laws that govern elections, especially registration requirements, absentee voting, and the location and hours that the polls are open. The impact of these variables, singularly and together, on the decision of whether or not to cast a ballot is the principal focus of this section.

The second and third parts of the chapter study influences on the vote. First, the partisan basis of politics is examined. How have political attitudes changed over the years, and how do they affect the ways people evaluate the campaign and shape their actual voting decisions? Models of voting behavior are presented and then used to help explain contemporary voting patterns.

Next, the social basis of politics is analyzed. Here we look at the electorate's demography, its socioeconomic divisions, and the public's various beliefs and the values upon which those beliefs are based. Our objective is to discuss the relationship between electoral groups and their voting behavior. Primary emphasis is placed on the formation of party coalitions and their evolution through the 1990s into the twenty-first century. The chapter concludes with a description of the groups that comprise the Republican and Democratic electoral coalitions today.

TURNOUT

Who votes? In one sense, this is a simple question to resolve. Official election returns indicate the number of voters and the states, even the precincts, in which people voted. By easy calculation, the percentage of voting-age population (VAP) who actually cast ballots for president can be determined: 55.2 percent in 1992, 49.1 percent in 1996, 51.3 percent in 2000, and 56.7 percent in 2004.[1]

But there is a problem with these figures. They include people who are old enough to vote but may not be eligible to do so: noncitizens; most of the people who are currently incarcerated in penal institutions; in some states, ex-felons and ex-military who were dishonorably discharged from the armed forces; and citizens who do not meet their state's residence requirements. If these people are excluded, then the percent voting increases by about 4 to 5 percent.[2] Professor Michael McDonald, a political scientist who studies turnout figures, concluded that 63.8 percent of the voting-eligible population (VEP) actually did so in 2004.[3]

Registration is also required in most states in order to vote; naturally, failure to complete the registration requirement or to keep it active by voting on a regular basis can result in the disenfranchisement of otherwise eligible voters. In the United States, 72 percent of adult citizens were registered to vote in 2004. Of those who were registered in that year, 88.5 percent reported that they voted.[4]

But can people be trusted to tell the truth about whether or not they voted, or will most people say what they think is the right answer, which, of course, is to say, "I voted? Unfortunately, more people say that they are going to vote than actually do so, and after the election, more people indicate that they have voted than actually have done so. Pollsters anticipate inflated responses to the question of voting. To get at a more accurate figure, they often ask questions about past voting practices, questions such as "By the way, where do people vote around here?"

After the elections, survey researchers weigh the responses they receive on the basis of the official results, knowing full well that approximately 15 to 20 percent more people will claim that they voted than actually did.

VOTING IN AMERICAN ELECTIONS

Voting turnout in the United States has varied markedly over the years. A variety of legal, social, and political factors have contributed to this variation. The next section documents these shifts and explains them within the context of the political environment.

Turnout Before the Twentieth Century

The Constitution empowers the state legislatures to determine the time, place, and manner of holding elections for national office. Although it also gives Congress the authority to alter such regulations, Congress did not do so until after the Civil War. Thus, the states were free to restrict suffrage, and most did. In some states, property ownership was a requirement for exercising the franchise; in others, a particular religious belief was necessary. In most, it was essential to be white, male, and over twenty-one.[5]

In the first national election, only about 11 percent of the adult population participated. The presidential vote was even lower since most of the electors were designated by the state legislatures and not chosen directly by the people. Prior to 1824, voters remained a relatively small percentage of the eligible population, in the range of 20 to 25 percent. Without a tradition of participation in politics or a well-entrenched party system during this period, the general public deferred to the more politically prominent members of the society in choosing their state's elected officials.[6]

Turnout began to increase in the 1820s, spurred by a political reform movement. Known as Jacksonian Democracy, this movement advocated a greater role for the public in the electoral process. By the 1830s, most states had eliminated property and religious restrictions, thereby extending suffrage to approximately 80 percent of the adult white male population. Turnout expanded accordingly.[7]

The rise of competitive, popular-based parties in the 1840s, along with campaigns directed at the entire electorate, boosted participation. Professor Walter Dean Burnham estimated turnout in the range of 70 to 80 percent for eligible voters throughout the remainder of the nineteenth century, although these percentages may be misleading because of the coercive and sometimes fraudulent voting practices that occurred during the era of machine party politics, during which the parties ran the elections, provided the ballots (distinguished by color), oversaw the voting, mobilized their partisans, and got them to the polls, sometimes early and often.[8]

Reforms at the end of the nineteenth and beginning of the twentieth century, however, reduced some of the more flagrant attempts to influence the election outcome. States began to monitor the conduct of elections more closely and more impartially. They adopted the Australian ballot and instituted secret voting; no longer could party poll watchers determine people's vote by the color of the ballot they dropped into the box. Registration procedures were introduced to prevent nonresidents and noncitizens from voting. These reforms improved the integrity of the electoral process, but they also reduced the percentage of the population that voted.

The growth of one-party politics in the South following the Civil War and the removal of federal troops contributed to the declining turnout in that region of the country. Despite the ratification of the Fifteenth Amendment in 1870, which removed race and color as qualifications for voting, the size of the southern electorate actually decreased after the Civil War. A series of restrictive state laws, such as poll taxes, literacy tests, and "private" primaries in which only whites could participate, plus the imposition of more restrictive residence requirements substantially reduced the proportion of adults in the South that voted.

Turnout During and After the Twentieth Century

Decreasing competition in the North and West at the end of the nineteenth century had much the same effect. It reduced the percentage of the population that voted, as did the extension of suffrage to women in 1919. Although the size of the eligible electorate doubled in the 1920s, turnout declined because newly enfranchised voters do not vote with the same regularity as people who have been exercising the franchise for some time. In 1924, only 44 percent of the voting aged population cast ballots. Within a period of thirty years, turnout had declined almost 40 percent.[9]

Although voter participation grew moderately during Franklin Roosevelt's presidency and the post–World War II era, it decreased again following the 1960 presidential election, an election in which 64 percent of the adult population voted. Part of the decline had to do with the expanding base of the electorate; part with growing voter disillusionment, heightened by the war in Vietnam, the Watergate scandal, and a series of lack-luster presidential candidates; and part with the weakening of the major parties' grassroots organizations and their increased dependence on television advertising.

Beginning in the 1960s, suffrage rights were expanded. In 1961, the District of Columbia was granted three electoral votes, thereby extending the right to vote to its residents in presidential elections (Twenty-third Amendment); in 1964, the collection of a poll tax was prohibited in national elections (Twenty-fourth Amendment); in 1971, the right to vote was extended to all citizens eighteen years of age and older (Twenty-sixth Amendment).

Moreover, the Supreme Court and Congress began to eliminate the legal and institutional barriers to voting. In 1944, the Court outlawed the white-only primary.[10] In the mid-1960s, Congress passed the Civil Rights Act (1964) and the Voting Rights Act (1965). The latter banned literacy tests in federal elections for all citizens who had at least a sixth-grade education in a U.S. school. Federal officers were sent to facilitate registration in districts in which less than 50 percent of the population was registered to vote. Amendments to the Voting Rights Act have also reduced the residence requirement for presidential elections to a maximum of thirty days.

These legal initiatives broadened the opportunities for people, particularly minority ethnic and racial groups, to participate in the electoral process. However, it took years before voting practices of these groups caught up with their new voting opportunities.

Table 3.1 indicates contemporary turnout numbers in recent presidential elections based on voting-age population (VAP).

Comparative Turnout in Western Democracies

As the percentages in Table 3.1 reveal, turnout has been mediocre at best. A smaller percentage of the population in the United States votes compared with many other democratic countries. (See Table 3.2.)

Why is turnout in American elections lower than many other democracies? Unlike some countries, the United States does not impose penalties on those who fail to register and vote; nor does it have a national system for automatic registration as do other democracies. Moreover, the day of the election is a workday in the United States, whereas in most other countries, it is Sunday or a holiday.

Another factor that contributes to a lower turnout percentage in the United States is the winner-take-all system of voting, which discourages participation in noncompetitive electoral districts.

Influences on Turnout

Why don't people vote? Does low turnout indicate voter satisfaction or alienation? Does it contribute to stability or create conditions for instability within the democratic political system? What party and which programs benefit and which suffer when so many people do not vote? The next part of the chapter answers these questions.

Legal Constraints

Some citizens have lost their right to vote. As previously mentioned, people convicted of a felony or dishonorably discharged from the military cannot vote

TABLE 3.1 | Suffrage and Turnout in the Twentieth and Twenty-First Centuries

Year	Voting-Age Population (VAP)	Turnout	Percent of the VAP
1900	40,753,000	13,974,188	35.0
1920	60,581,000	26,768,613	44.0
1932	75,768,000	39,732,000	52.4
1940	84,728,000	49,900,000	58.9
1952	99,929,000	61,551,000	61.6
1960	109,672,000	68,838,000	62.8
1964	114,090,000	70,645,000	61.9
1968	120,285,000	73,212,000	60.9
1972	140,777,000	77,719,000	55.5
1976	152,308,000	81,556,000	53.5
1980	164,595,000	86,515,000	52.6
1984	174,447,000	92,653,000	53.1
1988	182,600,000	91,602,291	50.2
1992	189,044,000	104,426,659	55.2
1996	196,507,000	96,277,564	49.1
2000	205,815,000	105,586,284	51.3
2004	215,694,000	122,295,345	56.7

Sources: Population for 1900 and 1920 are based on estimates and early census figures that appear in Neal R. Peirce, *The People's President* (New York: Simon & Schuster, 1968), 206; copyright renewed © 1979 by Neal R. Peirce. Reprinted by permission of Yale University Press. Population figures from 1932 to 1984 are from the U.S. Department of Commerce, Bureau of the Census, *Statistical Abstract of the United States* (Washington, D.C.: Government Printing Office, 1987), 250. Figures from 1988 to the present were compiled from official election returns supplied by the Federal Election Commission (www.fec.gov/pubrec/federalelections2004.shtml)

in many of the states. These restrictions have disproportionately impacted African-American males, disenfranchising about one out of every seven.[11] Currently, only two states, Maine and Vermont, allow people who are in jail to vote.

In addition, registration requirements have also inhibited voting. Congress tried to deal with this problem in 1993 by its enactment of the "Motor-Voter" bill, which requires states to permit registration by mail and provide registration forms at convenient state-wide offices such as motor vehicles, military recruitment, and welfare services.

The law took effect in 1995, and the number of people registered to vote has increased a little. Twenty-six million new registrants were added between 1996 and 2004, but 12.6 million people were removed from registration lists and 10.7 million were listed as inactive. Moreover, the VAP increased by about

TABLE 3.2 | INTERNATIONAL VOTER TURNOUT (IN PERCENTAGES)

Country	Year	Type of Election	Turnout of Eligible Voters
Australia	2004	Parliamentary	94.6
Austria	2004	Presidential	70.8
Belgium	2005	Parliamentary	90.5
Brazil	2005	Referendum	78.2
Canada	2004	Parliamentary	61.2
France	2007	Presidential	84.0[+]
Germany	2005	Parliamentary	77.7
Greece	2004	Parliamentary	76.5
India	2004	Parliamentary	57.7
Israel	2003	Parliamentary	67.8
Mexico	2003	Legislative	41.7
Poland	2005	Presidential*	49.7/51.0
	2005	Parliamentary	40.6
Russia	2003	Parliamentary	55.7
South Africa	2004	Parliamentary	76.7
South Korea	2004	Parliamentary	60.0
Spain	2004	Parliamentary	77.2
Switzerland	2003	Parliamentary	45.4
Ukraine	2004	Presidential*	74.2/81.1
United Kingdom	2005	Parliamentary	61.4
United States	2004	Presidential	63.8
	2006	Legislative	40.4

*Two rounds.

[+]Second round.

Source: "Electionguide.org: voter turnout." www.electionguide.org/voter-turnout2003.php (also 2004 and 2005) (accessed January 20, 2006). Updated by author with data from the Federal Election Commission and the United States Census Bureau, "News Releases of July 28, 2004 and May 26, 2005" www.census.gov/Press-Release/www/releases/archives/voting/002278.html (accessed January 20, 2006) and www.census.gov/Press-Release/www/releases/archives/voting/004986.html (accessed January 20, 2006).

10 million people, so the bad news from the perspective of a democratic electoral process is that voter registration in the United States has not even kept pace with population growth.[12]

The youngest group of eligible voters was expected to increase their electoral participation the most as a result of the Motor-Voter law. Although eighteen- to twenty-four-year-olds have traditionally had the lowest registration rates (in the range of 30 to 40 percent), they have much higher driving rates

BOX 3.1	REGISTERING TO VOTE

It is easy to register to vote. All you have to do is go to the Web site of the Election Assistance Commission and download the National Voter Registration form. All states but two (New Hampshire and Wyoming) will accept this form. North Dakota does not require registration. The booklet containing the form also lists the name and addresses to which it should be sent in your state (www.eac.gov/register_vote.asp).

You can also do any of the following to register:

- Contact your state's chief election official. In most states, it is the secretary of state; in some, it is the head of the Board of Elections; in a few, it may be the lieutenant governor.
- Go to your nearest department of motor vehicles, military recruitment, or public assistance office to obtain a copy of the registration form. Complete it, and give it to the appropriate person at the office at which you have obtained the form.
- Access the Web site of an organization called Rock-the-Vote at www. rockthevote.org, which will help facilitate your online registration.

(85 percent have driver's licenses). By making registration available at the same time and place where people get or renew their driver's licenses, it was thought that the law would increase the number of registered voters in the lowest age cohort. It did in 2004, but the youngest group of voters still have the lowest rate of turnout of all age groups. (See Box 3.1, "Registering to Vote," for how to register to vote.)

Convenience Issues
In addition to the registration requirements of most states, other factors contribute to nonvoting, particularly for younger Americans. Geographic mobility is one. Going away to college makes voting more difficult. Students need to return home or obtain absentee ballots.

Moreover, many young people have not yet developed the habit of voting. Peer pressure to do so may be low as well because so many in this younger age group have not voted or even registered. Thus, it is the older generation with whom young people interact as they move into voting age— parents, teachers, community, and religious leaders—that exercise greater influence on who votes. Older voters provide the critical information and model civic behavior that affects the initial decision of many young people, whether or not to vote.

The act of voting, however, increases the likelihood of doing it again and again. Finding the correct location, getting to the polls, and figuring out how to use the machines or punch cards are no longer obstacles once a person has voted. However, for people who have limited English language skills and for people with various mental and physical handicaps, voting can still be difficult. The bottom line, however, is that over time, voting becomes a habit, a ritual that people dutifully follow on most election days.[13]

Psychological and Political Attitudes

Personal feelings and beliefs are important in motivating people to vote. Interest in the election, concern over the outcome, feelings of civic pride, and political efficacy (the belief that one's vote really counts) are factors that affect how regularly people vote.[14] Naturally, those who feel more strongly about the election and who have the most interest in it are more likely to participate in the campaign and more likely to turn out on Election Day.

From the late 1960s until the mid-1980s, partisan attitudes weakened. The proportion of people within the body politic identifying themselves as independents increased. Since party allegiance is a motivation for voting, the decline in partisan identification contributed to the decrease in turnout. As a group, independents are 12 percent less likely to vote than are strong partisans.[15]

Another factor that has reduced turnout is lower voter efficacy, the belief that one can make a difference and that voters can change the way government works or public officials behave. Political efficacy has declined since the late 1960s. This decline, combined with the weakening of partisan attitudes, has also contributed to lower turnout. According to Paul R. Abramson, John H. Aldrich, and David W. Rohde, three political scientists who have researched and written about voting since the 1980 election, "the combined impact of this attitudinal change accounts for 80 percent of the decline of turnout [between 1960 and 2004], with the decline in political efficacy being three times as important as the decline in partisan loyalties."[16]

Nonetheless, for many, voting is a civic responsibility; for others, it is a matter a personal conviction; and as we have mentioned, it can even become a habit, one reason that turnout tends to increase with age. With advances in medicine, the point at which senior citizens stay informed and involved has been extended to the mid to late seventies with correspondingly higher voting rates for people ages sixty-five and over.

Social and Economic Factors

Several social and economic variables correlate with turnout. They include education, income, and occupational status, which also correlate with one another. As people become more educated, as they move up the socioeconomic ladder, and as their jobs gain in status and income, they are more likely to vote.

Education has a larger impact than any other single social characteristic on voting.[17] The reason education is so important is that it provides people with the skills for processing and evaluating information; for perceiving differences among the parties, candidates, and issues; and for relating these differences to personal values and behavior.

Education also increases a person's stake in the system, interest in the election, and concern over the outcome. Since the lesson that voting is a civic responsibility is usually learned in the classroom, schooling may also contribute to a more highly developed sense of responsibility about the importance of voting in a democracy.[18]

Given the relationship of education to turnout, why should the rate of turnout have declined from the 1960s through most of the 1990s when the general level of education in the United States during this period increased? The answer is that the attitudinal factors of decreasing partisanship and efficacy countered the increase in education. Had educational levels not increased, turnout would have been even lower.[19] The larger number of younger voters who entered the electorate, the so-called Generation "Xers," who voted at a lower rate than their elders, even when their elders were their age, have also decreased the proportion of the population that votes.[20]

Another contributing factor may be the expansion of poverty in the United States and the growing gap between the rich and poor. People with lower levels of income tend to have a lower sense of personal efficacy. They either do not see or are pessimistic about how the outcome of the election will affect them, so why vote?

Environmental Factors

In addition to legal, attitudinal, and social factors, the environment in which elections occur also affects turnout. The weather may be important. Three political scientists, Brad T. Gomez, Thomas G. Hansford, and George A. Krause examined the impact of weather on turnout. They found that rain reduces turnout by 1 percent per inch of rain. Snow also decreases voter participation in elections, primarily in rural areas.

The lack of competition decreases turnout. The less competitive the electoral environment, the lower the turnout is likely to be. To the extent that presidential strategies are targeted to the Electoral College, not to the general population, overall turnout will suffer in those states that the presidential campaign neglects because they are conceded to one side or the other.

Take the 2004 election, for example. Turnout was up from its 2000 level, almost twice as much in the battleground states (8.3 percent) than in non-battleground ones (4.7 percent).[21] With one exception, South Dakota, which had a very competitive Senate race involving the Senate Minority leader, Tom Daschle and a former member of Congress who was opposing him, all the other states that had the largest increases were key states for the 2004 presidential contest. (See Table 3.3.)

The level of competition alone cannot explain the variance between 2000 and 2004 since most of these states in which turnout increased the most were also key battleground states in 2000, but the intense effort both parties made to mobilize the vote in these states in 2004 did boost turnout. Both party and nonparty groups devoted more money and resources to get-out-the-vote activities, personally contacting voters at a higher rate than in 2000. In 2004, 43 percent said that they were personally contacted by a party compared to 35 percent four years earlier.[22] Personal contact and communication bring out the vote.

Issues within the states—eleven of them had ballot initiatives opposing marriage by same-sex partners—and others that had competitive candidate races also contributed to higher turnout.

TABLE 3.3 | TURNOUT VARIATION IN THE STATES

Largest Percentage Increases in 2004			Highest Rates of Turnout	
State	**Based on**		VAP	VEP
South Dakota	10.8	Minnesota	76.7	79.2
Arizona	10.1	Wisconsin	73.0	76.6
Ohio	10.0	Maine	72.0	73.1
Colorado	9.9	North Dakota	70.8	71.5
Nevada	9.8	Oregon	70.6	74.0
Florida	9.3	Montana	69.9	70.2
Minnesota	8.4	New Hampshire	68.9	71.5
Pennsylvania	8.1	Iowa	68.8	71.3
Michigan	8.1	South Dakota	67.0	68.3
Oregon	8.1	Missouri	66.3	68.5

Source: States with the largest percentage increase: Michael P. McDonald, "Up, Up and Away! Voter Partic-ipation in the 2004 Presidential Election," *The Forum*, II (Post Election, 2004) (www.bepress.com/forum/vol2/iss4/art4); states with the highest turnout: U.S. Census Bureau, Current Population Survey, November 2004.

Finally, situational variables help explain fluctuations in the vote. In 2004, the highly polarizing candidacy of George W. Bush, the controversy over the war in Iraq, and the domestic environment—the threat of terrorism and the spike in gas prices—energized both Republicans and Democrats and got them out to vote.

In short, the campaign and the environment matters as far as election turnout is concerned.

TURNOUT AND DEMOCRACY

What difference does it make that some people do not vote? It makes a great deal of difference.

Turnout affects perceptions of how well the democratic electoral system is functioning. Low turnout suggests that people may be alienated, lack faith in the candidates and parties, think that the government is and will remain unresponsive to their needs and interests, and most importantly, believe that they cannot achieve change through the electoral process.[23]

Low turnout also impacts representation and public policy decisions. Who gets what relates in large part to the influence they have in election outcomes and government decisions. The connection between low economic status and nonvoting results in a class bias that undercuts the democratic character of the American political system. It widens the participation gap between the haves and have-nots.[24] This gap has produced an electorate that is not representative of the population as a whole, that is, an electorate that is better educated and has higher incomes than the general public. To the extent that government responds to the electorate rather than to the general population, government policies take on a "have" rather than "have not" coloration.

This class bias in voting produces a tragic irony in American politics. Those who are most disadvantaged, who have the least education, and who need to change conditions the most, actually vote the least. Those who are the most advantaged, who benefit from existing conditions and presumably from the public policy that contributes to those conditions, vote most often.

TURNOUT AND PARTISANSHIP

Obviously, turnout has partisan implications as well. Since the Democratic Party draws more of its electoral support from those in the lower socioeconomic groups, people with less formal education and fewer professional opportunities, lower turnout thus has tended to hurt that party more than the GOP. See Table 3.4 for demographic turnout trends.

The common wisdom is that, all things being equal, the larger the turnout the better the Democrats will do. In 1960 and 1976, increases in turnout did favor the Democrats and resulted in two very close victories. The relatively high Democratic turnout in these two elections overcame the advantage the Republicans usually gain from having a larger proportion of their rank-and-file vote.[25] Similarly, in the 2000 presidential election, a late surge of support for Gore gave him a popular vote victory although he lost in the Electoral College.

Republican strategists, surprised by the larger turnout the Gore campaign generated, studied the election day tactics, particularly the efforts of organized labor and the African-American community that increased the Democratic vote. Determined not to be outmaneuvered again, the Republicans devised a turnout strategy for 2004 in which potential Republican voters were targeted, canvassed, and contracted by local volunteers within seventy-two hours before the vote. They successfully tested their plan in the 2002 Senate midterm elections.

The party budgeted $125 million dollars for this effort in 2004. It used the money to expand its data bank of likely Republican voters, train community volunteers who would implement the plan, and set up a communications system to contact likely Republican voters during the campaign and in the seventy-two hours preceding the vote. It was a masterful effort that utilized new technologies to identify potential GOP supporters and older, time-tested, on-the-ground campaigns to contact them. In contrast, the Democrats spent $60 million on turnout efforts in 2004. They depended largely on organized labor, 527 groups, and paid campaign workers to get out their vote.[26]

The Republican strategy was more successful. The Committee for the Study of the American Electorate estimated that the Republicans increased their partisan turnout more than the Democrats in the battleground states.[27]

TABLE 3.4 | Turnout 1980–2004 (Numbers in Thousands; Civilian Noninstitutional Population Who Reported That They Voted)

Years

Population Characteristics	2004	2000	1996	1992	1988	1984	1980
White	60.3	60.4	56.0	63.6	59.1	61.4	60.9
Black	56.3	54.1	50.6	54.0	51.5	55.8	50.5
Hispanic*	28.3	27.5	26.7	28.9	28.8	32.6	29.9
Gender							
Male	56.3	53.1	52.8	60.2	56.4	59.0	59.1
Female	60.1	56.2	55.5	62.3	58.3	60.8	59.4
Age							
18 to 24 years	41.9	32.3	32.4	42.8	36.2	40.8	39.9
25 to 44 years	52.2	49.8	49.2	58.3	54.0	58.4	58.7
45 to 65 years	66.6	64.1	64.4	70.0	67.9	69.8	69.3
65 years and over	68.9	69.9	67.0	70.1	68.8	67.7	65.1
South Percent Voted							
Race							
White	61.7	58.2	57.4	64.9	60.4	63.0	62.4
Black	61.8	53.2	51.4	53.8	55.6	58.9	52.8

*Hispanics may be of any race.

Source: U.S. Census Bureau, "Current Population Reports," November 2004, Table A-9 (modified by author) (www.census.gov/population/www/socdemo/voting.html)

The strategy was less successful in the 2006 midterm elections, however, because Republican partisans lacked the enthusiasm they had two years earlier for President Bush and GOP candidates for Congress.

Mobilizing the base is the key to winning an Electoral College and popular vote majority in today's highly polarized political environment. Appeals to independent voters and to partisans of the other party have become correspondingly less important. The turnout strategy that the Republicans used in 2004 also confirms the findings of political scientists that personal contact, strong feelings, and partisan allegiances are keys to maximizing turnout.[28]

Not only does partisan orientation affect turnout, but also it has a major impact on voting behavior. The next part of the chapter examines the role of political identity, the ebbs and flows of partisan feelings, and the impact of ideology on partisanship and voting behavior.

THE PARTISAN BASIS OF POLITICS

Why do people vote as they do? Considerable research has been conducted to answer this question. Initially, much of it has been done under the direction of the Center for Political Studies at the University of Michigan. Beginning in 1952, the Center conducted nationwide surveys during presidential elections that have been titled American National Election Studies (ANES).[29]

To identify the major influences on voting behavior, a random sample of the electorate is interviewed before and after each election. Respondents are asked a series of questions designed to reveal their attitudes toward the parties, candidates, and issues. On the basis of their answers to these questions, researchers have amassed a wealth of data to explain the voting behavior of the U.S. electorate.

A MODEL OF THE U.S. VOTER

One of the earliest and most influential theories of voting behavior based on the Michigan survey data was presented in a book entitled *The American Voter* (1960).[30] The model on which the theory is based assumes that individuals are influenced by their partisan attitudes and social relationships in addition to the political environment in which the election takes place. In fact, these attitudes and those relationships condition the impact of that environment on individual voting behavior.

According to the theory, people develop attitudes early in life, largely as a consequence of interacting with their families, particularly their parents and other significant elders.[31] These attitudes, in turn, tend to be reinforced by neighborhood, school, and religious associations.

Psychologically, it is more pleasing to have beliefs and attitudes supported than challenged. Socially, it is more comfortable and safer to associate with "nice," like-minded people, people with similar cultural, educational, and religious experiences, than with others who do not share the same values, beliefs, and experiences. This desire to increase one's "comfort level" in social relationships explains why the environment for most people reinforces rather than challenges their values and beliefs most of the time.[32]

Attitudes mature and harden over the years. The older people become, the less amenable they are to change. They are more set in their ways and their beliefs. Consequently, their behavior is more predictable.

Political attitudes are no exception to this general pattern of attitude formation and maintenance. They too are developed early in life, are reinforced by association, grow in intensity, and become more predictable with time.

Partisanship

Of all the factors that contribute to the development of a political attitude, identifying with a political party seems to be the most important. It affects how people see campaigns, how they evaluate candidates and issues, and how they vote on election day. Party identification operates as a conceptual framework, a mindset, a lens through which the campaign is understood and the candidates evaluated. Partisan allegiances provide cues for interpreting the issues, for judging the candidates, and for deciding whether or not to vote. If the decision is to vote, partisanship influences for whom the vote is cast. The stronger these attitudes, the more compelling the cues; conversely, the weaker the attitudes, the less likely they will affect perceptions during the campaign and influence voting on election day.[33]

When identification with a party is weak or nonexistent, other factors, such as the personalities of the candidates and their issue positions, are correspondingly more important. In contrast to party identification, which is a long-term stabilizing factor but one that can be modified or even changed over time, candidate and issue orientations are shorter term and more variable, often shifting from election to election.

Partisanship may be a factor even for those who do not identify with a political party. People who claim that they are independent, that they vote for the best person regardless of party, or that they simply do not know whether they are Democratic or Republican may still display partisan voting tendencies.

Although partisan allegiances affect perceptions of the candidates and issues, perceptions of the candidates and issues over time can also affect allegiances toward the parties. It is a two-way street in which people's perceptions can be reinforced or challenged by what happens during and after campaigns.

To summarize, partisanship is stable but not static. It can vary in intensity.[34] It tends to be lower during bad times for the party in power and higher during good times.

Candidate and Issue Orientations

People form general impressions about candidates on the basis of what they know about the candidates' experiences, political leadership capabilities, and their personal character. For an incumbent president seeking reelection, accomplishments in office provide much of the criteria for evaluating how well the incumbent has done. For the challenger, it is the potential for office as demonstrated by personal experience, knowledge, confidence, and assertiveness, plus a host of other leadership qualities that help determine public perceptions of their qualifications.[35]

Other characteristics, such as trustworthiness, integrity, empathy, and candor, may also be relevant. Much depends on the nature of the times. In the aftermath of a presidency besmirched by scandal or lacking in candor, integrity and honesty assume more importance than at other times when the problem has been weak or indecisive leadership.

Candidates' stands on the issues, however, seem less critical than do their partisan affiliation and their own potential for office or performance in it. The principal reason for downgrading the importance of issues is the low level of information and awareness that much of the electorate has.

To be important, issues must be salient. They must attract attention; they must hit home. Without personal impact, they are unlikely to be primary motivating factors for voting. In addition, candidates must take sufficiently different positions on the issues for voters to decide which of those positions are most acceptable. To the extent that the candidates' issue positions are not known or are indistinguishable from one another, their respective personal images become a stronger influence.

Ironically, that portion of the electorate that can be more easily persuaded, weak partisans and independents, tend to have the least information.[36] Conversely, the most committed also tend to be the most informed. They use their information to support their partisanship.

The relationship between degree of partisanship and amount of information has significant implications for a democratic society. The traditional view of a democracy holds that information and awareness are necessary to make an intelligent voting decision. However, the finding that those who have the most information are also the most committed, and that those who lack this commitment also lack the incentive to get more information, has upset some of the assumptions about the motivation for acquiring information and using it to vote intelligently.

A More Refined Theory of Voting

The model of voting behavior first presented in 1960 has engendered considerable controversy. Critics have charged that the theory presumes that most of the electorate is uninformed and vote habitually rather than rationally. One well-known political scientist, the late V.O. Key, even wrote a book dedicated to "the perverse and unorthodox argument. . .that voters are not fools."[37]

Key's contention was that most voters are not automatons and that most of their voting decisions are not solely or even primarily the product of their psychological dispositions and social pressures. Even though voters may have limited information, they use it to arrive at reasoned political judgments based in large part on their values, beliefs, and perceptions. They take into account their present situation, their beliefs about government, and their assessments of how the country is doing under its current leadership and will do in the future. In the words of political scientist, Samuel Popkin:

> They consider not only economic issues but family, residential, and consumer issues as well. They think not only of their immediate needs, but also of their needs for insurance against future problems; not only about private good but also about collective goods.[38]

How do they do this? What criteria do they use in making judgments?

Morris Fiorina, in his provocative study *Retrospective Voting in American National Elections* (1981), tried to answer these questions. Utilizing a rational choice model adopted from economics, Fiorina argued that voting decisions are calculations people make on the basis of their accumulated political experience. They make these calculations by assessing the past performance of the parties and their elected officials in light of the promises they made and political events that have occurred. Fiorina called this a retrospective evaluation.[39]

Retrospective evaluations are not only important for influencing voting in a given election, they are also important for shaping partisan attitudes, which Fiorina defined as "a running tally of retrospective evaluations of party promises and performance."[40] In other words, the running tally is a summary judgment of how well the parties and their leaders have done and are doing. Over time, that judgment can change. In the short run, however, it is fairly stable. How have these partisan attitudes evolved over the past several decades, and how they have impacted voting behavior?

Shifts in Partisanship and Voting Behavior

The initial model of voter behavior was based on research conducted in the 1950s. During that decade, approximately three-fourths of the electorate identified with one of the major parties, half of them strongly. (See Table 3.5.) The rest of the VAP was, for the most part, uninterested, uninformed, and uninvolved. Nor did they hold strong ideological views.[41] The two major parties were heterogeneous, although they differed on economic issues, particularly about the role of government within the economy.

Nonetheless, during this period, the parties organized the presidential campaigns, raised most of the money for them, provided the skilled political operatives, and used their grassroots organizations to reach and turn out their base of supporters. Advertising was done primarily in newspapers and on radio; personal contact was deemed important.

The Weakening of Partisanship: The Late 1960s to the Mid-1980s

Much has changed since then. Television became a primary communication link between candidates and the electorate. Public opinion polls became more accurate and dependable. Not only did they become a source of information about the views and preferences of the electorate, but candidates also began to use polls and focus groups to design and market their campaign appeals as well as test how their messages were being received. Television became the principal instrument for projecting these appeals to the electorate.

Accompanying the communications revolution were significant social and economic changes as well as international developments. During the 1960s and continuing into the 1970s, the United States experienced an unsuccessful war in Southeast Asia and a civil rights movement at home. Both of these events divided the American electorate, particularly the Democratic Party. The Watergate scandal, culminating in President Nixon's resignation and his pardon by President Ford, adversely impacted on the Republican Party, shrinking its base.

Both major parties suffered as a result of these events. There was a drop-off in the percentage of the VAP who identified with a party and, concurrently, an increase in the proportion of self-proclaimed independents. Not only did partisan identification decrease, but party loyalties also became weaker.

As might have been expected from the weakening attachments to political parties, there was also an increase in split-ticket voting. The statement, "I vote for the best person, regardless of party," was often heard during this period.

As elections became more candidate-centered, candidate organizations competed with party committees for money, personnel, and political consultants. The candidates placed greater emphasis on personal imagery and the use of television advertising to project it. Media gurus began to replace grassroots organizers as key campaign staff.

Not only were campaigns more candidate focused, but they also became more issue oriented. Debates over social and economic policy became more common as clearer ideological differences began to emerge between the major parties on such issues as civil rights, abortion, and school prayer. The Vietnam War also created divisions between doves and hawks (doves were those who favored ending the war and withdrawing American forces as soon as possible, and hawks were those who wanted the forces to remain until the United States secured a military victory). This division carried over into the 1980s.

In the short run, the Republicans benefited. Weakening support for the dominant party, the Democrats, and the greater stress put on personal images allowed Republicans to run for office without hiding their political affiliation. The GOP's more conservative policies, and especially its opposition to preferential treatment for minorities, coincided with the views of many Americans, especially those living in the South.

As the country prospered and the middle class grew, people became more conservative. They evidenced less sympathy for policies that trumpeted social, economic, and political equality, if not in theory, then in practice. They also became more leery of legislating social policy and of using government to promote that policy and redistribute resources within society.

The Democrats lost their status as the majority party by the end of the 1970s and the plurality party by the mid-1980s. The major parties have remained at rough parity with one another since then. Although the Democrats still hold a slight advantage in party identifiers, that advantage is reduced when turnout is taken into account.

The Reemergence of Partisanship: Mid-1980s to the Present
The weakening of partisanship that began in the late 1960s was short-lived, however. Partisan voting patterns reemerged in the 1980s as the policy differences between the major parties became clearer, and two quite different governing philosophies were debated by political elites and ultimately put before the American voters.

The Republican blueprint for the future, articulated by Ronald Reagan, Newt Gingrich's "Contract with America," and George W. Bush had government playing a smaller and less regulatory role in the economic and social spheres while focusing instead on law and order and national security issues. In contrast, the Democrats continued to see government as an important instrument for addressing social and economic inequities and redistributing resources.

Democrats agreed with Republicans on the need for a strong defense in the Cold War and the war on terrorism but placed greater emphasis on the need to achieve international cooperation. In contrast, Republicans were more desirous of using the country's military power as a diplomatic instrument as well as an armed force to promote national interests and security.

These diverging domestic and foreign policy perspectives contributed to an aligning of partisan attitudes along ideological lines with the Democrats the more liberal party and Republicans the more conservative. The alignment of ideology with partisanship resulted in the two major parties becoming more internally cohesive and externally distinct from one another.

Not only did partisan allegiances strengthen during this period, but partisan cleavages within government also became more pronounced. There was more party-line voting in Congress, more partisan divisions over judicial appointments, more strident partisan rhetoric, and less civility in government.

The number of moderates elected to Congress declined. Conservative Southern Democrats, who frequently sided with the Democrats on economic issues and with the Republican on budget and tax matters, were replaced by even more conservative Republicans, while moderate Republicans, especially from the Northeast, who sided with the Democrats and moderated their position on some social issues, have been replaced by liberal Democrats. Political polarization, heightened by partisan parity and divided government, became the norm not the exception since 1968.

These changes affected the disposition of the American electorate. Partisan voting patterns in federal elections became more apparent. The proportion of strong party identifiers began to increase. Although the proportion of self-identified independents did not vary very much, the majority of independents began to exhibit more partisan voting patterns. The term "independent leaners" is now used to describe these voters. Split-ticket voting declined. And while candidate imagery continued to play an important role in political advertising and news coverage, much of that imagery was imbedded within the prism of partisanship.

There is no doubt that political elites, candidates and office holders, have become polarized; and most political scientists also concede that party activists have become more ideological, more polarized, and much more influential during the nomination stage of the electoral process. The depth to which these partisan and ideological cleavages have affected the polity is less clear and has become a contentious issue among political scientists. There are two schools of thought. One view, put forth by Professor Morris Fiorina and some of his colleagues at Stanford University, argues that the polarization is not nearly as extensive or as deep within the general population as it is among those in power.[42] The Fiorina School sees the public as much less ideological, less active, and less overtly partisan in their attitudes and beliefs, although they do concede that there has been a shifting of public issue positions along ideological lines. However, instead of identifying this shift as evidence of polarization, they see it as a "sorting" of issue opinions that may have been prompted by the clearer, ideological choices put forth by candidates and elected officials to the public or by a natural alignment of the public's policy views with its partisan political predilections.[43]

In contrast, the Polarization School believes that the ideological divisions run deep within the electorate and perhaps even within the population. They point to the persistence of partisan voting patterns and partisan presidential evaluations since the end of the 1980s, the decline in split-ticket voting, the increase in electoral activity,[44] and the success of partisan appeals in turning out voters in recent elections. If the public were not primed for such appeals, they argue, the turnout campaigns would not have been nearly as effective as they were in 2004.[45]

The debate over the degree of social polarization has serious implications for politics and government. For the parties, it calls into question the extent to which they can accommodate the diversity of views and interests within the country as a whole. Can parties claim to be big tents, large enough to attract and welcome all those who choose to enter? At its core, the issue is the ability of the two-party system to sustain itself in an increasingly heterogeneous society.

For candidates, the dilemma is whether to moderate policy views and appeal to those in the middle of the political spectrum by taking a centrist approach, or direct their messages to core supporters who tend to be more ideological.

For those in government, the issue is representational as well. To what extent do elected leaders represent the views of the body politic when articulating and pursuing ideological policy positions? To what extent should they remain true to their beliefs and to the core partisan supporters that nominated them, or should they be more willing to compromise on a range of policy issues for the sake of political accommodation? Put another way, is there a disconnect among those in government, the American electorate, and the population as a whole? Answering these questions correctly is the challenge and the key to political success in the United States today.

In summary, partisan orientation remains a strong influence on how people evaluate candidates or issues, and ultimately on how they vote. It is a relatively stable orientation, but one that can change over the years with events and circumstances and as new people enter and older ones leave the electorate.

Today, partisanship has been reinforced by ideology and to some extent also by religious orthodoxy, a topic we address in the next section when we examine the impact of social factors on partisanship, turnout, and voting behavior. Table 3.5 indicates partisan preferences of the American people since 1952.

THE SOCIAL BASIS OF POLITICS

When individuals develop attitudes and opinions, they are also influenced by the associations they have with others and by the groups with which they are affiliated. That social influences can affect voting behavior is a theory first postulated by Paul F. Lazarsfeld, Bernard R. Berelson, and others who examined the sociology of electoral politics almost fifty years ago in their groundbreaking studies, *The People's Choice* and *Voting*.[46]

Although more attention has been devoted to the psychological influences on voting behavior since the publication of *The American Voter* in 1960, a more recent study by Paul Allen Beck and others lends support to the thesis that the social context in which elections occur matters. Beck and his associates found that intermediaries between the candidates and voters—individuals, media, and groups—provided information that contributed to voters' decisions. The intermediaries had most effect on those voters who were less tied to parties, and for the most part, were also less informed and interested in electoral politics. Coming into contact with others who had political information and enthusiasm for the parties, candidates, and/or issues brought the election to people who might otherwise have avoided it.[47]

Personal contact is important. Politicians have believed this proposition for a long time; more recently, experimental and field research by political scientists Donald P. Green and Alan Gerber has confirmed the conclusion that personal contact increases the vote, ". . . as a rule of thumb, one additional vote is produced for every fourteen people who are successfully contacted by canvassers."[48]

We now turn to these intermediaries and their influences on voting behavior, specifically to the groups that are part of the major parties' electoral coalitions and the support they provide party candidates in presidential elections.

THE NEW DEAL REALIGNMENT

Political coalitions form during periods of partisan realignment. The last time a classic realignment occurred was in the 1930s. Largely as a consequence of the Great Depression, the Democrats emerged as the dominant party.[49] Their electoral coalition, held together by a common belief that the government should play a more active role in dealing with the nation's economic problems, supported Franklin Roosevelt's New Deal program. Those in more dire economic circumstances generally subscribed to this view; they had few other options. On the other hand, many of the owners and executives of still solvent businesses saw government intrusion into the free enterprise system as a threat to the capitalist system. They opposed much of Roosevelt's domestic legislation and remained Republican in attitude and vote.

The Democrats became the majority party during this period by expanding their base. Since the Civil War and the withdrawal of federal troops, the

TABLE 3.5 | PARTY IDENTIFICATION, 1952–2004* (IN PERCENTAGES†)

Party Identification	1952	1956	1960	1964	1968	1972	1976	1980	1984	1988	1992	1996	2000	2004
Democrat	47	44	45	52	45	41	40	41	37	36	35	38	34	33
Strong	22	21	20	27	20	15	15	18	17	18	17	18	19	17
Weak	25	23	25	25	25	26	25	23	20	18	18	20	15	16
Independent§	23	23	23	23	30	35	37	34	34	36	39	34	40	39
Leaning Democrat	10	6	6	9	10	11	12	11	11	12	14	14	15	17
Nonpartisan	6	9	10	8	11	13	15	13	11	11	12	8	12	10
Leaning Republican	7	8	7	6	9	11	10	10	12	13	13	12	13	12
Republican	27	29	30	25	25	23	23	23	27	28	26	29	25	28
Strong	14	14	14	14	15	13	14	14	15	14	15	13	12	12
Weak	13	15	16	11	10	10	9	9	12	14	11	16	12	16
Apoliticals														
"Don't know"/other	4	4	3	1	1	1	1	2	2	2	1	1	1	0

*The survey question was "Generally speaking, do you usually think of yourself as a Republican, a Democrat, an Independent, or what?" If Republican or Democrat, "Would you call yourself a strong (R) (D) or a not very strong (R) (D)?" If Independent, "Do you think of yourself as closer to the Republican or Democratic Party?"

†Percentages may not equal 100 due to rounding.

§The people who fall into this category are those who declare themselves to be Independent, but in follow-up questions indicate that they may lean in a partisan direction.

Sources: American National Election Studies (ANES), Inter-University Consortium for Political and Social Research, Center for Political Studies, University of Michigan, 1952–2004. www.electionstudies.org

Democrats had enjoyed solid support in the South. White Protestants living in rural areas dominated the southern electorate; African Americans were largely excluded. Only in the election of 1928, when Al Smith, the Catholic governor of New York, ran as the Democratic candidate, was there a sizable southern vote for a Republican candidate at the presidential level. As a Catholic and an opponent of prohibition, Smith was unacceptable to many southern, white Protestants.

Catholics also voted Democratic even before the 1930s. Living primarily in the urban centers of the North, they became an increasingly important component of the Democrats' electoral coalition as their numbers grew in the population. Facing difficult economic circumstances, social discrimination, and, for many, language barriers, Catholic immigrants turned to big-city bosses for help; what they were expected to give in return was their support for the boss and the candidates that he and the party organization supported. In 1928, for the first time, a majority of the cities in the country voted Democratic. Catholic support for Smith and the Democratic Party figured prominently in this vote.

The harsh economic realities of the Great Depression enabled Roosevelt to expand Democratic support in urban areas even further, especially among those in the lower socioeconomic strata. Outside the South, Roosevelt's political coalition was differentiated along class lines. It attracted people with less education and income and those who were unemployed, underemployed, or had lower-paying jobs. Organized labor, in particular, became a reliable Democratic ally. Since the New Deal period, labor unions have remained a core group within the Democratic Party's electoral coalition.

In addition to establishing a broad-based, blue-collar, working-class coalition, Roosevelt also lured specific racial and ethnic groups, such as African Americans and Jewish Americans, from their former Republican roots. African Americans, who lived outside of the South, voted increasingly Democratic for economic reasons, whereas Jewish Americans supported Roosevelt's liberal domestic programs and his anti-Nazi foreign policy. Neither of these groups provided the Democratic Party of the 1930s with a large number of votes, but their long-term allegiances to that party has given the Democrats a secure and dependable base among these racial and religious minority groups.

In contrast, during the same period, the Republican Party shrank. Not only were Republicans unable to attract new groups, they were unable to prevent the defection of people whose economic plight made the Democratic program more appealing. Although the Republicans did retain the support of the business and professional classes, their working class base eroded. Republican strength remained concentrated in the Northeast, particularly in the rural areas.

Evolving Political Coalitions: The 1950s–1970s

The coalitions that were restructured during the 1930s and 1940s held together for another twenty years. During this period, African Americans and Jewish

Americans increased their identification with and support of the Democratic Party and its candidates. Although Catholics, for the most part, stayed Democratic, their vote fluctuated more at the presidential level. Catholic support for John Kennedy, a Catholic, reached a high of 78 percent of the total Catholic vote in 1960. The Democrats retained majority Catholic support through the 1970s.

Protestants remained Republican with the exception of less educated, lower-income fundamentalist and evangelic groups that voted Democratic, largely for economic reasons. Concentrated in the South and border states, these fundamentalist and evangelical Christians voted overwhelmingly for Jimmy Carter, a born-again Christian, in 1976.

Prior to the 1980s, there were no major partisan distinctions in gender preferences although some cleavages among different age cohorts were evident. Younger voters, attracted by the liberal policies of Democratic candidates and older Americans who had benefited from these policies, particularly Social Security, gave the Democrats more support, while newly affluent more conservative voters became increasingly Republican.

Socioeconomic Shifts

The changes that did take place in the 1950s and early 1960s emanated primarily from the growth of a larger and more populous middle class and its movement from the cities to the suburbs. In the short run, the nation's postwar prosperity did not result in a complete partisan realignment. People who gained in economic and social status did not, as a general rule, discard their partisan loyalties unless and until they objected to some of the social changes that were occurring during this period: Democratically initiated civil rights legislation followed by Affirmative Action policies, Supreme Court decisions on abortion and school prayer, and the movement by feminists for greater equality in the workplace. Over time, however, rising economic prosperity made the Republicans' policy positions more attractive to a growing and more prosperous middle class.

Coincidentally, the Democrats' labor base began to shrink. In 1952, organized labor represented about 25 percent of the American electorate. Today, it constitutes less than 15 percent.

Regional Shifts

More dramatic than this economic erosion of the Democrats' electoral coalition was the defection of Southern Democrats, a group that had been solidly Democratic since the end of the Civil War. The political attitudes and partisan allegiances of whites in the South began to change as a consequence of the national Democratic Party's support of civil rights. Harry Truman's order to integrate the military and his backing of the 1948 Democratic Convention platform's civil rights plank led to a walkout of southern delegates at the party's nominating convention, the third party candidacy of Strom Thurman, and a decline in the Democratic presidential vote in the South. In 1948, Harry

Truman won 52 percent of the southern vote, compared with Roosevelt's 69 percent four years earlier. Although Adlai Stevenson and John Kennedy carried the South by reduced margins, the southern white Protestant vote for president went Republican for the first time in 1960. And it has continued to become more Republican since then.

The Republicans also gained strength in the Southwest with the movement of population to this area of the country; in contrast, the coastal areas in the Northeast and on the Pacific Coast have become more Democratic.

PARTY PARITY AND THE REALIGNMENT OF ELECTORAL COALITIONS: 1980–PRESENT

The 1980s saw the end of Democratic dominance and the growth of the Republican Party. The GOP achieved parity with the Democrats during this period.

The Republicans

President Ronald Reagan gave voice and structure to a rejuvenated conservative, Republican coalition. The composition of this coalition includes southern whites, Protestant fundamentalists and evangelicals, and other economic and national security conservatives already aligned with the Republican Party. The coalition is disproportionately white, male, and increasingly middle-aged.

Southern Whites   Since the 1980s, southern whites have continued to shift their political allegiances from the Democrats to the GOP. They have given Republican presidential candidates a majority vote in six of the last seven elections. In fact, they have been the most Republican area of the country, more apt to vote Republican at the national level than any other region. In the 1994 midterm elections, Republican congressional candidates won a majority of the southern vote for the first time since Reconstruction.[50] In subsequent elections, the Republicans maintained their southern majority, picking up five open Senate seats in 2004.[51]

The only recent Democratic presidential candidate to do well in the South was Arkansas governor, Bill Clinton, who managed to split the southern vote with Robert Dole in 1996. Since then, Democratic presidential candidates have done poorly in the South. Had it not been for the growth of the African-American electorate in that region of the country, and more recently, the Hispanic population, the defection of the southern states from the Democratic camp would have been even more sweeping.[52]

Protestant Fundamentalists and Evangelicals   Another major shift from the Democrats' electoral coalition to the Republican's has been among orthodox religious believers that have been attracted to the Republican Party by its support of traditional family values. Beginning in the 1980s, Protestant fundamentalist and evangelical churches became better organized and more involved in national politics. Establishing organizations such as the Moral Majority, Christian Coalition, the Family Research Council, and a host of anti-abortion groups, Protestant fundamentalists and evangelicals have become active within the Republican Party's nomination process and a dependable component of its electoral coalition.

People who attended mainline Protestant churches, however, did not become as unified as their fundamentalist and evangelical brethren on the social issues which the Republican Party advocated. As a consequence, they have been somewhat less supportive of Republican candidates than Christian fundamentalist groups. Much depends on the theological and ideological orientation of the churches and their congregations.

John C. Green, a student of religion and politics, has differentiated among Protestant groups on the basis of their participation in church-related activities and the orthodoxy of their religious beliefs. Those who have the greatest involvement, who attend church services most regularly, who subscribe to more literal readings and interpretations of the Bible, are more likely to vote Republican. Those whose theological views are more nuanced, who are less engaged in church-related activities, and who attend services less regularly tend to be more liberal in their social outlook and less Republican in their political behavior.[53]

Green's "traditionalist-modernist" distinction within the Protestant religious community extends to other religions as well, to Catholics that subscribe to the Church's doctrine and regularly attend Mass and even orthodox Jews.

The key variable predicting voting behavior is the regularity of religious worship. People who attend services regularly are more apt to vote Republican than those who attend less regularly or not at all.

The sectarian-secular divide, evident for at least the past two decades, is applicable for white America. It does not extend to racial minority groups whose allegiances to the Democratic Party are more deeply rooted in that party's economic and social policy positions than they are in its attitude toward religious values and practices.

Men and Married Women   A gender gap has also been apparent since 1984. Males have been more attracted to the Republican Party and women to the Democratic Party.[54] The gap had been in the range of 4 to 8 percent until 1996, when it rose to 11 percent and remained at about that level in 2000. It was reduced to the 4 to 8 percent range in 2004 but grew again in the 2006 midterm elections and may grow even further in 2008 if the Democrats nominate a woman as their presidential candidate.

When the gender gap was largest during the 1990s, political pundits and news media commentators used the term "soccer moms" to describe the women with young children who supported Democratic candidates because of their stands on such issues as education, health care, equality in the workplace, and the environment. The drop in female support for the Democratic presidential candidate in 2004 was attributed to "security moms," older married women who were concerned about their family's personal security in an age of terrorism.[55]

The gender gap is larger among whites than nonwhites and larger among those with more formal education than less. It is also greater among those who are unmarried than those who are married and those without children than those with them.[56]

Middle Aged and Getting Older   The Roosevelt Democrats are being replaced by generations whose experiences with government are less positive than during the 1930s and 1940s. As a consequence, middle-aged and older Americans today are more receptive to Republican appeals of less government in the economic and social spheres but for a strong government role in national security. The 2004 presidential election was the first in which the over sixty-five vote was almost evenly divided. Prior to that election, voters over sixty-five tended to be more Democratic than Republican.

How then can the contemporary Republican electoral coalition be described? Beginning in the 1980s and continuing into the twenty-first century, the Republican coalition has become whiter, more middle class, more rural, more male, more religious, and more conservative. Republicans have gained support in the South and Southwest, but have lost it in the Northeast and on the Pacific Coast. In size, their coalition is almost as large as the Democrats', and when turnout is taken into account, it is as large as the Democrats'.

The Democrats

The Democrats' electoral coalition has frayed from its New Deal days; Democrats no longer constitute the majority; their coalition has shrink in size, become more diverse in composition, and more concentrated geographically. They have become a party in which ethnic and racial minorities and, increasingly, women and people with a secular views constitute core constituencies.

Democrats still receive overwhelming support from those with the lowest incomes and those who live in the cities. However, the relatively small sizes of the latter two groups within the electorate as a whole make them a less important voting bloc than they used to be.

Racial and Ethnic Minorities   The Democratic electoral coalition has retained and even increased its support among African Americans and Hispanics. Today, more than 75 percent of African Americans consider themselves Democrats and 10 percent Republicans compared to the late 1950s when almost 25 percent considered themselves Republican.[57] With their increased loyalty to the Democrats, African Americans have become a larger and more important component in the Democrats' core constituency.

The flip side of this increase in support has been that the party's positions on economic and social issues, particularly on civil rights and welfare benefits, have alienated some white working-class voters whose allegiances to the Democrats have declined over the past three decades.[58]

Hispanic voters have become another increasingly important component of the Democrats' electoral coalition. With the exception of Cuban Americans concentrated in South Florida, a majority of Hispanic voters identify with the Democratic Party, and two-thirds of them tend to vote for its candidates on a regular basis. Clinton received the support of almost three out of four Hispanic voters in 1996, and Gore, almost two out of three in 2000. In 2004, the small number of Hispanic voters within the exit poll sample made it did difficult to calculate accurately the group's turnout and vote although Bush's support from this group did increase over his 2000 Hispanic vote.[59] The concentration of Hispanic voters in the Southwest has made this area more competitive today for Democratic candidates.

Coastal Residents   The Northeast has become more Democratic but not primarily as a consequence of population movement. The Republican Party's increasing ideological rigidity, particularly its social agenda, has alienated some of old-line moderate Republicans from this area. New Hampshire, the last bastion of GOP strength, went Democratic at the presidential level in 2004 and at the congressional level (the House of Representatives) in 2006. The mid-Atlantic and Pacific Coast states have also become more Democratic. Competition between the parties tends to be greatest in the Midwest, an area in which most of the battleground states critical to winning an Electoral College majority are located.

Seculars   The movement of Protestant fundamentalists to the Republican Party has left the Democrats with a more secular base. With the exception of the Jewish community, which has remained in the Democrats' electoral coalition, and Muslims who have more recently reacted to the domestic security measures and foreign policies of the Bush administration by voting Democratic, the party lacks the strong religious base it had in previous eras.

Catholic support has declined particularly among the older-line Catholic groups, primarily Irish and Italian. Despite the fact that Catholic John Kerry ran on the Democratic ticket in the 2004 presidential election, the Catholic vote was almost evenly divided between Kerry and Bush. Had it not been for expansion of the Hispanic population, the drop in Catholic support for the Democrats would have been even greater. Again, the more traditional the religious beliefs and practices of Catholics, the less likely they are to vote Democratic.

Similarly, people who are not affiliated with a religious institution or who are not practicing their religious beliefs and heritage are much more likely to consider themselves Democrats.

Old and Young   There are also interesting age and educational distinctions between contemporary Democratic and Republican voters. People who came of voting age during the Roosevelt presidency remain the Democrats' most loyal age group, but they are passing from the scene. Their children do not share their strong Democratic allegiances. In recent elections, the youngest voters, however, have exhibited Democratic voting preferences.[60] Those in the youngest age cohort tend to be more tolerant of changing social mores and more supportive of the Democrats' liberal policy positions on many social issues.

Partisan voting trends are also evident on the basis of sexual orientation. According to the exit polls in recent elections, more than 70 percent of those who indicated that they were homosexual or lesbian voted Democratic. However, only a relatively small percentage of voters, about 4 percent, admit to being gay.[61]

Finally, it is interesting to note that the Democrats receive support from those who have the least and the most education. The less educated are more likely to be in the lower socioeconomic categories and thus more responsive to the Democrats' economic policy positions; those with the most education may be more receptive to the Democrats' stand on equity issues.

In summary, the Democrats are a party of racial, ethnic, and religious minorities; young and old; most and least educated; women; and those living in Metropolitan areas, primarily on the East and West Coasts. Gallup Poll data on group voting patterns since 1996 is presented in Table 3.6.

What conclusions can we draw about the social basis of politics today? It is clear that the old party coalitions have evolved. Today, the parties remain at rough parity with one another. Their parity gives groups within their respective electoral coalitions more clout than they otherwise would have. Defections and turnout matter in presidential elections.

TABLE 3.6	VOTE BY GROUPS IN PRESIDENTIAL ELECTIONS, 1996–2004							
	1996			2000			2004	
	Clinton	Dole	Perot	Gore	Bush	Nader	Kerry	Bush
NATIONAL	50.0%	41.0%	9.0%	48.7%	48.6%	2.7%	48.5%	51.5%
Sex								
Men	45	44	11	45	52	3	44	56
Women	54	39	7	53	45	2	52	48
Race								
White (incl. Hispanics)	46	45	9	43	55	3	44	56
Nonwhite	82	12	6	87	9	4	83	17
Non-Hispanic white	x	x	x	42	56	2	43	57
Nonwhite (incl. Hispanics)	x	x	x	80	17	3	78	22
Black	x	x	x	95	3	2	93	7
Age								
Under 30 years	54	30	16	47	47	6	60	40
30–49 years	49	41	10	45	53	2	43	57

(continued)

TABLE 3.6 | CONTINUED

	1996			2000			2004	
	Clinton	Dole	Perot	Gore	Bush	Nader	Kerry	Bush
50–64 years old	x	x	x	50	48	2	48	52
65 years and older	x	x	x	56	42	2	52	48
50 years and older	50	45	5	53	45	2	50	50
Education								
College	47	45	8	46	51	3	48	52
High School	52	34	14	52	46	2	54	46
Grade School	58	27	15	55	42	3	69	31
Post-Grad	x	x	x	53	43	4	53	47
College Grad only	x	x	x	44	55	1	42	58
Some College	x	x	x	44	53	3	44	56
High School or Less	x	x	x	53	45	2	54	46
Region								
East	60	31	9	55	42	3	58	42
Midwest	46	45	9	48	49	3	48	52
South	44	46	10	45	54	1	43	57
West	51	43	6	48	47	5	48	52
Size of Community								
Urban	58	36	6	62	35	3	56	44
Suburban	47	45	8	47	51	2	46	54
Rural	44	43	13	38	60	3	46	54
Politics								
Republicans	10	85	5	7	92	1	5	95
Democrats	90	6	4	89	10	2	93	7
Independents	48	33	19	44	49	7	52	48
Conservative	x	x	x	27	71	2	20	80
Moderate	x	x	x	57	41	2	63	37
Liberal	x	x	x	84	9	7	88	12
Religion								
Protestants	44	50	6	42	55	3	38	62
Catholics	55	35	10	52	46	2	52	48
Attend Weekly	x	x	x	41	56	2	37	63

(continued)

	1996			2000			2004	
	Clinton	Dole	Perot	Gore	Bush	Nader	Kerry	Bush
Attend Monthly	x	x	x	47	51	2	45	55
Seldom/Never Attend	x	x	x	52	41	7	60	40
Marital Status								
Married	x	x	x	40	57	2	40	60
Not Married	x	x	x	59	36	3	60	40
Married Men	x	x	x	37	59	3	39	61
Married Women	x	x	x	41	56	2	42	58
Unmarried Men	x	x	x	49	42	5	55	45
Unmarried Women	x	x	x	66	31	2	64	36
Labor Union								
Union families	x	x	x	68	31	2	67	33
Gun Ownership								
Owner	x	x	x	38	59	2	35	65
Nonowner	x	x	x	56	41	3	56	44

National figures are based on actual election outcomes, repercentaged to exclude minor third-party candidates. Demographic data are based on Gallup Poll final preelection surveys, repercentaged to exclude "no opinions" and support for minor third-party candidates; results are then weighted to conform with actual election results.
Source: Gallup Poll, "Election Polls: Vote by Groups" (www.galluppoll.com/content/CI=9469)

SUMMARY

The electorate is not neutral. People do not come to campaigns with completely open minds. Rather, they come with preexisting attitudes and accumulated experiences that color their perceptions and affect their judgments, much as stimuli from the campaign affect those attitudes and experiences.

Of the political beliefs people possess, partisanship has the strongest impact on voting. It provides a perspective for evaluating the campaign and for deciding whether and how to vote. It is also a motive for being informed, for getting involved, and for turning out to vote.

Toward the end of the 1960s, there was a decline in the proportion of the population that identified with a political party. This decline, a product of disillusionment with both major parties, contributed to lower voter turnout. It also increased the importance of short-term factors on voting behavior. During this period, more people identified themselves as independent; there was more candidate and issue voting; and as a consequence, more split-ticket ballots.

The use of television as the primary channel through which candidates and parties communicated to the electorate, the weakening of the major parties' grassroots organizations, and the creation of separate candidate and party organizations required by the Federal Election Campaign Act, all worked to reduce the influence of the parties on voting behavior.

But the weakening of partisanship has proven to be temporary. A growing ideological debate, waged along partisan lines, has recast and restructured the parties, polarized the electorate, and produced more discernible partisan voting patterns. These trends began in the 1980s and continued into the twenty-first century. New gender, religious, and regional divisions have also emerged.

As the national party organizations got stronger, they improved their fundraising operations, purchased new communications technologies, and protected their incumbents through artful drafting of legislative districts. The national parties began to exercise more influence over the conduct of congressional, and to a lesser extent, presidential campaigns. They were more effective in recruiting candidates, helping them finance their campaigns, and identifying, targeting, and contacting potential supporters.

Group ties to the parties have shifted as well. The Democratic Party, which had become dominant during the New Deal period, lost the support of a majority of southern whites in presidential and congressional elections. It also suffered defections from other groups—non-Hispanic Catholics and Protestant fundamentalists and evangelicals. The Democratic labor base shrunk as union laborers declined as a proportion of the population.

Racial minorities, such as African Americans and Hispanics, however, have retained their loyalty to the Democrats as have Jewish Americans. Women have become much more supportive of Democratic candidates as have people with more secular views. The party improved its proportion of the vote in the Northeast, Pacific Coast, and more recently, in Southwest—the latter a result of Hispanic immigration.

The Republican electoral base has grown in size and diversity. That party made inroads among the growing middle- and upper-middle classes that found its stands on law and order, lower taxes, and limited government within the domestic sphere appealing. The Republican Party's emphasis on family values attracted the support of traditional religious adherents and practitioners who attend services on a regular basis. White men also became more Republican in outlook and voting behavior. In addition to the South, the GOP picked up strength in the Southwest and maintained its support on the Mountain states.

The shifting partisan coalitions have helped the Republicans more than the Democrats. In fact, the GOP seemed to be at the verge of becoming the dominant party until events during George W. Bush's second term, the war in Iraq, the tepid government response to Hurricane Katrina, and a corruption scandal primarily involving Republican members of Congress resulted in a Democratic victory in the 2006 midterm elections.

The changes within the political environment have important implications for presidential politics. They have produced a more ideological-based party system, one in which party moderates exercise less influence. They have also produced cleavages within the electorate along gender and religious lines, cleavages that supplement the income-based divisions evident since the 1930s.

Partisan voting patterns have reemerged, reinforced by ideology. The decline in independent voting has encouraged both parties to reach out to their base with the result that turnout in the 2004 presidential election and the 2006 midterm elections increased. The extent to which these trends will continue will likely depend on the perceived state of the economy and the nation's security as the next presidential election approaches and each party's ability to appeal to its core supporters and, simultaneously, to a broader cross-section of Americans.

 WHERE ON THE WEB?

- **Democracy Network**
  www.dnet.org
    A public interest site sponsored by the education fund of the League of Women Voters on which you can find out candidate positions on the issues as well as connect to grassroots groups on a variety of salient issues.

- **Democratic National Committee**
  www.democrats.org
    Information on Democratic Party history, rules, convention, and campaigns with links to Democratic youth and state party affiliates.

- **Green Party**
  www.gp.org
    Information on the Green Party, its rules, convention, and candidates.

- **League of Women Voters**
  www.lwv.org
    Provides information on candidates, their positions, and how to register and vote.

- **Reform Party**
  www.reformparty.org
    Information on the Reform Party, its rules, conventions, and candidates.

- **Republican National Committee**
  www.rnc.org
    Information on Republican Party history, rules, convention, and campaigns with links to Republican youth and state party affiliates.

- **Rock-the-Vote**
  www.rockthevote.org
    An organization whose goal is to encourage young people to register and vote by providing a registration form online, as well as details about how to obtain an absentee ballot.

- **Project Vote Smart**
  www.vote-smart.org
  An organization that provides a wealth of information on candidates and their issue positions and evaluates their performance in office.

EXERCISES

1. If you are a U.S. citizen, eighteen years of age or older, and haven't already done so, register to vote by accessing the Election Assistance Commission's Web cite at www.eac.gov and downloading the national voter registration form, completing it, and sending it to your state election officials. Alternately, access Rock-the-Vote at www.rockthevote.org, and provide that organization with information to begin the registration process.

2. Indicate all the services that the major parties provide their candidates in the general election by accessing their Web sites and going through their menu of services. Which of these services do you think will be most helpful to the presidential candidates in the coming election?

3. Go to the FEC Web site (www.fec.gov) or the League of Women Voters' Education fund at (www.dnet.org) to determine the states with the highest and lowest turnout of voters in 2004. Group these states on the basis of their turnout rates and then compare their registration requirements (also obtainable at the FEC site) to see if differences in these requirements help explain the turnout differential. In addition to registration requirements, what other factors might explain the differences in turnout?

4. Describe the composition of the major parties' electoral coalitions. On the basis of your description, locate interest groups that represent these groups of supporters. Access their Web sites, and note what they have done or plan to do to mobilize their supporters in the election.

SELECTED READINGS

Abramson, Paul R., John H. Aldrich, and David W. Rohde. *Change and Continuity in the 2004 Elections*. Washington, D.C.: CQ Press, 2006.

Black, Earl, and Merle Black. *The Vital South: How Presidents Are Elected*. Cambridge, M.A.: Harvard University Press, 1992.

Burnham, Walter D. "The Turnout Problem" in *Elections American Style*, edited by A. James Reichley. Washington, D.C.: Brookings Institution, 1987, 97–133.

Campbell, Angus, Philip E. Converse, Warren E. Miller, and Donald E. Stokes. *The American Voter*. New York: Wiley, 1960.

Fiorina, Morris, Samuel J. Abrams, and Jeremy C. Pope, *Culture War? The Myth of a Polarized America*. New York: Longman, 2006.

Green, Donald P., and Alan S. Gerber, *Get Out the Vote! How to Increase Voter Turnout*. Washington, D.C.: Brookings, 2004.

Highton, Benjamin. "Voter Registration and Turnout in the United States," *Perspectives on Politics*, 2 (September 2004): 507–515.

Keith, Bruce E., David B. Magleby, Candice Nelson, and Elizabeth Orr. *The Myth of the Independent Voter*. Berkeley: University of California Press, 1992.

Leege, David, and Lyman A. Kellstedt. *Rediscovering the Religious Factor in American Politics.* New York: M. E. Sharpe, 1993.

Lyons, William, and Robert Alexander. "A Tale of Two Electorates: Generational Replacement and the Decline of Voting in Presidential Elections." *Journal of Politics,* 62 (Nov. 2000): 1014–1034.

Miller, Warren E. "Party Identification, Realignment, and Party Voting: Back to the Basics," *American Political Science Review,* 85 (June 1991): 557–570.

Nagler, Jonathan. "The Effect of Registration Laws and Education on U.S. Voter Turnout," *American Political Science Review,* 85 (December 1991): 1395–1405.

Nie, Norman H., Sidney Verba, and John R. Petrocik. *The Changing American Voter.* Cambridge, M.A.: Harvard University Press, 1976.

Nivola, Pietro S., and David W. Brady, eds. *Red and Blue Nation? Characteristics and Causes of America's Polarized Politics.* Washington, D.C.: Brookings Institution, 2006.

Patterson, Thomas E. *The Vanishing Voter.* New York: Knopf, 2002.

Piven, Frances Fox, and Richard A. Cloward. *Why Americans Don't Vote.* New York: Pantheon, 1988.

Popkin, Samuel L. *The Reasoning Voter: Communication and Persuasion in Presidential Campaigns.* Chicago: University of Chicago Press, 1991.

Stanley, Harold W., and Richard G. Niemi. "Party Coalitions in Transition: Partisanship and Group Support, 1952–1996," in *Reelection 1996: How Americans Voted,* edited by Herbert F. Weisberg and Janet M. Box-Steffensmeier, New York: Chatham House, 1999: 162–180.

Tate, Katherine. "Black Political Participation in the 1984 and 1988 Presidential Elections." *American Political Science Review,* 85 (December 1991): 1159–1176.

Teixeira, Ruy A. *The Disappearing American Voter.* Washington, D.C.: Brookings Institution, 1992.

Wattenberg, Martin P. *The Decline of American Political Parties: 1952–1996.* Cambridge, M.A.: Harvard University Press, 1998.

Wolfinger, Raymond E., and Steven J. Rosenstone. *Who Votes?* New Haven, C.T.: Yale University Press, 1980.

Notes

1. U.S. Census Bureau, "Percentage of the Voting Aged Population Which Voted." Federal Election Commission Web site: www.fec.gov/pubrec/fe2004/tables.pdf.

2. Michael P. McDonald and Samuel L. Popkin, "The Myth of the Vanishing Voter," *American Political Science Review,* 95 (December 2001), pp. 963–974; Samuel L. Popkin and Michael McDonald, "Turnout's Not as Bad as You Think," *Washington Post,* (Nov. 5, 2000), pp. B1, B2.

3. Michael P. McDonald, "Up, Up and Away! Voter Participation in the 2004 Presidential Election," *The Forum,* II (Post Election), 2004. www.bepress.com/forum/vol2/iss4.

4. Kelly Holder, "Voting and Registration in the Election of November 2004," Census Bureau, March 2006. www.census.gov/prod/2006pubs/p20-556.pdf. See also "Current Population Survey," U.S. Census Bureau, November 2004, Table 1.

5. Although some states initially permitted all landowners to vote, including women, by 1807, every state limited voting to men. Michael X. Delli Carpini and Ester R. Fuchs, "The Year of the Woman: Candidates, Voters, and the 1992 Election," *Political Science Quarterly,* 108 (Spring 1993), p. 30.

6. Ronald P. Formisane, "Deferential-Participant Politics: The Early Republic's Political Culture, 1789," *American Political Science Review,* 68 (June 1974), pp. 473–487.

7. Delli Carpini and Fuchs, "The Year of the Woman," p. 30.

8. Despite these allegations, Walter Dean Burnham still maintains that the high turnout percentages were real, "not artifacts of either census error or universal ballot stuffing." Ibid, 117. Walter Dean Burnham, "The Turnout Problem," in *Elections American Style,* ed. A. JamesReichley (Washington, D.C.: Brookings Institution, 1987), pp. 112–116.

9. Peter F. Nardulli, Jon K. Dalager, and Donald E. Greco, "Voter Turnout in U.S. Presidential Elections: An Historical View and Some Speculation," *PS* (September 1996), p. 480.

10. In the case of *Smith v. Allwright*, 321 U.S. 649 (1944), the Supreme Court declared the white primary to be unconstitutional. In its opinion, the Court rejected the argument that parties were private associations and thus could restrict participation in their selection process.

11. Paul R. Abramson, John H. Aldrich, and David W. Rohde, *Change and Continuity in the 2004 Elections.* (Washington, D.C.: Congressional Quarterly, 2006), p. 83. In addition, thirty-two states prohibit those on parole from voting, and twenty-nine prohibit those on probation. Fox Butterfield, "Many Black Males Barred from Voting," *New York Times* (Jan. 30, 1997), p. A12; Michael A. Fletcher, "Voting Rights for Felons Win Support," *Washington Post* (February 22, 1999), pp. A1, A6.

12. "The Impact of the National Voter Registration Act of 1993 on the Administration of Elections for Federal Office, 2003–2004." A Report to the 109th Congress, June 30, 2005, Election Assistance Commission. www.eac.gov.

13. For a very interesting article on the life cycle and voting, see Eric Plutzer, "Becoming a Habitual Voter: Inertia, Resources, and Growth in Young Adulthood," *American Political Science Review,* 96 (March 2002), pp. 41–56.

14. Angus Campbell, Philip E. Converse, Warren E. Miller, and Donald E. Stokes, *The American Voter* (New York: Wiley, 1960), p. 102.

15. S. E. Finkel and P. B. Freedman, "The Half-Hearted Rise: Voter Turnout in the 2000 Elections," in Herbert Weisberg and Clyde Wilcox, eds., *Models of Voting in Presidential Elections: The 2000 Elections* (Stanford, C.A.: Stanford University Press, 2003), pp. 180–205.

16. Abramson, Aldrich, and Rohde, *Change and Continuity in 2004,* p. 99. The authors also note a decline in trust in government but conclude that this decline has had little affect on turnout. Ibid., p. 100.

17. Raymond E. Wolfinger and Steven J. Rosenstone, *Who Votes?* (New Haven, C.T.: Yale University Press, 1980), pp. 13–26.

18. Ibid., pp. 18–20, 35–36.

19. Abramson, Aldrich, and Rohde write, "turnout would have declined 22 percentage points," if educational levels had not risen. Abramson, Aldrich, and Rohde, *Change and Continuity in 2004*, p. 95.

20. Why the drop in turnout among the young? Younger people may not have perceived the national government as relevant to them as their parents and grandparents saw the government when they were young. Until the terrorist attacks of September 11, 2001, there was not an event of the magnitude of the great Depression and World War II that demonstrated the importance of government or events such as the Vietnam War, and race relations that illustrated the dangers of government to people who found these experiences disconcerting.

21. McDonald, *Up, Up and Away!* p. 2.

22. American National Election Studies. www.umich.edu/~nes/nesguide/toptable/tab6c_1a.htm (accessed January 20, 2004). See also Paul Allen Beck, Russell J. Dalton, Steven Greene, and Robert Huckfeldt, "The Social Calculus of Voting: Interpersonal, Media, and Organizational Influences on Presidential Choices," *American Political Science Review*, 96 (2002), pp. 57–74.

23. On the other hand, low turnout can also indicate a level of satisfaction since citizens are more likely to vote when they are angry than when they are contented.

24. Another related factor is the increasing percentage of single people and single parents in the voting-age population over the past fifty years. For a variety of reasons from time constraints to lower income levels, single adults do not turn out to vote as regularly as do married adults.

25. Michael D. Martinez and Jeff Gill, "The Effects of Turnout on Partisan Outcomes in U.S. Presidential Elections 1960–2000," *Journal of Politics*, 67 (Nov. 2005), pp. 1248–1274.

26. Dan Balz and Thomas B. Edsall, "Unprecedented Efforts to Mobilize Voters Begin," *Washington Post* (Nov. 1, 2004), pp. A1, A6.

27. "President Bush, Mobilization Drives Propel Turnout To Post-1968 High; Kerry, Democratic Weakness Shown." Committee for the Study of the American Electorate, Press Release, November 4, 2004.

28. Donald P. Green and Alan S. Gerber, *Get Out the Vote! How to Increase Voter Turnout.* (Washington, D.C.: Brookings, 2004).

29. Actually, a small interview/reinterview survey was conducted in 1948, but the results were never published. In contrast to the emphasis on political attitudes of the large-scale interview projects in the 1950s, the project in 1948 had a sociological orientation.

30. Campbell, Converse, Miller, and Stokes, *The American Voter*, p. 102.

31. Most political science research has been directed toward the effect of environment factors on attitude formation, factors such as parents, schools, religious institutions, and peer and adult relationships. More recently, however, research in genetics suggests that there may be a link between the genes people inherit and the beliefs and attitudes they formulate. Since genes help explain physical appearance, they may also contribute to psychological dispositions and orientations, intelligence, and even political attitudes. See John R. Alford, Carolyn L. Funk, and John

R. Hibbing, "Are Political Orientations Genetically Transmitted?" *American Political Science Review*, 99 (May 2005), pp. 153–167.

32. Campbell, Converse, Miller, and Stokes, *The American Voter*, pp. 146–152.

33. Ibid., pp. 133–136. In examining the concept of party identification, Michigan analysts have stressed two dimensions: direction and strength. Others, however, have criticized the Michigan model for overemphasizing party and under-emphasizing other factors, such as social class, political ideology, and issue positions. For a thoughtful critique, see Jerrold G. Rusk, "The Michigan Election Studies: A Critical Evaluation." Paper presented at the annual meeting of the American Political Science Association, New York (Sept. 3–6, 1981).

34. Janet M. Box-Steffensmeier and Renee M. Smith, "The Dynamic of Aggregate Partisanship," *American Political Science Review* (Sept. 1996), pp. 567–580; Ronald B. Rapoport, "Partisanship Change in a Candidate-Centered Era," *Journal of Politics* (Feb. 1997), pp. 185–199.

35. For a more extensive discussion of desirable presidential images, see Chapter 6 of this book and Benjamin I. Page, *Choices and Echoes in Presidential Elections* (Chicago: University of Chicago Press, 1978), pp. 232–265.

36. Campbell, Converse, Miller, and Stokes, *The American Voter*, pp. 143, 547. Independents that lean in a partisan direction tend to be better informed than those who do not. These independent leaners have many of the characteristics of party identifiers, including loyalty to the party's candidates. They do not, however, identify themselves as Republicans or Democrats.

37. Key studied the behavior of three groups of voters between 1936 and 1960: switchers, stand-patters, and new voters. He found those who switched their votes to be interested in and influenced by their own evaluation of policy, personality, and performance. In this sense, Key believed that they exercised an intelligent judgment when voting. V.O. Key Jr., *The Responsible Electorate* (Cambridge, M.A.: Harvard University Press, 1966), p. 7.

38. Samuel L. Popkin, *The Reasoning Voter* (Chicago: University of Chicago Press, 1991), p. 43.

39. Morris P. Fiorina, *Retrospective Voting in American National Elections* (New Haven: C.T.: Yale University Press, 1981), pp. 65–83.

40. Ibid., p. 84.

41. Philip E. Converse, "The Nature of Belief Systems in Mass Publics," in *Ideology and Discontent*, ed. by David E. Apter (New York: Free Press, 1964), pp. 206–261.

42. Morris Fiorina, Samuel J. Abrams, and Jeremy C. Pope, *Culture War? The Myth of a Polarized America* (New York: Longman, 2006).

43. Morris P. Fiorina and Matthew S. Levendusky, "Disconnected: The Political Class versus the People," in Peitro S. Nivola and David W. Brady, eds. *Red and Blue Nation? Characteristics and Causes of America's Polarized Politics* (Washington, D.C.: Brookings Institution, 2006), pp. 49–71; pp. 95–111.

44. According to data in recent American National Election Studies, the level of participation in elections has increased. More people gave money; contacted friends, neighbors, or acquaintances; attended rallies or other campaign events; and worked

for a candidate or party than in the past. American National Election Studies. www.electionstudies.org/nesguide/gd-index.htm#6.

45. See Alan I. Abramowitz, "Disconnected or Joined at the Hip?" In Nivola and Brady, *Red and Blue Nation?* pp. 72–85; Gary C. Jacobson, "Comment," Ibid., pp. 85–95.

46. Paul F. Lazarsfeld, Bernard R. Berelson, and Hazel Gaudet. *The People's Choice: How the Voter Makes Up His Mind in a Presidential Campaign.* (New York: Columbia University Press, 1948); Bernard R. Berelson, Paul F. Lazarsfeld, and William N. McPhee, *Voting: A Study of Opinion Formation in a Presidential Campaign* (Chicago: University of Chicago Press, 1954).

47. Paul Allen Beck, Russell J. Dalton, Steven Greene, and Robert Huckfeldt, "The Social Calculus of Voting: Interpersonal, Media, and Organizational Influences on Presidential Choices," *American Political Science Review,* 96 (2002), pp. 67–69.

48. Green and Gerber, *Get Out the Vote,* p. 34.

49. This description of the New Deal realignment is based primarily on the discussion in Everett Carll Ladd Jr., with Charles D. Hadley, *Transformations of the American Party System* (New York: Norton, 1975), pp. 31–87.

50. Thomas B. Edsall, "Huge Gains in South Fueled GOP Vote in '94," *Washington Post,* (June 27, 1995), p. A8.

51. Despite Republican gains in the South, it is still not as solidly Republican today as it was solidly Democratic from 1876 through 1944. According to political scientists Earl and Merle Black, Franklin Delano Roosevelt averaged 78 percent of the southern vote during his four presidential elections compared with 57 percent for Republican presidential candidates from 1972 to 1988. Black and Black, *The Vital South,* p. 27.

52. In 2000 and 2004, approximately one half of the Southern vote Gore and Kerry received came from African Americans and other minority racial and ethnic groups.

53. John C. Green, "The American Religious Landscape and Political Attitudes: A Baseline for 2004," Ray C. Bliss Institute of Applied Politics, University of Akron. www.uakron.edu/bliss/docs/Religious_Landscape_2004.pdf.

54. There is also a gender gap within the parties. In an analysis of voting behavior in presidential primaries from 1980 to 2000, Professor Barbara Norrander found women more likely to consider themselves partisans than men. The differences were greater among Democratic voters than Republicans. Barbara Norrander, "The Intraparty Gender Gap: Differences between Male and Female Voters in the 1980–2000 Presidential Primaries," *PS: Political Science and Politics,* 36 (April 2003), pp. 181–186.

55. There is little empirical evidence to support this anecdotal proposition.

56. Abramson, Aldrich, and Rohde, *Change and Continuity in 2004,* pp. 111–112.

57. Lyman A. Kellstedt, John C. Green, James L. Guth, and Corwin E. Schmidt, "Religious Voting Blocs in the 1992 Election: Year of the Evangelical?" *Sociology of Religion,* 55 (1994), pp. 307–326; Robert B. Fowler and Allen D. Hertzke, *Religion and Politics in America: Faith, Culture, and Strategic Choice.* (Boulder, C.O.: Westview Press, 1995).

58. For an extended discussion of the impact of race on the Democratic Party, see Robert Huckfeldt and Carol Weitzel Kohfeld, *Race and the Decline of Class in American Politics* (Urbana: University of Illinois Press, 1989).

59. The exit poll sample indicated that 42 percent of the Hispanic population had voted for Bush, but Hispanic and other pollsters disputed this figure as too high. Their surveys indicated anywhere from about one-third to 36 percent may have voted for Bush.

60. "Sub-group Voting Patterns," Gallup Poll, November, 2–5, 2006. www. galluppoll.com/content/Default.aspx?ci=24289&t=SQ (accessed November 13, 2006).

61. Ibid., p. 113.

THE NOMINATION

PART 2

4

CHAPTER

PARTY RULES AND THEIR IMPACT: THE LEGAL ENVIRONMENT

INTRODUCTION

Presidential nominees are selected by the delegates who attend their party's national nominating convention. The way those delegates are chosen, however, influences the choice of nominees and also affects the influence of the state and its party leadership.

State law determines the procedures for delegate selection. Today, these procedures also have to conform to the general guidelines and rules established by the national parties. Prior to the 1970s, they did not. Under the old system, statutes passed by a state legislature reflected the needs and desires of the political leaders who controlled that state. Naturally, these laws were designed to buttress that leadership and extend its clout.

Although primaries were held, many of them were advisory; the actual selection of the delegates was left to caucuses, conventions, or committees, which were more easily controlled by party officials. Favorite son candidates, tapped by the leadership, prevented meaningful contests in many states. There were also impediments to delegates getting on the ballot: high fees, lengthy petitions, and early filing dates. Winner-take-all provisions gave a great advantage to candidates backed by the party organization, as did rules requiring delegates to vote as a unit.

Popular participation in the selection of convention delegates is a relatively recent phenomenon in the history of national nominating conventions. It began in the 1970s when the Democratic Party adopted a series of reforms that affected the period during which delegates could be selected, the procedures for choosing them, and ultimately their behavior at the convention. Although these Democratic rules limited the states' discretion, they did not result in uniform voting practices in primaries and caucuses. Considerable variation still exists in how delegates are chosen, how the vote is apportioned, and who participates in the selection.

This chapter explores these rules and their consequences for the nomination process. It is organized into three sections. The first details the changes in party rules. The second considers the legal challenges to these rules and the Supreme Court's decisions on them. The third section examines the impact of the rules changes on the parties and their electorates.

REFORMING THE NOMINATION PROCESS

Historically, states set their own rules for nominating candidates to office with relatively little guidance from the national party. Some rules discouraged popular involvement; others encouraged it but made no effort to translate the public's evaluation of the candidates into delegate support for them. In very few states was the delegation as a whole representative, demographically or ideologically, of the party's electorate within that state.

Democratic Party reforms were intended to frame the decentralized nomination process. The party had two principal objectives in altering its rules to promote more internal democracy. Democrats wanted to encourage greater rank-and-file participation and to select delegates who were more representative of the party's electorate. The problem has been how to achieve these goals and still win presidential elections.

The Democratic Party has gone through two stages in reforming its delegate selection procedures. During the first, 1968–1980, it adopted a highly structured set of national rules aimed at achieving its two principal aims: greater participation and more equitable representation. It imposed these rules on the states. Since that time, the party has modified these rules to improve the chances of its nominees in the general election. Unlike the Democrats, the Republican Party has mandated very few national rules on its state parties. Republican state parties, however, have been affected by Democratic reforms, which have been implemented by the enactment of new election laws by the states.

Democratic Rules, 1968–1980

The catalyst for the rules changes was the tumultuous Democratic convention of 1968, a convention in which Senator Hubert Humphrey won the nomination without actively campaigning in the party's primaries. Yet the primaries of that year were very important. They had become the vehicle by which Democrats could protest the Johnson administration's conduct of the war in Vietnam. Senator Eugene McCarthy, the first of the antiwar candidates, had challenged Lyndon Johnson in the New Hampshire primary. To the surprise of many political observers, McCarthy received 42.4 percent of the vote, almost as much as the president, who got 49.5 percent.[1]

Four days after McCarthy's unexpectedly strong showing, Senator Robert Kennedy, brother of the late president and a political rival of Johnson, declared his candidacy for the nation's highest office. With protests against the war mounting across the country and divisions within the Democratic Party intensifying, Johnson bowed out, declaring that he did not want the nation's involvement in Southeast Asia to become a divisive political issue.

Johnson's withdrawal cleared the way for Hubert Humphrey, the vice president, to run. Humphrey, however, waited almost a month to announce his intentions. His late entrance into the Democratic nomination process intentionally precluded a primary campaign since filing deadlines had expired in most of the states. Like Johnson, Humphrey did not want to become the focal point of antiwar opposition, nor did he have a grassroots organization to match McCarthy's and Kennedy's. What he did have was the support of most national and state Democratic leaders, including the president.

The last big-state primary in 1968 was California's. In it, Kennedy scored a significant win, but during the celebration that followed, he was assassinated. His death left McCarthy as the principal antiestablishment, antiwar candidate, but he was far short of a convention majority. Despite the last-minute entrance of Senator George McGovern, who hoped to rally Kennedy delegates to his candidacy, Humphrey easily won the nomination.

To make matters worse for those who opposed Humphrey and the administration's war efforts, an amendment to the party platform calling for an unconditional end to the bombing of North Vietnam was defeated. McCarthy and Kennedy delegates felt victimized by the nomination process and the resulting Humphrey victory. They were angry. They demanded reform and eventually got it. A divided convention approved the establishment of a party committee to reexamine the rules for delegate selection.

Compounding the divisions within the convention were demonstrations outside of it. Thousands of youthful protesters, calling for an end to the war, congregated in the streets of Chicago. To maintain order, the police, under direction from Mayor Richard Daley, used strong-arm tactics to disperse the crowds. Clashes between police and protesters followed. Television news crews filmed these confrontations, and the networks showed them during their convention coverage. The spectacle of police beating demonstrators further inflamed emotions and led to calls for party reform, not only from those who attended the convention but also from those who watched it on television.

After the election, a commission, chaired initially by Senator George McGovern, was appointed to study procedures for electing and seating convention delegates and to propose ways of improving them. The commission recommended that delegate selection be a *fair reflection* of Democratic senti-ment within the state and implicitly, less closely tied to the wishes of state party leaders. Rules were approved by the party to make it easier for individuals to run as delegates, to limit the size of the districts from which they could be chosen, and to require that the number of delegates elected be proportional to the popular vote that they, or the candidates to whom they were pledged, received. A requirement that delegates be chosen no earlier than the calendar year of the election was also established.

Additionally, Democrats tried to prevent independents and, especially, partisans of other parties, from participating in the selection of Democratic delegates. The difficulty, however, was to determine who was a Democrat since some states did not require or even permit registration by party. When implementing this rule, the national party adopted a very liberal interpretation of Democratic affiliation. People that identify themselves as Democrats at the time of voting, or those requesting Democratic ballots, were considered to be Democrats for the purpose of participating in the primaries. This process of identification effectively permitted crossover voting, allowing Republicans or independents to cross over and vote in the Democratic primaries in some states. The only primaries that the Democratic rules effectively prohibited were *open primaries*, those in which voters are given the ballots of both major parties, discard one, and vote the other.

In addition to translating public preferences into delegate selection, another major objective of the reforms was to equalize representation on the delegations themselves. Three groups in particular—African Americans, women, and people under thirty—had protested their underrepresentation on party councils and at the conventions. Their representatives and others sym-pathetic to their plight pressed the party for more equitable representation. The reform commission reacted to these pressures by proposing a rule requiring that all states represent these particular groups in reasonable relationship to their presence in the state population. Failure to do so was viewed as *prima facie* evidence of discrimination. In point of fact, the party had established quotas. Considerable opposition developed to the application of this rule during the 1972 nomination process, and it was subsequently modified to require only that states implement affirmative action plans for those groups that had been subject to past discrimination.[2] The Democrats went one step further with respect to women. Beginning with its 1980 nominating convention, the party mandated that each state delegation be equally divided between men and women.

Still another goal of the reforms, to involve more Democrats in the selec-tion process, was achieved not only by the fair reflection rule but also by making primaries the preferred method of delegate selection. To avoid a challenge to the composition of their delegation, states switched to primaries in which delegates were elected directly by the people.[3]

Caucuses in which party regulars selected the delegates were still permit-ted, but they, too, were redesigned to encourage greater rank-and-file partici-pation. (See Box 4.1, "The Iowa Caucus: How It Works.") No longer could state party leaders vote a large number of proxies for the delegates of their

BOX 4.1 | THE IOWA CAUCUS: HOW IT WORKS

STAGES

Step 1: Caucuses are held in 2,142 precincts to choose more than 1,500 delegates to 99 county conventions.

Step 2: One month later, conventions are held in counties to choose the approximately 3,000 delegates to the 5 congressional district conventions.

Step 3: Conventions are held in congressional districts to elect district-level delegates to national party conventions. The same delegates also attend the state convention.

Step 4: State conventions elect at-large delegates to national party convention.

Democrats also select their state party and elected official delegates.

PROCEDURES FOR THE FIRST-ROUND PRECINCT CAUCUSES

Democrats: Only registered Democrats who live in the precinct and can vote may participate. Attendees are asked to join preference groups for candidates. A group must consist of at least 15 percent of those present to be viable. Nonviable groups are dissolved, and those who were members of them may join other viable groups. Much lobbying occurs at this stage of the meeting. Delegates are allocated to candidates strictly on the basis of each group's proportion to the caucus as a whole.

Republicans: Attendees, who must be eligible to vote but do not have to be registered as Republicans, cast a presidential preference vote by secret ballot, which is tabulated on a statewide basis. Delegates to the county conventions are then selected by whatever method the caucus chooses—either by direct election (winner-take-all) or proportionally on the basis of a straw vote.

choice. Caucuses had to be publicly announced with adequate time given for campaigning. Moreover, they had to be conducted in stages, and three-fourths of the delegates had to be chosen in districts no larger than those for members of Congress.

Other consequences, not nearly as beneficial to the goal of increased participation, were a lengthening of the process, escalation of its costs, candidate fatigue, public boredom, and increased internal division within the major parties. Since the contests at the beginning of the quest for the nomination received the most attention from the news media, candidates, and public, states began moving their primaries forward, "front-loading" the schedule and forcing candidates to start their campaigns in the years prior to the election, another trend that has continued and accelerated in recent elections.

Selecting convention delegates in primaries and caucuses made it more difficult for elected officials and party leaders automatically to attend the nominating conventions. As a consequence, their attendance declined. The absence of these leaders generated and extended cleavages between the nominees and their electoral coalitions on one hand and the party's organization and its leadership on the other. These cleavages created serious problems, which adversely affected the chances of the party's nominees in the general election, and in 1976, in governing the country. During the presidential campaign, the divisiveness impaired a unified organizational effort, tarnished the images of party candidates, and increased partisan defections. After the election, it made establishing an agenda and building a majority coalition more difficult.

In short, the early party reforms produced unintended consequences. These consequences—proliferation of primaries, lengthening of the process, divisiveness within the party, poor representation of elected leaders, reduction of the power of state party officials, and, most importantly, failure to win presidential elections and govern successfully—prompted the Democrats to reexamine and modify their rules for delegate selection beginning in the 1980s.

Reforming the Reforms: Democratic Rules, 1981–Present

The changes that have been made since 1980 fall into three categories: those that affect the time frame and procedures of the selection process, those that affect the representation of public officials and party leaders, and those that govern the behavior of delegates at the convention itself.

The objective of the original reforms, to encourage participation by rank-and-file party supporters and to reflect their sentiment in the allocation of delegates, was impeded by three problems: The first problem was that the states that held their primaries and caucuses early seemed to exercise disproportionate influence on the selection of the party's nominee. This situation created an incentive for other states to front-load the process, for candidates to expend most of their resources at the beginning of the campaign or as soon as they got them, and for participants to turn out more regularly at the beginning than at the end of the nomination process.

In 1996, almost two-thirds of all the convention delegates were selected within a forty-four-day period beginning mid-February and continuing through March 26, 1996. In 2000 and 2004, two-thirds of the delegates had been chosen by the end of the second Tuesday in March. And the schedule for 2008 is even more front-loaded with several large states moving their primaries to February 5, the first day on which the Democratic Party permits any state to hold its caucus or primary.

Not only is front-loading inequitable, increasing the influence of the states that hold their contests early and decreasing that of those which go later, but also it forces the candidates to campaign and raise money earlier and earlier. Retail politics, door-to-door campaigning, is being replaced by multistate media-oriented campaigns.

Front-loading advantages those candidates who begin with national recognition, are able to amass sizable war chests, gain organizational support within the party, and have telegenic skills for multi-media campaigning. It also has resulted in the determination of a nominee earlier in the year, which facilitates partisan unity. However, front-loading could also have the opposite effect in a field of strong candidates. If no one emerges with a large lead after most of the delegates have been selected, then there may not be enough delegates left to determine a winner before the nominating convention is held late in the summer. Such a situation would keep a party divided for several months, disadvantaging its nominee if the other party has already settled on a candidate.

Front-loading also disadvantages lesser-known candidates who need time to establish their credibility, raise money, and build an organization of professionals and volunteers, which they may be able to do if they are able to do better than expected in one of the early contests.

A second problem is the relatively small percentage of the vote, known as a *threshold,* which is needed for candidates to be awarded delegates. This small percentage has encouraged multiple candidacies, factionalizing the party and providing an incentive for those without national experience, reputation, and even party ties to run. By obtaining the votes of as little as 15 percent of those who participate in a primary or caucus, relatively unknown candidates can win delegates, gain public recognition, and use this recognition to build a constituency and become a national figure.

The third problem that the Democrats had to address was the various proportional-voting formulas that states used to allocate delegates. These formulas did not always reflect the popular vote in the state. And even when they did, the impact on the party was not always beneficial. For the national party, proportional voting theoretically extended the nomination process, adversely affecting the party and its nominees in the general election. For the state parties, proportional voting diffused power and reduced the collective influence of party officials. For the candidates, proportional voting sometimes discouraged them from investing resources in districts that were highly competitive and from which they could gain only minimal advantage and encouraged them to concentrate on less-competitive districts in which they enjoyed the most support. This concentration of resources tended to lower turnout, which may adversely affect turnout in the general election.

To modify the first of these problems, the party imposed a "window" during which primaries and caucuses could be held. Initially, the official period extended from the second Tuesday in March to the second Tuesday in June. Today, the calendar opens one month earlier on the first Tuesday in February, the 5th in 2008.

What to do with those states, such as Iowa and New Hampshire, whose laws require that they choose their delegates before others has been a perennial issue.[4] Believing that it could not conduct its own selection process in these states, the national party decided that the best it could do was establish the window and grant Iowa and New Hampshire exceptions to it. However, complaints within the party that these two states were unrepresentative of rank-and-file Democrats and that they skewed the selection process, benefiting two small states at the expense of the others, led the party to revisit the exceptions that it granted to Iowa and New Hampshire.

A Democratic Commission on Nomination Timing and Scheduling, meeting during 2005, proposed a modification of party rules that would give states incentives in the form of additional delegates if they scheduled their nomination contests later in the cycle.[5] The Commission also proposed adding one or two first-tier caucuses after Iowa and before New Hampshire and one or two new primaries after New Hampshire and before the window opened for the other states.

Unlike the Republican rules, which require approval of the previous nominating convention before they can go into effect, the Democrats simply need a majority vote of the Democratic National Committee, which approved the rule changes in August 2006 for the 2008 presidential nomination process.

Another change has involved modifications to the so-called fair reflection rule. One modification affected the minimum percentage of the vote necessary to be eligible for delegates; the other pertained to the methods by which the primary vote is allocated. After some experimenting with the minimum vote necessary to receive delegates, the Democrats settled on a 15 percent threshold.[6] The party also required that delegates be chosen strictly on the basis of the proportion of the vote they received in the primaries.

Still another was the addition of party leader and elected official delegates (PLEOs), known as *superdelegates*. Unhappy with the decreasing number of its party leaders and elected officials who attended the convention as delegates in the 1970s, the party wanted its leadership to participate in conventions. Their absence, particularly national elected officials, was thought to have contributed to the lack of support that the nominees received during the campaign and after the election. Jimmy Carter's difficulties in dealing with a Democratic Congress were cited as evidence of the need for closer cooperation between congressional party leaders and their presidential standard-bearer.

To facilitate closer ties, the Democrats established a new category of *add-on* delegates to be composed of PLEOs. One group of these add-on delegates, chosen from designated party leaders (including all members of its national committee) and from those who held high elected positions in government (including all Democratic governors and members of Congress plus a number of other national, state, and local officials), was to be unpledged. It was thought that this group of distinguished Democrats might be in a position to hold the balance of power if the primaries did not produce a winner, a situation that has not occurred since the rules were changed.

Additionally, the party also provided for the selection of pledged add-on delegates equal to 15 percent of the state's base delegation. Although these superdelegates have not been in a position to broker a divided convention, they have had an impact on the delegate selection process, reinforcing the front-runner's advantage. Naturally this advantage has incurred criticism from nonfront-runners who desire the selection process to be open and not dominated by national legislators and party officials.[7] Approximately 15 to 18 percent of the delegates in 2008 are expected to be superdelegates.

Finally, the Democrats have reversed a rule adopted in 1980 that delegates who are publicly committed must vote for the candidate to whom they are pledged. Democratic delegates today can vote their consciences, although when they are initially selected as pledged delegates, they must sign an advanced pledge of presidential preference to ensure that they are supporters of the candidates who have slated them to run as their delegates. Under the circumstances, it is unlikely that many delegates will change their minds at the convention, unless the candidate to whom they are pledged encourages them to do so.

REPUBLICAN RULES

The Republicans have not changed their rules after each recent national convention as the Democrats have. Nor can they do so. It is the Republican convention itself that approves the rules for choosing delegates for the next Republican convention. Under normal circumstances, these rules cannot be altered by the Republican National Committee or by special commissions the party creates.

Republicans, however, have been affected by the Democratic rules changes in several ways. Since state legislatures enact laws governing party nominations, and since the Democrats controlled many of these legislatures in the 1970s and 1980s when primary laws were changed to conform to the new Democratic rules, some of the reforms were literally forced on the Republicans by the states. Moreover, the Republicans have also made changes of their own to eliminate discrimination and prevent a small group from controlling the nomination process.

Unlike the Democrats, the Republicans have not mandated national guidelines for their state parties. Although they do not have a window period during which all primaries and caucuses must be held, their nominations process is as heavily front-loaded as the Democrats'. Prior to the 2000 nomination, the GOP tried to encourage states to hold their nomination contests later in the cycle by offering them additional convention delegates if they did so. There were few takers, however, prompting the national committee to appoint an advisory commission to study the process and recommend changes.

Chaired by former senator and party chairman Bill Brock, the Commission recommended the implementation of a population-based nominating system in which states would be placed in one of four groups, based on their population size rather than geographic location, and then would conduct their primary election or the first stage of their caucus selection on the same day. The group containing the least-populated states would go first, and the one with the most populated states would go last with the dates on which the four groups would hold their contests spaced approximately one month apart.

Opposition to the plan quickly developed from the large states fearful that the nominee would be effectively determined before they had a chance to vote. Concerns were also expressed about the added costs to the candidates if they had to compete for four months, much less the wear and tear they would encounter. Not wanting the issue to divide the 2000 convention and interfere with his launch for the presidency, George W. Bush opposed the recommendation. The Republican Rules Committee, controlled by Bush delegates, decided not to propose the change to the convention.

Whereas the Democrats prescribe a minimum threshold to receive delegate support, the Republicans do not. Their threshold varies from state to state. Whereas the Democrats impose proportional voting, the Republicans do not. They permit winner-take-all voting within districts or within the state at large. Such a voting system greatly advantages front-runners, who can win the large states. In 1988, George H. W. Bush won 59 percent of the popular vote in states holding some type of winner-take-all voting on Super Tuesday but won 97 percent of the delegates from those states, giving him an almost insurmountable lead over his principal opponent that year, Robert Dole. In 1996, Dole, the Republican front-runner, was similarly advantaged and built a huge delegate lead in the winner-take-all states. As part of its recommendations to improve the delegate selection process, the party's advisory commission on nomination reform proposed that all delegates be allotted to candidates on a proportional basis, but the Rules Committee of the 2000 convention did not support this change either.

Finally, the Republicans do not have special categories of delegates for party leaders and elected officials, although their state and national leaders have traditionally attended Republican conventions in greater proportion than their Democratic counterparts. Nor do the Republicans require that 50 percent of each state delegation be women. Since the 1980s, the proportion of women at Republican conventions has ranged from 29 percent to 44 percent.

A summary of delegate selection rules for the 2004 nomination appears in Table 4.1.

THE LEGALITY OF PARTY RULES

As previously mentioned, party reforms, to be effective, must be enacted into law. Most states have complied with the new rules. A few have not, sometimes resulting in confrontation between these states and the national party. When New Hampshire and Iowa refused to move the dates of their respective primary and caucuses into the Democrats' window period in 1984, the national party backed down. But previously, when Illinois chose its 1972 delegates in a manner that conflicted with new Democratic rules, the party sought to impose its rules on the state.

In addition to the political controversy that was engendered, the conflict between the Democratic National Committee and Illinois also presented an important legal question: Which body—the national party or the state—has the higher authority on delegate selection? In its landmark decision, *Cousins v. Wigoda*, 419 U.S. 477 (1975), the Supreme Court sided with the national party. The Court stated that political parties were private organizations with rights of

TABLE 4.1 | DELEGATE SELECTION RULES

	Democrats	Republicans
Rank-and-file participation	Open to all voters who want to participate as Democrats.	No national rule.*
Apportionment of delegates within states	75 percent of base delegation elected at congressional district level or lower; 25 percent elected at large on a proportional basis.	No national rule; may be chosen at large.
Party leaders and elected officials	Current members and former chairs of the national committee, all Democratic members of Congress, former House Speakers and minority leaders and Senate party leaders, current and past presidents, vice presidents, and all Democratic governors.	None.
Composition of delegations	Equal gender division; no discrimination; affirmative action plan required with goals and timetables for specified groups (African Americans, Native Americans, and Asian/Pacific Americans).	No gender rule but each state is asked to try to achieve equal gender representation; "Positive action" to achieve broadest possible participation required.
Time frame	First Tuesday in February to second Tuesday in June. Exceptions: Iowa, New Hampshire, and in 2008, Nevada and South Carolina.	No national rule.
Allocation of delegates	By proportional vote. Only in primaries or caucuses.	May be selected in primaries, caucuses, or by state committee on basis of a proportional vote or by direct election within congressional districts or on an at-large basis.
Threshold	15 percent.	No national rule.
Delegation voting	May vote their conscience.	No national rule.
Enforcement	Automatic reduction in state delegation size for violation of time frames, allocation, or threshold rules.	Each state party to enforce its own rules; certain types of disputes may be appealed to the national party.

*Republican national rules prescribe that selection procedures accord with the laws of the state.

association protected by the Constitution. Moreover, choosing presidential candidates was a national experience that states could not abridge unless there were compelling constitutional reasons to do so. Although states could establish their own primary laws, the party could determine the criteria for representation at its national convention.

Crossover voting in open primaries prompted still another court test between the rights of parties to prescribe rules for delegate selection and the rights of states to establish their own election law. Democratic rules prohibit open primaries. Four states had conducted this type of election in 1976. Three voluntarily changed their law; a fourth, Wisconsin, did not. It permitted voters, who participated in the primary, to request the ballot of either party. The national party's Compliance Review Commission ordered the state party to design an alternative process. It refused. The case went to court. Citing the precedent of *Cousins v. Wigoda*, the Supreme Court held in the case of *Democratic Party of the U.S. v. Wisconsin ex. rel. La Follette*, 450 U.S. 107 (1981) that a state had no right to interfere with the party's delegate selection process unless it demonstrated a compelling reason to do so. It ruled that Wisconsin had not demonstrated such a reason; hence, the Democratic Party could refuse to seat delegates who were selected in a manner that violated its rules.[8]

In the case of *California Democratic Party v. Jones*, 530 U.S. 567 (2000), the Supreme Court reiterated its judgment by invalidating California's "blanket" primary system, which voters had approved in a 1996 ballot initiative. The new procedure required that state officials provide a uniform ballot in which voters, regardless of their partisan affiliation, could vote for any candidate of any party for any elected position. Naturally, the parties were upset by the possibility that their nominees could be determined by people who did not consider themselves partisans of that party. Four California state parties, including the Democrats and Republicans, went to court to challenge the constitutionality of the initiative, claiming that it violated their First Amendment right to freedom of association. The Supreme Court agreed. Its majority opinion held that the blanket primary system represented "a clear and present danger" to the parties and was therefore unconstitutional.

Although these Court decisions have given the political parties the legal authority to design and enforce their own rules, the practicality of doing so is another matter. Other than going to court if a state refuses to change its election law, a party, particularly a national party, has only two viable options: require the state party to conduct its own delegate selection process in conformity to national rules and penalize it if it does not do so, or grant the state party an exemption so that it can abide by the law of the state. In 1984, the Wisconsin Democratic Party was forced by the national Democratic Party to adopt a caucus mode of selection since the Republican-controlled legislature refused to change the state's open primary system.

The rule for allocating a specific number of delegates to the states has also generated legal controversy, but in this case, within the Republican Party. The formula that the Republicans use contains a bonus for states that voted Republican in the previous presidential election.[9] Opponents of this rule contend that it discriminates against the large states because bonuses are allocated regardless of size. Moreover, they argue that the large states are apt to be more competitive and thus less likely to receive a bonus. Particularly hard hit are states in the Northeast and on the Pacific Coast which have gone Democratic in recent elections. The Ripon Society, a moderate Republican organization, has twice challenged the constitutionality of this apportionment rule, but it has not been successful.

The Democratic apportionment formula, which results in larger conventions than the Republicans, has also been subject to some controversy, but not in recent years.[10]

THE IMPACT OF THE RULES CHANGES

The reforms to the nomination process have produced some of their desired effects. They have opened up the process by allowing more people to participate. They have increased minority representation at the conventions. But they have also reduced the influence of state and national party leaders over the selection of delegates, ultimately weakened the power of party leaders in the presidential electoral process, and have exacerbated divisions within the parties.

TURNOUT

One objective of the reforms was to involve more of the party's rank and file in the delegate selection process. This goal has been partially achieved. In 1968, before the reforms, only 12 million people participated in primaries, approximately 11 percent of the voting-age population (VAP). In 1972, the first nomination contest held after the changes were made, that number rose to 22 million. In 1988, it peaked. With two contested nominations, turnout increased to 35.1 million, approximately 21 percent of the VAP. It remained relatively high in 1992, dipped in 1996, rose in 2000, and dipped again in 2004. Approximately 16.3 million people voted in the 2004 Democratic primaries, less than 10 percent of the eligible voters.[11]

The level of participation also varies. It has always been greater in primaries than caucuses. In Iowa, which traditionally holds the first caucus, only about 4 percent of the VAP participate, despite extensive media coverage.

Turnout tends to be greater in states that hold their contests earlier (11.4 percent voted in the primaries through Super Tuesday, 2004) than in those that hold them later in the process and greater in those in which there is more competition than in states in which there is less. New Hampshire generally has a high turnout; in 2004, 23.5 percent of the state's eligible population voted in the Democratic primary.[12]

Not only does turnout vary among states, it also varies among population groups within them. The better-educated, higher-income, older members of society vote more often than do younger, less-educated, and poorer people. In general, the lower the turnout, the greater the demographic differences between voters and nonvoters. Although this pattern of participation has persisted in recent elections, the success of the Jackson campaigns in 1984 and 1988 in attracting minority voters and, to a much lesser extent, the campaign of Pat Robertson in 1988, which appealed to white, evangelical Protestants, muted some of the differences that had existed between primary voters and their party's electorate in these elections.

There have also been claims that primary voters tend to be more ideologically extreme in their political beliefs than the average party voter, with Democrats being more liberal and Republicans more conservative than their party as a whole. Strong empirical evidence has not been found to support this contention although studies have shown southern Democrats who participate in their party's primary tend to be more moderate than the southern electorate as a whole.[13] For most of the country, primary voters do not appear to be more ideologically extreme than people who vote in the general election, but convention delegates who represent them do.[14]

Finally, higher turnout in the nomination process benefits the parties because it encourages more partisans to participate. It also informs and energizes the party's electorate, thereby priming it for the general election. The long gap between the primaries and the general election, however, reduces that priming effect.

REPRESENTATION

A principal goal of the reforms was to make the national nominating convention become more representative of people who identified themselves as partisans. Before 1972, the delegates were predominantly white, male, and well educated. Mostly professionals whose income and social status placed them considerably above the national mean, they were expected to pay their own way to the convention. Large financial contributors, as well as elected officeholders and party officials, were frequently in attendance.

In 1972, the demographic profile of convention delegates began to change. The proportion of women rose substantially. Youth and minority participation, especially in Democratic conventions, also increased. Since 1976, when the Democrats changed from a quota system to an affirmative action commitment, the representation of minorities has remained fairly constant. The percentage of women has increased, largely as a consequence of the Democratic requirement that half its delegates be women. But attendance by those under age thirty, a group that has been removed from the specified minorities list, has not kept pace.

Despite the changes in composition, the income and educational levels of the delegates have remained well above the national average. Most of the delegates have much more formal education than do their party's rank and file.

It is more difficult to determine the extent to which ideological and issue perceptions of recent delegates have differed from those of their predecessors and from the electorate as a whole. In general, convention delegates tend to be more conscious of issues than their party's rank and file. Their issue stands confirm the partisan-ideological cleavage. Republican and Democratic delegates consistently take more conservative and liberal positions respectively, on a range of policy matters. If these positions were plotted on an ideological continuum, they would appear to be more consistent (or ideologically pure) than the partisan electorate they represent and much more consistent (or pure) than the general public.

The delegate selection process seems to have contributed to the purity of these ideological beliefs. Party activists tend to have the strongest ideological beliefs, which in turn, motivate their involvement in party politics. To the extent that this involvement has resulted in the election of more issue purists and fewer partisan pragmatists, compromise in government has become more difficult.

In summary, despite the reforms, there continue to be differences between the ideological and demographic characteristics of convention delegates and those of their partisan brethren and of the electorate as a whole. Convention delegates reflect some demographic characteristics of their party's rank and file more accurately than in the past, but they are not necessarily more ideologically in tune. In fact, delegates have tended to widen the differences between the beliefs and attitudes of Republicans and Democrats. Whether this trend makes contemporary conventions more or less representative is difficult to say. One thing is clear: obtaining equitable representation, rewarding partisan activism, maintaining an open nomination process, unifying the party, and winning elections are difficult goals to achieve, particularly during the same election cycle.

PARTY ORGANIZATION AND LEADERSHIP

Although increasing turnout and improving representation have been two desired effects of the reforms, weakening the state party organizations and their leadership has not. Yet this development seems to have been a consequence of the reforms as well. By promoting internal democracy, the primaries initially created divisions within party organizations that already had been weakened by new modes of campaigning, the loss of patronage opportunities, and the growth of social services by state and local governments. Moreover, the rules changes have encouraged the proliferation of candidates, which in turn has led to the creation of separate electoral organizations that can rival the regular party organization and weaken its organizational capacity to affect the presidential electoral process.

Party leaders can still use their influence with the state legislature to help determine the date on which the nomination contest will be held and the rules that govern it, and they can use their organization to support a particular candidate, but they can no longer dictate the composition of their state delegation to the national nominating convention. Why then did party leaders go along with the national party reforms to create a more open and accessible system process by which convention delegates would be selected in their state? To some extent, they did so to avoid the delegation's being challenged by the national party. However, their support of reforms varied, largely on the basis of whether their views converged or diverged with the dominant views of those people within their state most likely to participate in the selection process.[15]

The nominees are affected as well. Political scientists have argued that the more divisive the nomination process, the more likely that it will adversely affect the successful nominee's chances in the general election.[16] Other factors, such as the quality of the candidates and the particular environment in which the election occurs, also impact the final general election results.[17]

A divisive nomination process is usually perceived as a liability from the standpoint of the party and the winning candidate. Undergoing rigorous and critical examination by candidates for the party's nomination can damage a nominee's image at the beginning of the general election campaign. Candidates who avoid a challenge for the nomination do not have to contend with this problem. However, it often is the potential vulnerability of a candidate that encourages others to seek the nomination in the first place. Challenges and perceived vulnerability go hand-in-hand.

WINNERS AND LOSERS

Rules changes are never neutral. They usually benefit one group at the expense of another. Similarly, they tend to help certain candidates and hurt others. That is why candidates have tried to influence the rules and why the rules themselves have been changed so frequently. Candidate organizations and interest groups have put continuous pressure on state and national parties to amend the calendar and rules to increase their own clout in the selection process.

Clearly, the prohibition of discrimination, the requirement for affirmative action, and the rule requiring an equal number of men and women in state delegations have improved representation for women and minorities, and coincidentally, reduced the proportion of white male delegates. For candidates seeking their party's nomination, this change has necessitated that slates of delegates supporting a candidate be demographically balanced to ensure that a multitude of groups are included.

The openness of the process and the greater participation by the party's rank and file have encouraged those who have not been party regulars to become involved and have created opportunities for outsiders to seek their party's nomination. Businessman Steve Forbes (1996 and 2000), ministers Jesse Jackson (1984) and Pat Robertson (1988), columnist Pat Buchanan (1992, 1996, and 2000), and former Senator Paul Tsongas (1992), and to some extent even governors Michael Dukakis (1988) and Bill Clinton (1992), former Senator Bill Bradley and Senator John McCain (both in 2000), and Barack Obama (2008) have literally come out of political nowhere to run for their party's nomination. Senator John Kerry also was not well known beyond his home state of Massachusetts when he began his presidential quest in 2003.

On the other hand, the more the process concentrates the number and location of primaries at the beginning of the delegate selection process, the more those who have access to the largest amounts of money and the most political endorsements, particularly from governors who control their state party organizations, are likely to benefit.

All of this has affected the candidates' quests for the nomination and their ability to govern if elected. It has made campaigning more arduous and governing more difficult. It has created incentives for candidates to promise more than they can deliver. Thus, the quest for the nomination and what it takes to win may ultimately weaken a newly elected president by hyping performance expectations and then generating discontent when these expectations cannot be realized. We turn to these issues in the next chapter where we discuss the strategies and tactics of the nomination campaign.

SUMMARY

The delegate selection process has changed dramatically over the past forty years. Originally dominated by state party leaders, it has become more open to the party's rank and file as a consequence of the reforms initiated by the Democratic Party. These reforms, designed to broaden the base of public participation and increase the representation of the party's electorate at its nominating convention, have affected the Republicans as well, even though the GOP has not chosen to mandate national guidelines for its state parties, as the Democrats have. Supreme Court decisions that give the national parties the authority to dictate rules, new state laws that conform to these party rules, and public pressure to reflect popular sentiment and improve representation have led to a greater number of primaries and more delegates selected in them for both major parties.

Public participation has increased somewhat, although turnout levels have varied from one nomination process to another. The date of the contest, the level of intraparty competition, the amount of money spent, and other candidate-related factors help explain these variations. But the bottom line is that many less people follow the nomination contests closely and vote in them compared to the general election. In short, the democratization of the nomination process has had limited impact on the American electorate.

It has, however, shifted power within the parties from state party officials to rank-and-file activists. It has also resulted in better demographic representation of partisans at their party's national nominating conventions. Whether it has also provided better attitudinal representation is less clear, although as we have noted in the previous chapter, the major parties today are more internally cohesive and externally distinctive than they had been prior to 1980.

WHERE ON THE WEB?

- **Democratic National Committee**
www.democrats.org
   Information on Democratic Party history, rules, convention, and campaigns with links to Democratic youth and state party affiliates.

- **Green Party**
www.gp.org
   Information on Green Party candidates, the party's platform, press releases, and state party affiliates.

- **Republican National Committee**
www.rnc.org
   Information on Republican Party history, rules, convention, and campaigns with links to Republican youth and state party affiliates.

- **Wikipedia**
http://en.wikipedia.org/wiki/United_States_presidential_primary
   An online encyclopedia.

EXERCISES

1. Party officials in New Hampshire strongly objected to the changes in the Democratic caucus and primary schedule for 2008. What was the nature of their arguments? (You can find this information on the DNC Web site [www.democrats.org] by searching for the Commission on Presidential Nomination Timing and Scheduling.) How would you evaluate New Hampshire's arguments from the perspectives of that state, the candidates, and the national Democratic Party?
2. Write a brief essay on the history of the Democratic and Republican Parties from information they provide on their Web sites.
3. Have the Democratic and Republican Party reforms in the nomination improved or hurt the democratic character of the parties and of presidential elections? What changes would you suggest to make the nomination process even more democratic?

SELECTED READINGS

Atkeson, Lonna Rae. "Divisive Primaries and General Election Outcomes: Another Look at Presidential Campaigns." *American Journal of Political Science*, 42 (1998): 257–261.

Bartels, Larry M. *Presidential Primaries and the Dynamics of Public Choice*. Princeton, N.J.: Princeton University Press, 1988.

Cook, Rhodes. *The Presidential Nomination Process: A Place for Us?* Lanham, M.D.: Rowman and Littlefield, 2004.

Day, Christine L., Charles D. Hadley, and Harold W. Stanley, "The Inevitable Unanticipated Consequences of Political Reform: The 2004 Presidential Nomination Process," in *A Defining Moment*, edited by William Crotty. Armonk, N.Y.: M.E. Sharpe, 2005: 74–86.

Geer, John G. *Nominating Presidents: An Evaluation of Voters and Primaries*. New York: Greenwood, 1989.

Mayer, William G., and Andrew E. Busch. *The Front-Loading Problem in Presidential Nominations*. Washington, D.C.: Brookings, 2004.

Norrander, Barbara. "Ideological Representativeness of Presidential Primary Voters." *American Journal of Political Science*, 33 (Aug. 1989): 570–587.

——. "The End Game in Post-Reform Presidential Nominations." *Journal of Politics*, 62 (Nov. 2000): 999–1013.

Polsby, Nelson W. *The Consequences of Party Reform*. New York: Oxford University Press, 1983.

Shafer, Byron E. *Quiet Revolution: The Struggle for the Democratic Party and the Shaping of Post-Reform Politics*. New York: Russell Sage Foundation, 1983.

NOTES

1. McCarthy's name was on the ballot, but the president's name was not. The regular Democratic organization in New Hampshire had to conduct a campaign to have Democrats write in Johnson's name.

2. The groups that were initially singled out were Native Americans, African Americans, and youth. Subsequently, the list of affected groups has been altered by the addition of Hispanics, Asian/Pacific Americans, and women, and by the deletion of youth. In 1992, the party also added those with physical disabilities to the groups protected against discrimination.

3. Some states still hold a presidential preference vote with a separate election of delegates by a convention. Others connect the presidential vote and delegate selection on an at-large or district basis. By voting for a particular candidate or delegates pledged to that candidate (or both), voters may register their presidential choice and delegate selection at the same time and by the same vote. The number of these primaries has increased as a consequence of the rules changes.

4. Iowa and New Hampshire both have laws that require their contests to be the first caucus and primary, respectively. They obviously gain advantages by doing so. The candidates come and visit with voters often. The news media also arrive in force to cover the beginnings of the next campaign. There is an economic gain as well. New Hampshire estimates that it took in $264 million from its 2000 primaries. "First in the Nation: The New Hampshire Primary; What It Means to the State and the Nation," published by the State of New Hampshire, 2000, p. 4.

5. The Democratic Party commission recommended that the calendar be divided into four stages. The states that held their nomination contests during the first stage, the two-week period beginning with the first Tuesday in March, would receive additional delegates equal to 15 percent of their total number of pledged delegates; if they held their election during stage two, the three-week period beginning the third Tuesday in March, they would receive an additional 20 percent; if their selection date was in the third stage, the three-week period that begins the second Tuesday in April, they would be allocated an additional 30 percent; if they held it after that and before the end of the Democratic nomination process, the second Tuesday in June, they would be entitled to an additional 40 percent.

6. In 1984, the Democrats had raised the minimum vote needed to obtain delegates to 20 percent in caucuses and up to 25 percent in primaries. This change was designed

to help nationally known candidates, such as Walter Mondale who was running that year for the Democratic nomination, and reduce the factionalizing effect that a large number of candidates could have on the party. After losing in 1980, the Democrats hoped the change would enable the eventual winner to emerge earlier, be a candidate of national prominence, and be better positioned to challenge the Republicans in the general election. Naturally, these changes hurt minority candidates such as Jesse Jackson, whose supporters were concentrated in districts with large minority populations. Although Jackson received votes in districts that had a white majority, he was unable to achieve the minimum required percentage in many of them. Thus, his 19 percent of the popular vote in 1984 translated into only 10 percent of the delegates. Owing to pressure from Jackson and others, the Democrats lowered the minimum threshold in 1988 to 15 percent and have kept it there since then.

7. A proposal by Jesse Jackson to decrease the number of PLEOs by eliminating the automatic inclusion of members of the party's national committee, however, was rejected by the very people who were to be excluded, the Democratic National Committee in 1990.

8. In another decision by the Supreme Court, also involving open primaries, the power of parties (in this case, state parties) to establish rules for nominating candidates was affirmed. In December 1986, the Supreme Court, in the case of *Tashjian v. Republican Party of Connecticut,* 479 U.S. 208 (1986), voided a Connecticut law that prohibited open primaries. Republicans, in the minority at the time in Connecticut, had favored such a primary as a means of attracting independent voters. Unable to get the Democratic-controlled legislature to change the law, the state Republican Party went to court, arguing that the statute violated its First Amendment rights of freedom of association. In a 5 to 4 ruling, the Supreme Court agreed, and struck down the legislation.

9. The formula Republicans use to determine the size of each state delegation is complex. It consists of three criteria: statehood (six delegates), House districts (three per district), and support for Republican candidates elected within the previous four years (one for a Republican governor, one for each Republican senator, one if the Republicans won at least half of the congressional districts in one of the past two congressional elections, and a bonus of four and one-half delegates plus 60 percent of the electoral vote if the state voted for the Republican presidential candidate in the previous election).

10. Under the plan used since 1968 and modified in 1976, the Democrats have allotted 50 percent of each state delegation on the basis of the state's electoral vote and 50 percent on the basis of its average Democratic vote in the past three presidential elections. The rule for apportionment was challenged in 1971 on the grounds that it did not conform to the "one person, one vote" principle, but a court of appeals asserted that it did not violate the equal protection clause of the Fourteenth Amendment.

11. Rhodes Cook, "2004 Democratic Primary, Caucus Analysis." www.rhodescook.com (accessed July 16, 2006).

12. Curtis Gans, "2004 Primary Turnout Low." www.american.edu/ccps/files/Files/csae030904.pdf; Linda L. Fowler, Constantine J. Spiliotes, and Lynn VaVreck, "The Role of Issue Advocacy Groups in the New Hampshire Primary," in

David B. Magleby, ed., *Getting Inside the Outside Campaign* (Provo, Utah: Brigham Young University, 2000), p. 31.

13. Earl Black and Merle Black, *The Vital South: How Presidents Are Elected* (Cambridge, M.A.: Harvard University Press, 1992), p. 268.

14. Barbara Norrander, "Ideological Representativeness of Presidential Primary Voters," *American Journal of Political Science*, 33 (Aug. 1989): pp. 570–587.

15. Scott R. Meinke, Jeffrey K. Staton, and Steven T. Wuhs, "State Delegate Selection Rules for Presidential Nominations, 1972–2000," *Journal of Politics*, 68 (Feb. 2006): pp. 180–193.

16. James I. Lengle, "Divisive Presidential Primaries and the Party Electoral Prospects, 1932–1976," *American Politics Quarterly*, 8 (1980): pp. 261–277; James I. Lengle, Diana Owen, and Molly Sonner, "Divisive Nomination Campaigns and Democratic Party Electoral Prospects," *Journal of Politics*, 57 (1995): pp. 370–383.

17. Lonna Rae Atkeson, "Divisive Primaries and General Election Outcomes: Another Look at Presidential Campaigns," *American Journal of Political Science*, 42 (Jan. 1998): pp. 256–271.

Campaigning for the Nomination

CHAPTER 5

INTRODUCTION

Rules changes, finance laws, and press coverage have affected the strategies and tactics of the candidates. Today, entering primaries is essential for everyone, even an incumbent president. No longer can a front-runner safely sit on the sidelines and wait for the call. The winds of a draft may be hard to resist but, more often than not, it is the candidate who is manning the bellows.

In the past, candidates carefully chose the primaries they entered and concentrated their efforts where they thought they would run best. Today, they have much less discretion, particularly at the beginning of the process, when press coverage is essential. Before 1972, it was considered wise to wait for an opportune moment in the spring of the presidential election year before announcing one's candidacy. Today, planning for a nomination run starts years in advance. Candidates usually establish exploratory committees following the midterm election. These committees help potential candidates test the water. The money they raise during the preelection stage of the nomination process helps them pay for travel, staff, and other expenses. Developing a donor list, gaining organizational support, and obtaining visibility in the news media and standing in the polls is particularly important during this early period.

BASIC STRATEGIC GUIDELINES

Every nomination campaign has to make a number of strategic decisions: when to begin the quest for the nomination and what type of organization to create; how to raise the necessary funds and to whom to turn to do so; how and where to spend resources; on what issues to focus, to which groups to target specific appeals, and how to project a presidential image when doing so; how to obtain sufficient and favorable news coverage and when to supplement that coverage with paid advertising; how to criticize one's opponents yet be in a position to gain their support after winning the nomination; and finally, how to position the campaign after becoming the preordained nominee in the period before the national nominating conventions.

Plan Far Ahead

Creating an organization, devising a strategy, and raising the amount of money necessary to conduct a national campaign all takes time. These needs have prompted potential aspirants for their party's nomination to set up exploratory committees, leadership PACs, and other precampaign organizations; hire personnel; contract with political consultants; raise money; and visit Iowa and New Hampshire more than two years before the caucuses and primaries will be held.

Some candidates have announced their intentions of running years in advance. George McGovern did so in January 1971; similarly, long-shot Jimmy Carter began his quest in 1974, almost two years before the 1976 Democratic convention. By the end of 2006, eleven Democratic and Republican candidates had either officially declared their candidacy or set up exploratory committees to evaluate their chances for their party's 2008 nomination; by the end of January 2007, that number had increased to nineteen (nine Democrats and ten Republicans) with others, not yet in the race, still considering running.

The first Democrat to do so was former Alaska Senator, Mike Gravel, who said on April 17, 2006 that he would use the campaign as a forum to advocate national ballot initiatives and a national sales tax to replace the federal income tax. Gravel's press conference, however, attracted few reporters, none of whom responded when he twice asked for questions. Finally a representative of the Associated Press asked him about his initiative plan.[1]

Even incumbent presidents plan for their renomination well in advance of the election year. President Clinton did so in the winter of 1994, following his party's defeat in the midterm elections. However, the president never formally announced his candidacy in order to convey the impression that his actions and decisions during this period were motivated solely by the demands of the presidency, not by his desire to remain in office for another term. President George W. Bush, anxious to avoid his father's belated and unsuccessful quest for reelection, began planning his campaign from almost the moment he was declared the winner of the 2000 election. In his first three years in office, Bush took 40 percent of his domestic trips from the White House to states he won or lost by 6 percent of the vote or less.[2]

CONCENTRATE EFFORTS IN THE EARLY CONTESTS

Doing well in the initial caucuses and primaries, raising money, gaining visibility, and organizing the campaign and staffing it with political professionals are the principal aims of most candidates today. The early contests are particularly important for lesser-known aspirants, less for the number of delegates they can win than for the amount of publicity they can get, the number of people they can meet, and the momentum they can generate.

Personal contact is very important in this period because it informs and motivates potential supporters and may produce contributors and volunteers down the road. The small states provide these "living-room" opportunities that are lost in multistate media campaigns.

Iowa

By tradition, the first official selection of delegates occurs in Iowa. Jimmy Carter in 1976, George H. W. Bush in 1980, Gary Hart in 1984, and John Kerry in 2004 got great boosts from their unexpectedly good showings in this state. Conversely, Ronald Reagan in 1980, John Glenn in 1984, George H. W. Bush in 1988, Robert Dole in 1996, and Howard Dean in 2004 were hurt by their disappointing performances. In 2000, Iowa simply confirmed the front-runners' status that George W. Bush and Al Gore enjoyed over their rivals.

Winning or coming in a strong second in Iowa can enhance the fortunes of a lesser-known candidate. A good example was Gary Hart's performance in 1984. He received only 16.5 percent of the Democratic vote, compared with front-runner Walter Mondale's 48.9 percent. But Mondale's victory was expected; Hart's second-place finish was not. As a consequence, Hart shared the media spotlight with Mondale but profited from more laudatory coverage.

John Edwards' second-place finish in 2004 with 32 percent compared to 38 percent for the winner, John Kerry, did not produce as much of a media bounce for him in large part because of Howard Dean's poor showing and his antics on election night. Trying to encourage his disappointed workers and supporters, Dean gave a passionate speech ending with a yell that looked to television viewers as if he had lost control of himself. Kerry's victory and Dean's scream, which was replayed over and over on the news during the week following the caucus, dominated the headlines and led the news, much to the dismay of the Edwards' campaign. In the words of his campaign manager, Nick Baldick, "... the story out of Iowa, instead of being Kerry-Edwards, was Dean's scream. We came within a couple of thousand votes of winning Iowa and got buried in the ninth paragraph."[3]

The Iowa caucus has been more important for lesser-known candidates than those with national reputations. The victories of Carter (1976), Bush (1980), and Hart (1984) gave these candidates opportunities to establish their credentials, opportunities that they might not have had in a big state primary. Although a defeat or poor showing by a front-runner such as happened to Reagan, Bush, and Dole in 1980, 1988, and 1996, respectively, slows their

"WILL SOMEBODY PLEASE SEND ME BACK TO SQUARE ONE?"

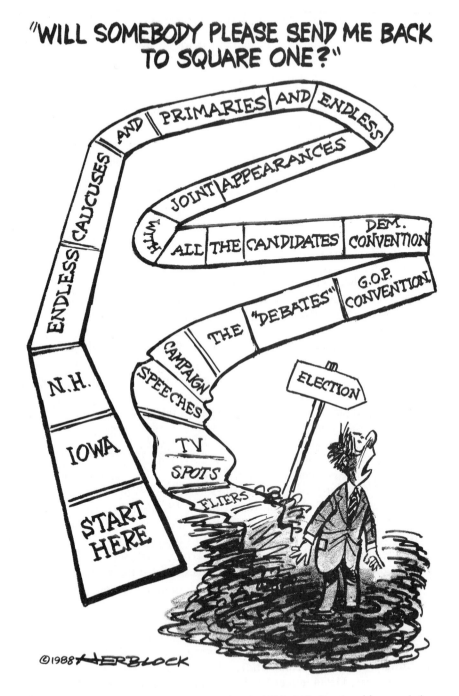

Source: Herblock, *Washington Post*, November 1, 1988, A18. Reprinted by permission.

momentum it does not necessarily terminate their candidacy. Front-runners have other opportunities made possible by their larger war chests, greater organizational support, and more political capital.

For lesser-known candidates, it is a different story. A loss or poor showing in Iowa may be the beginning of the end as it was for Richard Gephardt in 2004. Although Gephardt had been in politics for many years, run for president previously, served as the Democratic leader in the House of Representatives, and enjoyed the support of organized labor, his campaign created little enthusiasm, money, and national attention. Coming from neighboring Missouri, he saw Iowa as his principal opportunity to establish viability as a presidential candidate. He put all of his resources into that state and declared it make-or-break for him. His fourth place finish with only 11 percent of the vote doomed his candidacy. He dropped out of the race the next day.

The importance of the Iowa caucus has diminished in recent presidential campaigns because of the front-loading of the nomination process. With the New Hampshire primary scheduled nine to ten days later and an increasing number of primaries following it, there is simply not enough time to parlay success in Iowa into generating the resources for a major campaign effort as Carter did in 1976 and Hart tried to do in 1984.

Even though the Iowa caucus is no longer a stepping stone to the nomination, and no Democratic candidate who has won Iowa ever won the presidency,[4] candidates continue to spend a disproportion amount of time and money in that state because it is the first official contest; it generates a lot of media coverage; and aspirants are afraid that their campaign will be downgraded in the eyes of the public, contributors, and the news media if they skip it.

Iowa "winners" also face another problem. Expectations of their future performance increase, and media coverage tends to become more critical. Professor Craig Allen Smith describes the Iowa caucus as a "Venus fly-trap for presidential candidates," a description he embellishes in the following manner:

> Dramatic logic lures them to the sticky leaves of the precinct caucuses where, prodded by journalists and Iowans, they pour more and more of their time, money, people, and strategic options into the gaping mouth of the plant until, at the very moment of victory, it snaps shut on their ability to win subsequent contests. Iowa provides no significant delegates, its New Hampshire momentum is soon reversed, its Super Tuesday momentum is transient, and the resources it devours are rarely recovered.[5]

New Hampshire

After Iowa, attention turns to New Hampshire, traditionally the first state to hold a primary in which the entire electorate participates.[6] Candidates who do surprisingly well in this primary have benefited enormously. Eugene McCarthy in 1968, George McGovern in 1972, Jimmy Carter in 1976, Gary Hart in 1984, Bill Clinton in 1992, Pat Buchanan in 1996, and John McCain in 2000 all gained visibility and credibility from their New Hampshire performances, although none had a majority of the vote and only Carter and McCain had pluralities. Bill Clinton actually came in second with 25 percent of the vote in 1992, 8 percent less than former Massachusetts Senator, Paul Tsongas. Clinton's relatively strong showing, however, in the light of allegations of marital infidelity and draft dodging made his performance more impressive in the eyes of the news media than Tsongas' expected win. Tsongas was not considered to be a viable candidate; Clinton was. Similarly, John McCain's impressive victory in 2000 over front-runner George W. Bush by 18 percent elevated him overnight from just another candidate to serious contender. John Kerry's win over fellow New Englander Howard Dean confirmed his status as the Democratic front-runner and Dean's as an unviable option. (See Box 5.4 "Front-Runner Strategies in 2004.")

Like Iowa, New Hampshire also receives extensive media attention. Together, these two states usually account for the bulk of prenomination television coverage on the national news. For this reason alone, nonfront-runners have to contest this initial primary even though their odds of winning it are not great. However, unless they can demonstrate their voter appeal, they are not likely to gain the financial and organizational support, much less the press coverage, necessary to mount a serious challenge to the front-runner in the ensuing contests.

Candidates have more options after New Hampshire, particularly when multiple states hold their caucus or primary on the same date. Nonfront-runners tend to concentrate their limited resources on a few states, those in which they believe (and their polls suggest) that they will do best. Thus, in 2000, John McCain skipped Iowa and focused his efforts after New Hampshire on his home state of Arizona, and subsequently, directed them to South Carolina and Michigan. McCain gained a short-term advantage from this strategy, largely on the basis of his victories in New Hampshire and Michigan. Similarly, in 2004, Wes Clark and Joe Lieberman began in New Hampshire and then directed their efforts in one or two states holding primaries the next week.

In contrast, front-runners usually have sufficient resources to campaign everywhere. The early caucuses and primaries present a situation in which they can use their advantages of money, media, and momentum to eliminate or preclude competition, demonstrate their electability, perhaps even the inevitability of their nomination. And even if they lose several early caucuses and primaries, they can still add to their delegate lead and recover later on as Reagan, Mondale, and George H. W. Bush did after their second-place finishes in Iowa, and George W. Bush did after his disappointing loss to McCain in New Hampshire.

RAISE AND SPEND BIG BUCKS EARLY

Having a solid financial base at the outset of the nomination process provides a significant strategic advantage. It allows a presidential campaign to plan ahead, to decide where to establish its field organizations and how much media advertising to buy, as well as where and on which groups to focus that advertising. It is no coincidence that those candidates who raise and spend the most money tend to win their party's nomination.[7]

The impact of early money is particularly significant for candidates who do not begin the quest for their party's nomination with a national reputation, candidates such as Michael Dukakis in 1988, Bill Clinton in 1992, Howard Dean and John Edwards in 2004, and Mitt Romney and Barack Obama in 2008. The ability to raise relatively large amounts of money early, particularly in comparison with one's rivals, gives a candidate an edge in gaining media recognition, building organizational support, raising even more money, and discouraging potential rivals from entering the race.

In fact, the amount of money raised is frequently viewed by the press as a harbinger of future success or failure in the primaries. Howard Dean's campaign is a good illustration. Dean raised more money than did any of his Democratic rivals in 2003, almost $40 million, much of it from small donations. The press took notice. He rose in the polls. By November, he was the acknowledged Democratic front-runner. Similarly, Hillary Rodham Clinton and Barack Obama's fund-raising in the first quarter of 2007 reinforced their poll status as the leading Democratic candidates for the party's 2008 presidential nomination.

Early money is considered important for several reasons. It buys recognition for those who need it. Steve Forbes bought that recognition in 1996 with the expenditure of more than $42 million, much of it his own money. But as noted, public recognition also brings increased scrutiny by the news media and increased criticism by the other candidates.

Early money can buy viability. The press evaluates the candidates in part on the basis of how much money they can raise and how willing people are to contribute. Candidates who cannot raise much money are not usually taken seriously by the news media and by other potential contributors, even if they are well known, as was Elizabeth Dole was in 2000. Six of the twelve Republican candidates for the 2000 nomination were forced to terminate their quest for their party's nomination three months *before* the first caucus and primary. All cited financial reasons for their withdrawal.

Another important reason for having money upfront is that it gives a candidate the opportunity to hire an expert staff and develop a deep field organization in the early primary states. In the event of an early mishap, such an organization can come to the rescue as it did in South Carolina for George W. Bush after his defeat in New Hampshire in 2000. Front-loading also forces the candidates to spend more money earlier and earlier. Thus, the heavily front-loaded nomination schedule in 2008 has increased the importance of fund-raising in the year before the election and contributes to the advantage of well-funded candidates.

Two principal consequences follow from the need for early money: the financial campaign in the years before the nomination, the so called *invisible primary*, has assumed greater importance than in the past, and nonfront-runners are disadvantaged even more than they were previously unless they are independently wealthy. The odds against a little-known outsider using Iowa, New Hampshire, and the other early states to obtain the resources necessary to compete seriously for the nomination have increased in recent years.

GAIN MEDIA ATTENTION

Candidates cannot win if they are not known. Gaining visibility is most important at the beginning of the nomination process when the electorate starts to pay some attention to the contests that loom ahead. Since lesser-known aspirants are not as likely to have large war chests, unless they are independently wealthy or have substantial sums left over from previous campaigns, they need free media. Their problem is that coverage and public recognition go hand-in-hand. Better-known candidates get more coverage precisely because they are better known and thus considered more likely to do well. It is not news when a long shot loses; it is news when a front-runner does. On the other hand, when a long shot does well in raising money, gaining endorsements, drawing crowds, and winning straw votes and especially delegates, the press follows the story of the "conquering hero."

Free Media
What can nonfront-runners do to gain more coverage? They can stage events, release a stream of seemingly endless faxes and tapes to local media outlets, leak unfavorable information about their opponents, and solicit invitations to appear on talk/entertainment programs on radio and television. Here's how Pat Buchanan's 1996 campaign manager described a typical media-oriented day in Iowa before that state held the first nominating caucus:

> Gregg [Mueller, the press secretary] and Pat would get up at about five in the morning, get some coffee, get in the minivan, and go from one TV station to the other, in the local market, wherever they had morning shows and they would do a live segment on every morning television show.
>
> Then they'd come back to the hotel, read through the newspapers and at 10 A.M., we'd go out and do our theme event for the day—drive whatever our message was, get out a press release, which we faxed out everywhere and let that, hopefully, resonate into the newspapers.
>
> At noon, we'd go back to the television stations, if they would have us, or else we'd drive into a new market . . . all the time that they would be driving the van, Greg would have Pat on the cell phone doing radio interviews . . . Buchanan would literally go from one station to the other to the other, go back to the hotel, maybe take a nap in the afternoon, then you go out at 5 P.M. and you do the evening TV stations. If you literally saturated the local TV market, you try to get to the next one. You try to maximize the amount of time you could get on TV in a state while you were there.[8]

Participating in debates against their political opponents has become increasingly important for most candidates. During the 2003–2004 campaign for the Democratic nomination, there were fifteen debates among the Democratic contenders. Although debates among party candidates spark local interest and educate the partisan electorate, they rarely receive much national media coverage. The first televised debate in the 2004 nomination cycle occurred on May 3, 2003, more than fourteen months before the Democratic convention. In the 2007–2008 election cycle, the debates began even earlier. However, the first was carried on only one major broadcast network although not on most of its local affiliates. The all-news cable networks do carry a few of the nomination debates but primarily only the ones that the networks actually sponsor. Is it any wonder that prenomination debates do not have much national impact unless, of course, one of the candidates makes a major faux pas or claim that is deemed newsworthy?

In general, there has been a decline in the amount of time given to election news on the broadcast networks and an even larger decline in the number of candidate stories that appeared on the evening news shows. On the other hand, the 24-7 cable networks have increased their coverage as have the Web sites of the major news networks.

With campaign news sources more dispersed, candidates must pay close attention to what viewers are watching. Increasingly, they must design and present their own messages via paid advertising. Free media is not sufficient nor is receiving favorable coverage automatic. John McCain and Bill Bradley both received a higher percentage of positive spin than their front-running opponents—Bradley, prior to New Hampshire, and McCain after New Hampshire, yet they were unable to convert that good coverage into enough votes to win subsequent primaries. Similarly, in 2004, all the Democratic candidates received favorable coverage according to a study by the Center for Media and Public Affairs, a nonpartisan organization, that conducts content analyses of how the candidates are evaluated in the evening news on the broadcast network. The Center reported that 75 percent of the "spin" on the Democrats was positive. Of the major contenders, Edwards received the best press and Dean the worst. However, even Dean's coverage was still more favorable than unfavorable.[9]

Paid Media

Advertisements remain one of the most effective ways to communicate with voters. Studies have shown that people tend to retain more information from candidate commercials than they do from the broadcast networks' evening news.[10] As a result, campaigns continue to spend the bulk of their revenues on political advertisements. Box 5.1 provides a description of the 2004 Democratic nomination advertising campaign and a sample of the ads.

DEVELOP A DEEP AND WIDE ORGANIZATION

The concentration of primaries and caucuses also requires that candidates create a deep and wide organization, one that can attend to the multiple facets of the campaign and do so in many states simultaneously. But achieving this objective has become increasingly difficult with the front-loading of the primaries, even for well-financed candidates. As a consequence, the deep

| BOX 5.1 | THE AIRWARS OF 2003–2004: THE CONTESTED PHASE OF THE DEMOCRATIC NOMINATIONS |

A critical component of the nomination campaign is conducted electronically, over the airways, on cable, via satellite, and over the Internet. Most campaigns spend over half their funds on designing, targeting, and presenting their messages in the form of advertisements. The election of 2004 was no exception. A record amount of money was spent on political commercials by the candidates, political parties, and nonparty groups.

The first round of political advertising for the 2004 nomination took place in the campaign preseason during 2003. The bulk of the early advertising was directed toward the first contests in Iowa and New Hampshire.

The Candidates: Their Personal Images and Policy Appeals

The air wars were initially fought among the Democratic candidates. Most of them designed their early ads to introduce themselves—their qualifications and campaign appeals—to the Democratic electorate. Kerry was the Vietnam veteran who understood, "the courage of Americans to do what is right for this country;" Edwards, the candidate from working class parents, who stated his firm belief, "America works best when it works for all of us"; and Dean, the anti-establishment candidate, who claimed to be the only one of the principal Democratic candidates who opposed the war in Iraq from the outset. Dean's ads proclaimed: "The only way to beat George Bush is to stand up to him." The message of Wes Clark, the former general, was "he's led armies, forged coalitions, and helped negotiate a peace—don't we need a president like that?" Richard Gephardt, the former minority leader of the House claimed to be the middle class candidate; "I believe that what is good for the middle class is good for America." Joe Lieberman was presented as the candidate who does "what is right, even if it is not easy."[11]

The Kerry campaign designed and aired the most ads, forty-two in all. Most of them ran in the period from November 2003 through January 2004. In these ads, both Kerry and others testified to his military service, his later opposition to the Vietnam War, and his years in the Senate, particularly as a member of the Senate Foreign Relations Committee. In the words of Bob Strum, Kerry's media adviser, "The whole notion of the advertising was that Kerry was the person who could take on Bush."[12]

Dean ran twenty-one ads, most of them of the stand-up variety with the candidate criticizing George W. Bush. Dean advertised early but unevenly. His ads appeared in August 2003 but not September, in October but not November. They were back up again in the middle of December.[13] Many of Dean's ads first appeared on his Web site to gage the reaction of his supporters.

Edwards' ads were distinguished by their positive tone, the rural setting in which they occurred, and the town meeting format that had Edwards in his shirt sleeves talking to small groups of people about his roots, growing up in humble conditions in the South. The structure of the ads and story Edwards told did not vary very much but after a while, Edwards' media advisers dressed him up to make him look more presidential.[14]

Gephardt ran both positive and negative ads. The positive ones emphasized his government service and his proposal for health care that he personalized by talking about his son who had cancer. The negative ads went after Dean, reinforcing the news media's line that the Vermont governor's careless statements and limited experience indicated that he was not ready for prime-time television, much less for the presidency.

Clark's ads were distinctive by their black-and-white color, their relatively long length of 60 seconds, and their documentary style. Joe Slade White, who created the ads, stated: "I wanted the initial ads to be memorable because everybody else had been up on the air for months. These were coming in November and I wanted them to be dramatic ... I wanted his story to be different so we did black-and-white still photography opening with the dramatic theme of being wounded in Vietnam,"[15]

Round 1 Illustrating The Democratic Advertising Wars

A Dean 30-Second TV Spot

Image: Gephardt, Kerry, and Edwards standing with President Bush and Senator Trent Lott.

Audio: *[Narrator]* "Where did the Washington Democrats stand on the war? Dick Gephardt wrote the resolution to authorize war. John Kerry and John Edwards both voted for the war. Then Dick Gephardt voted to spend another $87 billion there. Howard Dean has a different view."

Image: Dean.

Audio: *[Dean speaking]* "I opposed the war in Iraq, and I'm against spending another $87 billion there. I'm Howard Dean, and I approve this message because our party and our country need new leadership."[16]

A Kerry 30-Second TV Spot

Image: Children playing on playground covered with snow. As Kerry, wearing a ski jacket, comes on the screen, the children, dressed warmly, run down a hill.

Audio: *[Kerry speaking]* "For nearly thirty years, we've talked about reducing America's dependence on Mideast oil. And here we are today, more dependent on foreign oil than ever. It's time to make energy independence a national priority, and to put in place a plan that frees our nation from the grip of Mideast oil in the next ten years. Because no child growing up in America today should ever have to go to war for oil. I'm John Kerry, and I approved this message."

Sources: Howard Kurtz, "Dean Chides Rivals on War," *Washington Post,* January 14, 2004, A6; and Jim Rutenberg, "Kerry's Call for Energy Independence," *New York Times,* December 26, 2003, A24.

Altogether, Democratic candidates spent $51.3 million on their television advertising in the 100 top media markets in the United States in their quest for their party's nomination according to Professor Ken Goldstein, director of a major research project tracking political advertising.[17] Of that amount, $10.7 million was expended in Iowa, $14 million in New Hampshire, and $14.1 million in the states that held primaries on February 3, 2004.[18] Dean spent the most, $11 million, closely followed by Clark and Kerry who spent $10.7 million and $10.6 million, respectively.[19]

organization rarely extends beyond the early states. In those states, it must also be supplemented by group activity, such as the pro-life and Christian Coalition groups that helped Pat Buchanan in 1996 and George W. Bush in 2000; organized labor and teacher's groups that came to the aid of Al Gore, particularly in Iowa and New Hampshire in 2000; and the veterans and firefighters who manned the telephone banks and campaigned door to door for John Kerry in Iowa in 2004. All the candidates supplement their organizational support with volunteers increasingly contacted by word of mouth or via the Internet.

George H. W. Bush benefited enormously from the backing and organizational support of state parties in New Hampshire, South Carolina, and Illinois in 1988, as did his son in the early contests in Iowa, South Carolina, and Virginia in 2000. Similarly, Bill Clinton owed his first primary victory in Georgia in 1992 to the active campaign of Governor Zell Miller and his party organization.

The major task of any organization is to mobilize voters and build electoral coalitions among core partisan groups.[20] Media coverage is necessary but not sufficient. Having an organization in the field is deemed especially important in caucus states in order to get supporters and sympathizers to the precinct meetings, which are less well known than the voting places at which people cast their primary ballots and also vote in the general election. In both caucuses and primaries, telephone banks must be established, door-to-door canvassing employed, and appropriate material mailed or hand delivered. It is also necessary to create the impression of broad public support and generate excitement. These activities involve a large grassroots effort.

Eugene McCarthy, George McGovern, and to a lesser extent Bill Bradley recruited thousands of college students to ring doorbells, distribute literature, and get supporters out to vote in 1968, 1972, and 2000. Jimmy Carter had his "Peanut Brigade," a group of Georgians who followed him from state to state in 1976. Jesse Jackson effectively used African-American churches to recruit volunteers and raise money for his presidential campaigns in 1984 and 1988, while Pat Robertson in 1988 depended on the 3 million people who signed petitions urging him to run for president.

One of Howard Dean's biggest disappointments in 2004 was his campaign's failure to create an efficient grassroots operation from the 500,000 people who provided their e-mail addresses or blogged on his Web site. The Dean volunteers who came to Iowa lacked political savvy and organizing skills. Their dress and manner branded them as outsiders, reducing their ability to persuade Iowans of the merits and viability of Dean's candidacy.[21] Barack Obama faces a similar task in 2008, converting bloggers for Obama into workers and voters for his campaign.

MONITOR PUBLIC OPINION

With intentions clear, money in hand, events planned and scheduled, and an organization in place, it is necessary to monitor public sentiment, appeal to it, and try to manipulate it, all at the same time. To achieve these goals, state polls and focus groups are considered essential. However, they did not become part and parcel of the nomination process until the middle of the twentieth century.

Republican Thomas E. Dewey was the first to have private polling data available to him when he tried unsuccessfully to obtain the Republican nomination in 1940. John F. Kennedy was the first candidate to engage a pollster in his quest for the nomination. Preconvention surveys conducted by Louis Harris in 1960 indicated that Hubert Humphrey, Kennedy's principal rival, was potentially vulnerable in West Virginia and Wisconsin. On the basis of this information, the Kennedy campaign decided to concentrate time, effort, and money in these predominantly Protestant states. Victories in both helped demonstrate Kennedy's broad appeal, thereby improving his chances for the nomination.

Today, all major presidential candidates commission their own polls. These proprietary surveys provide critical information about the beliefs and attitudes of voters, their perceptions of the candidates, and the kinds of appeals that are apt to be most effective, as well as which of them seem to be working best. Bill Clinton used polls to great advantage in 1992 to develop and target an economic appeal and to respond to allegations about his personal character. He used them even more in 1995 to reposition himself and launch his reelection bid following the Democrats' debacle in the 1994 midterm elections. The entire Clinton advertising campaign in 1995 and 1996 was developed and monitored through careful and constant Democratic polling; George W. Bush campaigns in 2000 and 2004 also relied on data from surveys and focus groups as have done the principal candidates of both parties in the 2007–2008 election cycle.

The use of focus groups to gauge the public's reaction to words and phrases as well as to evaluate the potential impact of candidate appeals has become an increasingly valuable tool for speechwriters and media consultants. Almost all campaign advertising is pretested by such groups to gauge likely public reactions. Adjustments may then be made before the ad is actually aired, if it is aired. A negative response by the focus group may kill the ad entirely.

Dick Morris, the political strategist behind Clinton's reelection campaign, described how he and his aides crafted the president's media advertising on the basis of focus group reactions:

> We prepared several different rough versions of the ads, called animatics, which [pollster] Mark Penn would arrange to test at fifteen shopping malls around the nation. After the Republicans began to attack us in their own ads, Penn tested the opposition ad and our reply at the same time to measure their relative impact. Penn's staffers would set themselves up in a mall and invite shoppers one by one to fill out a short questionnaire about Clinton, Dole, and their own political views. Then they would show the voters the ad we wanted to test. Afterward the shopper would fill in the same questionnaire and Penn would measure any changes in opinion. . . .

Based on the mall tests, we decided which ad to run and whether to combine it with elements from ads that did not do as well. We worked for hours to make the ad fit thirty seconds. Then we'd send the script to Doug Sosnik, the White House political director, who gave it to the president for his OK.[22]

The Bush and Kerry campaigns utilized similar procedures in 2004.

Telephone polling can also be a guise for getting out the vote, for pushing a vote, or even for suppressing one. In 1992, George H. W. Bush's supporters in New Hampshire countered Pat Buchanan's criticism with a telephone campaign directed at women who were read statements that Buchanan had made about their fitness to have a career. The choice of the statement was designed to produce a negative effect. Similarly, in 2000, supporters of McCain and Bush raised questions about their opponents' religious tolerance to get out their own religious supporters.[23] Poll results can also be used to build momentum, increase morale, and affect media coverage. The amount of coverage is important because the more coverage candidates have, particularly during the early months, the more volunteers they can attract and the more money they can raise.

The benefits of appearing to be popular and viable suggest why candidates have also used their private polls for promotional purposes. A good example from the past is Nelson Rockefeller, who tied his quest for the Republican nomination in 1968 to poll data. Since he did not enter the primaries, Rockefeller's aim was to convince Republican delegates that he, not Richard Nixon, would be the strongest candidate. Private surveys, conducted for Rockefeller in nine large states, five important congressional districts, and the nation as a whole, one month before the Republican convention, indicated that he would do better against potential Democratic candidates than Richard Nixon. Unfortunately for Rockefeller, the final Gallup preconvention poll, fielded two days after former President Dwight Eisenhower endorsed Nixon, did not support these findings. The Gallup results undercut the credibility of Rockefeller's polls as well as of another national poll that had Rockefeller in the lead and thus effectively ended his chances for the nomination.

Another use of private polls is to raise money. Contributors are more motivated to give to candidates whom they believe stand a reasonable chance of winning. Thus, the release of poll data to potential donors and even to the news media is often designed to demonstrate a candidate's electability.

Although polls directly affect a candidate's strategy, tactics, and fundraising, their impact on the general public is less direct and much less pronounced. Despite the fears expressed by politicians, there are few empirical data to suggest that polls generate a *bandwagon effect*, a momentum for a candidate that causes others to jump on board. There is, however, some evidence of a relationship among the candidate's standing in the polls, success in the primaries, and winning the nomination. What is unclear is whether the public opinion leaders win because they are more popular or whether they are

TABLE 5.1 | REGISTERED VOTERS' KNOWLEDGE OF CANDIDATES, JANUARY 19–FEBRUARY 2, 2004

	1/19 Before Iowa	1/26 After Iowa But Before N.H.	2/2 After N.H.
Knew Clark was a general	53%	61%	67%
Knew Dean was governor of Vermont	52	50	52
Knew Edwards was the son of a mill worker	17	17	27
Knew Edwards was a trial lawyer	19	29	36
Knew Clark was a decorated veteran	26	26	27
Knew Kerry was a decorated veteran	34	47	56
Knew Dean wanted to abolish all of Bush's tax cuts	27	31	29
Knew Dean opposed the war in Iraq	44	43	46

Source: "Democratic Primary Knowledge," National Annenberg Election Survey, February 6, 2004.

more popular initially because they are better known and ultimately because they look like winners.

DESIGN AND TARGET A DISTINCTIVE PERSONAL IMAGE AND POLICY MESSAGE

The information obtained from polls and focus groups is used to create and sharpen leadership images and to target these images to sympathetic voters. In designing an appeal, candidates must first establish their credentials, then articulate a general approach, and finally discuss specific policy problems and solutions. For lesser-known candidates, the initial emphasis must be on themselves: who they are and what is their experience, especially their qualifications for the presidency.

With the exceptions of Joe Lieberman, John Kerry, Dick Gephardt, and African-American activist, Al Sharpton, 40 percent or more of the population had not heard of any of the others at the end of 2003, only a few months before the Iowa caucus and the New Hampshire primary.[24] And even those who had, they knew very little.[25] Table 5.1 indicates the public's level of knowledge of the Democratic candidates as the nomination contests got underway.

Thus, the first and essential tasks are to gain name recognition, project a leadership image, and develop a distinctive policy appeal. Kerry, Clark, and Graham pointed to their personal experience: Kerry a much decorated Vietnam War veteran, Clark a four-star general who commanded U.S. forces in the Balkans, and Graham the senior Democrat on the Senate Intelligence Committee. They did so to establish their leadership credentials in light of the terrorist attacks and the war in Iraq.

Dean's opposition to that war gave him an initial advantage when appealing to Democratic activists who were particularly critical of the administration's Iraq policy. The other Democratic contenders had fewer qualifications to trumpet and policy positions to stress other than their criticism of the Bush administration. Within the domestic arena, first Gephardt, and then Dean and Kerry introduced comprehensive health plans; Lieberman stressed his moderate policy positions; and all the candidates criticized the administration's penchant to relieve the tax burden on the rich in the light of spiraling budget deficits.

In general, the candidates' issue positions and image projections do reach voters. The Annenberg Public Policy Center at the University of Pennsylvania, which studied policy agendas and image projections in recent presidential elections, found that people gain greater awareness and knowledge of the candidates and their positions as the nomination process advances, particularly in states in which the candidates actively campaigned.[26]

Annenberg researchers also examined the impact of political endorsements and campaign attacks on the electorate. They concluded that endorsements and attacks can inform voters and influence their behavior on election day.

Similarly, attacks, particularly those that become items in the news, also can have an effect. In the 2000 nomination campaign, ads criticizing McCain for voting against breast cancer research and against environmental legislation and Bradley for his overly ambitious and expensive health care plan took their toll on the reputations and evaluations of both candidates. Aimed primarily at moderates, both independents and partisans, who were thinking about voting for these anti-establishment candidates, the ads undermined their credibility as clear-thinking, public officials with a sophisticated understanding of the complexities of contemporary policy. In 2004, the avalanche of negative commercials by the Gephardt and Dean campaigns against each other in Iowa turned off undecided voters and made it difficult for both candidates to extend their base of support.

In short, what candidates say and do matters. Their appeals and attacks can inform, inflame, and influence the electorate. They may not be the only factors that affect an election's outcome, but they do seem to have an impact.

MAKE EFFECTIVE USE OF COMMUNICATION TECHNOLOGIES

In addition to the advertising, other communication channels are also used to reach voters. One of the distinctive aspects of nomination campaigns since the beginning of the 1990s has been the propensity of candidates to circumvent the national networks entirely for less expensive local media. Campaigns design products and events for expanded local news. Products include videotapes; opposition research, usually anonymously leaked; tailored interviews with local anchors; and made-for-television events. Computer-targeted telephone calls, candidate Web sites, and popular blogs are also used to reach out to voters.

The Internet has become an essential vehicle for building a core group and involving members of that group in campaign activities. The potential of political cyberspace is enormous. Cheap, quick, and accessible to an increasing portion of the electorate, it has become a mechanism for soliciting contributions, primarily small ones, building a staff and a cadre of volunteers, and getting them to attend campaign events and participate in get-out-the-vote drives.

In 2000, John McCain collected over $7 million in donations from Web site appeals, much of it after his surprisingly strong showing in New Hampshire.[27] Similarly, Howard Dean, Wesley Clark, John Kerry, and to a lesser extent, the other 2004 Democratic candidates also used their sites to solicit money, to provide information about their campaigns, and to respond rapidly to attacks made against them. (See Box 5.2, "Nonfront-Runner Strategies in 2004," for a discussion of Dean's innovative use of this technology in the 2003–2004 nomination process.) In January 2007, Senator Hillary Rodham Clinton announced her candidacy on her Web site, and Barack Obama got a big initial boost from college students who started blogs on behalf of his presidential candidacy.

Campaigning on the Internet is not without its problems, however. Squatters have registered Web addresses and then demand large sums from the campaigns to give them up. Parody sites and linkages have mushroomed in recent years. Unsubstantiated rumors circulate widely and rapidly on the Web. Security has also become a problem as Web sites become targets of political opponents and hackers who want to damage candidates by invading their sites.

Nonetheless, the Internet offers campaigns many compelling opportunities. It has become a vehicle for reaching out, particularly to the younger generation, whose online sophistication generally exceeds their political knowledge and activity. It is a way to convert passive observers into more active participants and a means by which candidates can communicate directly with their online electorate, and most importantly, to do so without press distortion. Speeches and rallies can be carried live or made readily available to users; ads can be viewed in their entirety; and reactions can be solicited and suggestions encouraged.

Candidates can also use their sites to maintain a campaign archive for the news media as well as a screen on which to alert the press to new and potentially newsworthy happenings and events. Communicating this information to the news media is important since most major news outlets maintain their own Web sites and must keep them current.[28]

| BOX 5.2 | NONFRONT-RUNNER STRATEGIES IN 2004 |

The Rise and Fall of Howard Dean

For political pundits, campaign operatives, and the news media, the big news of the 2003–2004 Democratic nomination process was the rise and fall of Howard Dean. When Dean announced his presidential ambitions in the fall of 2001, few took him seriously. How could a political unknown from a small, rural state have a realistic chance of winning the Democratic Party's presidential nomination? It was not 1976, when a poisonous political climate in Washington (the Watergate scandal and President Gerald Ford's pardon of Richard Nixon) and an extended Democratic primary process allowed Georgia Governor Jimmy Carter to parlay early and surprising victories in Iowa, New Hampshire, and Florida into a nomination victory.

Nor did Dean fit the mode of successful Democratic presidential candidates. He did not come from a southern state as Carter and Clinton did. He was not associated with the moderate wing of his party as both ex-presidents were. In fact, his support of a bill to grant civil unions to same-sex adults in Vermont was seen as a major liability for a presidential candidate in the general election. He did not have a lot of wealthy backers, a national political organization, or even much public recognition. Few people had ever heard of him as he began his quest.[29] How then did he become the Democratic front-runner, and why did his campaign collapse so quickly?

Dean's rise to prominence was a result of his innovative campaign appeal and a successful strategy to build a base of core supporters by using the Internet. Recalling the idealism of the 1960s, Dean talked about empowering people who felt alienated by the policies and practices of the Bush administration; and he categorically opposed the war in Iraq. Dean's clear-cut opposition to that war in Iraq contrasted sharply with the support that most of the other Democratic contenders had given the president in their votes for a resolution supporting the use of force, if necessary, and for appropriations to fund the military action.

Dean used the Internet effectively to solicit funds, to involve those who accessed his Web site in the activities of his campaign, and provide them with information to convince others to join the cause. Live and recorded speeches, advertisements, and even responses to criticisms of Dean made by opposing candidates or the news media were available on his Web site.

Dean raised more money than any of the other Democratic candidates in the year prior to the election, and he did so from small donors. His broad-based financial support suggested that he was tapping into a large segment of the Democratic base and possibly beyond it, reaching and energizing young people, and thereby giving credence to his campaign.

The Dean campaign maintained an ongoing conversation with people who frequented his Web site. The campaign requested comments and suggestions from those who accessed the site and posted them on the blog, which became an ongoing political forum. Campaign officials, including manager Joe Trippi, spent hours communicating with people who had asked questions and made recommendations. By the end of 2003, the names of 500,000 subscribers were in the campaign's data bank, ready to be mobilized for the caucus and primary campaigns.[30]

Dean's rhetoric, fund-raising, and Internet operations were newsworthy. They attracted the attention of the reporters who evaluate the candidates in the year before the election on the basis of the money they raise, the recognition they gain, the distinctiveness of their campaign, their standing in the polls, the endorsements they get, and the seriousness with which they are viewed by their opponents within their party and by the other party.

Dean scored well in all these categories. That he exceeded initial expectations was also newsworthy. He became the front-runner in the fall of 2003. Al Gore and several labor unions endorsed him in December 2003; these endorsements from political insiders, however, raised questions about Dean's status as an outsider and anti-establishment fighter.

Being number one also meant being the number one target. Dean did not fare well under the microscope of news media attention and attacks by his political opponents. His words and actions during the period in which he was the governor of Vermont were used against him. As governor, he had once called Medicare "a bureaucratic disaster" and cautioned against creating a national health system modeled on it; as candidate, he advocated strengthening and expanding the benefits of the Medicare program. As governor, he had disparaged the Iowa caucus, saying that it was "controlled by special interests"; as candidate, he appealed to Iowans for their votes. When Dean left the governorship, he ordered many of his files closed for ten years; as candidate, he railed against the secrecy of the Bush White House and the president's failure to disclose his National Guard records. After the capture of Saddam Hussein, Dean asserted that America was no safer than before the Iraqi dictator was apprehended, a claim that most Americans rejected.

Dean's campaign comments were highlighted as evidence that he lacked the temperament, thoughtfulness, and truthfulness to be president. He was rebuked for implying that his brother (who had been missing and believed dead since he traveled to Southeast Asia in 1974) had served in the military when he had not done so, rebuked for stating that U.S. policy in the Middle East was unbalanced and unfair, and rebuked for a comment, "I still want to be the candidate for guys with Confederate flags in their pick-up trucks", that some interpreted as racist. Dean's opponents asked: Was he ready for prime time? Could he be elected if he were the Democratic nominee?

Dean's temperament, particularly the anger and emotion he displayed, also raised questions about his mental balance and emotional stability. His "screaming" speech to supporters after his disappointing finish in the Iowa caucuses was played and replayed by the news media, became the target of late-night comics, and served as fodder for new jingle writers. Had he snapped under the pressure? Would he do so in the White House?

The Dean campaign also suffered from internal staff strife. Joe Trippi, a political consultant who had become the campaign manager, and Kate O'Connor, Dean's long-time aide, did not get along well, nor was Trippi able to exercise tight control over campaign operations. Critics pointed to the campaign manager's poor administrative skills, his abrasive manner, and his tendency to talk but not listen.[31] Trippi did not have a close personal relationship with Dean. After the disappointing showing in Iowa, Trippi left the campaign, and Dean named a new campaign manager, but by then, it was too late.

The knockout strategy, which the campaign adopted after Dean emerged as the Democratic front-runner, also boomeranged. The plan, designed in the fall of 2003, was to utilize the campaign's financial advantages and Dean's high standing in the polls to score a one-two knockout punch in Iowa and New Hampshire, and thereby make it unlikely that any candidate could overtake him. To achieve this goal, the campaign spent heavily from June 2003 to January 2004: $9.2 million for advertising;[32] $5.1 million for direct mail; $7.5 million for operational costs, including staff salaries; $2.2 million in travel; plus money for campaign paraphernalia, shipping, rental equipment, food, and lodging. Of the $41 million raised in 2003, only $9.7 million remained at the beginning of 2004. The Dean campaign also began the election year with a $1.2 million debt.

(*continued*)

| BOX 5.2 | NONFRONT-RUNNER STRATEGIES IN 2004 *continued* |

© REUTERS/Jim Bourg/Landov.

In short, Dean had squandered his financial lead by advertising before Democrats were tuned to the contest, by expanding his staff too quickly, and by decentralizing the campaign's decision-making structure too much. Nor did his Web supporters congeal into an effective grassroots force.[33] One hand seemed to be working against the other.[34] Dean's performance in Iowa and New Hampshire provided little incentive for supporters to dig more deeply into their pockets. His campaign collapsed around him.

Following his defeats in Iowa and New Hampshire, Dean reorganized his campaign staff, put their salaries on hold, and targeted his efforts toward the few states in which he believed he had a chance—Michigan and Wisconsin—but to no avail. His quest for the Democratic Party's presidential election had ended abruptly. A month later he endorsed John Kerry, although he vowed to keep his Internet-based organization alive. Despite the failure of Dean's campaign, his outreach efforts had struck a responsive cord among Democratic activists, and his skilled use of the Internet became the model for other candidates to follow.

The Other Democratic Contenders in 2004

The other Democrats, encouraged by polls that showed the president's declining numbers and increasing vulnerability, began their campaign by directing their criticisms toward the White House rather than each other. Each also tried to establish his or her own credibility by demonstrating knowledge of the issues; making specific policy proposals; extending an appeal to a cross-section of Democratic partisans, disaffected independents, and Republicans; and presenting what each hoped would be perceived as a presidential leadership image.

At the same time, however, each of the Democrats had to identify and hopefully energize a particular constituency within the party as the core upon which a broader electoral coalition could be built and sustained. For Gephardt, it was organized labor with a regional focus on the Midwest; for Edwards, it was the rural poor, the South, plus a financial base of trial lawyers;[35] for Lieberman, it was party moderates. For the other Democrats who were less well known and regarded as fringe candidates, it was primarily the African-American community and the remnants of Jesse Jackson's rainbow coalition for Sharpton, minority and liberal women for Mosley-Braun, and disaffected, anti-war liberals for Kucinich. Senator Bob Graham, the first to drop out, was unable to establish a base, sufficient financial backing, or enough public interest to remain on the news media's radar screen as a serious candidate. Faced with health issues of his own, he decided to drop out before being counted out.

Kerry's early status as Democratic front-runner, the most experienced and initially, the best funded of the candidates, Dean's meteoric rise in the polls during the fall in 2003, and the limited financial resources and visibility available to the other hopefuls made the nonfront-runner strategy their only viable option.

Gephardt Gephardt's weak fund-raising in the 2003 exploratory phase of the campaign and his need for the endorsement of the giant AFL-CIO labor union, required that he be perceived as Iowa's early leader and eventual winner if he were to have a chance to raise the resources and gain acceptance as the possible Democratic nominee.[36] However, Dean quickly became the poll leader in Iowa and elsewhere, leaving the Gephardt campaign little alternative but to take him on directly in the debates leading up to Iowa, in the advertising directed to that state, and in his own speeches and rallies.

Gephardt's strategy put him and Dean into a collision course as the Vermont Democrat pursued his own "one-two knockout strategy" for Iowa and New Hampshire. Thus, Dean also felt that he also had no choice but to take on Gephardt directly.[37] Their fight became increasingly negative as Gephardt reinforced the "not-ready-for-prime-time" label that the news media and other Democrats were pinning on Dean. In the end, Gephardt achieved part of his objective. He stopped Dean, but he also stopped himself. His weak third-place finish with only 11 percent of the Iowa Democratic vote allowed others to write him off as a viable contender. He dropped out the next day. Meanwhile, the Dean-Gephardt confrontation in Iowa allowed Kerry and Edwards to take the high road.

Edwards Edwards, however, was unable to make the most of his Iowa opportunity. Instead of his second-place finish becoming the second biggest story of the Iowa campaign following Kerry's victory, it was overshadowed by Dean's poor showing and his famous scream. As a result, Edwards did not get the bounce he anticipated and needed to make him the most viable alternative to Kerry.

Edwards' campaign had started well. He raised the most money in the first quarter of 2003. His strategy was to use his fund-raising success, his speaking abilities, and his Southern roots to present himself as the most electable Democrat despite his lack of experience and relatively low profile in the Senate.

Edwards did not expect to win in Iowa. He hoped for a fourth- or fifth-place finish that would keep him in the running. Similarly, in New Hampshire with two candidates

(continued)

BOX 5.2 | NONFRONT-RUNNER STRATEGIES IN 2004 *continued*

from neighboring states, a third-place finish for Edwards might be more newsworthy than either Dean or Kerry coming in first or second.[38] The next state to hold a primary, South Carolina, was the state in which Edwards was born and the neighbor of the state he represented in the Senate, North Carolina. If Edwards could demonstrate support in the South, his backers hoped that he would be perceived as an alternative to a liberal Democrat from New England, and thus the Democrat who had the best chance to win the presidency, given the Carter and Clinton experiences. Had not Dean's rise and demise and Kerry's comeback become the two big stories of the 2004 nomination process and had Edwards done better in the South—he only won South Carolina—his strategy might have worked, but it did not. He subsequently got the consolation prize, however, the vice presidential nomination.

Lieberman The biggest disappointment was the Lieberman campaign. Although his presidential ambitions were well known, Lieberman had promised Al Gore who had chosen him as his running mate in 2000 that he would not run if Gore decided to do so in 2004. Thus, the Lieberman campaign could not get underway until Gore decided in December 2002, at the height of George W. Bush's post 9/11 popularity, that he would not seek the presidency in 2004. By waiting, Lieberman lost valuable time for fundraising and early campaign activity. That he embraced the war in Iraq also hurt him with Democratic partisans who were increasingly critical of the Bush administration's foreign policy.

Liberman's strategy, skip Iowa and concentrate on New Hampshire, was premised on the belief that he could be the beneficiary of a cross-over Republican vote similar to the way McCain had gained Democratic and independent voters in that state in 2000. In the words of his deputy campaign manager, Brian Hardwick, "We always thought there was an opportunity for us in New Hampshire because of what McCain had been able to do with the independents in New Hampshire in 2000. . . . We knew that with two neighboring candidates, Dean and Kerry, a strong third place was really what you needed to get out of New Hampshire, and that was all predicated on Gephardt or Dean winning in Iowa."[39] Lieberman actually moved into the state, renting an apartment for he and his wife. But Kerry's Iowa victory, Wes Clark's entrance into the contest, and the latter's potential appeal in New Hampshire undermined Lieberman's strategy, reduced his already low war chest, and left him with few options after coming in fifth with only 9 percent of the vote. Winning nowhere the following week, he was forced to drop out of the race.

Clark Wesley Clark was the last to enter the 2004 Democratic primaries and caucus. A career military officer, West Point graduate, and Rhodes Scholar, Clark had risen to the rank of General. He was the commander of U.S. operations in the Balkans, a military action that occurred during the Clinton administration. Many Democrats saw Clark as an attractive candidate. He had strong national security credentials, opposed the war in Iraq, and had moderate policy views. Born and raised in Arkansas, he was close to the Clintons although he had been forced to resign by Clinton because of his public statements in support of the use of American ground troops in Serbia, an action that the administration opposed.

Lacking political experience, entering the campaign late on September 17, 2003, without a public record, he was a blank slate, an Army General that some disaffected

Democrats, unhappy with Dean and the other candidates, supported because they thought he had the best chance to defeat President Bush. But Clark floundered immediately. He declared himself a candidate before he had an organization. He could not answer a question asked about *his* position on the war. He did not know where to go, which contests to enter, or what to say. It took him several more months to hire staff, get his Web site up and running, and decide on a strategy.

Clark's first strategic decision was not to compete in Iowa. With limited funds, no troops on the ground, and not being well known in a state in which the others had been campaigning for several months, Clark believed that he had little chance of winning. He did not want to be lost in the pack. According to political strategist, Josh Gottheimer, "We went with the strategy that Dean would win Iowa and would probably win New Hampshire. We'd come in a very strong second in New Hampshire and then, on February 3 or so on, we would do very well down South after the others were knocked out."[40]

The strategy, which seemed on its surface to be plausible, turned out in the end to be wishful thinking. Clark finished a distant third in New Hampshire with only 13 percent of the vote. The following week he came in second to Kerry in Arizona, New Mexico, and North Dakota; first by less than 1 percent over Edwards in Oklahoma; and well behind Edwards, Kerry, and even Al Sharpton in South Carolina. The following week was more of the same. Clark ended his abortive campaign on February 10th after he lost the southern states of Tennessee and Virginia to Kerry with Edwards coming in second in both.

Pulpit Candidates   The rest of the Democrats were seen as fringe candidates with no serious chance of winning. For them, the campaign was an end in itself. They used it as a pulpit, much like Jesse Jackson had done in 1984 and 1988, Pat Robertson in 1988, Jerry Brown in 1992, and columnist and commentator Pat Buchanan in 1992, 1996, and 2000.

Pulpit candidates cannot afford large staffs, high-priced consultants, or much, if any, paid media. They depend on volunteers, free media, and events to which all the candidates are invited. They run because they want a podium to promote particular issues, to draw attention to themselves and their causes, and/or to represent the communities that they believe are not being adequately represented by establishment candidates.

Carol Moseley-Braun did not want the Democratic Party to take its large female constituency for granted. She thought it important that there be a woman candidate. The biggest applause line in her abbreviated campaign was "Take the men-only sign off the White House door." But Moseley-Braun could not campaign for long. She lacked the stature to raise sufficient funds, even among women. Her war chest of less than $600,000 was the smallest of all the Democrats. She dropped out before the Iowa caucus.

Rev. Al Sharpton had greater name recognition. He had been at the forefront of various social protests. He gave voice to many of the concerns of those at the lower end of the socioeconomic scale. A critic of the war in Iraq and the administration's pro-business economic and social policies, he presented the other side, often with great wit during the debates among the Democratic candidates. His campaign helped energize the African-American community after its disappointment in the Electoral College outcome of the 2000 presidential election.

Dennis Kucinich, a liberal member of Congress and former mayor of Cleveland, was also an outspoken critic of Bush's Iraq policy, his use of executive power, his unilateral approach to foreign and domestic policy making, and restrictions placed on Americans' civil rights and political liberties by the administration in the name of fighting terrorism. But his campaign lacked money, organization, and visibility. He stayed in the race but had little effect on it.

NOMINATION STRATEGIES

Timing, finance, organization, and communications affect the quest for delegates. They help shape the candidates' strategies and tactics for the nomination. Generally speaking, there have been two successful contemporary prototypical strategies, one for lesser-known aspirants and another one for front-runners. Jimmy Carter used the first of these strategies successfully in his quest for the nomination in 1976. In his run four years later, Carter adopted the second strategy. Since that time, most of the principal contenders have employed one of these strategies or variations of them in their attempts to win their party's nomination.

THE NONFRONT-RUNNER APPROACH: "STEPPING-STONES TO PROMINENCE"

Nonfront-runners lack the resources for victory: money, media, and organization. Their objective must be to obtain these resources as quickly as possible. The most effective way to achieve this objective is for candidates to run hard and fast at the outset: enter the early contests, do well, gain media attention, and generate momentum with a large delegate lead—all to demonstrate their viability as serious contenders capable of winning the nomination and being elected president of the United States.

Jimmy Carter pursued such a strategy in 1976; since then, it has since become the principal nonfront-runner model. Hamilton Jordan, Carter's campaign manager, who designed this basic game plan two years before the election, described the initial assumptions upon which this strategy was based:

> The prospect of a crowded field coupled with the new proportional representation rule does not permit much flexibility in the early primaries. No serious candidate will have the luxury of picking or choosing among the early primaries. To pursue such a strategy would cost that candidate delegate votes and increase the possibility of being lost in the crowd. I think that we have to assume that everybody will be running in the first five or six primaries.
>
> A crowded field enhances the possibility of several inconclusive primaries with four or five candidates separated by only a few percentage points. Such a muddled picture will not continue for long as the press will begin to make "winners" of some and "losers" of others. The intense press coverage, which naturally focuses on the early primaries plus the decent time intervals, which separate the March and mid-April primaries, dictate a serious effort in all of the first five primaries. Our "public" strategy would probably be that Florida was the first and real test of the Carter campaign and that New Hampshire would just be a warm-up. In fact, a strong, surprise showing in New Hampshire should be our goal which would have tremendous impact on successive primaries.[41]

Jordan's plan worked. Dubbed the person to beat after his victories in the Iowa caucus and New Hampshire primary, Carter, with his defeat of George Wallace in Florida, overcame a disappointing fourth place in Massachusetts a week earlier and became the acknowledged front-runner. The Carter effort in 1976 became the strategic plan for George H. W. Bush in 1980, Gary Hart in 1984, John McCain in 2000, and most of the Democratic candidates in 2004. Unlike Carter, however, the others were not successful.

Doing well in the early caucuses and primaries is important but no longer has the payoff it had for Carter. The front-loading of the selection process has reduced the "bump" that Iowa and New Hampshire can give to a victorious nonfront-runner. Yet, candidates have few other options to increase their name recognition and demonstrate their electability at the beginning of the nomination process.

The benefits of an early win are enormous for nonfront-runners. Their victory, no matter how slight, confounds the odds, surprises the news media, embarrasses the front-runner, and energizes the nonfront-runner's candidacy. (See Boxes 5.2 and 5.3.) Media coverage expands; fund-raising is made easier; volunteers join the organization; endorsements become more likely; and momentum can be generated, at least in the short run.

On the other hand, early losses for nonfront-runners doom their candidacy, forcing them to withdraw, usually on the pretext of lacking sufficient funds to continue. There is no prize for coming in second, except perhaps a prime time convention speech. News media often speculate that candidates who demonstrate some popular appeal would make good vice presidential candidates, but the fact of the matter is that successful nominees rarely choose their principal opponents to run with them. The only recent exceptions to this rule was Reagan's selection of George H. W. Bush, who was not his first choice, in 1980, and Kerry's selection of Edwards in 2004, who was his first choice.

THE FRONT-RUNNER STRATEGY: AMASSING DELEGATES

For front-runners the task is different. They do not need to gain recognition or establish their credentials. They do need to maintain their viability as candidates and extend their electoral coalitions. To do so, their strategy is simple and straightforward—take advantage of the advantages they already have: recognition as the potential nominee, the political influence that recognition conveys, and superior resources in the form of money, staff, endorsements, press coverage, volunteers and the ability to wage a multistate campaign. Front-runners use these resources to discourage challengers, acquire as many delegates as quickly as possible, and build an insurmountable lead.

A front-runner's advantages are most potent at the beginning of the nomination process when the perceived gap with the other candidates is widest. The front-loading of the primaries provides an additional benefit because it makes it more difficult for lesser-known opponents to use an early win to gain momentum. Thus, most front-runners try to deliver a knockout blow in the early rounds when their challengers are least able to compete with them. Scott Reed, Robert Dole's 1996 campaign manager, describes how this scheduling helps the front-runner:

> [I]f we were well funded and well organized, we'd be able to take advantage of the condensed period. We also recognized that even if we did stumble early in New Hampshire or Iowa—and we recognized in early January that we might—it would be very difficult for somebody else to capitalize with the next six, seven, or eight primaries happening so quickly. We were the only campaign that had gone out and registered actual delegates to run in all the other states; the other campaigns had missed a few states here and there.[42]

BOX 5.3	THE LESSONS OF JOHN MCCAIN'S UNSUCCESSFUL QUEST FOR THE REPUBLICAN PRESIDENTIAL NOMINATION IN 2000 FOR HIS 2008 NOMINATION CAMPAIGN

John McCain's challenge to George W. Bush in 2000 turned out to be one of the biggest surprises and news stories of that nomination campaign. It failed but provided the candidate with valuable lessons for his subsequent quest in 2008.

McCain started slowly in 1999. He had a small staff, little money, and responsibilities that kept him in the Senate for much of the year. Moreover, he lacked the credentials of successful Republican nominees in the past. He was not considered a party loyalist; he had not previously run a national campaign; he had few political endorsements, he had few major financial backers, and he had no discernible grassroots operation. What he did have, however, was a leadership image from his service in Vietnam, and a fighter image from his Senate campaigns against special interests, pork barrel legislation, the tobacco industry, and soft money. Moreover, McCain exuded confidence and conviction, two traits that bode well for a presidential candidate.

Although McCain did not begin his presidential quest until months after his Republican rivals, he had no choice but to target the early primaries and try to use them as stepping-stones to the nomination. However, he did make one strategic decision that worked to his advantage—not to compete in the first caucus in Iowa. That decision enabled him to conserve his resources and avoid an in-the-pack finish. As attention shifted to New Hampshire, he was the only Republican who had not lost to George W. Bush, a fact alone that earned him notoriety.

Unlike Bush, who followed his handlers' advice religiously, McCain was very much his own campaign manager. He called the shots, hated to read set speeches, and preferred unscripted remarks and discussions with the public. The image he presented, a straight shooter, free spirit, and a candidate who pledged to always tell truth, made him a refreshing contrast to the more programmed Bush. But it also made him prone to mistakes, to emotional outbursts, to anger—all of which suggested that perhaps he was not temperamentally suited for the presidency.

The Senator's appeal to patriotism, public service, and political reform resonated well with Republicans in New Hampshire, as well as with independent voters and Democrats around the country. Core Republicans, however, were not as moved by his rhetoric or his record. They regarded him as a renegade, undependable. Nor were McCain's priorities those associated with the ideological conservatism of Ronald Reagan, policies such as smaller and less intrusive government, Christian family values, lower taxes, and economic individualism.

During his campaign, Senator McCain had excellent relations with the press. In fact, he was a media favorite. The access he gave to reporters, the no-nonsense image he conveyed to the public, and the competition he generated resulted in expansive coverage and a favorable press.[43]

McCain's game plan was to do well in New Hampshire, gain the media spotlight, become George W. Bush's principal challenger, and then use the recognition he would receive from a victory in the first primary to raise money, get volunteers, and gain momentum for the next contest. The plan worked splendidly for a while. McCain won 48 percent of the New Hampshire vote compared to Bush's 30 percent and Steve Forbes's 13 percent. The Senator's unexpectedly large victory put Bush on the defensive, hastened the departure of other Republican candidates, and added $7 million dollars to McCain's war chest. But it also raised expectations for McCain's performance in the next contest in South Carolina, a state in which Bush enjoyed the backing of the Republican establishment, the Christian Coalition, a powerful force in that state, and pro-tobacco groups whom McCain had alienated by his antismoking crusade. These groups went after McCain personally and politically, focusing on his Senate record, his loyalty to the Republican Party, and even rumors about his private life. Operating at the grassroots level, the anti-McCain groups contacted millions of voters by phone and mail, raising questions about McCain's religious convictions, his moral turpitude, and his stands on abortion, school prayer, and civil rights.

Initially, the Senator responded to these attacks with attacks of his own. However, when the press made negative campaigning an issue, McCain abruptly pulled his negative ads. He pledged not to go negative even though the pro-Bush groups continued their anti-McCain campaign. In the end, Bush won handily, gaining an overwhelming proportion of the Christian Coalition vote; McCain's New Hampshire bubble had burst, and his momentum slowed appreciably.

The primaries then moved to more friendly territory for McCain, his home state of Arizona and Michigan, states in which religious conservatives were not nearly as strong as in South Carolina. Although the Republican establishment in both states endorsed Bush, and conservative anti-abortion and anti-tax groups mounted grassroots campaigns against him, McCain was able to overcome this opposition by appealing to independent and Democratic voters. He won both contests.

At this point, McCain looked viable. His campaign was raising money. He was appealing to a cross-section of voters. In fact, hypothetical polls against the likely Democratic candidate, Al Gore, actually showed McCain running better than George W. Bush, thereby supporting the Senator's contention that he, not George W. Bush, was Al Gore's worst nightmare.

The next three contests, the Washington and Virginia primaries and caucus election in North Dakota, proved disappointing to McCain and essentially undercut the boost that he received from his Arizona and Michigan victories. Facing on-the-ground opposition again, state rules that prohibited cross-over voting by independents and Democrats, and a resurgent Bush campaign, McCain lost in each of these states. A failed tactical gamble sealed his fate in Virginia. Speaking to voters in the southern part of the state, an area known for its religious fundamentalism, McCain denounced two of Virginia's most prominent fundamentalist ministers, Jerry Falwell and Pat Robertson, as "agents of intolerance" and "forces of evil," comments that united the Christian Coalition and brought out an unusually large vote against McCain, whereas moderate Republicans seemed unmoved by McCain's remarks.[44]

The next week was Super Tuesday, a date on which twelve Republican primaries and two first-round caucuses were to be held. McCain could not match Bush's money or organization. Although he won four out of the five New England primaries, he lost everywhere else, including the delegate-rich states of California, Ohio, and New York. With his opponent's delegate lead all but insurmountable, having come within $1 million of his spending limit because he had been forced to accept federal funds and Bush had not, the race was essentially over. McCain announced he would reevaluate his campaign. He went home to Arizona.

The lessons for 2008 were clear. McCain had not established sufficient credibility among Republicans. He had alienated fundamentalist Christians, a core constituency within the party. He lacked the support of most Republican state party leaders; he did not have a genuine grassroots movement in states in which only Republicans could participate in the caucuses and primaries. He did not start his campaign early enough, did not raise sufficient funds, did not accept criticism easily, and did not consult sufficiently with campaign professionals. His independence, so appealing to the general public, had

BOX 5.3

THE LESSONS OF JOHN MCCAIN'S UNSUCCESSFUL QUEST
FOR THE REPUBLICAN PRESIDENTIAL NOMINATION
IN 2000 FOR HIS 2008 NOMINATION
CAMPAIGN *continued*

backfired with core Republicans; his dependence on federal matching funds limited his competitiveness over the long haul. Moreover, his appeal to independent and Democratic voters, an asset in the general election, proved to be a mixed blessing at best, and a detriment at worst, in the primaries. Clearly, McCain had much to change in his statements and actions as a Senator, in his personal image and policy appeal as a candidate, and in his campaign strategy and tactics if he was ever going to be a serious contender for the Republican presidential nomination.

His metamorphosis began in the early years of the Bush administration. Initially, his relationship with President Bush remained chilly, although he did address Republican delegates at the party's 2000 and 2004 conventions, publicly support Bush's candidacy for election and reelection, and appeared with the Republican candidate on the campaign trail. In the Senate, McCain became less of a renegade and voted more along party lines. As the 2008 nomination approached, McCain showed his solidarity with Protestant fundamentalists on social issues. He gave a 2006 commencement address at Liberty University and campaigned extensively for Republican candidates in the midterm elections of that year. Meeting with Republican leaders and benefactors during the prelude to the 2008 party nominations, he emphasized his conservatism and his loyalty to basic Republican principles. He backed the president's surge strategy in Iraq. McCain realized that the key to his success in the 2008 Republican caucuses and primaries was placating the partisan base, not appealing to independents and Democrats.

Walter Mondale pursued a front-runner strategy in 1984, as did Democrats Al Gore in 2000, John Kerry in 2004, and Hillary Rodham Clinton in 2008. All Republican front-runners, beginning with Ronald Reagan in 1980, adopted this approach as well. Democrats Michael Dukakis and Bill Clinton used variations of this strategy in 1988 and 1992: spending heavily upfront, employing large professional staffs, and seeking (and receiving) political endorsements. These resources produced early payoffs—delegate leads that encouraged most of their opponents to drop out and gave them, as front-runners, a hedge against any future losses against the candidates who remained.

For those who are unchallenged, the nomination strategy is obviously different. They can use their position to launch their presidential campaign as Reagan did in 1984, Clinton in 1996, and Bush in 2004. The key here is to have sufficient resources at the beginning of the nomination cycle to discourage challengers and have sufficient flexibility to respond to critics. (See Box 5.4, ''Front-Runner Strategies in 2004.'')

| BOX 5.4 | FRONT-RUNNER STRATEGIES IN 2004 |

Running as the Incumbent: George W. Bush

George W. Bush's political advisers began planning his reelection campaign from the moment he was declared the victor in the 2000 election. Their announced goal was to raise $200 million even though Bush did not anticipate a challenge. Raising large sums of money in advance of the caucuses and primaries is the best way to discourage challengers. Bill Clinton used a similar approach in 1996. George H. W. Bush did not in 1992, and as a consequence was weakened by conservative columnist, Pat Buchanan, who nearly defeated the president in the New Hampshire primary.

Incumbents use the money they raise to staff their reelection team, establish an ongoing research operation and a policy agenda, conduct surveys and focus groups, and develop and air campaign advertisements prior to the convention, commercials that will be directed against their general election challenger once that person wins enough delegates to become the *de facto* opponent.

Having money upfront also gives an incumbent the flexibility to respond to criticism by other party candidates in their quest to be their party's nominee. President Clinton has used his early war chest for still another purpose—to document his moderate policy positions in contrast to the Republicans' more conservative views as evidenced by their 1994 Contract with America and the budget cuts they tried to impose on the Clinton administration, cuts that precipitated the closure of government in the winter of 1995–1996.

Bush did not have a similar problem in 2004. The terrorist attacks of September 11, 2001 had established his policy agenda and enlarged his leadership image. Moreover, he faced a cooperative Republican Congress in the last two years of his first term. Nonetheless, the money proved to be a powerful indicator of the president's continued popularity among Republicans in general and the business community in particular, a good omen for the general election. Although the administration was careful not to use federal buildings, notably the White House, to hold fund-raising events, it did carefully coordinate its fund-raising activities with public events held in the same city on the same day so that the taxpayers footed the bill for most of the president's travel. Clinton had utilized a similar strategy four years earlier.

There was an added benefit in combining the presidential and the political—public visibility during the day and private meetings with GOP benefactors in the evening; the former was open to the press and the latter was closed. A key advantage that incumbents possess is their presidential status; the president is not just another candidate. The perquisites of the office are used to showcase the incumbent as a national and international leader. The president stands behind the official seal, emphasizing policy achievements and future goals.

Moreover, the Republicans had artfully designed a scheduling advantage in the planning of their 2004 nominating convention. They had chosen to hold their convention in late August as close to the anniversary of the September 11, 2001 terrorist attacks as possible. Not only did such scheduling fit into the administration's principal campaign theme, "Leadership in an Age of Terrorism," but it effectively gave the Bush-Cheney reelection committee more time to spend the millions they raised in the preconvention period and a more condensed time frame to spend the federal funds for the general election.

Bush's large war chest and extensive endorsements from elected Republican leaders allowed his campaign to go into action the moment his Democratic opponent became clear. The first anti-Kerry ads were aired in early March 2004, at the time when Kerry, the consensus Democratic candidate, was even with the president in the pre-election polls. The object of the initial phase of the Bush advertising campaign was to drive up Kerry's negatives

(continued)

| BOX 5.4 | FRONT-RUNNER STRATEGIES IN 2004 *continued* |

by criticizing his voting record in the Senate and also use that record to illustrate the stereotype by which the Republicans hoped to define Kerry, a consummate politician, a man without strong personal beliefs who went with the popular view of the moment. This stereotype was intended to draw a vivid and unmistakable contrast with Bush, who was projected by his advertisements as a strong leader; a man of conviction, courage, compassion, and consistency; and a person of faith, who knew what had to be done and would do it.

Bush ran a highly disciplined campaign as he had done four years earlier. He was highly scripted, played it safe, and avoided mistakes. Moreover, he stuck with his principal constituencies—the Christian right on social issues; the business community, both large and small on economic issues; and Republican conservatives and national security hawks on foreign policy and defense issues. The fight against terrorism was the overriding theme, designed to coalesce and expand the party's electoral constituency. Despite the reemergence of a highly polarized polity, the president's strategy successfully maintained the cohesiveness of the Republican base and provided the president with the foundation he needed to structure his general election campaign.

Running as the Challenger: John Kerry

As the Democratic nomination process got underway, John Kerry was the early favorite. A wealthy man himself, he also had access to money. A strong campaigner, he had been elected to the Senate for three terms; in his previous election, he had come from behind to defeat the then sitting governor of Massachusetts, William Weld.

Kerry had contemplated running for president for several years. He formed his exploratory committee at the end of 2002; two months later, he hired a well-known, Democratic political consulting firm; and in 2003, he began raising money. In September of that year, he officially announced his candidacy and began his campaign.

Kerry's speeches and manner suggested that he was running for president, not for the Democratic nomination. He focused on Bush, not on the other Democratic candidates. He directed his appeal to a broad cross-section of Democrats, not to a particular constituency within the party. Kerry was careful not to alienate anyone, so careful in fact that he hedged on his policy positions. He also seemed distant and aloof; he talked but didn't listen; his early speeches were not followed by question-and-answer periods. As a consequence, he excited few Democrats even though most conceded that he was their party's strongest candidate.

Anointed the early front-runner by the news media, Kerry used the accolade to reinforce his credentials for the presidency, to raise money from partisans and others who prefer to contribute to the likely nominee, and to gain endorsements and extend his political base.[45] But his front-running status proved to be illusionary. He had not

SUMMARY

In running for their party's nomination, candidates have to make a number of important strategic decisions. These include when to begin, how to organize, where to concentrate their campaign's early focus, how to raise money and on what to spend those funds, how to gain the necessary news media coverage, monitor public opinion, and design and target a distinctive appeal and simultaneously, create a presidential image. Making effective use of modern communication technologies is essential.

demonstrated that he had grassroots support, nor could he until the caucuses and primaries began. Moreover, being the front-runner raised expectations about his position in the polls, his fund-raising totals, and his capacity to energize Democrats, expectations that he could not realize. Once Dean began to capture the attention, money, and enthusiasm of party activists, Kerry's star began to fall.

More and more, the 2004 Democratic nomination process seemed to be a rerun of 1972's when the candidacy of Maine Senator Edmund Muskie, the presumptive favorite to win the 1972 Democratic nomination, imploded in New Hampshire; Dean's uplifting campaign paralleled that of George McGovern's, winner of the nomination but a big loser in the election, a parallel not lost on Dean's Democratic opponents or the Bush White House.

As Kerry fell in the polls and his contributions dried up, he seemed to be dead in the water by November 2003. Radical surgery was necessary if Kerry's candidacy were to survive. He fired his campaign manager and replaced him with Mary Beth Cahill, a long-time senior aide to Senator Ted Kennedy. He tried to become more personal, shortening his speeches, interacting more with his audience, and staying to answer questions. He mortgaged his house in Massachusetts for $6.4 million dollars and lent the money to his campaign so that he could stay on the air in Iowa and New Hampshire. And he got unexpected outside help.

Jim Rassman, a navy veteran who had served with Kerry in Vietnam, showed up at one of the candidate's rallies in Iowa and testified that Lt. Kerry had saved his life. He said, "I'm not a politician...I'm a registered Republican...I owe this man my life...He's going to get my vote."[46] It was an emotional moment; Kerry embraced him; their reunion brought credibility to Kerry's military service and to his heroism and the decorations that he received for it. It solidified his relationship with the veterans who were supporting his campaign in Iowa, and most importantly, it added the human dimension that had been missing from Kerry's campaign up to that point. Rassman's appearance and endorsement brought Kerry down to earth; it made him look real and gave credibility to his presidential qualifications. It allowed him to stay positive in vivid contrast to the negative Gephardt–Dean campaign. Finally, it elevated his stature as a presidential contender at the same time Dean's was being lowered by his careless, callous, off-the-cuff remarks.

The next six weeks evidenced a shift in public opinion from Dean to Kerry. The results of the Iowa primary suggested that the Massachusetts' Senator had successfully turned the corner. The results in New Hampshire reinforced that judgment. Kerry would soon emerge as the consensus candidate, the person who Democrats believe to have the best chance of defeating George W. Bush in the general election. But as Kerry was to discover later, being a consensus candidate does not generate nearly the enthusiasm that personal qualities such as strength, passion, and conviction, and a clear and consistent policy vision can evoke.

Tactical decisions on how to mobilize and allocate sufficient resources to build and maintain delegate support depend on the particular circumstances of individual candidates, the environment in which the state nomination contest occurs, and the time frame required for tactics to have an impact. But times have changed. The old-fashioned campaign run by state party leaders, the candidates who wing it and do not easily take advice from the professionals, and those that refuse to use the latest communication technologies are not likely to be successful.

The new technologies of the late twentieth and early twenty-first centuries have extended the reach but shortened the candidate's reaction time. Computers are now used to map and track political advertising; targeted appeals are calibrated to arouse particular emotions in selective political communities; and interactive campaigning on the Internet is now standard. The use of these technologies requires expertise and financial resources—another reason for having a large war chest early in the campaign. In general, there have been two successful prototypes for winning the nomination: the come-from-the-pack approach of the nonfront-runners, and the out-front, big bucks, challenge-me-if-you-dare approach of the leading candidates.

Nonfront-runners need stepping stones to the nomination. Their initial goal must be to establish themselves as viable candidates. At the outset, the key is recognition. Over the long haul, it is momentum. Recognition is bestowed by the news media on those who do well in the early caucuses and primaries; momentum is achieved through a series of prenomination victories that demonstrate electability. Together, recognition and momentum compensate for what the nonfront-runners lack in reputation and popular appeal. That is why nonfront-runners must concentrate their time, efforts, and resources in the first few contests. They have no choice. Winning will provide them with opportunities; losing will confirm their secondary status.

For the front-runners, the task is different and somewhat easier. They have to maintain their position as likely nominees, not establish it. This objective provides them with a little more flexibility at the outset, but it also requires a broad-based campaign with major resources raised and spent early. Front-runners must take advantage of their organizational and financial base to build a quick and insurmountable lead. Their principal danger is falling short of expectations and then running out of gas.

In the end, the ability to generate a popular appeal among the party's electorate is likely to be decisive. Only one person in each party can amass a majority of the delegates, and that is the individual who can build a broad-based coalition. Although specific groups may be targeted, if the overall constituency is too narrow, the nomination cannot be won. That is why most candidates tend to broaden and moderate their appeal over the course of the nomination process.

 WHERE ON THE WEB?

The Nomination Campaign
- **Democracy in Action**
  www.gwu.edu/~action/P2008.html or www.P2008.org
  > A Web site maintained by the Graduate School in Campaign Management of the George Washington University. Contains pertinent and up-to-date information on the current or next campaign with links to other sources.

- **Gallup Poll**
  www.gallup.com
  Check this site for up-to-date polling data and analyses.
- **National Journal**
  www.nationaljournal.com
  There are many news sources for following the presidential primaries and caucuses; the *National Journal's* site is one of the best.
- **New York Times**
  www.nytimes.com
  The *New York Times* prides itself on being a paper of record. You will find much information on the policy positions and speeches of the candidates in this newspaper as well as the latest delegate count and prenomination polls.
- **Politics1**
  www.politics1.com
  An online guide to current politics with links to other relevant sites for the 2004 election.
- **Polling Report**
  www.pollingreport.com
  Summarizes public polls on the election.
- **Yahoo**
  www.yahoo.com
  A comprehensive listing of articles on the nomination and election.

EXERCISES

1. Check the official and unofficial Web sites of the candidates and their Leadership PACs. (See Appendix B for a listing of these sites.) Use the information from these Web sites to compare and contrast their positions on the most controversial issues in the campaign. Then compare the personal images that they have tried to project. On the basis of these comparisons, whom do you support and why?
2. Follow the news of the nomination campaign from the perspective of a major newspaper, television network, and news magazine (see "Where on the Web" in Chapter 7, page 247). Is the coverage of different media and of the different candidates essentially the same? From which source did you learn the most about strategy and tactics? From which did you learn the most about the candidates themselves?
3. Analyze the nomination campaign on the basis of the candidates' basic appeals, strategies, and tactics. Use Internet sources from the candidates, the news media, and public interest Web sites to obtain the information you need for your analysis.

SELECTED READINGS

Burden, Barry. "The Nominations: Technology, Money, and Transferable Momentum," in Michael Nelson, ed. *The Election of 2004.* Washington, D.C.: CQ Press, 2005, 18–41.

Kennedy Institute of Politics. *Campaign for President: The Managers Look at 2004.* Landam, M.D.: Rowman & Littlefield, 2006.

Magleby, David B. *Getting Inside the Outside Campaign.* Provo, U.T.: Brigham Young University, 2000.

Mayer, William G. "The Basic Dynamics of the Contemporary Nomination Process: An Expanded View," in William G. Mayer, ed. *The Making of the Presidential Candidates 2000.* Lanham, M.D.: Rowman and Littlefield, 2004, 83–132.

—— ed. *In Pursuit of the White House, 2000.* Chatham, N.J.: Chatham House, 1999.

Smith, Craig Allen. "Candidate Strategies in the 2004 Presidential Campaign: Instrumental Choices Faced by the Incumbent and His Challengers," in Robert E. Denton, Jr., ed. *The 2004 Presidential Campaign.* Lanham, M.D.: Rowman & Littlefield, 2005, 131–151.

NOTES

1. Dana Milbank, "A Democrat Who Isn't Afraid to Take the Lead," *Washington Post* (April 18, 2006), p. A2.

2. Kathryn Dunn Tenpass and Anthony Corrado, "Permanent Campaign Brushes Aside Tradition," *Arizona Daily Star* (March 30, 2004). www.brookings.edu/views/oped/20040330corradotenpas.htm.

3. *Campaign for President: The Managers Look at 2004,* (Lanham, M.D.: Rowman & Littlefield, 2006), p. 77.

4. Jimmy Carter used Iowa to get to the presidency, but he did not actually win the caucus. He lost to a slate of uncommitted delegates.

5. Craig Allen Smith, "The Iowa Caucuses and Super Tuesday Primaries Reconsidered: How Untenable Hypotheses Enhance the Campaign Melodrama," *Presidential Studies Quarterly,* 22 (Summer 1992), p. 524.

6. New Hampshire brags that its primary has been the first in the nation since 1920. "First in the Nation," in *The New Hampshire Primary: What It Means to the State and the Nation,* (published by the State of New Hampshire, 2000), p. 26.

7. Professor Barbara Norrander also notes that in nomination contests between 1976 and 1988 some of the biggest spenders on the Republican side have also been the biggest losers. Barbara Norrander, "Nomination Choices: Caucus and Primary Outcomes, 1976–1988," *American Journal of Political Science,* 37 (May 1993), p. 361.

8. *Campaign for President: The Managers Look at '96,* Institute of Politics, Harvard University (Hollis, N.H.: Hollis Publishing, 1997), pp. 7–8.

9. "Campaign 2004—The Primaries: TV News Coverage of the Democratic Primaries" *Media Monitor,* 18 (March/April 2004).

10. Thomas E. Patterson and Robert D. McClure, *The Unseeing Eye* (New York: Putnam, 1976), p. 58.

11. Most of the substantive discussion of the advertising in the Democratic primaries comes from an excellent paper written by L. Patrick Devlin, an expert on political advertising and Professor Emeritus of Communication Studies at the

University of Rhode Island. Devlin presented his paper to students in my course on Presidential Electoral Politics at Georgetown University, November 2004. The title of his paper is "Contrasts in Presidential Primary Campaign Commercials of 2004."

12. Ibid., p. 4.

13. Ibid., p. 21.

14. Ibid., p. 12.

15. Ibid., pp. 25–26.

16. One of the new requirements imposed by the BCRA was that candidates appear on the ads their campaign sponsors, acknowledging that they approved the content of the ad.

17. "Bush, Dem. TV Adv. Near Equal," Wisconsin Advertising Project at the University of Wisconsin–Madison, using data from TNS Media Intelligence/CMAG. http://polisci.wisc.edu/tvadvertising/Press_Releases/Press_Release_PDFs/Release%202004%20March%2025th.pdf (accessed March 25, 2004).

18. Ibid; L. Patrick Devlin arrived at slightly different totals for Iowa, $12.4 million and New Hampshire, $10.7 million. Devlin, "Contrasts in Commercials of 2004," p. 32.

19. "Bush, Dem. TV Adv."

20. Dante J. Scala notes that the Democratic candidates who have been most successful in New Hampshire are those whose campaigns built such partisan coalitions. Dante J. Scala, "Rereading the Tea Leaves: New Hampshire as a Barometer of Presidential Primary Success," *PS: Political Science and Politics,* 36 (April 2003), pp. 187–192.

21. Craig Allen Smith, "Candidate Strategies in the 2004 Presidential Campaign: Instrumental Choices Faced by the Incumbent and His Challengers," in Robert E. Denton, Jr., ed. *The 2004 Presidential Campaign: A Communication Perspective* (Lanham, M.D.: Rowman & Littlefield, 2005), p. 141.

22. Dick Morris, *Behind the Oval Office* (New York: Random House, 1997), pp. 146–147.

23. Alison Mitchell, "More Complaints About Negative Phone Calls," *New York Times* (February 13, 2000), p. A27. In 2004, Republican officials in New Hampshire mounted a telephone campaign to jam Democratic call centers to prevent them from mobilizing voters on Election Day. The New England Regional Chair of the Republican Party was convicted of conspiring to commit interstate telephone harassment, although his conviction was later reversed on a judicial technicality on appeal. Two other party officials, however, pleaded guilty to telephone harassment and were given jail sentences for their crime.

24. "The 2004 Political Landscape: Evenly Divided and Increasingly Polarized," Pew Research Center for the People & the Press, November 5, 2003.

25. "Democratic Primary Knowledge," National Annenberg Election Survey, February 6, 2004.

26. Annenberg Center, "The Primary Campaign," 1, pp. 4–10; "About One Third of Super-Tuesday Democratic Voters Say They Know Enough to Make an Informed

Choice." www.annenbergpublicpolicycenter.org/naes/2004_03_knowledge-dem-candidates-supertuesday_02–27_pr (accessed February 27, 2004).

27. Neil Munro, "The New Wired Politics" *National Journal* (April 22, 2000), p. 1260.

28. According to a survey conducted by the Pew Research Center for the People and the Press, 11 percent of the population reported the Internet as their primary source of news about the 2000 election campaign and 21 percent about the 2004 campaign. *Trends, 2005*, p. 47.

29. In surveys conducted over the summer of 2003, the Pew Research Center for the People and the Press found substantial but decreasing portions of the population (63 percent in early July, 54 percent in August, and 43 percent in September) who had *not* heard of Howard Dean. See "The 2004 Political Landscape," the Pew Research Center for the People and the Press, question 27.

30. Brian Faler, "Dean Leaves Legacy of Online Campaign," *Washington Post* (February 20, 2004), p. A12; and Brian Faler, "Add 'Blog' to the Campaign Lexicon," *Washington Post* (November 15, 2003), p. A4.

31. Dan Balz and Jonathan Finer, "Dean Staff Shake-Up Long Coming," *Washington Post* (January 30, 2004), p. A7.

32. According to Mark Squire, a partner in the advertising firm that developed and aired the Dean commercials, "The whole strategy was wrapped into an early strike out punch. It is part of the reason we put so many resources into Iowa and New Hampshire." As quoted in Devlin, "Contrasts in Commercials of 2004," p. 15.

33. Craig Allen Smith, "Candidate Strategies," in Denton, *The 2004 Presidential Campaign*, p. 141.

34. Glen Justice and Jodi Wilgoren, "Figures Detail Dean's Slide from Solvent to Struggling," *New York Times* (February 2, 2004), p. A18.

35. Trial lawyers were unhappy with the tort reforms that the Bush administration and Republican Congress threatened to enact.

36. Steve Murphy, *Campaign for President: The Managers Look at 2004*, pp. 59–60.

37. Joe Trippi, Ibid., p. 71.

38. Nick Baldick, Ibid., p. 42.

39. Ibid., p. 64.

40. Ibid., p. 28.

41. Hamilton Jordan, "Memorandum to Jimmy Carter, August 4, 1974" in Martin Schram, *Running for President 1976* (New York: Stein & Day, 1977), pp. 379–380.

42. *Campaign for President '92*, p. 24.

43. "Campaign 2000," *Media Monitor*, p. 4.

44. Alison Mitchell, "Birth and Death of the 'Straight-Talk Express'," *New York Times* (March 11, 2000), p. A8.

45. Mark Mellman, *Campaign for President: The Managers Look at 2004*, p. 46.

46. Devlin, "Contrasts in Commercials in 2004," p. 6.

SPRING INTERREGNUM: CONSOLIDATING VICTORY AND POSTURING FOR THE ELECTION

CHAPTER 6

INTRODUCTION

Caucuses and primaries start earlier, and conventions occur later, leaving a period of four to five months from the time the nomination may be effectively determined to the time when the nominee is officially "crowned" as the party's standard-bearer. This interregnum is an important one for the prospective nominees and their parties. The nominees need to repair any damage that the competitive nomination process inflicted on their image, policy stands, and electoral coalition. The parties need to reenergize, reunify, and refocus their efforts on the forthcoming campaign. And they both need to keep the public focused on the forthcoming election and the merits of their candidacies and their policies.

THE NONCOMPETITIVE PHASE OF THE NOMINATION CAMPAIGN

Even after becoming the preordained nominee, it is necessary for a candidate to continue the campaign until the convention to raise money, unify the party, project a strong and desirable leadership image, and keep the public interested and informed about the forthcoming election.

REPAIRING THE DAMAGE

In a competitive nomination, the more negative the campaign, the more likely that the nominee's personal image will have been tarnished, policy positions questioned, and divisions within the party widened. Each of these election-oriented problems will require attention and a public campaign to overcome them.

Candidates may have to reintroduce themselves to the voters to regain the electorate's attention and to remove or at least reduce the negative stereotypes by which their partisan opponents, other party candidates, and the news media and late-night comics have characterized them. Biographical ads, reinforced by information given to the press, and convention speeches given by distinguished party leaders can alter a less-than-desirable image that remains after a bitter nomination campaign.

Bill Clinton faced this problem after winning the Democratic nomination in 1992. Savaged first by press allegations of womanizing, draft dodging, and smoking marijuana, and later by criticism of his centrist policy positions by his liberal opponent, former California governor, Jerry Brown, Clinton needed to recast his presidential image. To do so, his campaign designed a series of commercials that detailed the hardships and struggles that this poor boy from Arkansas encountered growing up and ultimately surmounted in his rise to political prominence. The ads, combined with talk show appearances in which the candidate reminisced about his upbringing, gradually muted Clinton's negative image.

The Clinton campaign was helped in its reconstructive efforts by the news media's diverting its critical focus from Clinton to Ross Perot and his reemergence into the presidential race, his third-party challenge to President George H. W. Bush, and the subsequent Republican attacks against him. In the words of pollster Stan Greenberg:

> We came out of the primaries in very difficult shape . . . our negatives were very high. I think the principal advantage we gained from Perot was his being on the scene in June and our having the space to use that period to rebuild our candidacy. Without Perot, we assumed that, as you had with Dukakis, . . . [the Republicans] would have been on attack in June, and it would have been hard for us to rebuild in that period.[1]

Al Gore faced a different type of image problem in the spring of 2000. He needed to establish his own leadership credentials by moving out of Clinton's shadow. The primaries had not enabled him to do so fully, in part because his opponent, Bill Bradley, had proven to be a weak challenger, and in part because Clinton remained a very active and visible president. To gain stature, Gore needed to stand on his own or be credited with some of the economic successes of the Clinton years. He chose initially to emphasize his independence, thereby distancing himself from the president and making it harder to claim credit for the administration's accomplishments.

John Kerry faced a different task four years later. Not as well known as Gore, he had to present his qualifications to the American people. Most importantly, he had to define himself, knowing that the Bush reelection committee would do so as well and in much less flattering terms.

But Kerry also faced a more immediate problem—money. His campaign had spent most of the funds he had raised to win the Democratic nomination, whereas the president's reelection committee was flush with cash. In the words of Mary Beth Cahill, Kerry campaign manager, ". . . after March 18th, I think the Bush campaign had $114 million cash-on-hand, and we had $2.3 million. So the disparity was pretty enormous and that was the first thing we had to address."[2]

Kerry had little choice but to spend the next several months concentrating on fund-raising while the Bush campaign unleashed its attacks against him, attacks that began in early March 2004. During this period, the Kerry campaign depended on the advertising by 527 groups, the *Media Fund* and *Moveon.org.* to defend his candidacy and attack Bush's. Both groups ran negative Bush ads, but they could not do so in coordination with the Democratic Party or the Kerry campaign. As a consequence, they did not do what the Kerry campaign would have liked them to do—define Kerry in positive terms. Erik Smith, President of the Media Fund, explained the Fund's predicament:

> We were by three of four weeks out in front of the Kerry campaign. We felt that we were better prepared, certainly at that point, to do the negative track. We did not know enough about how the Kerry campaign was going to develop and what their message was going to be and what they wanted or what they were doing or saying to be able help in that endeavor at all. We felt that we were better suited for the negative message, which we embraced and did. We did that for . . . eight weeks. The hope was that through our actions, we would show very clearly what we were setting out to do.[3]

Thus, the early definitions of Kerry were provided primarily by the Bush campaign, much to Kerry's disadvantage and dismay.

Bringing his opponent down to size was the first objective of Bush's anti-Kerry campaign; setting the foundation for the president's reelection efforts was the second. Almost immediately, the Bush campaign aired negative Kerry commercials that presented the Massachusetts senator as a flip-flopper who regularly voted on both sides of controversial issues, including supplementary funding for the troops in Iraq and Afghanistan.

The Kerry campaign did not respond directly to these allegations. Instead, they took time to reorganize themselves, raise money, and tailor the message that they were going to present to the American people: the John Kerry story, his career, his knowledge of the issues, his policy positions, and his character. Cumulatively, these ads comprised a biography that Kerry's campaign staff thought was more compelling than disjointed refutations of the various charges the Republicans were directing at him. Campaign director Mary Beth Cahill, put it this way:

> Ads that would have said John Kerry is not a "flip-flopper" in response would not have exactly served us well. We thought that giving people an eye into the man, his approach to running for president and what he wanted to do when he was there was the answer to that.[4]

By not directly confronting the flip-flopper accusation, however, Kerry inadvertently let the charges stick in the public's mind. His personal negatives increased; his standing in the polls declined; and he lost much of the luster that he had gained by winning the Democratic primaries. Bush's anti-Kerry message made it more difficult for the Democratic challenger to project his own image of leadership.

Bush accused Kerry of supporting tax increases, defense cuts, and legislation that would weaken homeland security. In defending charges that he had voted against a supplementary spending for U.S. forces in Iraq, Kerry did not help his case when he stated, "I actually did vote for the $87 billion before I voted against it."[5] The comment, which the Republicans repeated in their anti-Kerry ads, reinforced the flip-flopper image.

The negative campaign against Kerry may not have convinced Democrats, but it certainly convinced Republicans. After six months of Democrats in the news, the Republicans needed to energize their base. The anti-Kerry campaign helped achieve this objective.

In addition to typecasting Kerry negatively, the early Bush ads cast the president as the strong antiterrorism leader. Returning to the scene of the 9/11 attacks, the ads documented Bush's empathetic but tough, no-nonsense response. The first Bush commercials, however, contained the seeds of controversy. A two-second clip of firefighters at ground zero carrying a flag-draped stretcher, presumably covering human remains, evoked protests by those who felt that the Bush campaign was exploiting the tragedy for political purposes. The International Association of Firefighters, a union that had endorsed Senator Kerry, objected to the ads as did some victims' family members.[6]

As a consequence, the ads became a news item. Polls showed that a majority of Americans thought the backdrop of the World Trade Center following the attack was inappropriate for a political commercial, thereby pressuring Bush's media advisers to delete the objectionable material.[7] The ads still demonstrated the power of the event and the raw emotions it continued to evoke to the president's advantage. The president's strong and unwavering response to the terrorist attack became the principal image and message of the Bush reelection campaign.

The early preconvention advertising helped Bush's image more than Kerry's. People saw the president as the tougher, more resolute, and also more likable leader, although they saw Kerry as more knowledgeable, flexible, and willing to listen to diverse advice. A survey taken by the Annenberg Public Policy Center of the University of Pennsylvania illustrated the effects of the early advertising on public perceptions of the candidates. (See Table 6.1.)

TABLE 6.1 | PUBLIC PERCEPTIONS OF THE MAJOR PARTY CANDIDATES

March 21–April 7, 2004	All Respondents		Respondents in States with TV Ads		Persuadable Voters	
	Bush	Kerry	Bush	Kerry	Bush	Kerry
Cares about people like me	4.95	5.21	4.80	5.08	4.80	5.34
Inspiring	4.98	4.79	4.90	4.67	4.76	5.03
Strong leader	6.10	5.48	5.95	5.29	6.21	5.69
Trustworthy	5.26	5.13	5.20	4.98	4.68	5.02
Shares my values	5.15	4.89	5.04	4.71	4.82	5.13
Knowledgeable	5.94	6.34	5.84	6.02	5.61	6.51
Reckless	4.72	3.97	4.96	3.96	5.10	3.80
Steady	6.00	5.27	6.10	4.98	6.09	5.54
Says one thing, does another	4.84	5.32	4.86	5.20	5.79	5.10
Has right experience to be President	5.70	5.58	5.72	5.44	5.55	5.73
Easy to like	5.92	5.50	5.95	5.39	5.45	5.78
Will make tough decisions despite political pressure	6.24	5.03	6.02	4.76	6.04	5.37
Has clear vision	6.22	5.62	6.22	5.39	6.64	5.79
Changes mind for political reasons	5.22	5.88	5.13	5.72	5.84	5.23
Out of touch with people like me	5.10	4.93	5.25	4.80	5.60	4.65
Stubborn	6.70	5.02	6.79	5.24	6.87	5.13
Arrogant	5.68	4.88	5.60	4.85	5.99	4.39

Statement: "I am going to read you some phrases. For each one, please tell me how well that phrase applies to [George W. Bush/John Kerry]. Please use a scale from 0 to 10, where 0 means it does not apply at all, and 10 means it applies extremely well."

Source: "Public Considers Bush a Stronger Leader but More Stubborn While Kerry Is Seen as Less Reckless but Inconsistent," National Annenberg Election Survey, April 9, 2004.

REPOSITIONING AND REPRIORITIZING THE ISSUES

In addition to readjusting and refining their presidential image, nominees often have to reposition themselves after moving toward their party's ideological core during the contested phase of the nomination campaign. Traditionally, the spring interregnum allows them time to soften and broaden their policy appeal by moving back toward the center and reprioritizing issues for the general election.

Repositioning and reprioritizing can be tricky business, however, since the news media and opposition party are sure to point out the policy inconsistencies, and in doing so, raise questions about the candidates' credibility and dependability to follow through on campaign promises if elected.

With economic and international matters equally salient at the beginning of 2004, the Bush and Kerry campaigns emphasized different policy areas. Kerry stressed the country's economic problems, particularly its loss of jobs to other countries in which the cost of labor was cheaper. He promised to make economic growth and job creation priorities of his administration. He also spoke of the need for expanded health care coverage. By focusing on economic and social issues, Kerry hoped to take advantage of the public's predisposition to believe that Democrats deal more effectively with domestic issues than do the Republicans.

George W. Bush used different strategies in 2000 and 2004 when prioritizing and presenting his policy proposals. Forced to appeal to the conservative Republicans to win the GOP nomination in 2000, Bush then moderated his stands, softened his rhetoric, and moved toward the policy center in that election. He accentuated the positive, stressing issues of compassion such as education, housing, Medicare, and Social Security—issues that had special appeal to Democrats, and especially to women voters, and which would help mute the impression left by the competitive primaries that he was a hard-core conservative. By promoting Democratic issues, Bush was following the same strategy that Clinton used so successfully in 1995–1996 when he emphasized the Republican policy agenda but took more moderate positions than did their congressional leadership on crime prevention, a balanced budget, and improved defense.[8]

In 2004, however, Bush campaigned for president as if he were running for the Republican nomination. His conservative orientation was consistent with the policies of his administration, although he did place greater emphasis on domestic issues in the 2004 campaign than he was able to do as president after the terrorist attacks of September 11, 2001.

In his quest for reelection, Bush directed his appeal to his Republican constituency: to economic conservatives, he promised to extend the tax cuts that were enacted in his first term and to reduce the deficit by cutting domestic spending; to the national security conservatives, he promised to maintain a strong military with the equipment and weapons systems needed to meet the challenges that international terrorism and ethnic, national, and religious rivalries created in the twenty-first century; and to social conservatives, he promised to continue to promote his faith-based initiative and maintain his opposition to abortion, same-sex marriage, and government-supported stem-cell research.

Using a nomination strategy for the general election was an acknowledgement of the highly polarized political environment in the United States. Republican strategists operated on the basis of three assumptions: that the country was evenly divided between Republicans and Democrats; that most partisans had already made up their minds for whom to vote; and that the proportion of independent or swing votes had shrunk to a very small percentage of the population. Bush's advisers believe that they stood a better chance of winning by motivating their base rather than persuading the relatively few undecided voters.[9]

The flip side of establishing issue themes and policy positions is criticizing the opponent's positions. To make and remake a point, the criticism is frequently exaggerated. Exaggerations and outright distortions can have an impact on those who repeatedly see and hear the same claims. Presenting Kerry as a tax-and-spend Democrat, ads sponsored by the Bush campaign and the Republican Party made persist allegations that "John Kerry wants to raise taxes by $900 billion"; "John Kerry voted for higher taxes 350 times"; and "John Kerry wants to raise gasoline taxes by 50 cents a gallon." Ads by Kerry, the Democratic Party, and the 527 groups supporting his candidacy, countered that "George W. Bush favors sending American jobs oversees"; "Three million American jobs have been lost while George W. Bush has been president"; and "George W. Bush raided Social Security to pay for tax cuts for millionaires."[10]

An analysis by *Factcheck.org,* a public interest group that reviews the accuracy of political advertising, found all these claims to be misleading at best and gross exaggeration and incorrect assertions at worst. Yet, many of the people who saw the ads believed them, in large part because they did not have contrary information at their disposal.

In a very interesting analysis of deceptive political advertising and its impact during this spring interregnum period, Kenneth Winneg, Kate Kenski, and Kathleen Hall Jamieson found that: "A little more than half of Americans believed that George W. Bush favors sending American jobs overseas and John Kerry voted for higher taxes 350 times were truthful statements."[11] Their research also revealed that believability of the ads increased as they were shown over and over. More people in the battleground states, states in which the ads were shown, thought the ads were true than did people in the nonbattleground states, that saw the same ads less frequently. The researches also found that partisans were also more likely to believe negative statements about the opposing candidates than were those identified with that candidate's party and independents.[12]

These findings explain why it is so important for candidates who are attacked to respond forcefully and immediately to the accusations with which they are charged. Democrat Michael Dukakis found this out the hard way in 1988 as did John Kerry in 2004. (See Box 6.1"Excerpts from the Bush–Kerry Advertising Campaigns in the Interregnum Period.")

HEALING PARTISAN DISCORD

A third task that usually follows a competitive nomination battle and occurs before the convention is to reach out to partisans who supported other

| BOX 6.1 | EXCERPTS FROM THE BUSH–KERRY ADVERTISING CAMPAIGNS IN THE INTERREGNUM PERIOD |

A Bush Ad

Image: President Bush walking in the White House, interacting with members of Congress, sitting and deeply in thought. The words "The First 100 Days" flash across the screen with a White House backdrop. Then the message "John Kerry's Plan on Spending and Taxes" appears.

Audio: *[Female announcer]* "A President sets his agenda for America in the first 100 days. John Kerry's plan: to pay for new government spending, raise taxes by at least 900 billion dollars."

Image: The words "John Kerry's Plan: On the War on Terror" appear on the screen, followed by pictures of people; then another message: "Weaken Fight Against Terrorists."

Audio: "On the war on terror, weaken the Patriot Act used to arrest terrorists in America."

Image: The words "Delay Defending America" appear, followed by pictures.

Audio: "And he wanted to delay defending America until the United Nations approves."

Image: The words "John Kerry. Wrong on Taxes. Wrong on Defense."

Audio: "John Kerry: Wrong on taxes. Wrong on defense."

A Kerry Ad

Image: Split screen picture of Bush on television and newspaper headline "Bush Unveils Negative Ads Vs Kerry."

Audio: *[Narrator]* "Once again George Bush is misleading America."

Image: Split screen images of television and newspaper headline "Kerry has never *[highlighted in yellow]* called for a $900 billion tax increase."

Audio: "Kerry has never called for a 900 billion dollar tax increase. He wants to cut taxes for the middle class."

Image: White House backdrop with the words "Once again, George Bush is misleading America. Doesn't America deserve more from its president than misleading negative ads?" superimposed on screen and stated by announcer.

Sources: Jim Rutenberg, "Clearly the Candidate, Bush Takes on Kerry on Defense, Taxes and Terrorism," *New York Times,* March 13, 2004. A11; and JohnKerry.com, "Bush Misleading America," John Kerry Media Console, March 12, 2004 (online at http://www.JohnKerry.com/videos).

candidates for the party's nomination. The sooner such an effort is undertaken the better since the news media will continue to highlight rifts in the party and potential problems for the campaign.

A first step in this effort is to gain the endorsements, and hopefully active support, from primary opponents. Overcoming the bitterness often involves more than a handshake. Gestures are important. A prime time speech at the convention, an honorary role in the campaign, even the hint of a position in the new administration are some of the "consolation prizes" that may be offered.

George W. Bush faced such a reunification challenge following his victory over John McCain in 2000; he did not in 2004. Polls conducted over the course of Bush's first term in the White House indicated very high support among people who identified themselves as Republicans. Said Matthew Dowd, the chief campaign strategist for the Bush–Cheney ticket: "It helped that we had a candidate with a 93 percent approval rating among 46 percent of the country."[13]

As the consensus Democratic candidate, Kerry did not face a divided party either. But he did face the challenge of mobilizing its core constituencies: women, organized labor, African Americans, and Latinos, constituencies in which he had not generated much emotional appeal. To energize his base, Kerry emphasized the one issue upon which most all Democrats agreed: they did not like George W. Bush, and they considered the policies of his administration to be misguided and misdirected, hurting America's image in the eyes of the international community, and enlarging the gap between the rich and poor in the United States.

Just criticizing the Bush administration was insufficient, and Kerry knew it. He also had to establish his own leadership credentials. Kerry saw the forthcoming Democratic convention as the time and place to do so.

THE PRELUDE TO THE CONVENTIONS

Considerable planning and much hype go into the convention buildup. Media attention turns to the vice presidential selection, usually the only unknown item left before the big show. That choice is the presidential nominee's. The last time that a convention actually selected the vice presidential nominee rather than ratified the person whom the winning presidential candidate designated was in 1956 when Adlai Stevenson, the Democratic candidate, professed no choice between Senators John F. Kennedy and Estes Kefauver, both of whom were vying for the nomination. The convention chose Kefauver.

The selection of the vice presidential nominee is one of the most important decisions that the prospective nominee must make. It is a character judgment that reflects directly on the presidential nominee. Picking an experienced, well-respected person who might have been or perhaps could become a candidate for the presidency sometime in the future usually suggests a willingness to delegate power as well as share some decisional responsibility.

Another factor concerns the political benefit that the vice presidential nominee brings to the ticket. In the past, the vice presidential nominee has been selected primarily to provide geographic or ideological balance. Occasionally, demographic variables are also considered such as gender and age. John Kerry had geography in mind when he chose John Edwards, a southerner, as his running mate. He also saw Edwards as a powerful speaker who would excite the Democratic base.

Bill Clinton broke with tradition in 1992 when he chose a fellow southerner and moderate, Al Gore, to reinforce the New Democrat image that Clinton wanted to project to the American people. George W. Bush's selection of Dick Cheney—a former White House chief of staff, representative from Wyoming, member of the Republican House leadership, and defense secretary in his father's administration—brought experience, particularly in national security affairs, to the ticket, which Bush initially lacked as a state governor. The choice of a governing mate, more than a running mate, also broke with tradition and suggested an enhanced vice presidency in a Bush administration.

Because so much media attention is directed toward the vice presidential selection, nominees and their advisers try to keep their decisions secret for as long as possible. They want to create a situation in which the announcement can be made with as much hoopla and favorable commentary as can be mustered. In the words of Kerry's Communications Director, Stephanie Cutter, "We saw the V.P. roll out as the first big opportunity to generate national news coverage in a way that would continue to fill out Kerry's biography, put excitement behind the campaign, and introduce the new team for the new America . . ."[14]

The preoccupation with surprise, however, has often precluded adequate screening of the candidates for fear that the news media will find out the identity of the prospective choice before the presidential candidate announces it.

The worse case scenario of this charade occurred in 1972 when George McGovern selected Thomas Eagleton, a senator from Missouri, as his running mate. Although he had spoken with the Democratic governor of the state, the senator himself, and the Missouri press, McGovern had not been informed of Eagleton's hospitalization for depression and the shock treatments he received for it at the Mayo Clinic.[15] When this information was revealed by the news media, McGovern was caught in a dilemma—he could admit he made a mistake and drop Eagleton from the ticket, looking weak and perhaps mean-spirited in the process, or he could indicate that it wasn't a mistake and stick with him. Initially, McGovern chose the latter strategy. However, when medical authorities suggested that the malady was serious and too risky for a person who might become president, McGovern was forced to drop him and select another person.

George H. W. Bush faced a similar dilemma in 1988. Although he had chosen Indiana senator, Dan Quayle, in part because he wanted a person who could appeal to the next generation of voters, Bush was unaware of Quayle's mediocre record as a student or his family's help in getting him an appointment in the Indiana National Guard, which lessened the possibility of active duty service during the Vietnam War. Bush, who had been accused of being a "wimp," felt he could not back off when the going got tough. He stayed with

Quayle and won. George W. Bush and John Kerry did not face similar situations, though they too kept their choices to themselves until they were ready to make their public announcements.

In addition to the vice presidential selection, the prospective nominee also must oversee the planning for the national nominating convention. One objective is to avoid any problems, especially factional divisions that carry over from the primaries or are generated by a dispute over policy. A unified convention is viewed as the most successful way to launch a presidential campaign. Candidates and their handlers go to great lengths to orchestrate public events leading up to the convention. Nothing is left to chance.

Thus, George W. Bush let it be known in 2000 that he opposed changes to the traditional positions the party took in its platform so as not to alienate any group in the Republicans' core constituency and chose a running mate who was acceptable to all major party factions. Bush wanted an upbeat, people-oriented convention that emphasized positive imagery. As the poll leader going into the conventions, he and his staff did not want to rock the boat or break his momentum.

In 2004, Bush wanted to use the convention to launch his presidential campaign, present his second term agenda, and continue Republican criticism of the Democratic nominee. Kerry saw it as an opportunity to present his credentials for the presidency and his priorities if elected. Democrats decided that they wanted a positive convention, one that would convey optimism for the future. As a consequence, criticisms of Bush pertained to his policies not his character.

NATIONAL NOMINATING CONVENTIONS

National nominating conventions were at one time important decision-making bodies. They were used to decide on the party's nominees, platforms, and rules and procedures, as well as provide a podium for launching presidential campaigns. They also became an arena for settling internal party disputes, unifying the delegates, and getting ready for the general election campaign.

Today, however, they are not nearly as important or as newsworthy. They are theater, pure and simple. They are orchestrated for television and designed to present a picture of a cohesive and energized party that enthusiastically supports its nominees and its platform and optimistically launches its presidential campaign.

THE POLITICS OF CONVENTIONS PAST

Early conventions were brokered by party leaders who exercised considerable influence over the selection and actions of their state delegations. The leaders debated among themselves, formed coalitions, and fought for particular candidates and over credentials, rules, and platform planks. These internal disputes occurred within committees that were charged with credentialing the delegates, establishing the rules by which the convention would be governed, and drafting the platform on which the party would stand in the general election.

Twice in the twentieth century, Republican conventions were the scene of major credential challenges that ultimately determined the nominees. William Howard Taft's victory over Theodore Roosevelt in 1912 and Dwight Eisenhower's victory over Robert Taft in 1952 followed from convention decisions to seat certain delegates and reject others.[16]

Rules fights have also been surrogate disputes over the selection of the nominees. Until 1936, the Democrats operated under a rule that required a two-thirds vote for winning the nomination. James K. Polk's selection in 1844 was a consequence of Martin Van Buren's failure to obtain the support of two-thirds of the convention, although Van Buren had a majority. The two-thirds rule in effect permitted a minority of the delegates to veto a person they opposed.

In general, most convention rules are accepted without controversy. The most recent rules controversy occurred at the 1980 Democratic convention. At issue was a proposed requirement that delegates vote for the candidate to whom they were publicly pledged at the time they were chosen. Trailing Jimmy Carter by about 600 delegates, Ted Kennedy, who had previously supported this requirement, urged an open convention in which delegates could vote their consciences rather than merely exercise their commitments. Naturally, the Carter organization favored the pledged delegate rule and lobbied strenuously and successfully for it. Subsequently, the Democrats modified the rule. Today, delegates must reflect in good conscience the sentiments of those who elected them.[17]

The Democrats had a major policy dispute in 1948 that led to a walkout of delegates from several southern states. At issue was the party's stance in support of civil rights, a stand that the delegates from the southern states opposed. When they were unable to get the convention to change its position, several of the southern delegations left the convention and backed the States' Rights candidacy of Strom Thurmond for president. In 1964, Republican delegates fought over proposed amendments opposing extremism and favoring a stronger position on civil rights, amendments that delegates supporting Barry Goldwater defeated. The 1968 Democratic convention witnessed an emotional four-hour debate on U.S. policy in Vietnam. Although the convention voted to sustain the majority's position, which had the approval of President Johnson, the discussion, carried on television, reinforced the image of a divided party to millions of home viewers.

Before the choice of the nominee was dictated by the results of the caucuses and primaries, the delegates had to make that decision themselves by voting on the convention floor. Sometimes agreeing on a nominee took several votes. In 1924, Democratic delegates cast 103 ballots before they agreed on John W. Davis and Charles W. Bryan as their nominees; in 1932, they took four roll calls before obtaining the two-thirds vote they needed to nominate Franklin Roosevelt. After the two-thirds rule was changed to a simple majority, the Democratic conventions had much less difficulty agreeing on its nominees. In fact, the only other Democratic convention that took more than one ballot was in 1952 when it took three votes to nominate Adlai Stevenson. In 1940, Republican Wendell Willkie was selected on the eighth ballot, breaking a deadlock among Thomas Dewey, Arthur Vandenberg, and Willkie himself. Eight years later, Dewey was nominated on the third ballot.

Today a first ballot nomination is preordained by the results of the caucuses and primaries. There are few disputes that make it to the convention floor since the winning candidate controls a majority of the delegates. The objective is theatrical; the internal politics have already been settled.

CONTEMPORARY CONVENTIONS

Modern conventions are made-for-television productions. They are designed and organized by convention planners months before they are scheduled. And there is much to plan and orchestrate.

Size, Site, and Structure

Contemporary conventions are large and well orchestrated. The number of participants runs into the thousands. In 2004, the Republicans had 2,509 delegates and 2,344 alternates, while the Democrats had 4,319 delegates, some casting fractions of a vote, and 610 alternates. The 2008 conventions will be of similar size.

The demographic composition of the delegates tends to reflect their electoral constituencies. When the candidates for the nomination compose their slates of delegates, they try to balance the slates so as to achieve broad representation. Democratic rules require an even gender division. Republican rules do not. Nonetheless, the GOP has increased the proportion of women at its nominating conventions. In 2004, 44 percent of the Republican delegates were women.

Ethnic and racial minorities comprise a large part of the Democrats' electoral coalition. Almost 40 percent of the Democratic delegates in 2004 were minorities compared to 17 percent for the Republicans.[18] On the other hand, the Republicans, which usually benefit from the vote of active duty military and veterans, had a larger percent of veteran and military reservists (18 percent) than did the Democrats (11.5 percent).[19]

Although the convention is planned by representatives of the winning candidates, preliminary decisions, such as where to hold it and who should run it, are made by the party's national committee, usually on the recommendation of its chair and appropriate convention committees. An incumbent president normally exercises considerable influence over many of these decisions: the choice of a convention city, the selection of temporary and permanent convention officials, and the designation of the principal speakers. In choosing a site, many factors are considered: the size, configuration, and condition of the convention hall, transportation to and from it, financial inducements, the political climate, the geographic area, and the cultural ambiance of the city itself. For example, when detailing its logistic requirements for the party's

2008 convention, the Democrats asked cities bidding for the convention for 17,000 hotel rooms, 125 air-conditioned buses, and control over the convention site for a 3-month period, preceding and following the meetings. Security is also a factor.

Conventions are very costly. The federal government provides a grant to the major parties to hold their annual meetings. In 2004, that grant totaled $15 million, but that is only a drop in the bucket; it will be over $16 million in 2008. Local authorities contribute to nonadministrative costs, construction, transportation, and security. The rest comes from private donations. The Democrats raised an additional $36 million for their convention in Boston, and the Republicans raised an additional $53 million for theirs in New York in 2004.[20] They both will raise millions again in 2008.

Private donors who give large contributions receive a variety of convention-related perks from deluxe hotel suites, to box seats at the convention, to invitations to meet with the candidates and party leaders, to tickets to the receptions and other events. Major corporations and associations, whose lobbyists are frequently in attendance, provide transportation, food, and entertainment. It is a big party for the delegates, party leaders and elected officials, and the generous donors.

The delegates also spend a lot of money, which is a principal reason that cities bid to hold the meetings. The cities chosen to host the 2008 conventions are Denver for the Democrats and Minneapolis-St. Paul for the Republicans.

Timing is also important. Parties want to attract as large an audience as possible. Conventions have to be scheduled so as not to compete with other major events, such as the summer Olympics, or the traditional Labor Day holiday. Holding a convention last may be a financial advantage (as it was in 2004) for candidates who accept federal funds for the general election but not for the nomination period. It provides more time for spending private funds and less for spending limited public funds. Finally, candidates want to use the convention as a springboard to their general election campaign. Scheduling the convention at the end of the summer permits the campaign to follow without much interruption; holding it early may not. Thus, the Democrats chose to set their 2008 convention dates at the end of August (25–28); the Republicans decided to hold theirs even later (September 1–4).

Conventions have become faster paced and more varied than in the past, primarily to keep their viewing audience as long as possible. From the standpoint of the parties' convention planners, the more cogent the message and the more entertaining the proceedings, the more likely the convention will have a positive impact on the voters. Obviously, the press has a different objective and perspective.

Both the Democrats and the Republicans have traditionally turned to national party leaders to top positions. Governor Bill Richardson of New Mexico was the Democratic convention chair in 2004 and political activist, Ed Gillespie, was the Republican convention chair that year. The technicalities of scripting and staging the event are left to entertainment professionals, media consultants, pollsters, and party officials with national campaign experience.

Stimulus, Style, and Substance

Modern day conventions entertain, inform, and provide opportunities for party leaders to gain media attention; present the policy positions for which the party stands in its platform; and anoint their presidential and vice presidential candidates by formally nominating them. Ritual surrounds each of these functions.

Entertainment, Information, and Exposure   Conventions are full of speeches. Some of political oratory has been very powerful, occasionally eloquent, and almost always emotive, designed to "turn on" the delegates and their partisan brethren who are watching. The substance of the oratory is also readily predictable. The speakers trumpet the achievements of their party, eulogizing their leaders and criticizing, often harshly, their opponents. They also reinforce and validate the ideology and policy positions associated with their party by attributing the country's prosperity to these policies and its problems to their opponents'.

Most of the conventions are scripted. Speeches are usually written or approved by the top advisers for the nominee. Each of the four days of the meetings has an overall theme; the speakers are chosen with this theme in mind. They are also selected to reward politicians, including primary and caucus opponents, for their pledge of supporting the winning ticket, to acknowledge the elected leaders of the party and give them an opportunity to shine in the spotlight, and to provide a build-up to the climax, the nomination of the presidential and vice presidential candidates and their respective acceptance speeches.

In past conventions, there used to be a keynote address, which occurred early in the convention and was intended to unify the delegates, smoothing over any divisions that may have emerged during the preconvention campaign, and rouse them and the public for the forthcoming election.[21]

Recent conventions have not designated keynote speakers, but they have engaged in the usual criticism and praise that rouses the faithful and informs the public. In 2004, former Presidents Jimmy Carter and Bill Clinton and the party's 2000 presidential candidate, Al Gore, addressed the Democratic convention. They were put on the first day to bookmark the convention, beginning with its past leaders and ending with its 2004 nominee, John Kerry. Naturally, the Democrats, particularly the two ex-presidents, compared their successes with the failures of the current Republican administration. Carter was particularly critical of President Bush and his foreign policy. He said: "In the world at large, we cannot lead if our leaders mislead."[22] Clinton engaged his convention and television audience by praising Democratic nominee, John Kerry, and criticizing the Republicans for concentrating power and wealth in those who embraced their views, "leaving ordinary citizens to fend for themselves on important matters like health care and retirement security."[23]

Clinton's "rich person–average American" theme is one the Democrats have used repeatedly to emphasize the stereotype by which they label the Republicans and their nominees. In 1984, Governor Mario Cuomo of New York sounded a similar theme in his keynote address. Describing the United States as a tale of two cities, he chided the Reagan administration for pursuing policies that benefited the rich at the expense of the poor. In a folksy and humorous address at the 1988 Democratic convention, Ann Richards, then treasurer of Texas, ridiculed George H. W. Bush for being aloof, insensitive, and uncaring. She concluded sarcastically, "he can't help it. He was born with a silver foot in his mouth."[24] Richards's comment irritated George W. Bush, so much so, that he later resolved to run against her for governor, a race that he won.[25]

Speakers at the Republican convention have been equally dismissive of the Democrats and their candidates. In 2004, the GOP chose as one of its principal speakers, Zell Miller, former Democratic governor and senator from Georgia who had nominated Clinton in 1992. Miller lit into the Democratic Party "for its warped way of thinking" and Kerry for having weakened the military by his votes as a senator.[26] Vice President Dick Cheney was also extremely critical of Kerry's position on the war in Iraq. "Senator Kerry denounces American action when other countries don't approve, as if the whole object of our foreign policy were to please a few persistent critics," adding, "George W. Bush will never seek a permission slip to defend the American people."[27]

Amid the oratory of both conventions, delegates are shown movies, hear bands, and are given plenty of opportunity to applaud the speakers and shout their support. Within contemporary conventions, there are few unscripted events. Speakers that are deemed potentially controversial, such as Democrats Al Sharpton and Howard Dean were in 2004, are frequently scheduled early in the day's festivities before the broadcast networks began their prime time telecasts. Since that coverage has been limited in the past two conventions, some of the major addresses are not available on the broadcast networks, thereby reducing the size of the audience that watches them.[28]

Much of the convention is ritual and carefully orchestrated, but occasionally embarrassing incidents can and do occur.[29] Take the time in 1956 when Vice President Richard Nixon was to be renominated by the Republicans. Nixon was expected to be the unanimous choice after a movement to dump him from the ticket failed. When the roll of states was called for nominations, a delegate from Nebraska grabbed the microphone and said he had a nomination to make. "Who?" said a surprised Joseph Martin, chair of the convention, at this deviation from the script. "Joe Smith," the delegate replied. Martin did not permit the name of Joe Smith to be placed in nomination, although the Democrats were later to contend that any Joe Smith would have been better than Nixon.

It has become customary in recent conventions for the nominees' wives to speak, usually introducing their spouse as Elizabeth Dole and Hillary Clinton did in 1996, and Laura Bush and Tipper Gore in 2000. In 2004, Teresa Heinz

BOX 6.2	2004 CONVENTION THEMES AND SPEAKERS

Day 1	Day 2	Day 3	Day 4
Democratic Convention			
The Kerry-Edwards Plan for America's Future	A Lifetime of Strength and Service	Politics of Hope	Stronger at Home, Respect in the World
Jimmy Carter	Howard Dean	Jesse Jackson	Wes Clark
Al Gore	Teresa Heinz Kerry	Al Sharpton	Nancy Pelosi
Hillary and Bill Clinton	Barack Obama	Elizabeth and John Edwards	John Kerry
Republican Convention			
A Nation of Courage	People of Compassion	Land of Opportunity	A Safer and More Hopeful America
John McCain	Bill Frist	Mitt Romney	Tommy Franks
Rudolph Giuliani	Laura Bush	Zell Miller	George Pataki
	Arnold Schwarzenegger	Richard Cheney	George W. Bush

Kerry and Laura Bush spoke earlier in the proceedings. Box 6.2, "2004 Convention Themes and Speakers," lists the themes and major speakers at the 2004 Democratic and Republican nominating conventions.

Drafting a Platform   In addition to the speeches, color, and other ritual, conventions must approve the party's platform, which is a collective statement of the party's principal positions and agenda for the fall campaign. Contrary to popular belief, platforms are important even though few people read them in their entirety or know what is in them. They are important because they help shape the agenda for the government if the party is successful and wins control of Congress and the presidency.

   Political scientists have found that elected officials of both parties have a relatively good record of trying to redeem their campaign promises and platform planks. Although approximately three-quarters of party platforms contain high-sounding rhetoric and lofty goals, about one-fourth of them are fairly specific policy pledges. Of these, the majority have been proposed as laws or implemented as executive actions.[30] Party leaders in government follow through on their platform's promises because they believe in them personally, they want to maintain the cohesion of their electoral coalition, and many of them have been on the committee that drafted the platform or testified before it. Similarly, in all likelihood, the successful presidential candidate approved of the draft in committee before it was presented to the convention for ratification.

Party platforms also differ from one another, more now than in the past. In an examination of the Democratic and Republican platforms between 1944 and 1976, political scientist Gerald Pomper found that most of the differences were evident in the planks incorporated by one party but not by the other.[31]

Contemporary platforms have become more detailed and policy specific. Drafted with the party's electoral coalition in mind, they tend to have something for every relevant group. They also reflect the ideological differences that have come to divide Democrats and Republicans in recent decades. Box 6.3 "Excerpts from the 2004 Republican and Democratic Platforms," contrasts the 2004 Republican and Democratic Party platforms.

NOMINATING AND PRESENTING THE PRESIDENTIAL AND VICE PRESIDENTIAL CANDIDATES TO THE AMERICAN PEOPLE

The purpose and climatic end of the convention is to nominate the candidates and give them the opportunity to be seen and heard by the delegates, and most importantly, the electorate. Since the presidential nominees have been pre-ordained by the caucuses and primaries and known for many months by the public, and the choices for vice president have also been publicized, the most important purpose of the convention is to give the candidates a national podium to be seen and heard, to present themselves and their policy agendas to the country. Contemporary conventions try to maximize this exposure by separating the presidential and vice presidential addresses and building up to the acceptance speech by the presidential nominee.

In early conventions, it was customary for delegates simply to rise and place the name of a candidate in nomination without a formal speech. Gradually, the practice of nominating became more elaborate. Speeches were lengthened. Ritual required that the virtues of the candidate first be extolled before the candidate's identity was revealed. Today, with public speculation beginning months before and the selection of the nominee a foregone conclusion, the practice of withholding the name has been abandoned.

The custom of giving acceptance speeches by the presidential standard-bearers began in 1932 by Franklin Roosevelt. Before that time, conventions designated committees to inform the presidential and vice presidential nominees of their decisions. Journeying to the candidate's home, the committees would announce the selection in a public ceremony. The nominee, in turn, would accept in a speech stating his positions on the major issues of the day. The last major party candidate to be told of the nomination in this fashion was Republican Wendell Willkie in 1940.

Today, acceptance speeches are both a call to the faithful and an address to the country. They articulate the principal themes for the general election and the priorities the nominee attaches to them. They also provide insight into the qualifications of the party's presidential candidate.

BOX 6.3	EXCERPTS FROM THE 2004 REPUBLICAN AND DEMOCRATIC PLATFORMS

REPUBLICANS

DEMOCRATS

Foreign Policy: Iraq

As Republicans, we do not equivocate, as others have done about whether America should have gone to war in Iraq. . . . Our nation did the right thing, and the American people are now safer because we and our allies ended the brutal dictatorship of Saddam Hussein, halting his decades-long pursuit of chemical, biological, and nuclear weapons. President Bush had a choice to make: Trust a madman or defend America. He chose defending America.

This Administration badly exaggerated its case, particularly with respect to weapons of mass destruction and the connection between Saddam's government and al Qaeda. This Administration did not build a true international coalition, . . . disdained the U.N. weapons inspection process, and rushed to war without exhausting diplomatic alternatives, . . . did not send sufficient forces . . . , and . . . went into Iraq without a plan to win the peace.

War on Terrorism

The freedom we enjoy also makes us vulnerable to attack. Since September 11, 2001, President Bush, Vice President Cheney, the Congress, and governors across the country have taken significant steps to streamline the federal government to make it more effective at combating terrorism; tighten security at entry points like ports, airports, and borders; strengthen protections at critical infrastructures; and reduce the threats of bioterrorism and cyberterrorism.

Despite his tough talk, President Bush's actions against terrorism have fallen far short. He still has no comprehensive strategy for victory. . . . We must put in place a strategy to win—an approach that recognizes and addresses the many facets of this moral challenge, from the terrorists themselves to the root causes that gives rise to new recruits, and use all the tools at our disposal.

Taxes, Jobs, Economics

George W. Bush ran for President on a promise of lower taxes, so that people could keep more of the income they earned. He fulfilled that pledge. This year, 43 million families with children are receiving an average tax cut of $2,000. . . . Our Party endorses the President's proposals to make tax relief permanent. . . . We believe that good government is based on a system of limited taxes and spending. . . . The taxation system should not be used to redistribute wealth or fund ever-increasing entitlements and social programs.

We offer America a new economic plan that will put jobs first: tax reform to create jobs, a plan to reinvigorate manufacturing, and free and fair trade. . . . President Bush and the Republicans in Congress have ignored the middle class. . . . They have catered to the wealth of the richest instead of honoring the work of the rest of us. . . . We will cut taxes for 98 percent of Americans. . . . We must restore responsibility to our budget, or we will strangle opportunity for the next generation of middle-class Americans.

(continued)

| BOX 6.3 | EXCERPTS FROM THE 2004 REPUBLICAN AND DEMOCRATIC PLATFORMS *continued* |

REPUBLICANS

DEMOCRATS

Education

No Child Left Behind . . . was the most significant overhaul of federal education since 1965. . . . With this success, Republicans have transformed the debate on education. We have challenged low expectations and poor achievement, and we are seeing results. Now is the time to extend the progress we've made. . . . To take the reforms that we know are working in elementary schools and apply them up and down the education ladder—starting in early childhood education. . . . and finishing in high school.

In President Bush's America, our government ignores the shameful truth that the quality of a child's education depends on the wealth of that child's neighborhood. . . . Vast achievement gaps persist in America. Nearly half of African-American, Latino, and American Indian youth don't graduate high school. . . . We will expand and improve preschool and Head Start initiatives. . . . And we will undertake a national campaign to raise graduation rates by raising student achievement, expecting more from our schools, reaching out to troubled youth with mentoring and tutoring, and strengthening the basic high school curriculum.

Health Care

We must attack the root caucuses of high health care costs by: aiding small business in offering health care to their employees; empowering the self-employed through access to affordable coverage; putting patients and doctors in charge of medical decisions; reducing junk lawsuits and limiting punitive damage awards that raise the costs of health care; and seizing the cost-saving and quality-enhancing potential of emerging health technologies. It is also important that we reaffirm our Party's firm rejection of any measure aimed at making health care a government-run enterprise.

We believe that health care is a right not a privilege . . . Our goal is straightforward: quality, affordable health coverage for all Americans. . . . We will strength Medicaid for our families and expand the children's health care program created under President Clinton . . . we will offer individuals and business tax credits to make quality, reliable health coverage more affordable. At the center of our efforts will be a plan to reduce health costs.

Social Security

Social Security needs to be strengthened and enhanced for our children and grandchildren. . . . Personal retirement accounts must be the cornerstone of strengthening and enhancing Social Security.

We are absolutely committed to preserving Social Security. We oppose privatizing Social Security or raising the retirement age. We oppose reducing the benefits earned by workers just because they have earned a benefit from certain retirement plans.

REPUBLICANS	DEMOCRATS

Environment

Republicans know that economic prosperity is essential to environmental progress. Thanks to President Bush's strong leadership and the commitment of Congressional Republicans to reform and innovation, air pollution has been reduced, water quality has been improved, wetlands have been restored, and more than a thousand brownfield sites are being revitalized. . . . Our President and our Party strongly oppose the Kyoto Protocol and similar mandatory carbon emissions controls that harm economic growth and destroy American jobs.

. . . in President George Bush's government, where polluters actually write environmental laws and oil company profits matter more than hard science and cold facts, protecting the environment doesn't matter at all. We will make our air cleaner and our water purer. . . . We will foster a healthy economy and a healthy environment by promoting new technologies. . . . We reject the false choice between a healthy economy and a healthy environment.

Abortion

The unborn child has a fundamental individual right to life that cannot be infringed. We support a human life amendment to the Constitution. . . . We oppose public revenues for abortion and will not fund organizations that advocate it. We support the appointment of judges who respect traditional family values and the sanctity of innocent human life.

Because we believe in the privacy and equality of women, we stand proudly for a woman's right to choose, consistent with Roe v. Wade, and regardless of her ability to pay. We stand strongly against Republican efforts to undermine that right. . . . Abortion should be safe, legal, and rare.

Guns

Republicans and President Bush strongly support an individual's right to own guns . . . We applaud Congressional Republicans for seeking to stop frivolous lawsuits against firearms manufacturers, which is a transparent attempt to deprive citizens of their Second Amendment rights.

We will protect Americans' Second Amendment right to own firearms, and we will keep guns out of the hands of criminals and terrorists by fighting gun crime, reauthorizing the assault weapons ban, and closing the gun show loophole . . .

Marriage

We strongly support President Bush's call for a Constitutional amendment that fully protects marriage, and we believe that neither federal nor state judges nor bureaucrats should force states to recognize other living arrangements as equivalent to marriage . . .

In our country, marriage has been defined at the state level for 200 years, and we believe that it should continue to be defined there. We repudiate President Bush's divisive effort to politicize the Constitution by pursuing a "Federal Marriage Amendment." Our goal is to bring Americans together, not to drive them apart.

Source: Adapted from the 2004 Republican and Democratic Party platforms, http://www.nc.org/2004/2004 platformcontents and www.dems2004.com/AboutTheConvention.html

Harry Truman's speech to the Democratic convention in 1948 is frequently cited as one that helped to fire up the party. Truman chided the Republicans for obstructing and ultimately rejecting many of his legislative proposals and then adopting a party platform that called for some of the same social and economic goals. He electrified the Democratic convention by challenging the Republicans to live up to their convention promises and pass legislation to achieve these goals in a special session of Congress that he announced he was calling. When the Republican-controlled Congress failed to enact that legislation, Truman was able to pin a "do-nothing" label on it and make that label the basic theme of his successful presidential campaign.

In 1984, Democratic candidate Walter Mondale made a mammoth political blunder in his acceptance speech. Warning the delegates about the U.S. budget deficit that had increased dramatically during Reagan's first term, Democrat Mondale said that he would do something about it if he were elected president: "Let's tell the truth. Mr. Reagan will raise taxes, and so will I. He won't tell you. I just did." Democratic delegates cheered his candor, directness, and boldness; the public did not. He and his party were saddled with the tax issue throughout the *entire* campaign.

The 2004 acceptance addresses continued the practice of reiterating themes, emphasizing priorities, and illustrating character. John Kerry listed his goals as "Make America stronger and respected in the world" and "Restore trust and credibility to the White House." He promised to achieve these goals by increasing the size of the military, involving more of America's allies to share the burden of maintaining peace and security, investing in new technologies, improving health care, and strengthening, not privatizing Social Security.

To emphasize his own military service in Vietnam and his patriotism, Kerry began his remarks by saying, "I'm John Kerry, and I'm reporting for duty." He saluted, surrounded by Vietnam veterans, and the delegates roared. His emphasis on his Vietnam experience at the expense of other traits such as empathy, humor, even personal charm, proved in retrospect to be a mixed blessing after a Republican group, Swift Boat Veterans for Truth, disputed his record of service in Vietnam and pointed to his antiwar protests after leaving active duty.

President Bush pointed to his administration's achievements in education, Medicare, and the war on terrorism. He reiterated his domestic policies of simplifying the tax code and making his first term tax cuts permanent, increasing job training, partially privatizing Social Security, and remaining vigilant in the war on terrorism. He also stressed his support for the protection of marriage as a union between a man and a woman. In contrast to Kerry, Bush entered the convention from the back of the stage and walked toward the delegates and to the podium alone, suggesting that in the end it is the president and the president alone who must make the critical decisions.[32]

News Media Coverage of Political Conventions

Political conventions used to be major newsworthy events. Radio began covering national conventions in 1924 and television in 1956. Because conventions in the 1950s were interesting unpredictable events in which important political decisions were made, they attracted a large audience, one that increased rapidly as the number of households having television sets expanded. During the 1950s and 1960s, about 25 percent of the potential viewers watched the conventions, with the numbers swelling to 50 percent during the most significant part of the meetings.

The sizable audience made conventions important for fledgling television news organizations, which were beginning to rival newspapers for news reporting. Initially, the three major networks provided almost gavel-to-gavel coverage. They focused on the official events, that is, what went on at the podium. Commentary was kept to a minimum.

The changes in the delegate selection process that began in the 1970s had a major impact on the amount and type of television coverage as well as the size of the viewing audience. As the decision-making capabilities of conventions declined, their newsworthiness decreased, as did the proportion of households that tuned in and the amount of time spent watching them.

With the exception of the public broadcasting system (PBS), the major broadcast networks (ABC, CBS, and NBC) subsequently reduced their coverage. In 1992, they covered each of the conventions for a total of fifteen hours; in 1996, they reduced that coverage to twelve hours; in 2000, they covered eight and a half hours; and in 2004, it was just three hours each.[33]

Despite the practice of the 24-7 cable news channels and C-span to cover most of the convention proceedings, the proportion of Americans watching them has declined.[34] The Democratic convention had an audience size of 20.4 million in 2004 compared to 22.6 million for the Republicans. Only about 30 percent of households with televisions tuned in to them, and many of those who did, did so inadvertently for short periods of time.[35]

Since conventions are less newsworthy—a primary reason why a smaller proportion of Americans watch them—the reporters who cover the conventions have to search for news. Television cameras constantly scan the floor for dramatic events and human-interest stories. Delegates are pictured talking, eating, sleeping, parading, even watching the convention on television. Interviews with prominent party leaders and elected officials, rank-and-file delegates, and family and friends of the candidate are interspersed with the speeches, convention movies, and of course, the breaks for advertising.

To provide a balanced presentation, supporters and opponents are frequently juxtaposed. To maintain the audience's attention, the interviews are kept short, usually focusing on reactions to actual or potential political problems. There are also endless commentary, prognostications, and forecasts of how the convention is likely to affect voters and their decisions on election day.

When the conventions are over, however, they are rarely mentioned in the reporting of the campaign, although clips from convention highlights, especially from the acceptance speeches of the nominees, reappear in their advertising.

Coverage inside the convention is supplemented by coverage outside the hall. Knowing this, groups come to the convention city to air grievances and to protest. The most violent of these political demonstrations occurred in 1968 in Chicago, the city where the Democratic Party was meeting. Thousands of people, many of them students, marched through the streets and parks protesting U.S. military involvement in the Vietnam War. Police set up barricades, blocking, beating, and arresting many of the protestors. Claiming that the events were newsworthy, the broadcast networks broke away from their convention coverage to report on these activities and show tapes of the bloody confrontation between police and protestors. Critics charged that the presence of television cameras incited the demonstrators and that coverage was disproportional and distracted from the proceedings. In response, one network, CBS, reported that it had devoted only thirty-two minutes to these events out of its thirty-eight hours of convention coverage.[36]

At subsequent conventions, protests have occurred but have not received as much attention by the mainstream press. Even though there were some demonstrators in Boston and thousands in New York during the 2004 conventions, they received minimal attention and did not disturb the proceedings in either convention. Only alternative radio gave them substantial coverage.

The news media's orientation, which highlights conflict, drama, and human interest, obviously clashes with the party leadership's desire to present a united and enthusiastic front to launch their presidential campaigns. The clash between these two conflicting goals has resulted in a classic struggle for control between the news media and politicians. The convention managers have been more successful in orchestrating their meetings to achieve their objectives, which is a principal reason for the decline in broadcast news coverage.

Surveys conducted by the Annenberg Public Policy Center and The Joan Shorenstein Center on the Press, Politics, and Public Policy following the national party conventions in 2000 and 2004 found about half the television audience during the period when the conventions were in session indicated that they did not see any of the proceedings.[37] Of those who did watch some portion of them, the majority of these viewers said that they came upon the conventions while channel surfing, and for the most part, watched for only a few minutes.[38]

The surveys also reveal that convention watching varies with age. Those over fifty are much more likely to tune in for an hour or more than those twenty-nine and under. The Shorenstein Center reported that most of the young people who watch conventions do so inadvertently as compared with only half of those older than thirty.[39] Partisans watched their own convention more than the opposition's convention.[40]

Party officials, concerned with the declining participation and interest of young people in partisan national politics, created Web sites to attract the next generation of voters. They trumpeted the interactive character of their sites. In addition, thirty-five other Internet sites, dominated by news organizations, covered the conventions live. But "hits" on these news sites were down as well.[41]

In short, the big news of the 2000 and 2004 nominating conventions was that despite the increasing number of ways in which the electorate could follow them, despite each party's hype and public appeal, despite the news coverage of the conventions, more people did not watch them than did. Since conventions inform voters, the decline in the size of the audience watching them and the time during which they watch is an undesirable development for the candidates, the parties, and democratic elections.

Other than the presidential debates, the national party conventions provide the largest viewing audience for any election event. They also provide the most sustained period in which people can learn about the positions of the party and its nominees.

MINOR PARTY CONVENTIONS

Although the major parties get limited coverage on most of the broadcast networks, the minor party conventions get almost no coverage, not even on cable news networks. The absence of competition within most of these parties combined with the improbability of their candidates winning the election or even affecting its outcome explain the low visibility given to these events. The one exception was the Reform Party's conventions in 1996 and 2000, which received some coverage from the cable news and public affairs networks. The broadcast networks covered these conventions as items on their news shows.

H. Ross Perot, the party's founder and financial backer, had much to do with getting coverage in 1996, whereas the attraction in 2000 was the battle between supporters and opponents of Pat Buchanan, the former Republican who left that party to run as the Reform candidate.

In 1996, the Reform Party held a two-stage convention. At the first stage of the nomination process, Perot and his opponent, former Governor Richard D. Lamm of Colorado, were given an opportunity to address the assembled delegates. During the next week, partisans voted by regular mail or e-mail with the results announced at the second convention, which also provided another opportunity for the winning candidate, Perot, to announce his vice presidential selection and make his acceptance speech.

In 2000, there was also a mail ballot as well as a convention vote, but it was the organizational battle over Buchanan's candidacy in the months leading up to the convention that attracted media attention. The hard-ball tactics that Buchanan's supporters employed to oust state party officials who opposed his candidacy created deep divisions within the party and ultimately led to a walkout by delegates hostile to Buchanan. These angry delegates proceeded to hold their own convention, nominate their own candidates, and claim the Reform Party label as theirs, while Buchanan's backers nominated him as their Reform Party candidate. The dispute ended up in the courts that had to decide which of these two sets of candidates should be listed as the Reform nominees for 2000. Similarly, the Federal Election Commission had to determine which of them was entitled to the $12.6 million the party was to receive on the basis of Perot's 1996 vote. The commission chose Buchanan. Buchanan did not run in 2004, and the party's convention drew very little public attention.

The other minor party that received some national coverage in 2000 was the Green Party, which nominated consumer advocate and anticorporate crusader Ralph Nader. Holding its convention in June before those of the Republicans and Democrats, the Green Party gained coverage by virtue of

Nader's reputation as an outspoken critic of corporate America and special interest politics as well as early polls, which indicated that his candidacy could make a difference in the outcome of the Bush–Gore contest. In other words, Nader provided the party with visibility, and the party gave him a pulpit from which to articulate his beliefs. Nader did not receive the Green Party nomination four years later. He ran as an independent and also received the endorsement of the Reform party, which got him on the ballot in seven states, including Florida where he had won over 97,000 votes in 2000.[42]

ASSESSING CONTEMPORARY CONVENTIONS' IMPACT ON VIEWERS AND VOTERS

Do national nominating conventions have an impact on the election? Most observers believe that they do. Why else would the major parties devote so much time, money, and effort to these events? Why else would party leaders and academics concerned with civic education bemoan the reduction of convention coverage by the broadcast networks? Why else would the parties conduct focus groups, consult poll data, and even tally hits on their convention Web sites and monitor e-mail responses? And why else would people watch them when they know the identity of the nominees and have a general sense of the parties' political stands?

Political scientists also believe that conventions matter. They have hypothesized that there is a relationship between convention unity and electoral success. Since 1968, the party that appears to have had the most harmonious convention has emerged victorious. It is difficult, however, to say how much or even whether the unity contributed to the result or simply reflected the partisan environment that fostered that particular outcome.

In the short run, conventions almost always boost the popularity of their nominees and decrease that of their general election opponents. This boost is referred to as the convention "bounce," which tends to average about a 6 percent gain in the public opinion polls. The only recent nominees who did not get a bounce were George McGovern in 1972 and John Kerry in 2004. Kerry actually dropped 1 percent in the polls (2 percent among likely voters); in contrast, George W. Bush received a 2-percent bounce in 2004.[43] Table 6.2 indicates the bounces that nominating conventions since 1960 have given their party's nominees. Bounces, however, can be short-lived as President Bush discovered in 1992, Robert Dole in 1996, and George W. Bush in 2000.

The importance of conventions for the nominees is that they allow them to define themselves before a large audience. Thus, candidates such as George H. W. Bush and Al Gore, both vice presidents who were seen largely in the shadows of the more charismatic presidents with whom they served, finally had the opportunity to shine alone, and they did, albeit briefly. Self-definitions, however, are more important for challengers for whom less is known than incumbent presidents or even vice presidents running for the top position.

(continued)

TABLE 6.2 | CONVENTION BOUNCES, 1968–2004

	Candidates (winner)	Last Poll Before First Convention	Poll After First Convention (Challenger/Party)	Bounce for Challenger	Last Poll Before Second Convention	Poll After Second Convention (Incumbent/Party)	Bounce for Incumbent
1968	Nixon (R)	40	45	+5	NA	43	–
	Humphrey (D)	38	29	–	NA	31	+7
	Wallace (AI)	16	18	–	NA	19	–
1972	Nixon (R)	53	56	–	57	64	+7
	McGovern (D)	37	37	0	31	30	–
1976	Carter (D)	53	62	+9	57	50	–
	Ford (R)	36	29	–	32	37	+5
1980	Reagan (R)	37	45	+8	45	38	–
	Carter (D)	34	29	–	29	39	+10
	Anderson (I)	21	14	–	14	13	–
1984	Reagan (R)	53	46	–	52	56	+4
	Mondale (D)	39	48	+9	41	37	–
1988	Bush (R)	41	37	–	42	48	+6
	Dukakis (D)	47	54	+7	49	44	–
1992	Clinton (D)	40	56	+16	56	52	–
	Bush (R)	48	34	–	37	42	+5

TABLE 6.2 | CONTINUED

	Candidates (winner)	Last Poll Before First Convention	Poll After First Convention (Challenger/Party)	Bounce for Challenger	Last Poll Before Second Convention	Poll After Second Convention (Incumbent/Party)	Bounce for Incumbent
1996	Clinton (D)	52	48	–	50	55	+5
	Dole (R)	30	41	+11	38	34	–
	Perot	12	7	–	7	6	–
	Others/	6	5	–	2	5	–
	No Opinion	5	4	–	4	2	–
2000	Gore (D)	39	37	–	39	47	+8
	Bush (R)	50	54	+4	55	46	–
	Others/	6	5	–	2	5	–
	No Opinion	5	4	–	4	2	–
2004	Kerry	49	48	–1	48	48	–
	Bush	45	48	–	47	49	+2
	Others/ No Opinion	6	3	–	3	3	–

Source: Gallup Poll Data; David W. Moore, "Bush Bounce Keeps Going," Gallup Poll, September 17, 2004. http://www.Gallup.com/content/default.aspx?ci=13066&pg=1

The long-term impact is more difficult to measure. Nonetheless, political scientists have suggested three major effects of conventions on voters: (1) the conventions heighten interest, thereby increasing turnout; (2) they arouse latent feelings, thereby raising partisan awareness; (3) they color perceptions, thereby affecting personal judgments of the candidates and their issue stands.[44]

Each of these effects is supported by survey data taken before, during, and after recent conventions. The Shorenstein and Annenberg surveys found a substantial rise in public interest in the campaign immediately before, during, and after the Republican and Democratic conventions of 2000 and 2004 as well as more positive feelings toward the parties and their nominees.[45] As expected, partisans of each party respond more favorably during the week of their party's nominating convention.[46]

The reactions of partisans shore up support for their party's nominees, which is usually reflected in election polls conducted after the conventions.[47] They also provide viewers with information; for those who watched, the conventions help to clarify candidate images and policy positions.[48] In this way, they contribute to the knowledge necessary to making a more informed judgment.

The general public believes that they are important as well and that they learn about the candidates, issues, and parties from the conventions. A survey taken by the Shorenstein Center during the week of the 2004 Democratic Convention found that 40 percent of those surveyed said that they had learned a great deal or quite a bit compared to 23 percent who indicated that they had not learned much or anything about John Kerry from the convention.[49] These findings parallel those by the Annenberg Center that knowledge increases for those who watch the proceedings, particularly the candidate's acceptance speeches.[50] The Annenberg study concluded:

> The number of voters feeling they have learned enough about the candidates to make an informed choice continues to climb, albeit slowly. Whereas at the beginning of the year, only 20 percent felt they had learned enough, that number now stands at approximately 50 percent. The period of the conventions saw an increase of 10 percent in this figure.[51]

Researchers have also found that convention watchers tend to make their voting decisions earlier in the campaign.[52] Whether they make those decisions because they watch the convention or whether they watch the convention because they are more partisan and politically aware and have made or are making their voting decisions, is unclear, however. Nonetheless, a significant portion of the electorate claim that they decide for whom they will vote before or during the conventions. In 2004, that proportion was estimated at about two-thirds of the electorate.[53]

In short, conventions can have a powerful psychological impact on those who watch them for extended periods of time. They make viewers more inclined to follow the campaign after the convention is over and vote for their party's candidates. Conventions can energize participants. They can also have an organizational effect, fostering cooperation among the different and frequently competing groups within the party, encouraging them to submerge their differences and work toward a common goal.

CHARACTERISTICS OF THE NOMINEES

The nominations of relatively obscure governors by the Democrats in 1976, 1988, and 1992, and a former movie actor and California governor by the Republicans in 1980 indicate that changes in the preconvention process have affected the kind of people chosen by their parties. In theory, many are qualified. The Constitution prescribes only three formal criteria for the presidency: a minimum age of thirty-five, a fourteen-year residence in the United States, and native-born status. Naturalized citizens are not eligible for the office.

In practice, a number of informal qualifications have limited the pool of potential nominees. Successful candidates have usually been well known and active in politics, and have held high government positions. Of all the positions from which to seek the presidential nomination, the presidency is clearly the best. Only five incumbent presidents (three of whom were vice presidents who became president through the normal succession process) have failed in their quest for the nomination. It should be noted, however, that several others, such as Harry Truman and Lyndon Johnson, were persuaded to retire rather than face tough challenges.

Over the years, there have been a variety of paths to the White House. When the congressional caucus system was in operation, the position of secretary of state was regarded as a stepping-stone to the nomination if the incumbent chose not to seek another term. When national conventions replaced the congressional caucus, the Senate became the incubator for most successful presidential candidates. After the Civil War, governors emerged as the most likely contenders, particularly for the party that did not control the White House. Governors of large states possess a political base, a prestigious executive position, and leverage by virtue of their control over their delegations. They also have not been forced to take stands on as many controversial national issues as member of Congress must during their terms in office.[54] Today, the vice presidency is seen as a stepping-stone to the presidential nomination.

There are other informal criteria, although they have less to do with qualifications for office than with public prejudices over the years. Through 2004, only white males have ever been nominated for president by either of the major parties, although African Americans and women have sought the Democratic nomination. Until John F. Kennedy's election in 1960, no Catholic had been elected, although Governor Alfred E. Smith of New York was chosen by the Democrats in 1928 and John Kerry in 2004. Joseph Lieberman's selection as Al Gore's running mate is the first time a Jewish American has been nominated for that position. Michael Dukakis was the first candidate whose ancestry could not be traced to northern Europe, a surprising commentary on a country that has prided itself on its diversity for many years.

TABLE 6.3 | TOLERANCE IN VOTING FOR WOMEN AND MINORITIES FOR PRESIDENT

Generally speaking, do you think Americans are ready to elect a/an [RANDOM ORDER] as president, or not? (**in Percentages**)

	Gallup Poll (Sept. 2006)			Fox News/Opinion Dynamics Poll (Feb. 2007)		
	Ready	Not Ready	No Opp.	Ready	Not Ready	No Opp.
Woman	60	38	1	60	35	5
African American	58	40	2	69	24	7
Mormon	26	66	5	40	48	12
Gay or lesbian	7	91	2	13	82	5
Jew	55	42	3			
Hispanic	41	58	1			
Atheist	14	84	2			
Asian	33	64	2			
Twice Divorced				65	21	14

Source: Jeffrey M. Jones, "U.S. Ready for a Female President," October 3, 2006. www.gallup.com/content/ ?ci=24832&pg=1; Fox News/ Opinion Dynamics Poll, February 27–28, 2007 as reported in the Polling Report. www.pollingreport.com (accessed April 17, 2007).

The selection of a woman, Geraldine Ferraro, by the Democrats in 1984 for their vice presidential nomination, the candidacy of Elizabeth Dole for her party's 2000 presidential nomination, and the candidacy of Hillary Rodham Clinton in 2008 suggests that gender is much less of a barrier than it has been in the past. Similarly, discussion of General Colin Powell in 1996 as a potential Republican candidate and Barack Obama and Bill Richardson as Democratic candidates for the 2008 nomination also indicates that race and ethnicity may no longer be as much of a factor.

Public attitudes are changing. Polls taken after Lieberman's selection found an overwhelming percentage of those surveyed indicated that his Jewish religion made no difference to them. Gallup polls indicate a growing public tolerance toward electing people of various racial and religious backgrounds to the nation's highest office. A 2006 Gallup survey found that being a woman, an African American, or a Jew no longer automatically disqualified an individual in the minds of most Americans.[55] However, a significant proportion of the population would still not vote for a mormon, an atheist, or a homosexual for president. (See Table 6.3.)

Personal matters, such as health and family life, can also be factors. After Alabama governor George Wallace was disabled by a would-be assassin's bullet in 1972, even his own supporters began to question his ability to with-stand the rigors of the office. As noted previously, Senator Thomas Eagleton was forced to withdraw as the Democratic vice presidential nominee in 1972 when his past psychological illness became public. Before George W. Bush announced Dick Cheney's selection as his running mate, he had his father, former President George H. W. Bush, inquire about Cheney's medical condition. Cheney had suffered three heart attacks in the 1980s, but was described by his Houston doctors as in excellent health. Democratic candidates John Kerry and Bob Graham had much-publicized operations for cancer and heart disease, respectively, at the beginning of the 2003–2004 election cycle. Republicans John McCain, Rudolph Guiliani, and Fred Thompson have been treated for cancer, McCain on at least two occasions. Today, presidential and vice presidential candidates are expected to release detailed medical reports on themselves.

Family ties have also affected nominations and elections, as the father–son relationship between the Adams and the Bushes, and the marriage between Bill and Hillary Clinton demonstrate. There have been only two bachelors elected president, James Buchanan and Grover Cleveland.[56] During the 1884 campaign, Cleveland was accused of fathering an illegitimate child and was taunted by his opponents with "Ma, Ma, Where's my Pa? Gone to the White House, Ha! Ha! Ha!" Cleveland admitted responsibility for the child, even though he could not be certain he was the father.

Until 1980, no person who was divorced had ever been elected. Andrew Jackson, however, married a divorced woman, or at least a woman he thought was divorced. As it turned out, she had not been granted the final court papers legally dissolving her previous marriage. When this information became public during the 1828 campaign, Jackson's opponents asked rhetorically, "Do we want a whore in the White House?"[57] Jackson and Cleveland both won. That a candidate has been divorced and remarried seems to have little impact or even gain much notoriety today, but whether being divorced more than once has an impact remains to be seen.

Adultery is another matter. Senator Edward Kennedy's marital problems and his driving accident on Chappaquiddick Island, off the coast of Massachusetts, in which a young woman riding with the senator was drowned, were serious impediments to his presidential candidacy in 1980. Gary Hart's alleged "womanizing" forced his withdrawal in 1988 and made his reentry into Democratic presidential politics problematic. On the other hand, Bill Clinton was elected despite allegations of Gennifer Flowers that she had a long-term relationship with him while he was governor of Arkansas. Clinton, however, feared that he would not have been renominated and reelected if the Monica Lewinsky affair had become public before the 1996 Democratic Convention and general election campaign.

Nonetheless, Bill Clinton's nomination in 1992, despite the allegations of marital infidelity, marijuana smoking, and draft dodging, and in 1996, despite a pending sexual harassment suit by an Arkansas employee and the ongoing Whitewater investigation, as well as George W. Bush's self-admitted binge drinking as a younger man suggest that the electorate is more concerned about contemporary behavior than they are with previous relationships and behavior of the distant past.

The informal qualifications of the presidential nominee in general extend to vice presidential candidates as well.

SUMMARY

With the end of the competitive stage of the caucuses and primaries coming earlier and earlier, candidates who emerge victorious have to continue campaigning right up until their national convention even though their nomination may be secure. During this interregnum, which in 2004 lasted more than four months for the Democrats and almost five for the Republicans, the winners must consolidate their base, unify their party, and gain the support and endorsements of their nomination opponents. In addition, they may have to raise money for the party, and if they do not accept federal funds, they also need to raise it for themselves. They have to plan their general election strategy, developing and testing the themes they want to articulate, the policy stands they want to emphasize and those they don't, and the personal images they desire to project. Moreover, they have to stay in the news, avoid mistakes, and build their campaign organization. There is little rest for the weary.

As the nomination process now preordains the party's presidential candidate and control of the committees that set the rules, review the credentials, and draft the platform, the national nominating conventions have become more scripted than spontaneous, more glamour than substance, and more entertainment than news. It is politics as theatre, Hollywood style. Great effort goes into scripting and orchestrating the meetings to present a good show, one that will attract viewers, emphasize certain policy goals and positions, and create or reinforce leadership images.

The parties still see their conventions as important events that provide a favorable environment for beginning their fall campaigns. From the perspective of convention planners, the goals are to generate and illustrate partisan unity and enthusiasm for the nominees, inform and energize the partisans who watch it, and provide media exposure for the politicians who attend it—exposure that may help them in their reelection campaigns and also will be salve for their egos. From the perspective of the party, the goals are to raise the spirits and hopes of its workers, both delegates and the partisans at home; obtain even more donations; mobilize the faithful; and educate the public. From the perspective of the nominees, the goals are to demonstrate their broad-based policy appeals and strong leadership images.

The press that covers the convention have different objectives. Not oblivious to their public service function, they still need to maximize their viewing audience by reporting the convention as news, as well as presenting it as the party's public relations spectacular. To do this, they must find and report newsworthy events, especially those that are dramatic, divisive, and unexpected; provide analysis; and engage in endless prognosis about what it all means for the election and for the next government. The commercial broadcast networks seem to be giving up this task, leaving most of the coverage to the public broadcasting system, C-Span, and the cable news networks.

Although contemporary conventions are more theatrics than politics and more rhetoric than action, they continue to attract public attention, although less today than two or three decades ago. For those who watch, inadvertently or deliberately, conventions do increase awareness and shape perceptions of the candidates, parties, and their respective issue positions.

The impact of conventions varies with the attitudes and predispositions of those who watch or read about them. For partisans, conventions reinforce allegiances, making party identifiers more likely to vote and work for their party's nominees. For those less oriented toward a particular party, conventions deepen interest in the campaign; in 2000 and 2004, they also contributed to a more positive outlook about the candidates and their parties. In general, conventions provide the electorate with information with which to make a more informed voting decision; they also hasten that decision for a certain group of voters.

The changes in the nominating process have also affected the characteristics, qualities, and background of those gaining their party's nomination. Initially, they enlarged the selection zone for potential standard-bearers. It is unlikely that a Democratic convention before 1972 would have chosen a McGovern, Carter, Dukakis, or even Clinton, or that a former movie actor and governor would have come as close as Reagan did to defeating President Gerald Ford for the Republican nomination in 1976 and then winning the nomination for himself four years later. Moreover, the selection of a woman by the Democrats in 1984 and a Jew in 2000 as vice presidential nominees combined with the boomlet for other female and minority candidates suggests that gender, religion, and race may no longer be the critical criteria they once were for presidential and vice presidential standard-bearers. Times have changed; the electorate, reflecting the mores of the society, has become more accepting.

WHERE ON THE WEB?

The political parties are obviously a good source of information about their nominating conventions. Here again are the sites for the major parties and the Green and Reform Parties.

- **Democratic National Committee**
  www.dnc.org

- **Green Party**
  www.gp.org

- **Reform Party**
  www.reformparty.org

- **Republican National Committee**
  www.rnc.org
- **Democracy Network**
  www.dnet.org

EXERCISES

1. Compare the Democratic and Republican conventions on the basis of their schedules, the tenor of their televised speeches, and their video presentations. Which did you find more interesting and why?
2. Compare the acceptance speeches of the major party candidates for the presidential and vice presidential nominations. On the basis of your comparison, indicate to what extent these speeches previewed the principal appeals of the candidates in the general election. Compare these appeals to those of the minor party candidates.
3. To what extent do the major party platforms today reflect the increasing ideological content of contemporary politics? Are there any major areas in which the major parties take similar stands and/or use similar rhetoric today?
4. Contrast the major party platforms with those of two third parties, one on the left of the political spectrum and one on the right. Would you categorize the major parties as centrist? Are they still within the mainstream of American public opinion?
5. Looking back toward the previous presidential campaign, indicate which parts of the winning party's platform and promises of the winning candidate were enacted into law and which planks and promises were not. Were there any promises or platform planks that the winners ignored?
6. Examine the inauguration address of the newly elected president and any other major addresses made within the first 100 days in office to see which of the party's platform positions are highlighted and which are not. On the basis of your analysis, do you think that platforms are important agenda setters for the new administration?

SELECTED READINGS

Adler, Wendy Zeligson. "The Conventions on Prime Time," in *The Homestretch: New Politics,* edited by Martha FitzSimon and Edward C. Pease. New York: The Freedom Forum Media Studies Center, 1992, 55–57.

Cammarano, Joseph, and Jim Josefson, "Putting It in Writing: An Examination of Presidential Candidate Platforms in the 1992 Election." *Southeastern Political Review,* 23 (June 1995): 187–204.

Davis, James W. *National Conventions in an Age of Party Reform.* Westport, C.T.: Greenwood Press, 1983.

Holloway, Rachel L. "Political Conventions of 2004: A Study in Character and Contrast," in *The 2004 Presidential Campaign: A Communication Perspective,* edited by Robert E. Denton, Jr.. Lanham, M.D.: Rowman & Littlefield, 2005: 29–73.

Maisel, L. Sandy. "The Platform-Writing Process." *Political Science Quarterly,* 108 (Winter 1993–1994): 671–698.

Pavlik, John V. "Insider's Guide to Coverage of the Conventions and the Fall Campaign," in *The Homestretch*, 40–54.

Shafer, Byron E. *Bifurcated Politics: Evolution and Reform in the National Party Convention*. Cambridge, M.A.: Harvard University Press, 1988.

Smith, Larry David, and Dan Nimmo. *Cordial Concurrence: Orchestrating National Party Conventions in the Telepolitical Age*. New York: Praeger, 1991.

NOTES

1. *Campaign for President: The Managers Look at '92* (Hollis, N.H.: Hollis Publishing, 1994), pp. 184–185.

2. *Campaign for President: The Managers Look at 2004* (Lanham, M.D.: Rowman & Littlefield, 2006), p. 87.

3. Ibid., p. 223.

4. Ibid., p. 87.

5. John Tierney, "We Got a Check from Whom?" "Political Points," *New York Times* (April 4, 2004), p. A12.

6. Elisabeth Bumiller and David M. Halbfinger, "Amid Criticism of Campaign Ad, Bush Will Visit a 9/11 Memorial," *New York Times* (March 6, 2004), p. A11.

7. "Majority Considers Bush Ads' 9/11 Images 'Inappropriate,'" National Annenberg Election Survey, March 12, 2004. www.annenbergpublicpolicycenter.org/naes/; and Jeffrey M. Jones, "Campaign 2004 Out of the Gates," Gallup Poll, March 16, 2004. www.gallup.com/content/login.aspx?ci=11002.

8. Alison Mitchell, "Bush Strategy Recalls Clinton on the Trail in '96." *New York Times* (April 18, 2000), p. A18.

9. Matthew Dowd, *Campaign for President, 2004*, p. 100.

10. These specific claims were the ones analyzed by Kenneth Winneg, Kate Kenski, and Kathleen Hall Jamieson in their article, "Detecting the Effects of Deceptive Presidential Advertisements in the Spring of 2004," *American Behavioral Scientist,* 49 (Sept. 2005): pp. 114–128.

11. Ibid., p. 125.

12. Ibid.

13. *Campaign for President, 2004*, p. 200.

14. *Campaign for President, 2004*, p. 91.

15. George McGovern, conversation with author.

16. In both cases, grassroots challenges to old-line party leaders generated competing delegate claims. The convention in 1912 rejected these challengers and seated the regular party delegates, producing a walkout by Roosevelt's supporters and giving the nomination to Taft. Forty years later, the delegates denied the nomination to Taft's son by recognizing the credential of delegates pledged to Eisenhower and rejecting those supporting Senator Taft. There was no delegate walkout in 1952.

17. During the 1976 Republican convention, the Reagan organization proposed a rules change that would have required Gerald Ford to name his choice for vice president before the convention's vote for president, as his opponent, Ronald Reagan had done. Ford's supporters strongly opposed and subsequently beat this amendment. As a consequence, there was no way for Reagan to shake the remaining delegates loose from Ford's coalition.

18. According to a survey conducted by the Democratic National Committee, 20 percent of the delegates were African American, 11.6 percent were Hispanic, 3.9 percent were Asian-Pacific, 1.7 percent were Native American, and 3.9 percent gay, lesbian, or transsexual. www.den.org/2004/conv/demdelegates.htm (accessed October 19, 2004).

19. CNN, "Delegate Explainer." www.cnn.com/ELECTION/2004/special/president/convention/rnc/delegate (accessed July 21, 2006).

20. "New Campaign Finance Institute Analysis Charts Leap in Private Financing of Political Conventions," Campaign Finance Institute. www.cfinst.org/pr/060303.htm (accessed July 21; 2006).

21. The keynoter for the party that does not control the White House usually sounds a litany of failures and suggests that the country needs new leadership. Naturally, the keynoter for the party in office reverses the blame and praise. Noting the accomplishments of the administration and its unfinished business, the speaker urges a continuation of the party's effective leadership and policy successes.

22. Jimmy Carter, "Speech at Democratic Convention," July 26, 2004. www.cnn.com/2004/ALLPOLITICS/0726/dems.carter.transcript/index.html (accessed July 20, 2006).

23. Bill Clinton, "Speech at Democratic Convention," July 26, 2004. www.cnn.com/2004/ALLPOLITICS/07/26/dems.clinton.transcript/index.html (accessed July 20, 2006).

24. Ann Richards, "Address to the Democratic Convention in Atlanta, Georgia, on July 19, 1988," as quoted in *Congressional Quarterly,* 46 (July 23, 1988): p. 2024.

25. In recent years, there have been other newsworthy speeches. Pat Buchanan gave one of his rousing campaign speeches on opening night of the 1992 Republican convention. Endorsing the president for reelection, Bush's former challenger unleashed a scathing attack on the Democrats and Bill Clinton. The delegates loved the speech, but the news media saw it as harsh and mean-spirited conservative rhetoric and described it as such to viewers.

26. Zell Miller, "Speech at the Republican Convention," September 1, 2004. www.cnn.com/2004/ALLPOLITICS/09/01/gop.miller.transcript/index.html (accessed July 20, 2006).

27. Richard Cheney, "Speech at the Republican Convention," September 2, 2004. www.cnn.com/2004/ALLPOLITICS/09/02/gop.cheney.transcript/index.html (accessed July 20, 2006).

28. Barack Obama's moving speech before the 2004 Democratic convention was scheduled before the major broadcast networks began their prime time coverage as was Jimmy Carter's and Al Gore's opening night address for the Democrats. There

was no broadcast network coverage of the first night of the GOP convention when John McCain and Rudolph Giuliani spoke.

29. Michael Moore, the documentary film maker who made the movie, *Fahrenheit 911*, that was so critical of President Bush, was credentialed as a member of the press corps at both the Democratic and Republican 2004 conventions. Somehow he was seated next to former President Jimmy Carter, who also had been very critical of Bush in his address. Putting these two critics together embarrassed the Democratic convention planners who wanted to convey a positive, upbeat message to the American people.

30. Gerald M. Pomper, "Control and Influence in American Politics," *American Behavioral Scientist,* 13 (Nov./Dec. 1969): pp. 223–228; Gerald M. Pomper with Susan S. Lederman, *Elections in America* (New York: Longman, 1980), p. 161; Jeff Fishel, *Promises and Performance* (Washington, D.C.: CQ Press, 1994), pp. 38, 42–43.

31. Pomper, "Control and Influence," p. 161.

32. The symbolism, which the Republican convention planners purposively conveyed about the loneliness of the job, paralleled a similar image that the Democrats conveyed in 1980 in a political commercial that showed a single light late at night in the White House with an announcer intoning that the president's job is never done.

33. Jim Rutenberg, "Network Anchors Hold Fast to Their Dwindling 15 Minutes" *New York Times* (July 26, 2004), pp. A1, A7.

34. A report by the Joan Shorenstein Center on the Press, Politics, and Public Policy found that the television audience was between 15 million and 27 million households in 2004. During the hours of only cable coverage, the audience did not exceed 10 million. "Election Interest is up Sharply But Convention Interest is Not," July 21, 2004.

35. Rachel L. Holloway, "Political Conventions of 2004: A Study in Character and Contrast," in Robert E. Denton Jr., *The 2004 Presidential Campaign: A Communication Perspective* (Lanham, M.D.: Rowman & Littlefield, 2005), p. 68. See also "National Convention Ratings," Nielsen Media Research, as appears in the *New York Times* (July 26, 2004), p. 7.

36. "Republicans Orchestrate a Three-Night TV Special," *Broadcasting* (Aug. 28, 1972), p. 12.

37. Kathleen Hall Jamison, et al., "The Public Learned about Bush and Gore from Conventions; Half Ready to Make an Informed Choice," Annenberg Public Policy Center, (Aug. 25, 2000), p. 2; "GOP Convention Struggles for Audience," *Vanishing Voter* (Aug. 11, 2000). www.vanishingvoter.org/releases/08-2500conv.shtml.

38. Thomas E. Patterson, "Lessons from the Last Convention," *Vanishing Voter* (Aug. 13, 2000), p. 23. "GOP Convention Struggles for Audience," *Vanishing Voter* (Aug. 11, 2000), p. 24. Jamison, et al., "The Public Learned about Bush and Gore from Conventions," p. 2; "Americans Say National Party Conventions Still Important," *Vanishing Voter* (Aug. 5, 2004), p. 1. www.vanishingvoter.org/releases/08-13-00conv-1.shtml and www.vanishingvoter.org/releases/080504.shtml (accessed September 8, 2004).

39. Shorenstein Center, "Election Interest is up Sharply," (July 21, 2004).

40. Thomas E. Patterson, *The Mass Media Election* (New York: Praeger, 1980), pp. 72–74.

41. PC Data Online, a firm that monitors traffic on news sites, reported a 14 percent drop in the number of people who accessed these sites during the conventions. Howard Kurtz, "Web Coverage Does Not Spark Convention Interest," *Washington Post* (Aug. 15, 2000). www.washingtonpost.com/wp-dyn/articles/A24614200Aug.14.html.

42. Shankar Vedantam, "An Outsider Tries to Shake the 'Spoiler' Label," *New York Times* (June 26, 2004), pp. A1, A6.

43. Kerry had hoped that his choice of John Edwards on July 6, 2004, the well-planned and orchestrated Democratic convention three weeks later, and his acceptance speech would have given him a sizable bounce in the polls, but his support actually dropped, more from likely voters than the population as a whole. Why? The fact that the viewing audience was smaller than in previous years, the Democrats did not engage in Bush-basing at their Convention, and the Swift Boat Veteran for Truth's ads that followed on the heels of the Democratic convention may have contributed to Kerry's drop.

44. Thomas E. Patterson, *The Mass Media Election* (New York: Praeger, 1980), pp. 72–74.

45. Jamison, et. al. "The Public Learned about Bush and Gore from Conventions," p. 2; "Voter Involvement Index," *Vanishing Voter*. www.vanishingvoter.org/graphs/vi08-20-00.shtml.

46. Jamison, "The Public Learned," p. 2.

47. Gallup Poll, "Bush up 54 to 37 Percent over Gore at GOP Convention," August 7, 2000.

48. Jamieson, et. al. "The Public Learned About Bush and Gore," pp. 3–5; "Conventions Boost Americans Issue Awareness," *Vanishing Voter* (Aug. 30, 2000).

49. "Americans Say Conventions Important," *Vanishing Voter* (Aug. 5, 2004). www.vanishingvoter.org/Releases/release080504.shtml.

50. "Despite Limited Convention Coverage, Public Learned About Campaign from Democrats, Annenberg Data Show," Annenberg Center for Public Policy (Aug. 29, 2004).

51. Ibid.

52. Patterson, *Mass Media Election*, p. 103.

53. Jeffrey M. Jones and Joseph Carroll, "Changing Minds in the 2004 Election? A Report on Gallup's Post-Election Panel Survey," Gallup Poll (June 3, 2005). www.gallup.com/content/default.aspx?16576&pg=3.

54. The House of Representatives has not been a primary source of nominees. Only one sitting member of the House, James A. Garfield, has ever been elected president, and he was chosen on the thirty-fifth ballot. In recent nominations, there have been House candidates, but they have not done well. Most lack national visibility, even those who have been in office for many years. Two House members are running in 2008, Duncan Hunter and Dennis Kucinich.

55. David W. Moore, "Little Prejudice Against a Woman, Jewish, Black or Catholic Presidential Candidate," Gallup Poll (June 10, 2003).

56. Historian Thomas A. Bailey reports that James Buchanan was once greeted by a banner carried by a group of women that read, "Opposition to Old Bachelors." *Presidential Greatness* (New York: Appleton-Century Crofts, 1966), p. 74.

57. Ibid.

THE PRESIDENTIAL CAMPAIGN

7 CHAPTER | ORGANIZATION, STRATEGY, AND TACTICS

INTRODUCTION

Elections have been held in the United States since 1789; campaigning by parties for their nominees began soon thereafter. It was not until the end of the nineteenth century, however, that presidential candidates actively participated in the campaigns. Personal solicitation was viewed as demeaning and unbecoming of the dignity and status of the presidency.

Election paraphernalia, distributed by the parties, first appeared in the 1820s; by 1828, there was extensive public debate about the candidates. Andrew Jackson, and to a lesser extent, John Quincy Adams, generated considerable commentary and controversy. Jackson's supporters lauded him as a hero, a man of the people, "a new or second Washington"; his critics referred to him as "King Andrew the first," alleging that he was immoral, tyrannical, and brutal.[1] Adams was also subjected to personal attack. Much of this heated rhetoric appeared in the highly partisan press of the times.

The use of the campaign to reach, entertain, inform, and mobilize the general electorate began on a large scale in 1840. Festivals, parades, slogans, jingles, and testimonials were employed to energize voters. The campaign of 1840 is best remembered for the slogan, "Tippecanoe and Tyler too"—promoting Whig candidates General William Henry Harrison, hero of the battle of Tippecanoe in the War of 1812, and John Tyler—and for its great jingles:

WHAT HAS CAUSED THIS GREAT COMMOTION?

(SUNG TO THE TUNE OF "LITTLE PIG'S TAIL")

What has caused this great commotion, motion, motion,
Our country through?
It is the ball a rolling on, on.
Chorus
For Tippecanoe and Tyler too—Tippecanoe and Tyler too,
And with them we'll beat little Van, Van, Van, [Martin Van Buren]
Van is a used up man, And with them we'll beat little Van.[2]

The successful Whig campaign made it a prototype for subsequent presidential contests.

THE EVOLUTION OF PRESIDENTIAL CAMPAIGNS

The election of 1840 was also the first in which a party nominee actually campaigned for himself. General William Henry Harrison made twenty-three speeches in his home state of Ohio.[3] He did not set a precedent that was quickly followed, however. It was twenty years before another presidential candidate took to the stump and then under the extraordinary conditions of the onset of the Civil War and the breakup of the Democratic Party.

Senator Stephen A. Douglas, Democratic candidate for president, spoke out on the slavery issue to try to heal the split that it had engendered within his party. In doing so, however, he denied his own personal ambitions. "I did not come here to solicit your votes," he told a Raleigh, North Carolina, audience. "I have nothing to say for myself or my claims personally. I am one of those who think it would not be a favor to me to be made President at this time."[4]

Abraham Lincoln, Douglas's Republican opponent, refused to reply, even though he had debated Douglas two years earlier in their contest for the Senate seat from Illinois, a contest Douglas won. Lincoln, who almost dropped out of public view when the campaign was underway, felt that it was not even proper for him to vote for himself.[5] He cut his own name from the Republican ballot before he cast it for others in the election.[6]

For their part, the Republicans mounted a massive campaign on Lincoln's behalf. They held what were called "Wide Awake" celebrations in which large numbers of people were mobilized. An account of one of these celebrations reported that

> The Wide-Awake torch-light procession is undoubtedly the largest and most imposing thing of the kind ever witnessed in Chicago. Unprejudiced spectators estimate the number at 10,000. Throughout the whole length of the procession were

scattered portraits of Abraham Lincoln. Banners and transparencies bearing Republican mottoes, and pictures of rail splitters, were also plentifully distributed. Forty-three bands of music were also in the procession.[7]

FROM PORCH TO TRAIN

Presidential candidates remained on the sidelines until the 1880s. Republican James Garfield broke the tradition by receiving visitors at his Ohio home. Four years later in 1884, Republican James Blaine made hundreds of campaign speeches in an unsuccessful effort to offset public accusations that he profited from a fraudulent railroad deal. Benjamin Harrison, the Republican candidate in 1888, resumed the practice of seeing people at his home, a practice that has been referred to as front-porch campaigning. Historian Keith Melder writes that Harrison met with 110 delegations consisting of almost 200,000 people in the course of the campaign.[8] William McKinley saw even more visitors over the course of his front-porch campaign in 1896. He spoke to approximately 750,000 people who were recruited and in some cases transported to his Canton, Ohio, home by the Republican Party.[9]

McKinley's opponent in that election, William Jennings Bryan, actually traveled around the country making speeches at Democratic political rallies. By his own account, he logged more than 18,000 miles and made more than 600 speeches, and, according to press estimates, he spoke to almost 5 million people, nearly collapsing from exhaustion at the end of the campaign.[10]

In 1900, Republican vice presidential candidate Theodore Roosevelt took on Bryan, "making 673 speeches, visiting 567 towns in 24 states, and traveling 21,209 miles."[11] Twelve years later, ex-president Theodore Roosevelt, once again took to the hustlings, only this time he was trying to defeat a fellow Republican president, William Howard Taft, for his party's nomination. Roosevelt won nine primaries, including one in Ohio, Taft's home state, but was denied the nomination by party leaders. He then launched an independent candidacy in the general election, campaigning on the Progressive, or "Bull Moose," ticket. His Democratic opponent, Woodrow Wilson, was also an active campaigner. The Roosevelt and Wilson efforts ended the era of passive presidential campaigning. The last front-porch presidential campaign was waged by Warren G. Harding in 1920.

FROM RALLY TO RADIO AND TELEVISION

Harding's campaign was distinguished in another way; he was the first to use radio to speak directly to voters. This new electronic medium and television, which followed it, radically changed presidential campaigns. Initially, candidates were slow to adjust their campaign styles to these new techniques.[12] It was not until Franklin Delano Roosevelt that radio was employed skillfully in political campaigns. Roosevelt also pioneered the "whistle-stop" campaign train, which stopped at railroad stations along the route to allow the candidate to address the crowds that came to see and hear him. In 1932, Roosevelt, who personally took a train to Chicago to accept his nomination, visited thirty-six states, traveling some 13,000 miles in his presidential campaign. His extensive travels, undertaken in part to dispel a whispering campaign about his health—he had polio as a young man, which left him unable to walk or even stand up unaided—forced President Herbert Hoover onto the campaign trail.[13]

Instead of giving the small number of speeches he had originally planned, Hoover logged more than 10,000 miles, traveling across much of the country. He was the first incumbent president to campaign actively for reelection. Thereafter, with the exception of Franklin Roosevelt during World War II, personal campaigning became standard for incumbents and nonincumbents alike.

Harry Truman took campaigning by an incumbent a step further. Perceived as the underdog in the 1948 election, Truman whistle-stopped the length and breadth of the United States, traveling 32,000 miles and averaging ten speeches a day. In eight weeks, he spoke to an estimated 6 million people.[14] While Truman was rousing the faithful with his down-home comments and hard-hitting criticisms of the Republican-controlled Congress, his opponent, Thomas E. Dewey, was promising new leadership but providing few particulars. His sonorous speeches contrasted sharply and unfavorably with Truman's straightforward attacks.

The end of an era in presidential campaigning occurred in 1948. Within the next four years, television came into its own as a communications medium. The number of television viewers grew from less than half a million in 1948 to approximately 19 million in 1952, a figure that was deemed sufficient in the minds of campaign planners to launch a major television effort. The Eisenhower presidential organization budgeted almost $2 million for television, and the Democrats promised to use both radio and television "in an exciting, dramatic way" in that election.[15]

The potential of television was evident from the outset. Republican vice presidential candidate, Richard Nixon, took to the airwaves in 1952 to reply to accusations that he had appropriated campaign funds for his personal use and had received money and other gifts from wealthy supporters, including a black-and-white cocker spaniel named Checkers. Nixon denied the charges but said that under no circumstances would he and his family give up the dog, which his children dearly loved. A huge outpouring of public sympathy for Nixon followed, effectively ending the issue, keeping him on the ticket, and demonstrating the impact television could have on a political career and a presidential campaign.

Television made mass appeals easier, but it also created new obstacles for the nominees. Physical appearance became more important as did oratorical skill. Instead of just rousing a crowd, presidential aspirants had to convey a personal message and compelling image to television viewers.

Television had other effects as well. It eventually replaced the party as the principal link between the nominees and the voters. It decreased the incentive for holding so many election events—rallies, parades, speeches—since many more people could be reached through this mass medium. It also required that campaign activities and events be carefully orchestrated and scripted, keeping in mind how they would appear on the screen and what images they would convey to voters. Off-handed comments and quips were discouraged because they invariably got candidates into trouble.

FROM ART TO SCIENCE

The people who organized and ran campaigns were also affected. Public relations experts were called on to apply mass-marketing techniques. Pollsters and media consultants supplemented and to some extent replaced old-style politicians in designing and executing strategies. Even the candidates seemed a little different. With the possible exception of Lyndon Johnson and Gerald Ford, both of whom succeeded to the presidency through the death or resignation of their predecessors, incumbents and challengers alike reflected the grooming and schooling of the age of mass communications. And where they did not, as in the cases of Walter Mondale, Michael Dukakis, and Robert Dole, they fared poorly.

The age of television campaigning is obviously not over, but the revolution in computing, communications technology, and in the collection and integration of large data sets of personal information has provided political organizations in general and parties in particular with opportunities to target and communicate with individuals, opportunities that they are now beginning to use to identify and turnout likely supporters.

This chapter and the one that follows discuss these aspects of modern presidential campaigns. Organization, strategy, and tactics serve as the principal focal points of this chapter, whereas news coverage, image and issue projection, and the impact of the media on campaigns are addressed in the next chapter.

The next section of this chapter describes the structures of modern presidential campaigns and the functions they perform. It examines attempts to create hierarchical campaign organizations but also notes the decentralizing pressures. The tensions between candidate organizations and the regular party structure are alluded to, as is the relationship between the campaign organization and the new administration.

The basic objectives that every strategy must address are explored in the section that follows. These include designing a basic appeal, creating a leadership image, sometimes coping with the incumbency factor, and building a winning geographic coalition. The last section of the chapter deals with tactics, describing the techniques for communicating a candidate's message, orchestrating the campaign, targeting and timing appeals, and finally, turning out the vote.

CAMPAIGN ORGANIZATIONS AND OPERATIONS

Running a campaign is a complex, time-consuming, nerve-racking venture. Constant emergencies and unexpected events must be dealt with as well as the numerous personal issues, heightened by the pace of work, the hours spent at it, and the egos of ambitious, mostly young, people, who get involved. Campaigns are hectic, fast-paced, and all-consuming experiences. Mistakes can be costly. Nonetheless, most of the people who work in political campaigns enjoy the experience.

Campaign organizations engage in a variety of broad-based operations, including advance work, scheduling, press relations, issue research, speech writing, polling and focus groups, media advertising, finances, legal issues, and more recently, computer-based technologies, Internet communications, and targeted outreach activities involving a variety of nonparty groups and associations.

All recent presidential campaigns have had large and increasingly specialized organizations. They are led by a chairperson who presides over the organization and usually acts as a liaison among the candidate, party, and public; a hands-on manager oversees the operation and coordinates the medium with the message; and a political director and several deputies supervise day-to-day activities. There is also a press secretary, speechwriters, and a research team to provide the news media with favorable information, draft speeches, and respond to opposition attacks. In addition, there are division chiefs for special operations, and a geographic hierarchy that reaches down to the state and local levels. Every campaign also has its professional pollsters, media consultants, strategists and grassroots organizers, plus an array of technical experts, including accountants, lawyers, computer geeks, and data analysts.

Within this basic structure, organizations have varied somewhat in style and operation. Most have been centralized, with a few individuals making the key strategic and tactical decisions; a few have been decentralized. Some have worked through or in conjunction with national and state party organizations; others have created their own field organizations. Some have operated from a comprehensive game plan; others have adopted a more incremental, design-it-as-you-go approach. In some, the nominees have assumed an active decision-making role; in others, the candidates defer to the principal campaign advisers who collectively make major strategic and tactical decisions.

REPUBLICAN STRUCTURES AND STAFFS

The Goldwater (1964), Nixon (1972), Reagan (1984), George H. W. Bush (1988), and George W. Bush (2000 and 2004) campaigns all exemplify the tight, hierarchical model in which a few individuals control decision making and access to the candidate. In Goldwater's case, his chief advisers were suspicious of top party regulars, most of whom did not support the senator's candidacy. They opted for an organization of believers, one that would operate in an efficient fashion.[16]

The same desire for control and for circumventing the party was evident in Richard Nixon's reelection campaign in 1972. Completely separate from the national party, even in title, the Committee to Reelect the President (known as CREEP by its critics) raised its own money, conducted its own public relations (including polling and campaign advertising), scheduled its own events, and even had its own security division. It was this division, operating independently from the Republican Party, which harassed the Democratic campaign of George McGovern by heckling his speeches, spreading false rumors, and perpetrating other illegal acts, including the attempted wiretapping of the Democratic National Committee headquarters at the Watergate Office Building.

The excesses perpetuated by individuals in this group illustrate both the difficulty of overseeing all the aspects of a large presidential campaign and the risk of placing nonprofessionals in key positions of responsibility. Had the more experienced Republican National Committee exercised greater influence over the president's reelection, there might have been less deviation from accepted standards of behavior.

The George W. Bush presidential campaigns of 2000 and 2004 were prototypes of well-run, well-coordinated political operations. Karl Rove, who had overseen Bush's gubernatorial campaigns, was the chief strategist and principal link to the candidate. He was assisted by an experienced team of Republican campaign professionals and a large number of volunteers. Figure 7.1 indicates the personnel, titles, and lines of authority of President Bush's 2004 reelection organization.

The Bush reelection committee coordinated closely with the White House. Early on, a process was established to differentiate lines of authority and spheres of decision making between top campaign and White House officials. Karl Rove was the linchpin with joint responsibilities in both political spheres. He initiated a "Breakfast Club" of the president's top advisers that met on weekends at Rove's home to evaluate the progress of the campaign and discuss strategy. White House communication chief, Dan Bartlett, and Karen Hughes, who traveled with the president, regularly interacted with top campaign officials. The fact that most of the principals had worked together on Bush's 2000 campaign and the White House staff facilitated their working relationships during the campaign.

The Bush campaigns of 2000 and 2004 maintained a war room that anticipated and reacted quickly to developments in the news and tactics used by the Kerry campaign. The staff also looked for targets of opportunities upon which to take the offense. A key objective of the Bush campaign was to reinforce Kerry's flip-flopper image. Operating twenty-four hours a day, the war room was peopled with college students and recent graduates who monitored Web sites, newspapers, magazines, talk shows, and even the late-night comics. Practically every statement that Kerry uttered was assessed for its "flip-flopper" potential. Faxes and e-mails were sent to the news media on a daily, sometimes even hourly basis, to alert them to Kerry mishaps and misstatements and to negative research that the staff dug up about Kerry and his fellow Democrats.[17]

DEMOCRATIC STRUCTURES AND STAFFS

Democratic campaign organizations have tended to be looser in organization and more decentralized in operation than have the Republicans. Until the

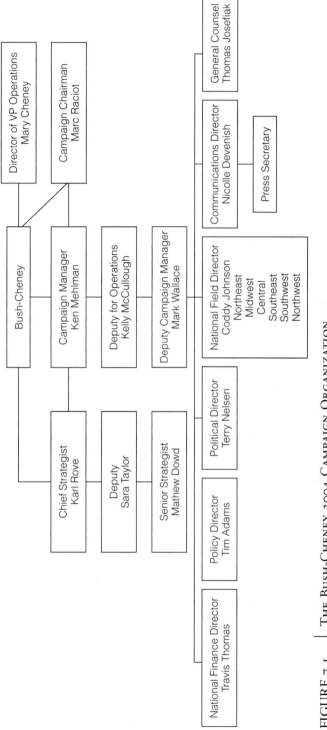

FIGURE 7.1   THE BUSH-CHENEY 2004 CAMPAIGN ORGANIZATION

1970s, the Democrats had stronger state parties and a weaker national base. As a consequence, their presidential candidates tended to rely more heavily on state party organizations than did the Republicans. In recent years, Democratic presidential campaigns have designated regional and state coordinators to oversee state party efforts on their behalf. These coordinators, placed on the payroll of the state parties to reduce administrative costs to the national campaign, also have served as intermediaries between the state party and the campaign organization.

Some of the Democratic presidential campaigns, such as those of Walter Mondale and Michael Dukakis, experienced difficulty in coordinating campaign activities. Others such as Bill Clinton's were well run, followed carefully designed strategic plans, and used a war room for tactical operations and rapid reactions to events.

Both Clinton campaigns relied heavily on pollsters to monitor the public mood. And both depended on a media team to design and target advertising. Clinton himself was heavily involved in these efforts, particularly in the early phases of both campaigns. As president, he ran weekly strategy sessions in which major issues were discussed and decisions were made.[18]

In contrast, the Democratic presidential campaigns of 2000 and 2004 suffered from organizational problems that resulted in campaign managers being changed, adjustments being made in how the candidate presented himself to the public, and some shifting of policy emphases. Fortunately for both campaigns, however, these problems surfaced fairly early, giving them time to regroup and redirect their political activities.

In general, Democratic presidential campaigns have been more dependent on outside groups for reaching and mobilizing voters than have their Republican counterparts, which have relied more heavily on their national and state party organizations. Figure 7.2 indicates the organization and principal players in the 2004 Kerry campaign.

TRANSITIONING TO GOVERNMENT

The organization of presidential campaigns, the key players in the organization, and their relationship to the candidate all have important implications for government. A campaign organization reflects a candidate's management style: how willing the candidate is to take advice, to delegate to others, and to make decisions and adhere to them or adjust them if the situation changes. Reagan's reliance on his campaign staff, his reluctance to second-guess his advisers, augured his White House staffing arrangement and his passive administrative style. In contrast, Clinton's penchant for details, his involvement in the campaign's strategic and tactical decisions, and his constant desire to assess the public mood before, during, and after he voiced his policy preferences were also reflected in the way in which he did business as president. Similarly, George W. Bush's hands-off style suggested the CEO management approach he has taken as president.

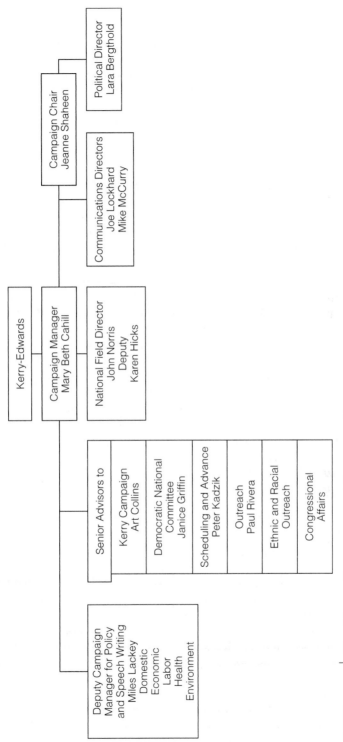

FIGURE 7.2 | THE KERRY-EDWARDS 2004 CAMPAIGN ORGANIZATION

A second way in which campaigns affect governance is through the personnel who are recruited for key administration positions, particularly for those in the White House. Many of the senior aides in the White House have also served in the inner circles of presidential campaigns, as have many junior aides. However, the success with which these campaign personnel have made the adjustment to White House staff has been mixed at best.

In George W. Bush's case, his chief political strategist, Karl Rove, continued to integrate and oversee political activities for the White House, activities that extended from scheduling presidential events, to taking policy positions, to monitoring information on public reactions for Bush and his administration, and to coordinating White House activities with the 2004 reelection campaign.

After the president's reelection, Rove continued to play an important political role in the White House as deputy chief of staff, chief political adviser, and chief Republican strategist for the 2006 midterm elections. His influence faded, however, after the Republicans' defeat in those elections. Others who have stayed on after their work in the Bush campaigns include the communications director for the 2000 campaign, Karen Hughes, and communications director for the 2004 effort, Nicole Devenish, both of whom occupied important White House positions. The president also retained his main policy advisers from his first campaign, Josh Bolton, Condoleezza Rice, and Lawrence Lindsay, plus those of his second. A host of other campaign workers were offered less senior White House and subcabinet positions. Ken Mehlman, the 2004 campaign manager, became chair of the Republican National Committee.

The relationship between the candidate's organization and the party's organization also impacts governance. Candidates who circumvent their party and its elected officials in the planning and conduct of their presidential campaigns, as Richard Nixon did in 1972, Jimmy Carter did in 1976, and, to a lesser extent, Bill Clinton did in 1992, find it more difficult to mobilize the necessary support in Congress to bridge the separation of powers and govern effectively. In contrast, candidates who do not circumvent their party and who are heavily invested in partisan political activities tend to do better.

STRATEGIC OBJECTIVES

Strategies are game plans, blueprints, and calculated efforts to convince the electorate to vote for a particular candidate. They include a basic appeal as well as a plan for implementing it.

Certain decisions cannot be avoided when developing an electoral strategy. These decisions stem from the rules of the system, the costs of the campaign, the character of the electorate, and the environment in which the election occurs. Each decision involves identifying objectives, allocating resources, and monitoring and adjusting that allocation over the course of the campaign. That is what a strategy is all about: It is a plan for directing campaign resources, targeting them to specific groups, and tracking their impact on the electorate.

Most strategies are designed before the race begins; a few may be forged during the election itself. In 1984, Reagan strategists developed an elaborate plan well before the Republican convention. George H. W. Bush's campaign plan in 1988, Clinton's in 1992 and 1996,[19] and George W. Bush's in 2000 and 2004 were also formulated well before their respective conventions met. In fact, the principals who were responsible for President George W. Bush's reelection campaign started almost immediately after the president took office in 2001 to plan for his next campaign.[20] Gore and Kerry adjusted their strategies during the campaign as do many candidates who find themselves behind.

DESIGNING A BASIC APPEAL

The first step in constructing a campaign strategy is fashioning a basic appeal. This appeal has two principal components: partisan images and policy positions and priorities. The objective is to frame the electoral choice in as advantageous a manner as possible.

Partisan Images

All things being equal, the candidates of the dominant party have an advantage that they try to maximize by emphasizing their partisan affiliation, lauding their partisan heroes, and making a blatant partisan appeal. When the Democrats were the majority, their candidates traditionally clothed themselves in the garb of their party. During the same period, the Republicans did not. Eisenhower, Nixon, and Ford downplayed partisan references, pointing instead to their personal qualifications and policy positions. As the partisan gap narrowed, Republican candidates became more willing to point to their partisan label. Today, both major party candidates wear that label proudly.

Identifying with the party is only one way in which the partisan orientations of the electorate are activated and reinforced. Recalling the popular images of the party is another. For the Democrats, common economic interests are still the most compelling cue for most of their party's electoral coalition. Perceived as the party of the average person, the party that got the country out of the Great Depression, the party of labor and minority groups, the Democrats do better when economic issues are salient as they were in 1992 and 1996.

Democratic candidates emphasize "bread-and-butter" issues, such as jobs, wages, education, and other benefits for the working and middle classes. The Democrats contrast their concern for the plight of the average American with the Republicans' ties to the wealthy and especially to big business.

The Democrats' sympathy for the less fortunate, however, has been a mixed blessing in recent years. Beginning in the 1970s and continuing into the twenty-first century, this sympathy has been perceived by some as antithetical to the interests of the middle class, particularly if big government programs are involved. Exploiting this perception, Republicans have repeatedly criticized their liberal, "tax-and-spend" opponents.

Bill Clinton sought to reassert his party's middle-class appeal in his presidential campaigns. Calling himself a "New Democrat," Clinton took pains to distinguish his own moderate policy orientation from the more liberal views of his Democratic predecessors and the more conservative positions of his Republican opponents. He presented himself as a change-oriented candidate in 1992 and as a builder of progress in 1996. In contrast, Al Gore and John Kerry took more populist approaches, emphasizing their desire to help working families and later pitching their economic appeals directly to middle-class voters.

Whereas economic issues have tended to unite the Democrats, social issues have been more divisive. Since the 1970s, Republican presidential candidates have taken advantage of these divisions by focusing on those matters on which the Democrats' electoral constituency was divided, issues such as school vouchers, welfare programs, free trade, affirmative action, and same-sex marriage. In doing so, the Republicans appealed to the fears and frustrations of moderate and conservative Democrats as well as reaffirmed their own support for the traditional American values of individual initiative, family responsibility, and local autonomy.

When foreign policy, national security, and more recently, homeland security issues are salient, Republican candidates have traditionally done better. In 1952, Eisenhower campaigned on the theme "Communism, Corruption, and Korea," projecting himself as the candidate most qualified to end the war. Nixon took a similar tack in 1968, linking Humphrey to the Johnson administration and the war in Vietnam. Four years later, Nixon varied his message, painting George McGovern as the "peace at any price" candidate and himself as the experienced leader who could achieve peace with honor. Gerald Ford was not nearly as successful in conveying his abilities in foreign affairs but compensated for his shortcomings by relying on Dr. Henry Kissinger as secretary of state and principal foreign policy spokesman. Reagan, despite his own lack of experience in foreign affairs, pointed to the Soviet invasion of Afghanistan and to the Iranian hostage situation to criticize Carter's foreign policy leadership. George H. W. Bush cited his experience in foreign affairs and his personal acquaintance with many world leaders in 1988, although his emphasis on foreign policy became a liability four years later with the Cold War over, the Persian Gulf War concluded, and the public preoccupied with a domestic economy in recession. Lacking his father's expertise in foreign affairs, George W. Bush did not stress foreign policy in his 2000 campaign, but he did in 2004 in the light of the terrorist attacks and his declaration of a war on terrorism. He defended U.S. involvement in Iraq, as a critical battlefield in that war.

The general perception that the Democrats are weaker in foreign and military affairs has prompted some of their recent standard-bearers to talk even tougher than their Republican opponents. In his 1976 campaign, Carter vowed that an Arab oil embargo would be seen by his administration as an economic declaration of war. In 1984, Walter Mondale supported the buildup of U.S. defenses, including Reagan's strategic defense initiative. In 1988, Dukakis spoke about the need for the United States to be more competitive within the international economic arena as did Clinton in 1992. Gore and Kerry emphasized the foreign policy expertise they gained in the Senate, their military service in Vietnam, and their support for a strong American presence in the international community of nations. Kerry criticized Bush for not sending more and better-equipped troops to Iraq.

Salient Issue Positions

The electoral environment affects the priorities and substance of a candidate's policy appeal. In 1992, the electorate was concerned about the economy, particularly the loss of American jobs abroad and the growing federal budget deficit. In 1996, with the economy strengthened, unemployment low, inflation in check, and a strong stock market, the electorate in general expressed satisfaction with the country's economic condition, a situation that favored the incumbent. The salient issues in 2000 were how to improve education, provide tax relief, and put Social Security and Medicare on a firmer financial foundation; in 2004, the war in Iraq was a primary concern, along with continuing budget deficits, unequal economic growth, the loss of American jobs abroad, and social issues such as same-sex marriage.

In general, economic issues tend to be the most recurrent themes in American elections. A poor economy helps the party that is out of power and hurts the incumbent's party. Ronald Reagan drove the economic problem home in 1980 with the question he posed at the end of his debate with President Jimmy Carter, a question directed at the American people: "Are you better off now than you were four years ago?" Similarly, James Carville, chief strategist of the 1992 Clinton campaign, kept a sign over his desk that read, "It's the economy, stupid." He did not want anyone in the Clinton organization to forget that the poor economy was the campaign's primary issue.

A strong economy helps the party in power but not to the extent that a weak one hurts it. Loss of jobs, increases in the cost of living and inflation, even skids in the stock market affect large numbers of people and become strong motivations for voting against the party and president on whose watch these problems occurred.

CREATING A LEADERSHIP IMAGE

Regardless of the partisan imagery and thematic emphases, candidates for the presidency must stress their own qualifications for the job and cast doubt on their opponents'. They must appear presidential, demonstrating those personal attributes and leadership qualities the voters consider essential.[21]

Accentuating the Positive

A favorable image, of course, cannot be taken for granted. It has to be created, or at least polished. Contemporary presidents are expected to be strong, assertive, and dominant. During times of crisis or periods of social anxiety, these leadership characteristics are considered absolutely essential. The strength that Franklin Roosevelt was able to convey by virtue of his successful bout with polio, Dwight Eisenhower by his military command in World War II, and Ronald Reagan by his tough talk, clear-cut solutions, and consistent policy goals contrast sharply with the perceptions of Adlai Stevenson in 1956, George McGovern in 1972, Jimmy Carter in 1980, and Walter Mondale in 1984 as weak and indecisive. Kerry suffered as well from the perception, heightened by the Republican campaign, that he vacillated, pontificated, and has made inconsistent policy judgments throughout his political career. These perceptions were reinforced by Kerry's lack of clarity on the policies he would pursue if elected.

For challengers, the task of seeming to be powerful, confident, and independent (one's own person) can best be imparted by a no-nonsense approach, a show of optimism, a conviction that success is attainable, and a clear, coherent, and consistent vision that can be converted into specific policy positions. John Kennedy's rhetorical emphasis on activity in 1960 and Richard Nixon's tough talk in 1968 about the turmoil and divisiveness in the country helped to generate the impression of a take-charge personality. Kennedy and Nixon were seen as leaders who knew what had to be done and would do it. Ronald Reagan's simple but direct language, his strong, consistent anti-communist views, his optimism and belief in America's strength and ingenuity, and the sincerity with which he presented his views contrasted sharply with Jimmy Carter's inaction during the Iranian hostage crisis, his penchant for self criticism, his demands for sacrifice, and his bland, emotionless rhetoric.

In addition to seeming tough enough to be president, it is also important to exhibit sufficient knowledge and skills for the job. In the public's mind, personal experience testifies to the ability to perform. John Kerry had only mixed success, however, in pointing to his military service and Senate record in preparing him for a presidency during crisis because both claims were subjected to considerable scrutiny throughout the 2004 campaign by Bush, the Republicans, and outside, pro-Republican groups.

Experience can also become an issue for candidates who have not held national office. State governors, particularly those from small states, need to prove that they handle a job as difficult, complex, and pressured as the presidency. George W. Bush had to overcome the lack of experience hurdle although his presence during his father's presidency mitigated this problem somewhat. What many candidates without national experience do is run against Washington, pointing out that they are not part of the problem so that they are better able to fix it. Obviously, such a strategy works only if the public has a lot of grievances against those in power. This was the message Jimmy Carter presented after Watergate and was probably the reason he was elected.

Empathy is also an important attribute for presidential candidates. People want a president who can respond to their emotional needs, one who understands what and how they feel. As the government has become larger, more powerful, and more distant, empathy has become more important. Roosevelt and Eisenhower radiated warmth. Carter, Clinton, and George W. Bush were particularly effective in generating the impression that they cared, whereas McGovern, Nixon, Dukakis, and Dole appeared cold, distant, and impersonal. Kennedy and Kerry, wealthy in their own right, repeatedly echoed a theme of economic popularism to demonstrate that they understood the problems of the poor and middle class. George W. Bush pointed to his own religious experience to connect with his Christian fundamentalist supporters.

Candor, integrity, and trust emerge periodically as important attributes in presidential image building. Most of the time these traits are taken for granted.

Occasionally, however, a crisis of confidence, such as Watergate or the Clinton impeachment, dictates that political skills be downplayed and these personal qualities stressed. Such crises preceded the elections of 1952, 1976, 2000, and 2008. In the first two of these elections, Dwight Eisenhower, a war hero, and Jimmy Carter, who promised never to tell a lie, both benefited from the perception that they were honest, decent men not connected with the "mess" in Washington. George W. Bush made much of the scandalous behavior in the Clinton administration during his nomination campaign, but much less during the general election campaign. However, he often repeated the line that brought him the most accolades from Republican audiences: "When I put my hand on the Bible, I will swear to not only uphold the laws of our land, I will swear to uphold the honor and dignity of the office to which I have been elected, so help me God."[22] In contrast, Gore pledged emphatically not to let the American people down in his 2000 campaign, and Kerry promised never to engage the American military in situations abroad without an exit strategy.

Character is important in elections when issues involving personal behavior preoccupy the administration in power. Character also tends to be more important when less is known about the candidates—at the beginning of their presidential quest. It is less important for an incumbent running for reelection because the electorate by then has a basis for evaluating the kind of president that person has made. (The character issue in 2004 is discussed in Box 7.1 "An Incumbency Balance Sheet.")

Highlighting the Negative
Naturally, candidates can be expected to raise questions about their opponents. These questions assume particular importance if the public's initial impression of the candidates is fuzzy, as it may be with outsiders who win their party's nomination. When Republican polls and focus groups commissioned by the Bush campaign in 1988 revealed Dukakis's imprecise image, Bush campaign advisers devised a strategy to take advantage of these perceptions and define Dukakis in ways that would discredit him. The strategy was based on the premise that the higher the negatives of a candidate, the less likely that candidate would be to win. Lee Atwater, architect of this strategy, put it this way: "When I first got into politics, I just stumbled across the fact that candidates who went into an election with negatives higher than 30 or 40 points just inevitably lost." [23] Honesty was the desired attribute that people mentioned most often in the 2007–2008 election cycle.[24]

In 1992, Bush also challenged the qualifications of his opponents. But here his campaign ran into a public relations problem generated by adverse reactions to his negative Dukakis campaign four years earlier and to the allegations about Ross Perot that were leaked to the media by supporters of Bush. Fearing that his first negative commercials would be greeted by a "there he goes again" refrain by the press, the Bush campaign delayed their airing and then introduced them with a touch of humor to soften their effect.[25] Still, voters were leery.[26]

Unlike Dukakis, who chose initially not to dignify Bush's attacks by replying to them, Clinton helped defuse the attacks against him by reacting quickly and forcefully. His rapid reaction not only deflected criticism, but it also enabled the Clinton campaign to keep the media focus on its main issue—the economy—not on the candidate's character.

The emphasis on negativity has continued in each subsequent election. In 1996, the Clinton campaign unleashed a barrage of press releases and advertisements that criticized Dole's voting record in the Senate. Dole countered with personal accusations against Clinton. In 2000, Gore's credibility, particularly his tendency to exaggerate his own importance and embellish stories he told, became the focus of Republican attacks after the first and second presidential debates in which the Democratic candidate misspoke several times. In contrast, the Democratic criticism of Bush was based on his competence, not his character. Democrats alleged that confusion over details and factual errors indicated that Bush lacked a deep understanding of the issues. In the words of news correspondent Cokie Roberts, "The story line is Bush isn't smart enough and Gore isn't straight enough."[27]

Negativity played a major role in the 2004 election. George W. Bush repeatedly defined his opponent, John Kerry in negative terms, calling him indecisive, inconsistent, and sometimes incoherent—a flip flopper. Kerry, who wanted to wage an upbeat, positive, and optimistic campaign, still was very critical of his opponent's economic and national security policies. His criticism was reinforced by news of the resistance in Iraq, spiking gasoline prices, and continuing problems of balancing the federal budget and international trade.

In summary, candidates try to project images of themselves that are consistent with public expectations of the office and its occupant and project images of their opponents that are not inconsistent with those expectations. Traits such as inner strength, decisiveness, competence, and experience are considered essential for the presidency, as are empathy, sincerity, credibility, and integrity. Which traits are considered most important vary to some extent with the assessment of the strengths and weaknesses of the incumbent and the needs of the times. Challengers try to exploit an incumbent's vulnerabilities by emphasizing the very skills and qualities that the incumbent president is said to lack.

In the 2004 campaign, Kerry tried to project his familiarity with the issues; his speeches were laden with facts and analyses. He also emphasized the need to be flexible, to work with others, and to listen to their recommendations, indirectly criticizing his opponent's lack of these traits—the president's stubbornness, his unilateral decision making style, and his unwillingness or inability to admit mistakes or even to reevaluate his policy judgments. Bush raised questions about Kerry's indecisiveness, his tendency to temporize, and the inconsistencies of his Senate record.

DEALING WITH INCUMBENCY

Claiming a leadership image requires a different script for an incumbent than for a challenger. Until the mid-1970s, when the media became more critical of presidential performance, incumbents were thought to have an advantage. (See Box 7.1 "An Incumbency Balance Sheet."), Between 1900 and 1972, thirteen incumbents

BOX 7.1	AN INCUMBENCY BALANCE SHEET

Incumbency can be a double-edged sword, strengthening or weakening a claim to leadership. Incumbents ritually point to their accomplishments, noting the work that remains, and sounding a "stay-the-course" theme; challengers argue that it is time for a change and that they can do better.

Advantages of Incumbency

Being president is thought to help an incumbent in the quest for reelection more often than not. The advantages stem from the visibility of the office, the esteem it engenders, and the influence it provides. The president is almost always well known. A portion of the population may even have difficulty at the outset in identifying challengers, although the extended nomination process contributes to the name recognition over time.

Moreover, incumbents are generally seen as experienced and knowledgeable, as leaders who have stood the tests of office in the office. Such a perception benefits them more often than not. Stability and predictability satisfy the public's psychological needs; the certainty of four more years with a known quantity is likely to be more appealing than the uncertainty of the next four years with an unknown one provided the performance in office for the incumbent during the past four years has been viewed as generally favorable. In the case of George W. Bush, partisans disagreed on his domestic record but were generally praiseworthy of his response to 9/11. Thus for Bush, the challenge was to keep the primary focus on terrorism, relegating other concerns to secondary importance.

Translated into strategic terms, the public's familiarity and comfort with incumbents permits presidents running for reelection to highlight their opponent's lack of experience, leadership qualities, and clear policy options and contrast these deficiencies with their own experience, leadership, and record of policy achievements. Carter used a variation of this tactic in 1980. He emphasized the arduousness of the job in order to contrast his energy, knowledge, and intelligence with Reagan's. Clinton contrasted himself with his opponent in another way in 1996. He portrayed himself as the candidate for the future and his seventy-three-year-old opponent as the link to the past. Both presidents Bush ran on their national security records. For George H. W. Bush, that record was not sufficient because of the economic recession; for George W. Bush, it was, in large part because the economy was not in recession and other grievances were not of the magnitude to defeat the president. Democratic pollster, Mark Mellman stated simply, "The reality is the country was not feeling the level of pain to oust an incumbent president."[28]

The ability of presidents to make news, to affect events, and to dispense the "spoils" of government can also work to their advantage. Presidents are in the limelight and can maneuver to remain there. Having a "bully pulpit" gives them an advantage in setting the campaign agenda in presidential as well as midterm elections. George W. Bush's emphasis on the war on terrorism in the 2002 midterm elections, especially his contention that rouge nations with weapons of mass destruction were a threat to U.S. security, illustrates how presidents can manipulate the campaign agenda to their own political advantage.

All recent presidents who have campaigned for reelection have tried to utilize the symbolic and ceremonial presidency, signing legislation into law in the Rose Garden of the White House, meeting heads of state in Washington or their own capitals, making speeches and announcements, holding press conferences, honoring military and civilians—all behind the presidential seal.

(*continued*)

BOX 7.1 | AN INCUMBENCY BALANCE SHEET *continued*

Clinton emphasized these presidential activities, giving rise to the term *constant campaign*. He all but obliterated the line between governing and campaigning. George W. Bush has done much the same.[29]

Presidents have another trump card. Presumably, their actions can influence events. They try to gear economic recoveries to election years. They also use their discretionary authority to distribute resources such as grants, contracts, and emergency aid to their political advantage. They must be careful, however, not to seem overtly partisan when doing so. Actions that they take that appear to be solely or primarily for political purposes, such as Ford's pardon of Nixon in 1974 or announcements of juicy federal government contracts during the election, can backfire.

The incumbency advantages extend to vice presidents seeking their party's presidential nomination but not nearly as much to their general election campaign. Of the four incumbent vice presidents who tried to succeed to the presidency directly from the vice presidency—Nixon (1960), Humphrey (1968), George H. W. Bush (1988), and Al Gore (2000)—only Bush was successful.

The difficulty that incumbent vice presidents face is that they cannot exert leadership from a position of followership. To establish their leadership credentials, vice presidents need to get out of their president's shadow; they have to separate themselves. If they do, it becomes that much more difficult for them to claim and share the successes of that administration. George H. W. Bush dealt with this problem by stating that he would pursue Reagan's agenda but do so in a kinder and gentler way. Moreover, he refused to indicate positions he had taken or advice he had given to Reagan, thereby casting his fate with his popular predecessor and forcing the electorate to judge him in 1988 on the basis of the performance of the administration in which he served.

Al Gore, on the other hand, articulated a popularist policy in contrast to the Clinton administration's more moderate, mainstream approach. Moreover, in his acceptance

---

sought reelection and eleven won; the two who lost, Taft in 1912 and Hoover in 1932, faced highly unusual circumstances. In Taft's case, he was challenged by the independent candidacy of former Republican president, Theodore Roosevelt. Together, Taft and Roosevelt split the Republican vote, enabling Democrat Woodrow Wilson to win with only 42 percent of the total vote. Hoover ran during the Great Depression, for which he received much of the blame.

Following the 1972 election, however, incumbents have not fared as well. All have sought reelection, but only Reagan, Clinton, and George W. Bush have been successful. Adverse political and economic factors help explain the defeats. The worst political scandal in the nation's history and the worst economic recession in forty years hurt Ford's chances, as did his pardon of the person who had nominated him for the vice presidency, Richard Nixon. In 1980 and 1992, a weak economy, a loss of confidence in the president's leadership abilities, and an anti-Washington mood contributed to Carter and George H. W. Bush's losses.

Today incumbents are advantaged or disadvantaged based on their perceived performance in office. Having a good record contributes to a president's reelection potential just as a poor record detracts from it. Bad times almost always hurt an

speech at the Democratic convention, Gore made a point of asking voters to support him on the basis of *his* policy goals, not Clinton's. "This election is not an award for past performance. I'm not asking you to vote for me on the basis of the economy we have. Tonight I ask for your support on the basis of the better, fairer, more prosperous America we can build together."[30]

Disadvantages of Incumbency

The challenges that contemporary presidents face, the persistent media criticism they encounter, and the anti-Washington, anti-politician mood of the contemporary electorate can offset the usual incumbency advantage.

In their campaigns for office, presidential candidates hype themselves, make promises, and create expectations. Once in office, however, they find these expectations difficult to meet. With the constitutional system dividing authority; the political system decentralizing power; and public opinion fluid, ambiguous, often inconsistent, and compartmentalized; it is difficult for presidents to build and maintain a governing consensus. Yet their leadership role demands that they do so—hence the gap between expectations and performance.

Persistent media criticism contributes to these difficulties. With radio and television talk-show hosts railing against them, their policies, and their behavior in office; with television and newspaper investigative reporters heightening public awareness of policy problems and inadequate governmental responses to them; and with network news coverage generally more critical of incumbents, particularly during presidential campaigns; presidents often find it hard to maintain a favorable leadership image, although Reagan was able to do so, and Clinton gained high job approval ratings during his last five years in office. George W. Bush's image was mixed as illustrated by his presidential approval scores that hovered around the 50 percent mark during his reelection campaign. On the issue of fighting terrorism, however, he received more praise than blame.

incumbent. A crisis, however, helps, at least in the short run. Rightly or wrongly, the public places most responsibility for economic conditions, social relations, and foreign affairs on the president. That a president may actually exercise little control over some of these external factors seems less relevant to the electorate than do negative conditions themselves, the desire that they be improved, and the expectation that *the president* do something about them.

Attributes such as personal favorability appear to be less important. Both Carter and George H. W. Bush had favorable personal ratings, yet both were defeated in their reelection attempts. Clinton's favorability evaluation was much less positive, yet he was easily reelected in 1996. However, his highly negative ratings in 2000 may have hurt Gore, or so Gore feared when he designed a strategy to separate himself from Clinton.

BUILDING A WINNING GEOGRAPHIC COALITION

In addition to designing a general appeal and addressing leadership and related incumbency issues, assembling a winning geographic coalition is also a critical strategic component of every presidential campaign. Since the election is decided in the Electoral College, the primary objective must always be to win a majority of the college, not necessarily a majority of the popular vote. In the words of George W. Bush's director of policy and media planning for his 2000 election campaign, Matthew Dowd, "We never put together a plan to win the popular vote. We put together a plan in the states that we targeted based on winning the Electoral College vote;"[31] Tad Devine, a senior adviser to John Kerry, uttered a similar refrain: "Strategically, our orientation was to win electoral votes in states that we considered battlegrounds. That is where we spent our time. That's where we sent our most precious resource—our candidates."[32]

Electoral College strategies almost always require candidates to campaign in the most competitive states, giving priority to those with the most electoral votes. These states are the most important in an Electoral College system because of the winner-take-all method by which the votes are allocated in all but two states (Maine and Nebraska)—hence the need to determine which states will be the most competitive states.

One criterion for assessing the level of competition, at least at the beginning of the election cycle, is the margin of victory in the previous presidential election. If that margin was within the range of +/−6 percent, the state is considered competitive; if the margin of victory exceeded that amount, it would probably not be unless a large influx or exodus of residents to or from that state occurred in the four years following the election. The influx of Hispanic immigrants in the Southwest, Colorado, and southern California is a case in point. States, which had long-established Republican voting patterns, such as Arizona and Colorado, have become much more competitive as a consequence of immigration from south of the border, while California, which had been competitive, is now tilting Democratic at the presidential level because of the growth of the Hispanic population.

Another strategic factor that can influence resource allocation strategies is the existence of a third party or independent candidate such as H. Ross Perot in the 1990s and Ralph Nader in 2000 and 2004. As noted previously, Nader's vote in Florida substantially exceeded the margin of Bush's 2000 victory, yet the Gore campaign prematurely decreased its advertising in that state, unaware that the Nader vote could be the difference between victory and defeat there. The Kerry campaign, determined not to make the same mistake four years later, worked hard at limiting Nader's ballot access and his popular vote in competitive states. (See Box 7.2 "Presidential Campaign Strategies in 2004").

In addition to the initial determination of how competitive the state may be, campaigns use public opinion polls to continuously monitor voter sentiment.[33] Polls that indicate a closer-than-expected race can trigger the expenditure of more resources by both sides; if the number of advertising buys or candidate appearances increase on one side, the other campaign usually takes notice, conducts its own poll, and if the findings confirm that opinion is becoming closely divided, adjusts its Electoral College strategy accordingly. Resource calculations are made primarily on the basis of polling data, the relative strength or weakness of the party organization in the state, the number of electoral votes that are at stake, and the availability of funds.

In building their Electoral College coalitions, candidates start with their base—areas that have been traditionally favorable to their party's nominees. Following the Civil War, the Democrats could depend on the "Solid South," while Republicans were stronger in the Northeast. Beginning in the 1960s, these areas began to shift their partisan allegiances. By the mid-1990s, the South was solidly Republican, and the Southwest was increasingly Republican, while the Northeast was becoming more Democratic. With the Rocky Mountain region strongly Republican, and the Pacific Coast states leaning Democratic, the focus of recent campaigns has been the Midwest, America's so called weather vane, a region that tends to reflect the country's mood.

Since 1968, Republicans who have won the presidency have concentrated their campaigns in the major battleground states in the Midwest. The three Democratic victories, by Carter in 1976 and Clinton in 1992 and 1996, were achieved by narrowing the Republican advantage in the South and winning a majority of the large industrial states.[34] When the Republicans are not able to take the South for granted, they must devote more resources to this area. Doing so enables the Democrats to compete more effectively in other regions of the country.

In 2000 and 2004, both parties focused their efforts on a few key battleground states. Each side began their campaign with about twenty states in play. As the campaign progressed, the number of competitive states decreased. Initially in 2004, Florida, Pennsylvania, and West Virginia were considered highly competitive, as were Oregon and Washington. By the end, these states had shifted in the direction of one candidate or the other, and as a consequence, both campaigns directed most of their resources to a few Midwest states—Ohio, Wisconsin, Missouri, Iowa, and Minnesota—plus three additional small states that polls indicated were too close to call: Nevada, New Hampshire, and New Mexico. Said Tad Devine, a senior Kerry adviser, "We were looking at the same geography. We knew ten months before that this thing was about winning two out of three of Ohio, Florida, and Pennsylvania. It wasn't that complicated."[35]

The concentration of both campaigns in the same key battleground states is evident from the advertising buys and candidate appearances of the presidential hopefuls plus party and nonparty group activity. (See Table 7.1.)

From the standpoint of the Electoral College, continuity, not change, has characterized the presidential vote in the first two elections of the twenty-first century. Only three states, New Hampshire, New Mexico, and Iowa, switched their vote from 2000 to 2004. The continuity of these voting patterns suggests that in 2008, the presidential election will again be concentrated in the Midwest, Southwest, and a few other small but competitive states. The home states of the candidates, population shifts in the South and Southwest, and a major event, such as a natural disaster or economic downturn that impacts disproportionately on a particular region of the country, could also affect the 2008 Electoral College strategy of each of the major parties' presidential

| BOX 7.2 | PRESIDENTIAL CAMPAIGN STRATEGIES IN 2004 |

George W. Bush: A New Strategy for Staying in Place
The components of Bush's 2004 election strategy were derived from the political environment in which the country found itself at the beginning of the twenty-first century, the character strengths George W. Bush demonstrated as president following the terrorist attacks on September 11, 2001, John Kerry's character weaknesses, and the advantages incumbents have in seeking reelection when national security issues are dominant.

The principal goal of the reelection strategy was to enlarge the Republican electorate since it was assumed that most of the electorate had already made up their minds and were strongly inclined to vote in accordance with their partisan loyalties. There simply were not many undecided voters as indicated in Table 7.2.

Learning from Experience This election strategy grew out of the failure of Bush's 2000 election campaign to win a popular vote victory. Republican strategists blamed themselves for not getting out the maximum Christian fundamentalist vote in 2000. They were determined not to repeat this tactical error again. In the words of Ken Mehlman, who initially headed the political office in the Bush White House and later directed the president's reelection campaign:

> The 2000 campaign convinced us of a lot of different things, but one of the most important things was that we needed a plan to try to expand the electorate and particularly expand our part of the electorate. There was a four-year plan to accomplish that, which included lots of different things. Fundamentally, it included two big things: one, to use the 2001 and 2002 elections to test out all kinds of different political tactics and make sure that we were being most effective in 2004. . . (turnout, television advertising—where we bought, how we bought it). But secondly, just as important, was a way of communicating to key audiences that would expand the electorate.[37]

| TABLE 7.2 | TIME OF VOTING DECISION IN THE 2004 ELECTION CAMPAIGN |

Question: When did you make up your mind?

Time Frame	2004
In the voting booth	1
On Election Day	1
In the last few days before the election	2
In the last week	4
Before that	92

Source: Jeffrey M. Jones and Joseph Carroll, "Changing Minds in the 2004 Election? A Report on Gallup's Post-Election Panel Survey," Gallup Poll, (June 3, 2005). http://www.gallup.com/content/default.aspx?16576&pg=3.

(continued)

BOX 7.2 | PRESIDENTIAL CAMPAIGN STRATEGIES IN 2004
continued

Expanding the Electorate: The Ground Campaign Republican efforts to improve partisan turnout began immediately after the 2000 presidential campaign. Fifty million dollars was spent in 2002 alone, developing and testing "victory-type" programs.[38] The GOP had become convinced that the old-style programs, "the traditional buying ads on three channels, doing some robo-calls, and doing some paid mail as a voter contact," were no longer sufficient.[39]

Republican political strategists decided that a multifaceted approach was necessary to identify and contact people with pro-Republican inclinations. Moreover, the volunteers who did the contacting should be known, personally or by reputation, by the people they contacted. The volunteers should live in the same communities as the people whose vote they were soliciting.[40]

The information necessary to direct such an appeal to the "right" people, those who would be most responsive, was available, but it had to be collected, integrated, and analyzed. The Republicans set about collecting and collating a huge data set in 2001. They combined lists of people who attended church regularly; belonged to certain groups with Republican leanings; subscribed to certain publications; listened to or watched certain networks, stations, or programs; contributed to a Republican candidate in the past; and/or lived in certain areas, Republican-leaning suburbs or more rural communities.

Step one was to identify these people; step two was to determine whether they were registered to vote (and if registered, with which party); step three was to focus on those who were not registered or who had not voted regularly in the past but had the characteristics of likely Republican voters; step four was to begin the process of contacting these so called "lazy Republicans," and get them registered and motivated to vote. In states that permitted voting before Election Day, the goal was to convince people to vote early because an early vote is considered a surer one than if it were cast on Election Day.

The plan required well-trained and committed partisans who could be counted on to initiate and maintain contacts with members of the targeted group. In the past, both parties had turned to paid organizers, party professionals, labor unions, nonparty groups, and even profit-making firms to turn out the vote. The Republican plan deviated from past grassroots efforts by depending primarily on community-based volunteers. Mehlman described it as a "bottoms-up" effort:

> We did not have outsiders come in. This was bottom up, not top down. What we tried to do was to provide channels for those people all over the country that supported this president to get their energies and their enthusiasms involved, and to figure out metrics by which we could figure our resource allocation.[41]

The strategy depended on intense, positive feelings toward the president and his party. In 2004, those feelings were present; by 2006, they had weakened considerably. Democrats also felt strongly and for the most part, negatively about Bush and/or his policies in 2004, but most did not feel as strongly about Kerry. In other words, Republicans displayed greater intensity toward Bush than Democrats did toward Kerry.

Another important component of the Republican ground campaign was its focus on the cultural issues. The eleven state ballot initiatives on gay marriage, the President's repeated reference to a constitutional amendment that would define marriage as a union between man and woman, and Bush's own and frequently stated beliefs about God and the sanctity of human life, all contributed to the success of the Republican's get-out-the-vote strategy.[42]

Focusing on the President's Character Strengths and His Opponent's Weaknesses A second strategic thrust of Bush's reelection campaign was the emphasis on leadership. The president had established his leadership credentials following the terrorist attacks on the World Trade Center and the Pentagon. Even if people disagreed with his policies, they acknowledged his attributes of strength, conviction, determination, and purpose. Bush had passed the leadership test; Kerry had not taken it in the minds of the American people. Stated Matthew Dowd, a senior strategist for the Bush campaign:

> There were a lot of people who never knew if Kerry wanted to cut and run—they didn't know what he wanted to do. On Election Day, a lot of them questioned whether or not he had a different plan than the President. In the end, the majority of voters said, I trust the President more than John Kerry on Iraq.[43]

The Bush campaign replayed its leadership qualities card again and again, comparing the president's actions after 9/11 to his challenger's equivocation, lack of clarity, and penchant for reversing himself. The Republicans believed that on the national security issue, Kerry had not demonstrated qualities of leadership that would make him an acceptable alternative to Bush during a war on terrorism. Here's how campaign manager, Ken Mehlman, put it:

> If you look historically, when people reject an incumbent because they are worried about an issue that's out there, they reject the incumbent because they think the challenger has a certain quality that helps deal with the issue they are worried about. In 1980, the public viewed the Iranian Hostage Crisis as evidence that Jimmy Carter was a weak leader, which they always thought, and they wanted a strong leader, Ronald Reagan. In 1992, . . . when people heard economic news they didn't think was good enough, they wanted a guy who was going to focus on the economy. That had always been Clinton's definition. . . . If people thought Iraq was really messed up and was a tougher battle than before, then they wanted someone who would be a strong leader. . . . [Kerry] did have national security experience, but he wasn't defined as a strong leader as the President was.[44]

It's Terrorism Stupid Keeping the focus on the war on terrorism also worked to Bush's advantage even though the news from Iraq was generally negative. The president and his surrogates dealt with bad news by reminding the electorate about the war on terror, that Iraq was a second front in that war, and as important, that Kerry seemed to be talking out of both sides of his mouth.

The campaign also kept the president focused on the issue that aids incumbents the most, threats to the nation's security. When these security issues are salient, incumbents tend to be reelected. Moreover, since the end of World War II, the public has placed more confidence in the Republicans' ability to be tougher in foreign affairs than the Democrats'.[45]

Being the incumbent helped Bush as well. The Bush Reelection Committee tried to maximize their incumbency advantages by using the bully pulpit to frame the campaign debate, shielding Bush from the press, and using the backdrop of the White House and the presidential seal to distinguish George W. Bush from his Democratic challenger.

(continued)

BOX 7.2 PRESIDENTIAL CAMPAIGN STRATEGIES IN 2004
continued

John Kerry's Strategy: "Anything You Can Do, I Can Do Better"
With the electorate divided evenly along partisan lines and Kerry's leadership qualities disputed, the Democratic challenger did not have an obvious or easy road to take to the White House. In fact, he began with several disadvantages. The five-week period following the Democratic convention and before the Republican one was the biggest according to campaign manager Mary Beth Cahill.[46] Going silent after his acceptance speech undercut whatever momentum the convention gave to Kerry and made him a target for his Republican critics, especially the Swift Boat Veterans for Truth. (See Chapter 8, page 284.)

A second problem concerned the president's personal favorability ratings that precluded a campaign to demonize him. Kerry went after Bush's policies with some success among Democrats but not among Republicans. Nor were the proportion of undecided independents large enough or angry enough at Bush for Kerry to gain a decisive edge.

Moreover, the issue of change was a mixed one for the Democrats. The critical news on Iraq, high gasoline prices, spiraling deficits, and limited job opportunities for people without the requisite skills provided Kerry with some targets of opportunity on policy issues but not on the overall leadership question.

Advocating leadership change in times of crisis is difficult for challengers unless they can demonstrate that the incumbent's policies or actions were responsible for the crisis *and* that the challenger has demonstrated superior leadership qualities to deal with such a crisis. The Kerry campaign did not try to tag Bush with the responsibility for 9/11, only with a failed policy in Iraq; and as we have already noted, Kerry's personal character traits did not add up to Bush's for dealing with another 9/11 situation in the minds of most Americans.

At the heart of tactics are communications, the messages that are directed to audiences and those that reach the electorate indirectly after being mediated by the news media. Most people will not experience a campaign directly—they will not attend an event, line a parade route, call in a question on a talk show, or volunteer their money or services to the campaign—but they will hear about it from acquaintances, read about it in newspapers and magazines, and see and hear it on radio television, and the Internet.

We turn first to the efforts of the campaign to reach, engage, and mobilize as large an audience as possible: how they do it, what communications they use, and what the impact those communications have on voting behavior. Then we turn to campaign events themselves that often have an impact beyond the audience that attends it. Here we discuss advancing the event, choreographing it, and enhancing the candidate's style and interactive skills.

CAMPAIGN OUTREACH: THE MEDIUM AND THE MESSAGE

There are a variety of ways to convey a political message, including door-to-door canvassing, direct mail, e-mail and other communications on the Internet,

Policy The Kerry strategy was composed of three basic parts: policy change, leadership acceptability, and partisanship. Within the policy dimension, Kerry and the Democrats tried to separate Iraq from the war on terrorism, criticize economic policies of the Bush administration and Republican Congress as skewed toward the rich, and promote their concern for family values. However, the backing Kerry received from individuals and groups that were pro-choice, pro gay rights, and pro separation of church and state, and the positions Kerry took on these issues, undercut his pro-family values' claim on social issues in the minds of social conservatives.

Personal Leadership Nor was Kerry able to evoke the passions among Democrats that Bush was able to generate among Republicans, making it more difficult for the Democrats to enlarge their partisan base than it was for the Republicans to enlarge theirs. The Bush campaign, Republican campaign ads, and nonparty groups such as the Swift Boat Veterans for Truth raised questions about Kerry's leadership potential, which the Kerry campaign was unable to refute satisfactorily.

Democratic groups were successful, however, in minimizing the impact of the Nader campaign. State Democratic Party organizations impeded ballot access for Ralph Nader in several key states such as Oregon and Pennsylvania. Similarly, Kerry ads and talking campaigns in the battleground states reminded voters that a vote for Nader was a vote for Bush. In the end, the Nader campaign did not appreciably affect the results as it had four years earlier.

But the bottom line was that Kerry was unable to convince an American electorate dubious of Bush's foreign and economic policies, much less his conservative ideological approach on social issues, that he could provide stronger, more dependable, more coherent leadership in the war on terrorism. In the end, that inability proved fatal.

and indirectly, through the news and entertainment media. At the local level, door-to-door campaigning may be a viable option, but personal contact is also time-consuming and volunteer-intensive.[47] Beginning in the 1960s and continuing through the 1980s, candidates and parties devoted more of their resources to mass-marketing techniques. Turnout dropped as a consequence.

Today, advances in communications technology, particularly the ability to direct appeals to specific groups of voters, have rejuvenated grassroots campaigns. Both parties have invested millions of dollars in new computer-based data set and programs to identify potential supporters, persuade them of the merits of their candidates, and get them out to vote. Labor unions and other nonparty groups took the lead for the Democrats, while the Republican National Committee designed, tested, and conducted its highly successful 2004 turnout effort.

The results of the parties' outreach activities are shown in Table 7.3, data collected by David B. Magleby and Kelly D. Patterson for the nonpartisan Campaign Finance Institute. In 2004, 71 percent of the voters in battleground states reported being contacted by telephone by someone active in one of the campaigns, 76 percent by direct mail, and 27 percent by personal visits or contacts as indicated in Table 7.3.

TABLE 7.3 │ GRASSROOTS CAMPAIGNING IN 2004 (IN PERCENTAGES)

Intensity of Campaigning	Battleground	Nonbattleground
Contacted personally to vote early	27	9
Contacted personally	23	14
Received letter or mail	76	54
Received request to donate money	26	25
Received telephone call	71	52
Received e-mail	15	13

Source: David B. Magleby and Kelly D. Patterson, "Stepping Out of the Shadows? Ground War Activity in 2004," in Michael B. Malbin, ed. *The Election After Reform: Money, Politics, and the Bipartisan Campaign Reform Act.* (Landam, M.D.: Rowman and Littlefield, 2006): (Table 8.1).

Communicating the Message

Of the various ways to reach the electorate, personal visits and conversations in the workplace or during leisure activities are the most effective but also the most labor-intensive. Telephone calls can also have an impact, but it varies with the messenger and the message. Both parties use recorded appeals by party and group leaders to mobilize various ethnic, racial, and religious communities. In 2004, Bill Clinton, Jesse Jackson, and John Kerry recorded messages to Democrats as did George W. Bush, Laura Bush, George H. W. Bush, and Arnold Schwartzenegger to Republicans.

Candidate interviews that are carried by radio and television, major speeches and candidate appearances, and campaign advertising are all designed to reach people who learn about the campaign primarily through the news media. One recent change has been the shift from the national broadcast networks to local affiliates and specialized cable channels to target groups of voters in the most cost-effective way. Developments in the communications media, specifically in satellite technology, enable candidates to remain in a studio and talk with local anchors around the country. Electronic town meetings and press conferences have now become standard fare.

The 2004 election saw the expansion of campaign activity on the Internet, an easy and cheap way to reach voters who access campaign Web sites and provide their e-mail addresses. Younger voters have become an attractive target for e-mail communication. Direct mail has also been used to convey a specific message to a specific audience. It tends to have greater impact on those who are less educated, particularly those who do not receive a lot of other mail.

Designing and Testing the Message

Candidates are normally very careful about their public utterances. Knowing that the press focuses on inconsistencies and highlights controversies, they tend to stick to a prepared script that coordinates themes, positions, pictures, and words. Reagan did so successfully in 1984. His campaign introduced a new theme every ten days to two weeks and keyed the president's speeches to it. Situations that might have distracted public attention or confused it were carefully controlled.

Speeches and policy statements are constructed on the basis of survey research and focus group testing and are targeted to certain groups. Frequently, code words are used to generate a reaction from the group. The message is often compartmentalized. Groups get only those positions and priorities that the campaign has determined to be most in accord with their opinions and beliefs. Other candidate stands and beliefs are not conveyed. The problem with such specialized messages is that they can lead to unrealistic expectations that the newly elected or reelected president cannot achieve.

Timing the Message

In addition to what to say, how to say it, and to whom, timing is also an important consideration. Candidates naturally desire to build momentum as their campaigns progress. The 1996 Clinton campaign was one of the most successful in adhering to a timed plan for communicating various messages to the voters. In the year before the election, the president emphasized his centrist and moderate positions, co-opting many of the Republicans' policy stands in the process. As the nomination campaign got under-way, he talked about family values and showcased himself in various presidential roles, in stark contrast with the Republican candidates who were criticizing one another's qualifications for the presidency. During the general election campaign, Clinton remained on his presidential pedestal, emphasizing the accomplishments of his administration and his desire to build a "bridge to the future."

In the 2000 election, Bush allocated his resources evenly over the course of the campaign, whereas Gore spent more heavily in the final weeks. However, the Republican National Committee, which had more money on hand than did its Democratic counterpart, made up the difference by running ads on Bush's behalf.

ORCHESTRATING THE POLITICAL EVENT

Staging a campaign event is not easy. The appearance of the stage, the timing of the speech or rally, the dignitaries invited and where they sit, the size and manner of the audience, the facilities for press coverage, the videotaping of the event for the campaign, and of course, the candidate's dress, speech (and the sound bites written in it), and interaction with those present must be planned in detail well ahead of the event. Nothing should be left to chance.

Advance

Whether appearing in person or on television, much advance work is necessary. Jerry Bruno, who advanced Democratic presidential campaigns in the 1960s, described his tasks as an advance man, tasks that have not changed all that much over the years:

> It's my job in a campaign to decide where a rally should be held, how a candidate can best use his time getting from an airport to that rally, who should sit next to him and chat with him quietly in his hotel room before or after a political speech, and who should be kept as far away from him as possible.
>
> It's also my job to make sure that a public appearance goes well—a big crowd, an enthusiastic crowd, with bands and signs, a motorcade that is mobbed by enthusiastic supporters, a day in which a candidate sees and is seen by as many people as possible—and at the same time have it all properly recorded by the press and their cameras.[48]

Bruno's efforts are indicative of the great lengths to which modern campaigns go to prevent uncontrolled and unanticipated events from marring a presidential candidate's appearance.

The Bush campaign of 2004 took the art of crowd control to new heights. Almost all Bush events required tickets, and the Republicans monitored their distribution. In most cases, tickets went to party workers, campaign volunteers, and political donors. Protestors, evident at some Bush events, were kept outside and at a distance; if one protestor or a small group of them managed to slip in and displayed critical posters, banners, or even t-shirts, or heckled the president, they would be escorted out by campaign security personnel. Town meeting participants were screened, selected in advance, and rehearsed. Camera crews, hired by the Bush-Cheney campaign, recorded the events and distributed video film clips to local and regional television.

The Kerry campaign, while well organized, was not nearly as efficient as Bush's. It too distributed tickets for events but did so through labor unions or local and state party organizations. Pledges of loyalty were not required for admission. In fact, Kerry would frequently quip, "I trust nobody here had to sign a loyalty oath to get in."

Personal Style of the Candidates
George W. Bush is a disciplined campaigner. In both his presidential campaigns, he stayed on message, did not ad lib, and talked to his audience in language that usually evoked favorable responses and considerable applause. When religious conservatives made up a substantial portion of the audience, Bush would make frequent references to foundational Christian values: marriage, family, religion, the sanctity of every life, and God-given freedom and human rights; when the audience was composed of business leaders and independent entrepreneurs, the president unleashed his litany of fundamental economic values; individual initiative, private ownership, lower taxes, and America as a land of opportunity. In 2004, regardless of the composition of the audience, Bush would almost always return to his central campaign theme: the terrorist threat and his personal resolve to defend the security of the American people with "whatever it takes."

Relations with the press, however, changed dramatically in the two campaigns. In 2000, Bush interacted with the news media, particularly with the reporters who traveled with him on the campaign trail; in 2004, the press was kept at a distance. Questions were discouraged; interviews were rare, but e-mails and faxes from campaign headquarters and from the communications operation on the president's plane were plentiful. There were also ample photo opportunities given to the news media in settings that made Bush look presidential and/or regal, popular, and friendly.

The Bush campaign was determined to avoid controversies caused by off-the-cuff remarks. In his 2000 campaign, Bush had experienced such a situation, which diverted focus from the message and marred the image of the candidate. Not realizing a microphone in front of him was open, the candidate used a scatological metaphor to characterize a *New York Times* reporter to vice presidential candidate Dick Cheney, who, in turn, replied, "big time." Sixteen years earlier, Bush's father had used a similar epithet.[49]

Occasionally, one-liners have worked to a candidate's advantage, at least in the short run. When Republican vice presidential nominee Dan Quayle compared his Senate experience with John F. Kennedy's in his debate with Lloyd Bentsen, the Democratic candidate shot back, "I served with Jack Kennedy; I knew Jack Kennedy; Jack Kennedy was a friend of mine. Senator, you are no Jack Kennedy."[50] Quayle, shaken by Bentsen's blunt reply, remained on the defensive for the remainder of the debate.

Although Kerry, like Bush, had standard stump speeches, he would digress from the text more than his Republican opponent did. The challenger's style was to criticize Bush's policies but not Bush personally. Kerry talked more about domestic issues; he was, however, very critical of the president's judgment and his management of the war in Iraq, but the alternatives the Democratic challenger presented were not nearly as clear-cut as Bush's, thereby reinforcing the equivocator mantra that Bush and his Republican surrogates placed on Kerry. After Kerry's early nomination experience in which he was accused of being aloof and unapproachable, the Democratic nominee took questions and interacted more with the press corps. Kerry was more accessible to the news media than was Bush in the 2004 campaign.

SUMMARY

Throughout much of the nineteenth century, presidential campaigns were run by the political parties on behalf of their nominees. The goal of the campaign was to energize and educate the electorate with a series of public activities and events. Beginning in the 1840s, but accelerating in the 1880s, presidential candidates themselves became increasingly involved in the campaign. By the 1920s, they had become active participants, using radio, later television, and more recently, the Internet, to reach as many voters as possible.

Advances in transportation and communications have made campaigns more complex, more expensive, and more technologically sophisticated. These advances require considerable activity by the candidates and their staffs. Strategy and tactics are now more closely geared to the technology of contemporary politics and run by campaign professionals: pollsters, media consultants, direct mailers, grassroots organizers, lawyers, accountants, database collectors and analysts, and Internet operatives. Their inclusion in the candidate's organization has made the coordination of centralized decision making critical. It has also produced several complementary organizations, that of the candidate, the party, outside groups and coalitions, and when an incumbent is running, the White House.

The job of campaign organizations is to produce a unified and coordinated effort. Most presidential campaigns follow a general strategy based on the prevailing political attitudes and perceptions of the electorate, the reputations and images of the nominees and their parties, and the geography of the Electoral College. The strategy includes designing a basic appeal, creating a leadership image, dealing with incumbency (if appropriate), and allocating campaign resources in the light of the Electoral College.

In projecting their basic appeal, Democratic candidates have emphasized their party label and those "bread-and-butter" issues that have held their coalition together since the 1930s. Republican candidates, on the other hand, did not emphasize partisanship until the 1980s when the Republicans gained parity with the Democrats, focusing instead on domestic and foreign policy problems. They also stressed character issues.

Part of the strategy of every presidential campaign is to project an image of leadership. Candidates do this by trumpeting their own strengths and exploiting their opponent's weaknesses. They try to project those traits that the public desires in their president, traits that are endemic to the office and resonate with the public mood at that time.

An established record, particularly by presidents seeking reelection, shapes much of that leadership imagery. That record may contribute to or detract from the candidates' reelection potential. In good times, incumbents have an advantage; in bad times, they do not. When national security issues are salient, incumbents usually benefit; when economic issues are paramount, they do not. Being president, making critical decisions, and exercising the powers of the office is evidence of the leadership skills that challengers have to demonstrate, thereby giving incumbents an advantage.

When allocating resources, the geography of the Electoral College must always be considered. Each party begins with a base of safe states. In the 1980s, that base was thought to be larger for the Republicans than for the Democrats. Population movements to the South and the West resulted in a regional advantage for the Republicans, one that allowed them greater flexibility in designing their general election strategy. In the 1990s, however, the Democrats seemed to gain an advantage in the Northeast and Pacific Coast. Today, no party has a lock on the Electoral College.

The level of competition within states is another factor that affects campaign strategy and resource allocation. Less than one-half of the states are truly competitive at the beginning of the race and usually less than a dozen at the end. Time, effort, and money are concentrated within the most competitive states; the rest of the country witnesses the campaign primarily in the news and by word of mouth; they do not see the candidates in person except perhaps at a fund-raiser during the preelection period; they do not see many if any of the political commercials, except if they are controversial and become news in and of themselves; and they receive less personal and computer-generated communication than do those in the key battleground states.

The candidates' strategies influence the conduct of their campaigns, but their tactics tend to have greater and more direct effect on day-to-day events and get-out-the-vote activities. Key tactical decisions include what communication techniques are to be used, when, and by whom. They also include what appeals are to be made, how, when, and to whom.

Campaign events are designed to project and reinforce the candidate's image and policy appeals and to critique those of the opponent's. Everything is carefully planned from the composition of the audience, to the positioning of the cameras, to the script for the candidate and others who may also address the crowd, to the sitting arrangement on the platform.

The event is only one component of the campaign. In addition, policy and personal appeals are directed to specific groups with three goals in mind: turning out as large a partisan electorate as possible; translating partisan orientations into voting behavior; and generating a mass appeal that will attract independents and partisans of the other party.

In the end, the methods that mobilize the electorate by getting people excited about a candidate are likely to generate the most impact in turning out and influencing the vote. Much of the campaign is filtered through the news media, however. The next chapter explores this mediation and its impact on the election.

WHERE ON THE WEB?

Many of the *Where on the Web* sites listed in Chapter 5 will be useful for the general election as well.

- **Campaigns and Elections**
  www.campaignline.com
    Posts articles that have appeared in the magazine *Campaigns and Elections*.
- **24-7 News Networks: CNN; Fox News; MSNBC**
  www.CNN.com
  www.foxnews.com
  www.msnbc.com
    Contain news, investigatory, and feature stories on the presidential campaign.

- **C-SPAN: The Road to the White House 2008**
  www.cspan.org

  Provides C-SPAN programming on the campaign as well as candidate appearances, speeches, student surveys, and political debates.

- **Gallup Poll**
  www.gallup.com

  Contains the latest polling data on the campaign. Gallup is one of the premier polling organizations.

- **National Journal**
  www.nationaljournal.com

  Of the many news sources for following the presidential primaries and caucuses, the *National Journal's* site is one of the best.

- **New York Times**
  www.nytimes.com

  The *New York Times* prides itself on being a paper of record. You will find much information on the policy positions and speeches of the candidates in this newspaper as well as the latest delegate count and prenomination polls.

- **Politics1**
  www.politics1.com

  An online guide to current politics with links to other relevant sites for the 2004 election.

- **Polling Report**
  www.pollingreport.com

  Summarizes ongoing public polls on the 2004 election.

Exercises

1. Assess how the candidates targeted their appeals in the most recent presidential election. What appeals have they directed toward their own partisans, especially to the principal groups in their party's traditional electoral coalition, and how have they dealt with independents and others, including those who say they support third-party candidates?
2. Indicate the initial geographic strategies of the major party candidates in 2004 and then how those strategies changed over the course of the campaign. Now compare these strategies to those you believe that should or will be employed in 2008. Design a resource allocation memo for the candidate of your choice.
3. How have the tactics of presidential campaigns changed over the years? To what extent have the theories of mass marketing affected political campaigns?
4. Write a memo for your party's presidential candidate on the most effective ways to use the Internet to reach, energize, and motivate partisans and those without partisan affiliations.

5. List the type of activities that a contemporary "war room" for a presidential candidate must do.

SELECTED READINGS

Institute of Politics, John F. Kennedy School of Government, Harvard University, ed. *Campaign for President: The Managers Look at 2004*. Landam, M.D.: Rowman & Littlefield, 2006.

Jamieson, Kathleen Hall, and Paul Waldman, eds. *Electing the President 2000: The Insiders' View*. Philadelphia: University of Pennsylvania Press, 2001.

McCubbins, Mathew D., ed. *Under the Watchful Eye: Managing Presidential Campaigns in the Television Era*. Washington, D.C.: Congressional Quarterly Press, 1992.

Melder, Keith. *Hail to the Candidate: Presidential Campaigns from Banners to Broadcasts*. Washington, D.C.: Smithsonian Institution Press, 1992.

Morris, Dick. *Behind the Oval Office*. New York: Random House, 1997.

Nader, Ralph. *Crashing the Party: Taking on the Corporate Government in an Age of Surrender*. New York: St. Martin's Press, 2002.

Ornstein, Norman, and Thomas Mann, eds. *The Permanent Campaign and Its Future*. Washington, D.C.: AEI/Brookings, 2000.

Tenpas, Kathryn Dunn, *Presidents as Candidates*. New York: Garland, 1997.

Troy, Gil. *See How They Ran: The Changing Role of the Presidential Candidate*. New York: Free Press, 1991.

White, Theodore H. *The Making of the President: 1960*. New York: Atheneum, 1988.

—— *The Making of the President, 1964*. New York: Atheneum, 1965.

—— *The Making of the President, 1968*. New York: Atheneum, 1969.

—— *The Making of the President, 1972*. New York: Atheneum, 1973.

—— *America in Search of Itself: The Making of the President, 1956–1980*. New York: Harper & Row, 1982.

Woodward, Bob. *The Choice*. New York: Simon & Schuster, 1997.

NOTES

1. Keith Melder, *Hail to the Candidate: Presidential Campaigns from Banners to Broadcasts* (Washington D.C.: Smithsonian Institution Press, 1992), pp. 70–74.

2. Ibid., p. 87.

3. Ibid., p. 88.

4. Marvin R. Weisbord, *Campaigning for President* (New York: Washington Square Press, 1966), p. 45.

5. Historian Gil Troy writes that Lincoln's avoidance of anything that smacked of political involvement was in fact a political tactic that he used throughout the campaign, emphasizing passivity and partisanship. Gil Troy, *See How They Ran: The Changing Role of the Presidential Candidate* (New York: Free Press, 1991), p. 66.

6. Weisbord, *Campaigning for President*, p. 5.

7. Melder, *Hail to the Candidate*, p. 104.

8. Ibid., p. 125.

9. Keith Melder, "The Whistlestop: Origins of the Personal Campaign," *Campaign and Elections*, 7 (May/June 1986), p. 49.

10. William Jennings Bryan, *The First Battle* (1896; reprint, Port Washington, N.Y.: Kennikat Press, 1971), p. 618.

11. Melder, *Hail to the Candidate*, p. 129.

12. Weisbord, *Campaigning for President*, p. 116

13. Franklin Roosevelt had been disabled by polio in 1921. He wore heavy leg braces and could stand only with difficulty. Nonetheless, he made a remarkable physical and political recovery. In his campaign, he went to great lengths to hide the fact that he could not walk and could barely stand. The press generally did not report on his disability. They refrained from photographing, filming, or describing him struggling to stand with braces.

14. Cabell Phillips, *The Truman Presidency* (New York: Macmillan, 1966), p. 237.

15. Stanley Kelley, *Professional Public Relations and Political Power* (Baltimore: Johns Hopkins Press, 1956), pp. 161–162.

16. Karl A. Lamb and Paul A. Smith, *Campaign Decision Making: The Presidential Election of 1964* (Belmont, C.A.: Wadsworth, 1968), pp. 59–63.

17. Jim Rutenberg, "In Bush's War Room, the Gloves Are Always Off," *New York Times*, (July 14, 2004), pp. A1, A18.

18. There was, however, a clash of personalities at the outset of the 1996 Clinton campaign. The principal antagonists were chief strategist Dick Morris along with the campaign operatives he brought on board and senior White House staffers who saw their roles as advisers and felt their access to the president threatened by the Morris group. However, these differences were muted by the apparent success of the Clinton campaign, the president's steady rise in the polls, and the joint strategy sessions, which the president conducted. The friction ended with Morris's resignation from the campaign after allegations of his weekly liaison with a Washington "call girl" became public. However, the strategic plan, which Morris had developed, continued to guide the campaign.

19. In the words of James Carville, principal Clinton strategist in 1992:

    By the time the convention had come, we had spent a lot of time, a lot of money, a lot of research on determining what it was that we wanted to do. By mid-June, . . . we had a pretty good idea of the things that we needed to accomplish, of the nature and depth of our problems, and how we wanted to solve them and accomplish our objectives. . . . Strategically, we knew 85 percent of what we wanted to do by late June.

    James Carville, in Charles T. Royer, ed. *Campaign for President: The Managers Look at '92* (Hollis, N.H.: Hollis Publishing, 1994), p. 194.

20. George W. Bush believed that his father had made a major error by not considering his reelection as a component of the political power he was able to exercise as president. The younger Bush was determined not to repeat this error.

21. An excellent examination of presidential traits appears in Benjamin I. Page, *Choices and Echoes in Presidential Elections* (Chicago: University of Chicago Press, 1978), pp. 232–265. The discussion that follows in the text is based in part on Professor Page's description and analysis.

22. George W. Bush, "Acceptance Speech at the Republican National Convention," www.georgebush.com (August 3, 2000).

23. Thomas B. Edsall, "Why Bush Accentuates the Negative," *Washington Post* (Oct. 2, 1988), p. C4.

24. Lydia Saad, "Republicans and Democrats Seek Similar Qualities in 44th President," Gallup Poll, April 4, 2007. www.gallup.com/content/default.aspx?ci=27088.

25. Fred Steeper, in Royer, *Campaign for President*, p. 192.

26. A survey conducted by the Times Mirror Center for the People & the Press in early October 1992 found that 50 percent of those who saw the Bush advertisements felt that they were not truthful compared with 35 percent for the viewers of Clinton's ads. Times Mirror Center for the People & the Press, "Campaign '92: Air Wars." (Oct. 8, 1992), p. 2.

27. Howard Kurtz and Terry M. Neal, "Bush Team Devised Truth Trap That's Tripping Gore," *Washington Post* (Oct. 15, 2000), p. A11.

28. Institute of Politics, Harvard University, ed. *Campaign for President, The Managers Look at 2004* (Landam, M.D.: Rowman & Littlefield, 2006), p. 138.

29. Elisabeth Bumiller, "Keepers of Bush Image Lift Stagecraft to New Heights," *New York Times* (May 16, 2003), pp. A1, A20. See also George C. Edwards III, *Governing by Campaigning* (New York: Pearson/Longman, 2007).

30. Al Gore, "Acceptance Speech to the Democratic National Convention," www.algore 2000.com (Aug. 17, 2000).

31. Kathleen Hall Jamieson and Paul Waldman, eds. *Electing the President 2000: The Insiders' View* (Philadelphia: University of Pennsylvania Press, 2001), p. 45.

32. *Campaign for President 2004*, p. 153.

33. Matthew Dowd in Jamieson and Waldman, *Electing the President*, p. 45.

34. Since 1960, the only Democratic presidential candidates who have been able to win in the South were southerners such as Jimmy Carter (Georgia), who carried much of the South in 1976 but not in 1980, and Bill Clinton (Arkansas), who won approximately half the southern states in 1992 and 1996.

35. *Campaign for President 2004*, p. 196.

36. During the Republican primaries and caucuses, Dole emphasized his Senate leadership role in contrast to the less impressive resumes of his challengers; after he had effectively won the nomination and the Senate got mired in controversy, Dole changed his tactical focus and resigned from the Senate to become "Citizen Dole." When the citizenship role did not close the gap with an incumbent president, Dole turned to substantive issues, specifically, his proposal to cut income taxes by 15 percent. When the tax issue failed to generate the desired response, the Dole campaign changed its focus to other policy issues. Failing again to gain much

leverage from these issues, Dole turned his attention to the president, first emphasizing Clinton's liberalism and then, his "character issue." Dan Balz, "In Challenger's Quest, Tactics More Prominent Than Strategy," *Washington Post* (Oct. 25, 1996), pp. A1, 18.

37. Mehlman, Ibid., p. 98.

38. Mehlman, Ibid., p. 102.

39. Mehlman, Ibid., p. 103.

40. The turnout strategy was supported by experimental and field research which found that personal contact is the key to turning out people who are less likely to vote. Donald P. Green and Alan S. Gerber, *Get Out the Vote: How to Increase Voter Turnout* (Washington, D.C.: Brookings Institution, 2004).

41. *Campaign for President 2004*, p. 109.

42. Democrats pursued a similar strategy in the 2006 midterm elections, using ballot initiatives on minimum wage to get out their vote.

43. *Campaign for President 2004*, p. 193.

44. *Campaign for President 2004*, pp. 114–115.

45. Lydia Saad, "Republican Party Favored on Security Issues, Foreign Policy," Gallup Poll, (Jan. 15, 2004). www.gallup.com/content/?ci=10204&pg=1.

46. *Campaign for President*, p. 92.

47. The Kennedy organization in 1960 was one of the first to mount a campaign on the local level. Using the canvass as a device to identify supporters and solicit workers, Kennedy's aides built precinct organizations with the newly recruited volunteers. The volunteers, in turn, distributed literature, turned out the voters, and monitored the polls on election day. They were instrumental in Kennedy's narrow victory in several states.

48. Jerry Bruno and Jeff Greenfield, *The Advance Man* (New York: Morrow, 1971), p. 299.

49. Another well-reported incident, this one involving Vice President Nelson Rockefeller, occurred in 1976. It too was precipitated by heckling. The Republican vice presidential candidate of that year, Senator Robert Dole, accompanied by Rockefeller, was trying to address a rally in Binghamton, New York. Constantly interrupted by the hecklers, Dole and then Rockefeller tried to restore order by addressing their critics directly. When this approach failed, Rockefeller grinned and made an obscene gesture. The vice president's response was captured in a picture that appeared in newspapers and magazines across the country, much to the embarrassment of the Republican ticket.

   Democrats have also had their share of off-color embarrassing remarks. In 1972, Senator George McGovern, the Democratic nominee, had been heckled continuously at events; it was later discovered that many of these hecklers had been campaign workers and volunteers for the Committee to Reelect the President and had been instructed to disrupt the McGovern campaign. In one incident, a sign-carrying heckler yelled an obscenity at the Senator as he worked the crowd. McGovern replied with the off-color remark, "Kiss my ass," an assertion that suggested a forcefulness that many believed had been lacking in his campaign.

Similarly, to evidence a macho character that critics believed he lacked, George H. W. Bush said he "intended to kick ass" in his debate with Democratic vice presidential nominee, Geraldine Ferraro.

50. Lloyd Bentsen, "Transcript of the Vice Presidential Debate," *Washington Post* (Oct. 6, 1988), p. A30.

8 CHAPTER | MEDIA POLITICS

INTRODUCTION

Media and politics go hand in hand. The press has served as an outlet for divergent political views from the founding of the Republic. When political parties developed at the end of the eighteenth century, newspapers became a primary means for disseminating their policy positions and promoting their candidates.

This early press was contentious and highly adversarial, but it was not aimed at the masses. Written for the upper-, educated class, newspapers contained essays, editorials, and letters that debated economic and political issues. It was not until the 1830s that the elitist orientation of the press began to change. Technological improvements, the growth in literacy, and the movement toward greater public involvement in the democratic process all contributed to the development of the so-called penny press, newspapers that sold for a penny and were directed at the general public.

THE MASS MEDIA AND ELECTORAL POLITICS: AN OVERVIEW

The penny press revolutionized American journalism. Newspapers began to rely on advertising rather than subscriptions as their primary source of income. To attract advertisers, they had to reach a large number of readers. To do so, newspapers had to alter what they reported and how they reported it.

Prior to the development of the penny press, news was rarely "new"; stories were often weeks old before they appeared and were rewritten or reprinted from other sources. With more newspapers aimed at the general public, a higher premium was placed on gathering news quickly and reporting it in an exciting, easy-to-read manner.

PRINT MEDIA

Once newspapers became designed for the mass public, they began to help inform voting decisions for most of the electorate. The invention of the telegraph helped in this regard. The telegraph made it possible for an emerging Washington press corps to communicate information to the entire country. What was considered news also changed. Events replaced ideas; human-interest stories supplemented the official proceedings of government; and drama, and conflict were featured.

Stories of crime, sex, and violence captured the headlines and sold papers, not essays and letters on public policy. Joseph Pulitzer's *New York World* and William Randolph Hearst's *New York Journal* set the standard for this era of highly competitive "yellow journalism."[1]

Not all newspapers featured sensational news. In 1841, Horace Greeley founded the *New York Tribune,* and ten years later, Henry Raymond began the *New York Times*. Both papers appealed to a more-educated audience interested in the political issues of the day. After a change in ownership, the *New York Times* became a paper of record. Operating on the principle that news is not simply entertainment but valuable public information, the *Times* adopted the motto, "All the news that's fit to print." It published entire texts of important speeches and documents and detailed national and foreign news.

Toward the middle of the nineteenth century, newspapers began to shed their advocacy role in favor of more neutral reporting. The growth of news wire services, such as the Associated Press and United Press, and of newspapers that were not tied to political parties, contributed to these developments.

As candidates became more personally involved in the campaign, they too became the subject of press attention. By the beginning of the twentieth century, the focus had shifted to the nominees, so much so that at least one candidate, Alton Parker, Democratic presidential nominee for 1904, angrily criticized photographers for their unyielding efforts to take pictures of him while he was swimming in the nude in the Hudson River.[2] Despite the intrusion into their personal lives, candidates began taking advantage of the press's interest in them, using "photo opportunities" and news coverage to project their image and extend their partisan appeal.

BROADCAST MEDIA

With the advent of radio in the 1920s and television in the 1950s, news media coverage of campaigns changed once again. Radio supplemented the print media. Although it did not provide regular news coverage, radio excelled at covering special events as they were happening. The 1924 presidential election was the first to be reported on radio; the conventions, major speeches, and election returns were broadcast live that year. During the 1928 election, both presidential candidates, Herbert Hoover and Alfred E. Smith, spent campaign funds on radio advertising.

Radio lost its national audience to television in the 1950s but remained a favorite communications medium of candidates seeking to target their messages to specific groups in specific locations. A cheap and accessible electronic medium, radio continues to be used extensively.

The influence of television on presidential elections was first felt in 1952. The most important news event of that presidential campaign was a speech by General Dwight Eisenhower's running mate, Richard Nixon. Accused of obtaining secret campaign funds in exchange for political favors, Nixon defended himself in a television address. He denied accepting contributions for personal use, accused the Democratic administration of being soft on communism, criticized his campaign opponents, and vowed that he would never force his children to give up their dog, Checkers, who had been given to the Nixon family by political supporters. The emotion of the speech, and particularly the reference to Checkers, generated a favorable public reaction, ended discussion of the campaign funds, kept Nixon on the Republican ticket, and demonstrated the power of television for candidates in their campaigns.

Paid television advertising by the political parties also first appeared in the 1952 presidential campaign. The major broadcast networks extended their evening news reports to half an hour in 1963. By the end of the 1960s, television had become the principal source of election news for most Americans, and presidential campaigns in turn became made-for-television productions. Public events were staged with television in mind. On-air interviews, talk show participation, even the entertainment format have become part and parcel of the modern electoral campaigns.

During the 1970s into the 1980s, the evening newscasts had the largest audience. Newspapers trailed, with radio and news magazines lower down the list. One of the big changes during this period was the development and growth of cable news networks. Cable and satellite technologies began to acquire more subscribers and all-news formats, thereby fragmenting the number of news sources.

That growth has continued. Today, more than two-thirds of television households are wired for cable, and 21 percent have alternate sources such as satellite dishes.[3] The latest communication technologies include laser fiber optics, integrated circuits for high-speed transmission of digital images and data, and the Internet.

THE INTERNET

With about 75 percent of the population having some access to the Web, with the Internet's use as a primary and secondary news source growing (see Table 8.2 later in this chapter), and with more young people going online on a daily basis, the major candidates and parties have felt the need to incorporate the Web into their communication strategies. Besides being a relatively cheap and easy way to reach potential supporters, the Internet targets younger voters who might otherwise not see as much of the campaign, receive much of the direct mail, or be contacted personally by a campaign worker.

The Kerry and Bush campaigns used their own Web sites to provide up-to-date information, including the latest speeches, political news, forthcoming events, and all the political advertising that they aired on television and the documentaries they made about their candidates. They used the latest video streaming to do so. The sites also included testimonials from key figures in the political, sports, and entertainment arenas, lists of falsehoods and exaggerations made by the opposing candidate and party, and rebuttals to them. The Bush Web site had a "Kerry Gas Calculator," which could be used to find out how much additional money people would have to expend if a 50 cents per gallon tax were enacted, one which the Bush campaign claimed that Kerry supported. After the presidential debates, both sides lauded their candidate's responses, spinning their answers to their own partisan advantage.

Kerry, Bush, and many of the third-party candidates also maintained blogs. Following the model set by Howard Dean during the Democratic primaries, the blogs were intended to build and energize a political community, mobilize it during the campaign, and get bloggers out to vote on election day. The idea of the blog is to maintain an ongoing dialogue with those who access it in order to generate new ideas, build team spirit, and gain workers to turn out the vote. The blogs have also been used to issue alerts that something is about to happen, to make periodic appeals for money and volunteers, and to invite supporters to rallies and other campaign events. The parties created interactive sites with automated games to sustain interest and gain partisan backing.

Both major party campaigns have also advertised on the Internet in addition to showing their candidate's speeches and commercials on their own sites. They also ran commercials on national news sites, designed to pop up in the key battleground states, as well as targeted specific groups that access certain sites. The Bush campaign placed its education ads on such sites as *Parent's Magazine*, *Parenting, Better Homes and Gardens, Ladies Home Journal*, and the *Food Network*. The Kerry campaign ran an ad on *Google's* search engine. When anyone searched for "the economy" on *Google*, a Kerry commercial popped up.[4] Various communication devices with online capabilities, such as cell phones and Blackberries, have opened additional channels for communicating during campaigns.

This chapter examines these developments and their impact on presidential electoral politics. The first section discusses traditional "hard" news coverage of campaigns. It examines how network news organizations interpret political events and how candidates react to those interpretations. The "soft" news/entertainment format is explored in the second section. Here the chapter describes the techniques that candidates have used in recent campaigns to circumvent the national press corps. The third section turns to another news/entertainment feature—presidential debates. It describes the history of debates, their structure, staging, and impact on the electorate. Political advertising is the subject of the fourth section, in which some of the most successful advertisements are described, the increasing emphasis on negativity examined, and the effect of advertising on the voters' perceptions of the candidates assessed. The final section looks at the media's cumulative impact on voting choice.

TRADITIONAL COVERAGE: HARD NEWS

The modus operandi of news reporting is to inform the public. But the press does so with its own professional orientation—one that affects what is covered and how it is covered.

HORSE RACE JOURNALISM

Political scientist Thomas E. Patterson argues that the dominant conceptual framework in which the election is reported is that of a game. The candidates are the players and their moves (words, activities, images) are seen as strategic and tactical devices to achieve their principal goal, winning the election. Even their policy positions are frequently evaluated within this gaming framework, described as calculated appeals to certain political constituencies. Although Patterson argues that the gaming aspect of electoral politics is most pronounced at the beginning of the presidential selection process, he sees it as an organizing principle for the press throughout the entire election cycle.[5]

Why do the news media use the game, often described as a "horse race," as its primary focus? The answer is entertainment. Races are exciting. Viewing elections as a game heightens viewers' interest. Heightened interest, in turn, increases the size of the audience and, of course, the profits because advertising revenue is based on the estimated number of people watching, hearing, or reading a particular program or paper.

There is another reason. The game format lends an aura of objectivity to reporting. Rather than presenting subjective accounts of the candidates' positions and their consequences for the country, this format encourages the news media to present quantitative data on the public's reaction to the campaign. Public opinion surveys reported as news are frequently the dominant story during the primaries and caucuses, sharing the spotlight with other campaign issues, such as the character, strategies, and tactics of the candidates.

Covering campaigns as if they were sporting events is not a new phenomenon. In 1976, Thomas Patterson found about 60 percent of television election coverage and 55 percent of newspaper coverage was devoted to the campaign as a contest.[6] Michael J. Robinson's and Margaret Sheehan's analysis of the *CBS Evening News* during the 1980 election revealed that five out of six stories emphasized the competition.[7]

The emphasis on the game of politics continued through the 2000 presidential election with the contest as the principal content of the story. (See Table 8.1.) In the 2004 election, however, policy stories—the war on terror, the war in Iraq, spiraling oil prices, and a host of domestic issues combined—slightly exceeded the attention given to the race for president.

TABLE 8.1 | BROADCAST NETWORK EVENING NEWS COVERAGE OF PRESIDENTIAL ELECTIONS (LABOR DAY – ELECTION DAY), 1988–2004

Year	1988	1992	1996	2000	2004
Amount					
Number of Stories	589	728	483	462	504
Stories per Day	10.5	11.5	7.7	7.3	9.0
Total Minutes	1,116	1,402	788	805	1,070
Focus (percent of stories)*					
Horse Race	58	58	48	71	48
Policy Issues	39	32	37	40	49
Candidate Sound Bite					
Length (seconds)	9.8	8.4	8.2	7.8	7.8
Percent of Air Time	n/a	12	13	12	12
Tone (percent of favorable comments)					
Democratic Nominee	31	52	50	40	59
Republican Nominee	38	29	33	37	37

*Stories can include one or both focuses. Numbers do not add up to 100.

Source: Stephen J. Farnsworth, and S. Robert Lichter, "The Nightly News Nightmare Revisited: Network Television's Coverage of the 2004 Presidential Election," paper presented at the annual meeting of the American Political Science Association, Washington D.C., September 2005, Table 1, p. 31.

The problem with horse-race journalism is that it diverts public attention from substance to strategy. Instead of examining the merits and limitations of a candidate's proposal, journalists explore the underlying political motivations for making the proposal, moving from the *what* to the *why* in the process. Such a focus skews the information people receive; it also heightens the partisan political component of elections and reduces the substantive policy debate to which most people are exposed.

Until recently, there has also been a decline in the amount of campaign news that was available on the major broadcast networks. However, in 2004, that amount increased, reversing a decline that began in 1992. (See Table 8.1.) Once the campaign is underway, the principal candidates get approximately the same amount of coverage; third-party and independent candidates do not.[8] Contrary to popular belief, incumbents seeking reelection do not usually dominate the election news.

With the growth in the number of all-news networks on cable television and news sites on the Internet, the total amount of information available to the general public is larger today than in the past. However, so are the options for avoiding news programming entirely.

In fact, the proliferation of entertainment options on cable, satellite, and home videos may have contributed to a less knowledgeable electorate by providing alternatives to those who are less interested in political affairs, thereby widening the information gap between those who are politically active and those who are not.

The growth of news sources has also created more pressure on the all-news networks to find their niche rather than aim for a general audience with a more broad-brush, bipartisan approach. Fox News has successfully directed its news programming toward conservatives and Republicans; in contrast, CNN and National Public Radio attract more liberal, Democratically-oriented viewers and listeners. According to Professor Diana C. Mutz, differentiated approaches and audiences have contributed to the partisan political divide in the United States today by facilitating selective exposure, which in turn, reinforces rather than challenges the political attitudes that people have. This reinforcement has heightened the partisan divide and contributed to the current state of a polarized American polity.[9]

THE BAD NEWS SYNDROME

The tone of election coverage also tends to be negative. Incumbents usually receive more critical comments from nonpartisan sources, average Americans, than do challengers. In 1980, Jimmy Carter was treated more harshly than Ronald Reagan, and in 1984, Reagan was treated more harshly than Walter Mondale. Vice President George Bush, running for president in 1988, also fared poorly, but so did his Democratic rival, Michael Dukakis. Each received two negative comments for every positive one. In 1992 and 2004, the incumbents were the subjects of more critical remarks than were their challengers. Only Bill Clinton in 1996 fared better than Republican, Robert Dole. (See Table 8.1.)

More Republicans than Democrats perceive an ideological bias in political reporting. Most academic experts do not, although they admit that reporters and correspondents tend to be more liberal and Democratic but also point out that the owners and their editors are more Republican and conservative, findings that have been supported by empirical research.[10] However, content analyses of the coverage of presidential elections on the major broadcast networks' evening news shows conducted by the Center for Media and Public Affairs indicate that in the elections of 1984, 1992, 1996, and 2004, the Democratic presidential candidate got a higher percentage of good press than did his Republican opponent. In 1980, 1988, and 2000, neither party's candidate was advantaged.[11]

Why the bad press? Most academic experts see it as a consequence of the news media's role as watchdog of government. They also believe it has something to do with the press' understanding of what is newsworthy and what is not. Put simply, bad news seems to be more newsworthy than good news. A fresh face winning and an experienced candidate losing are news; an experienced one winning and a unfamiliar one losing are not. Similarly, the first time a candidate states a position, it may be newsworthy; the second time, it is old news; the third time it is not news at all. Since candidates cannot give new speeches every time they make an address, the news media that cover the candidates look for other things to report.

Verbal slips, inconsistent statements, and mistakes often become the focus of attention. Kiku Adatto found that "only once in 1968 did a network even take note of a minor incident unrelated to the content of the campaign."[12] In recent elections, however, there is much more frequent reporting of trivial slips. Roger Ailes, media director for George Bush's 1988 campaign, explained this phenomenon in the following manner:

> Let's face it, there are three things that the media are interested in: pictures, mistakes, and attacks. That's the one sure way of getting coverage. You try to avoid as many mistakes as you can. You try to give them as many pictures as you can. And if you need coverage, you attack, and you will get coverage.
>
> It's my orchestra pit theory of politics. If you have two guys on stage and one says, "I have a solution to the Middle East problem," and the other guy falls in the orchestra pit, who do you think is going to be on the evening news?[13]

The news media's penchant for reporting embarrassing misstatements encourages the candidates not to be spontaneous, not to be candid, and above all, not to make mistakes. But if misstatements are made or poorly chosen words are used, it also forces candidates to acknowledge errors, misstatements, and unbecoming episodes in their past to try to minimize any negative fallout. In 2000, Al Gore admitted that he made factual errors during the first presidential debate; George W. Bush conceded that he had once been arrested for drunk driving many years earlier; in his first debate with Bush in 2004, John Kerry said, "when I talked about the $87 billion, I made a mistake in how I talked about the war." He did not, however, say whether his vote had been a mistake. Bush, however, refused to reply to accusations that appeared in internal National Guard memos, and highlighted by CBS News, that he had not fulfilled his Guard responsibilities in the 1970s; the memos turned out to be forgeries.

A candidate's failure to provide the news media with information, pictures, or even the pose they desire can be a source of admonishment. Take the comment that ABC correspondent Sam Donaldson made to Michael Dukakis, who was playing a trumpet with a local marching band in the midst of his 1988 presidential campaign. Donaldson reported, "He played the trumpet with his back to the camera." As Dukakis played the Democratic victory tune, "Happy Days Are Here Again," Donaldson could be heard saying off-camera, "We're over here governor."[14]

Television news has an additional bias. As an action-oriented, visual medium, its content must move quickly and be capable of projecting a strong visual image on a screen. Television emphasizes pictures and deemphasizes words; less attention is devoted to what candidates say and more to how people react to their words and images. That is why campaign speeches are laden with sound bites and catch phrases, such as "Where's the beef?" "It is morning in

America," "Read my lips—No new taxes," "a bridge to the twenty-first century," "compassionate conservatism," and the "war on terrorism."

Emotion is more newsworthy than passivity; conflict is usually more newsworthy than consensus. Angry words and actions gain attention more easily than does reasoned debate. They also produce a more emotive response from the audience. Professor Diana C. Mutz argues that news coverage of strident rhetoric has contributed to partisan incivility and to more passionate partisan politics that characterizes the American political environment today.[15]

MEDIATED COVERAGE

From the candidates' perspectives, the bad news is magnified by the fact that they do not have the opportunity to tell their own stories in their own words on the news that is broadcast by the major networks. The average length of a quotation from candidates on the evening news in 1968 was 42.3 seconds. In 1988, it was 9.8 seconds; in 1992, it was 8.3 seconds. During the 1996 Republican primaries and caucuses, it dropped even further, averaging only 7.2 seconds, increasing to 8.2 seconds in the general election. And it has continued to decrease. In the past two presidential elections, the average sound bite has been only 7.8 seconds.

What is worse from the candidates' perspective is that the reporters and correspondents are on camera much longer than are the candidates, approximately seven times longer for most campaign stories.[16] The bottom line is that it is the networks' anchors and correspondents, not the candidates, who present election news to the voters. How they do so has even become a subject of news media coverage.

THE STORY LINE

In addition to the presumptions about the nature of network news and the format in which it is portrayed, there is also a framework into which that news is fitted. According to Patterson, a dominant story line emerges, and much of the campaign is explained in terms of it. In 1992, it was Pat Buchanan's surprising showing against Bush that was news, not Bush's easy wins over his Republican rival; it was the conservative-controlled Republican convention and platform that garnered the headlines during the summer of 1992, not the adulation that greeted Bush and his running mate, Dan Quayle at the convention; it was the president's inability to turn the election around, to "hit a home run" during his debates with Clinton and Perot that was news rather than Bush's plans for the future or even the character issues he raised about his opponents. In Patterson's words:

> Bush's bad press was mainly a function of journalistic values. The news form itself affected both the content and the slant of most of his coverage. Bush's story was that of a reelection campaign in deep trouble—much like the story of a baseball team that was favored to win the pennant but stumbled early and never regained its stride.[17]

Patterson describes this story line as the likely-loser scenario. It was the story of the Dole campaign in 1996. Portrayed as a weak opponent, hopelessly trailing the incumbent president, Dole's position in the race was used as the basis for evaluating and assessing the status of his campaign. Unfortunately for Dole, that evaluation was harsh. The news media repeatedly referred to his struggling campaign and his attempts to "jump-start" it, as if it had stalled. Thus, the horse race metaphor contributed to the likely-loser scenario into which the press fit the story of the Dole campaign.[18]

For Clinton, the story line was just the opposite. It was that of the front-runner who had a large lead and who had skillfully maneuvered to keep it. In this particular story, the press attributed Clinton's lead and inevitable success to a beneficial economic environment; superior resources, especially the perquisites of the presidency; and an extremely well-organized and well-run campaign. The news media's depiction of Ronald Reagan's 1984 presidential campaign was presented in a similar manner and provides yet another illustration of the press's use of the front-runner script.

Two other narratives, according to Patterson, are the bandwagon, in which one candidate builds a larger and larger lead over the course of the campaign as people join the bandwagon, and in the opposite scenario, the front-runner loses ground. In the first scenario, the image of strong and decisive leadership generates support; in the second, the image of weak and vacillating leadership contributes to the erosion. Jimmy Carter's primary spurt in 1976 provides an illustration of the bandwagon; his decline in the general election of 1980 exemplifies the losing-ground story.[19]

The story line in 2000 focused on the closeness of the race, attributed in part to the weaknesses of both candidates: Gore's personal shortcomings and Bush's lack of depth on the issues. A variant on the competition theme toward the end of the campaign was the spoiler scenario for Ralph Nader. In 2004, the focus was on leadership, Bush's leadership in the war against terrorism and the war in Iraq. In directing attention to the president, the news media made much of his polarizing candidacy to convey the hostile political climate in which the election was cast.

Patterson's point is that the press fit the news of the campaign into the principal story rather than creating a new story from the changing events of the campaign. Naturally, the perceptions of the news media affect the electorate's understanding of what is happening.

IMPACT OF THE NEWS MEDIA

What impact does the style and substance of election news coverage have on the voters? Studies of campaigning in the 1940s indicated that the principal effect of the print media was to activate predispositions and reinforce attitudes rather than to convert voters. Newspapers and magazines provided information but primarily to those who were most committed. The most committed, in turn, used the information to support their beliefs. Weeding out opposing views, they insulated themselves from unfavorable news and from opinions that conflicted with their own.[20]

Selective Perception
With the bulk of campaign information coming from the print media in the 1940s, voters, especially the most partisan voters, tended to minimize cross-pressures and strengthen their own preexisting judgments. In contrast, the less committed also had less incentive to become informed. They maintained their ignorance by avoiding information about the campaign. The format of news-papers and magazines facilitated this kind of selective perception and retention.

Television might have been expected to change this situation because it exposed the less committed to more information and the more committed to other points of view. Avoidance became more difficult, although the use of remote controls has rendered viewers less captive to the picture on a particular channel than they were when television first began to cover presidential cam-paigns. Similarly, the proliferation of cable channels provides viewers with many nonnews options as well as a variety of 24-7 news networks that possess discernible and different ideological orientations.

Television news also compartmentalizes more than the print press. The evening news fits a large number of stories into a thirty-minute broadcast (which includes only about twenty-three minutes of news). Of necessity, this limited time restricts the coverage that can be given to each item. Campaign stories average ninety seconds or less, the equivalent of only a few paragraphs of a printed account. Their brevity helps explain why viewers do not retain much information from this type of television coverage.

There has also been a fragmentation of news sources. The major broadcast networks have lost a substantial portion of the audience they had in the 1970s and 1980s to cable news networks and local news affiliates. The local affiliates in particular have become more important sources for news about campaigns. They devote more time to news coverage and have gained in audience size.[21] Viewers of cable news programs have also increased, with the Fox News Network enjoying the greatest growth. There has also been a polarization among regular viewers, with conservatives and Republicans preferring Fox, and liberals and Democrats favoring CNN.

Television news is still important because more people follow presidential campaigns on television than through any other medium. It is the prime source of news for approximately two-thirds of the population. Newspapers are a distant second, with only about 20 percent of the population; however, the most informed voters list newspapers as their principal source of news as indicated in Table 8.2.

Agenda Setting
Television news helps set the agenda for the campaign. It helps determine issue salience by emphasizing what is newsworthy and what is not. This emphasis frames the debate, the attention paid by candidates to specific policy and

TABLE 8.2 | Principal Sources of Campaign News, 1992–2004

Question: How have you been getting most of your news about the presidential election campaign? From television, from newspapers, from radio, from magazines or from the Internet? (Up to two answers were accepted.)

Main Source	1992	1996	2000	2004
Television	82	72	70	76
Broadcast				29
NBC	–	–	–	13
ABC	–	–	–	11
CBS	–	–	–	9
Cable				40
FOX	–	–	–	21
CNN	–	–	–	15
MSNBC	–	–	–	6
Local News	–	–	–	12
Newspapers	57	60	39	46
Radio	12	19	15	22
Magazines	9	11	4	6
Internet	–	3	11	21

Source: "Voters Liked Campaign 2004, But Too Much 'Mudslinging'," Pew Research Center for the People & the Press, (Nov. 11, 2004), p. 8. www.peoplepress.org/reports/display.php3?ReportID=23

character issues, and to some extent, the kinds of responses they have to provide. Media expert Michael J. Robinson believes that this agenda-shaping function directly affects the political elites. He argues that the press influences how political elites "relate" to the mass public and how those elites communicate political options.[22] In this way, the news media affect the conduct of the campaign.

The news media may have a direct influence on voters as well. They provide information that colors public perceptions of the candidates and parties, particularly the candidates' qualifications for leadership. From the perspective of those running for office, this coverage is harsh, and the reporters and commentators are adversarial. The candidates' motives are questioned, their speeches are summarized into a very few points or sound bites, their misstatements are highlighted, their character frailties stressed, and their policy positions criticized and often portrayed as inconsistent, or even hypocritical.

Media Bias

In a highly polarized political environment, the negativity of the press contributes to perceptions of media bias. In a survey taken after the 2004 presidential election, the Pew Research Center for the People and the Press found that 40 percent of Republicans felt that Bush's coverage was unfair; and they were right according to the Center for Media and Public Affairs, which monitors the "spin" on the broadcast networks evening news casts. The Center found that only 37 percent of the comments on Bush were positive compared to 59 percent for Kerry. (See Table 8.1.)

Perceptions of media bias have led to a loss of confidence in the press. Twenty years ago, a majority of people thought that the news media got their facts right. Today, a majority believes that they do not, that the news media lack compassion, and that they are too negative. Confidence in the press has dropped more sharply than public confidence in other American institutions.[23]

Yet even with all the negative coverage, most candidates conclude that critical coverage is better than no coverage, particularly in the early phases of the nomination process and especially for the candidates who do not begin with national reputations. At the outset of the process, media attention conveys credibility; it is an indication that the news media take a candidate seriously. That is why candidates try their utmost to get coverage.

Although the news tends to be concentrated and focused on certain issues, events, or personal traits, the press does not speak in a single voice. The fragmentation of news sources and the orientations of news networks provide some balance to campaign coverage, although the self-selection process by which people choose the news outlets they regard as fair and most believable tends to reinforce the partisan and ideological perspectives that voters bring to the election campaign.

NONTRADITIONAL COVERAGE: SOFT NEWS AND LOCAL COVERAGE

The way the news media cover elections, the manner in which they present criticism, and tone of their coverage have encouraged candidates to find ways of circumventing national press corps to reach their audiences directly. Since the 1990s, one of the methods for doing so has been appearances on talk-entertainment shows, the so-called "soft" news format. Another has been appearances on local news shows that carry a greater variety of human-interest stories in addition to the news within their regional focus.

Ross Perot pioneered the use of a soft news format on television, and Jerry Brown did so on radio. This new format provides a candidate-friendly environment in which to engage the electorate. Appearances on the morning and evening television news/talk shows (such as CBS's *The Early Show,* ABC's *Good Morning America,* NBC's *Today,* and CNN's *Larry King Live*) and syndicated programs on these and other networks, including MTV, have now become commonplace as have appearances on the light-night shows of Jay Leno and David Letterman, and Comedy Central's *The Daily Show* with Jon Stewart.

Here Bill Clinton plays his saxophone for Arsenio Hall. This appearance, like one on MTV, contrasted the younger, "swinging" Clinton with George Bush—a contrast that worked to Clinton's advantage.

Even incumbent presidents are expected to use this news/entertainment medium in their quest for reelection. President George H. W. Bush initially resisted in 1992, and when he finally consented to appear on talk show interviews, he seemed ill at ease, especially on MTV. Bill Clinton was just the opposite. His appearance on the *Arsenio Hall Show* before the Democratic convention in 1992, wearing sunglasses and playing his saxophone, portrayed him as a "real cool guy," someone with whom the audience could identify.

For Perot, talk show appearances constituted much of his "live" campaign, beginning with his announcement that he might run for president on *Larry King Live* in 1992 and again in 1996. Chris Dodd announced his candidacy for the 2008 Democratic nomination on *Imus in the Morning*. Asked why he chose that radio venue for making his announcement, Dodd said: "CBS said they would give me three minutes. I got 20 minutes on Imus."[24]

And the appearances on news/entertainment shows have continued, even accelerated, in subsequent presidential campaigns. Visits on the Oprah Winfrey Show and the late-night entertainment shows are now considered standard. Many of the Democratic contenders for their party's 2004 nomination appeared on *The Daily Show*; John Edwards even used his appearance to announce his candidacy.

Why would candidates subject themselves to the ridiculing humor of a Jon Stewart? The answer is the viewers—in Stewart's case, a much younger audience than newspaper readers or even network news watchers. Reaching out to a new group of potential voters can have a short-term and long-term impact for the candidates, and especially, their parties.

The talk-entertainment format offers a much less hostile environment than interviews by national reporters and network anchors. The candidates are treated better, more like celebrities than politicians. The hosts tend to be more cordial. They and the general public tend to ask softball questions in comparison to the hardball, "gotcha" journalism of the national media. Candidates also have more time to answer the questions on these shows than the brief comments that are aired on the news networks.[25]

The audience differences are also important. People who watch these shows tend to be less oriented toward partisan politics; thus they may be more open to the information presented by the candidates who appear on these programs. Incidental learning occurs; candidate images improve as a consequence of the time and discretion they are given to talk about personal and family matters; they appear more lifelike and likeable, less like stereotypical politicians.[26]

Variations of the talk-entertainment format are town meetings and call-in programs in which candidates answer questions posed by average citizens. By interacting with everyday folks, presidential candidates can demonstrate their responsiveness, sincerity, and empathy with the problems people face. Bill Clinton was particularly effective in such a setting during his two presidential campaigns.

Another advantage of doing the talk-entertainment circuit is that the candidates' appearances themselves may become newsworthy, thereby generating an even larger impact for the candidates when clips of their comments are rebroadcast or summarized on the news. Nor are the expenses associated with these appearances comparable to the costs of staging a major media event or even designing, testing, and airing an advertisement.

The diverse audience, the higher comfort level, and the greater ability of candidates to project their desired images by presenting seemingly spontaneous but often carefully crafted answers suggest that the soft news format will continue to be used by presidential campaigns to circumvent the national press corps and reach a portion of the general public directly.

Local news outlets offer candidates many of the same advantages that talk/entertainment shows provide: more time, greater visibility, less invasive questioning, a different audience, interaction with local luminaries, and an opportunity to illustrate their personal side—the human dimension.

PRESIDENTIAL DEBATES

Debates represent another "entertainment" component of presidential campaigns, one which candidates, particularly those who are behind, find useful. They see debates as an opportunity to improve their own images and damage their opponents'. Unlike most of their campaign rhetoric—speeches, statements, and responses to questions, debates are live and unedited, although the formats, agreed to beforehand, limit the time for responses. Moreover, the candidates' answers are usually prepared in advance, are carefully crafted, and are well rehearsed. Nonetheless, debates give those running for office greater latitude to present their thoughts as they want them to be presented and in doing so demonstrate some of their personal qualifications for the job.

The news media like the debate format as well because it generates interest and facilitates comparison. A debate is a newsworthy event that fits within the game motif. Debates attract larger audiences than speeches or most news coverage, although they are not a source of revenue for the television networks because advertisements are not permitted during the debates.

The public likes debates because they are more exciting and "real" than staged campaign events and canned stump speeches. Debates provide voters with comparable information. They generate interest; they are a spectacle to be seen and heard.

The first series of televised debates occurred in 1960. John Kennedy used them to counter the impression that he was too young and inexperienced. Richard Nixon, on the other hand, sought to maintain his stature as Dwight Eisenhower's knowledgeable and experienced vice president and the obvious person to succeed his boss in office.

In the three elections that followed, Lyndon Johnson and then Nixon, both ahead in the polls, saw no advantage in debating their opponents and refused to do so. Gerald Ford, however, trailing Jimmy Carter in pre-election polls, saw debates as his best opportunity to come from behind and win. The Carter camp, on the other hand, saw them as a means of shoring up his support. In 1980, the rationale was similar. From Reagan's perspective, it was a way to reassure the electorate about himself and his qualifications for office. For Carter, it was another chance to emphasize the differences between himself and Reagan, between their parties, and between their issue position and ideological perspectives.

By 1984, presidential debates had become so much a part of presidential campaigns that even incumbents could not avoid them without making their avoidance a major campaign issue. Thus, Ronald Reagan was forced by the pressures of public opinion to debate Walter Mondale, even though he stood to gain little and could have lost much from their face-to-face encounter. And in the 1992 election, George H. W. Bush's initial refusal to accept a plan for a series of campaign debates put forth by the Commission on Presidential Debates, a nonpartisan group that had organized the 1988 presidential and vice presidential debates, hurt him politically. Bill Clinton chided Bush repeatedly for his refusal to debate. Democrats dressed as chickens appeared at his campaign rallies. President Bush finally relented, telling his handlers, "I am tired of looking like a wimp."[27]

The issue in 1996 and again in 2000 was not whether to debate but whom to include. In 1992, Ross Perot and his running mate, Admiral James Stockdale, were invited to participate, and they did, to Perot's advantage but not to Stockdale's.[28] In 1996, Perot and his running mate, Pat Choate, were not asked.

The Bipartisan Commission on Presidential Debates, composed of five Democrats and five Republicans, concluded that Perot's candidacy was not viable, that he had no chance of winning the election even though his name appeared on the ballot in all fifty states and the District of Columbia. The Commission based its decision on Perot's standing in the polls, about 5 percent at that time, and on the judgment of a small number of political scientists and journalists, surveyed by the commission's staff and advisory council, who unanimously concluded that Perot not only could not win the election but would not carry a single state.[29]

The Commission on Presidential Debates employed similar reasoning in 2000 and 2004 when it excluded third-party candidates. In doing so, it established three criteria for inclusion in the debates: a candidate had to meet the test of constitutional eligibility (be a natural born citizen, thirty-five years of age or older, and a resident of the United States for at least fourteen years); be on the ballot in enough states to have a chance of winning a majority of the electoral votes, be organized in a majority of the congressional districts within the state; and demonstrate a sufficient level of electoral support by receiving an average of 15 percent or more in public opinion polls. That percentage was to be calculated by averaging preelection surveys of five different polling organizations. Not surprisingly, the only candidates to meet these criteria were the Democratic and Republican presidential nominees.

By bringing the candidates together on the same stage at the same time, the debates become major news, routinely covered by the news media. They attract more viewers than any other single event of the campaign. In 2004, more than 63 million people watch the first debate between President Bush and Senator Kerry. (See Table 8.3.)

Although presidential debates have now become part of the American electoral tradition, their number, scheduling, and format are still subject to arduous negotiation between the principal contenders and their staffs. In these negotiations, each side naturally wants to maximize its advantages. Candidates who are ahead in the polls when these negotiations occur, usually the incumbent, call the shots on the number of debates, their scheduling, and their rules. Ostensibly, the Commission on Presidential Debates hosts the events, but the candidates determine the procedures for conducting them. For example, President Carter refused to include independent John Anderson in the 1980 debate; in 1984, 1988, 1996, and 2004, incumbents Reagan, Vice President Bush, Clinton, and George W. Bush set the parameters. There was little their opponents could do but concur.

It was a different story, however, in 1992. With President Bush trailing in the polls, the campaign moving into the late September–early October period, and Clinton making an issue of Bush's refusal to debate, the president could not dictate the terms and had to accept a compromise that included formats that he and his advisers initially opposed.[30]

An agreement of understanding, drafted and approved by the major party candidates, specifies the rules. In 2004, one rule was that only the

TABLE 8.3 | PRESIDENTIAL DEBATES, 1960–2004

Year		Number of Debates	Average Estimated Size of the Television Audience (in Millions)	Percent of Households Watching
1960	Kennedy v. Nixon	4	77	60
1976	Carter v. Ford	4*	65	51
1980	Carter v. Reagan	1	81	59
1984	Mondale v. Reagan	3*	66	46
1988	Dukakis v. Bush	3*	66	36
1992	Bush v. Clinton v. Perot	4*	66	42
1996	Clinton v. Dole	3*	40	29
2000	Gore v. G. W. Bush	4*	40.6+	26
2004	G. W. Bush v Kerry	4*	53.5+	

*Includes one vice presidential debate.

+The average for just the three presidential debates.

Sources: Estimates of audience sizes for 1960–1992, "How Many Watched" *New York Times,* (Oct. 6, 1996), p. A25. Copyright © 1996 by the *New York Times.* Reprinted by permission. Estimates for 1996, "Debate Ratings Beat Baseball," Associated Press (Oct. 17, 1996). Copyright © 1996 by the Associated Press. Reprinted by permission. Estimates for 2000 and 2004 based on ratings by Nielsen Media Research. Reprinted by permission. Percentage of households reported in Thomas Patterson, *The Vanishing Voter* (New York: Random House, 2002), p. 122.

person talking would be seen on television; no cutaways to the other would be permitted. The television networks, however, were not parties to the agreement and did not abide by it. Sometimes they showed one of the candidates and sometimes both. Kerry took notes when Bush was talking; Bush did not, however, when Kerry spoke. To some, the president appeared bored, tired, or irritated. Moreover, during the first debate his suit jacket bulged in the middle of his back, suggesting to Democrats that he had a device feeding him the answers, an allegation that Bush's handlers vigorously denied. However, in the second and third debates, he wore a better fitting suit.

PREPARATION

Despite the appearance of spontaneity, debates are highly scripted, carefully orchestrated events. The candidates are coached and rehearsed. They often sound like their stump speeches and political commercials. There are exceptions, however. Richard Nixon in his first debate with Kennedy, and James

AP/Wide World Photo.

Stockdale in the 1992 vice presidential debate, did not prepare extensively for them and suffered by comparison with their more polished opponents.[31]

To get ready for the debates, candidates go over briefing books that their aides prepare, view videotapes of their opponents, and engage in mock debates with stand-ins playing their opponents' part. This extensive preparation is designed to ensure that there are no surprises, that the candidates anticipate the questions, and provide thoughtful answers that are consistent with their campaign themes, previous statements, and political advertising. The dry runs are also intended to avoid adlibs, gaffes, and misstatements that may get them into trouble.

In addition to the concern about substance and rhetoric, campaign media consultants also consider stylistic matters: how candidates look, how they dress, how they speak, and how they interact with the questioners and with their opponents. Kennedy and Carter talked faster than Nixon and Ford to create an action-oriented image in the minds of the viewers. Both tried to demonstrate their knowledge by citing many facts and statistics in their answers. Ford and Reagan spoke in more general terms, expressing particular concern about the size and structure of government. Reagan's wit and anecdotes in 1980, Bush's manner in 1988, and Perot's down-to-earth language and self-deprecating humor in 1992 conveyed a human dimension with which viewers could identify in contrast to their opponents' less "identifiable" responses. Dukakis was especially hurt by his reply to the question of whether he would favor an irrevocable death penalty for a person who raped and killed his wife. His matter-of-fact, rambling response sealed his technocratic, iceman image.

In 2004, Kerry's goal was to look presidential, sound authoritative, and evidence a command of the issues, while Bush wanted to emphasize his leadership traits in the war on terrorism. Both achieved their stylistic objectives, at least in the minds of their supporters.

STRATEGY AND TACTICS

Much calculation goes into debate strategy and tactics. Candidates need to decide which issues to stress and how to stress them; how to catch their opponents off guard or goad them into an error; and whether and how to respond to a personal attack and to criticism of their policy positions. In 1992, Clinton emphasized the need to change policy. In 1996, he took credit for his policies and the good times that followed from them. In 1992, he was critical of Bush on the issues, especially the economy; in 1996, he took the high road as president and did not engage in personal allegations of his opponent, even when Dole criticized him personally.

A strategic goal of most candidates during debates is to overcome any negative perceptions about them that have developed and, at the same time, magnify their positive attributes. For George W. Bush in 2000, this meant demonstrating his presidential potential—his command of the issues, communication skills, and leadership abilities. As vice president, Gore had already established his mastery of the issues and become a policy and political spokesman for the administration. What the vice president needed to do was convey a more human side and approachable manner. Bush achieved his strategic goals; Gore did not.[32]

In 2004, the situation was reversed. It was Kerry who had to demonstrate presidential qualities; Bush had already proven his. Kerry's challenge was to look presidential, sound authoritative, and show his command of the issues. And he did, although the contrast with the president was most apparent in the first debate when Kerry looked and sounded sharper than Bush. He jumped five points in the public opinion polls following that debate, while the president dropped three. Democrats were elated. According to the Bush campaign's communication director, Nicole Devenish, "There was a now buoyancy [in the Kerry campaign], and a new life breathed in, and a sense of momentum. Their press corps felt it, and they all felt it. They did a brilliant job spinning the instant polls."[33]

But the surge was short-lived. In the second and third debates, the president held his ground and rebounded in the polls. He ended the debates with the same amount of support that he had going into them. What happened, according to Bush campaign manager, Ken Mehlman, was that Kerry's base returned, but he did not gain among independents and Republicans.[34] (See Table 8.4.)

TABLE 8.4 | THE IMPACT OF PRESIDENTIAL DEBATES ON ELECTORAL SUPPORT, 1992–2004

1992

Time Sequence	Bush	Clinton	Perot	Other/Undecided
Before the Debates	33%	51%	10%	6%
After the First	34	47	13	6
After the Second	31	43	18	8
After the Third	34	43	17	6

1996

Time Sequence	Clinton	Dole	Perot
Before the Debates	52%	37%	5%
After the First	54	38	5
After the Second	52	41	5

2000

Time Sequence	Gore	Bush	Nader	Buchanan
Before the First	49%	41%	2%	1%
After the First	41	48	4	1
After the Second	44	47	3	1
After the Third	41	50	3	1

2004

Time Sequence	Bush	Kerry
Before the First	52%	44%
After the First	49	49
After the Second	49	48
After the Third	52	44

Sources: 1992 figures are based on the *Gallup Poll Monthly* (Sept. and Oct., 1992); 1996 figures are based on ABC News tracking poll of likely voters; 2000 and 2004 figures from Gallup Poll of likely voters, October 23, 2000 and October 18, 2004. http://www.gallup.com/content/?ci=13657

EVALUATION AND IMPACT

Debates usually help the challenger more than the incumbent because they provide a basis for comparison. Being on the same stage and answering similar questions enable a lesser known candidate to clarify his image, emphasize leadership qualities, and articulate policy positions. Kennedy (1960), Carter (1976), Reagan (1980), and George W. Bush (2000) benefited from their initial debates with their incumbent presidential or vice presidential opponent because they were able to satisfy questions about their knowledge of the issues, their relevant political experience, and their qualifications for president. Similarly, John Kerry was able to demonstrate his presidential leadership qualities in his first debate with President Bush in 2004.

In close races, debates can make a difference. They can convince the undecided for whom to vote and reinforce or counter preferences of weak partisans. They do so by increasing interest, clarifying issue positions, and shaping images.

But debates rarely shift public opinion on a large scale because most voters have their minds made up or at least have their partisan predilections intact before viewing the debates. In fact, they are attracted to the debates precisely because of their strong partisan feelings. In general, people who are more interested in the election are more likely to watch the debates; people who are more knowledgeable are more likely to learn from them; and people who have strong partisan inclinations are more likely to be convinced by them. Partisans see the debate through a political lens and root for their own candidate. As a result, a single, poor performance, such as Reagan's in his first debate with Walter Mondale and Bush's in his first debate with John Kerry, is unlikely to change the voting preferences of most partisans.

Normally, the vice presidential debate is not nearly as consequential as the presidential one. Fewer people watch it since that debate involves the number two players on the teams. But the debate can still raise or allay doubts about the vice president's capacity to fill in, if something were to happen to the president. In 1988, the vice presidential debate worked to Dan Quayle's disadvantage when his performance confirmed rather than challenged the impression that he was not up to the job. In 1992, Admiral James Stockdale, Perot's running mate, seemed unprepared, which left doubts in voters' minds whether he (and by implication, Perot) were qualified for the country's top two jobs. In 1996, Jack Kemp floundered on foreign affairs.[35] No such concerns were evident about either vice presidential nominee during their one debate in 2000 and 2004.

CAMPAIGN ADVERTISING

Candidates are marketed much like any commercial product. Advertising is used to gain attention, make a pitch, and leave an impression. The goal, of course, is to get the electorate to do something—vote for a specific candidate on election day.

Advertising allows candidates to say and do what they want. The trick is to make the commercials look real. Candidate-sponsored clips are not unbiased, and the public knows it. To refine advertisements and improve the odds that they project the desired messages, which in turn produce the desired effects, they are pretested before focus groups.

When they are not, they can do more damage than good. Such was the case when Michael Dukakis's staff created a photo opportunity in which their candidate wore an army helmet and rode in a combat-ready tank. The objective of the advertisement was to demonstrate Dukakis's support for the military and for a strong national defense policy. The situation, however, looked so silly and contrived that the Republicans countered with a commercial of their own in which a scene from the Dukakis ad was featured along with information about the Democratic candidate's opposition to a long list of military programs and weapons systems.

THE AD MAKERS

Media consultants specializing in political advertising are hired to supplement regular campaign staff to design, produce, and target the advertisements as well as buy time on media markets in states in which the campaign is focusing. Each campaign normally retains a firm to coordinate these activities.

Mark McKinnon directed the Bush–Cheney advertising effort in both campaigns. In 2000, he did so from his firm's headquarters in Austin, Texas; in 2004, he directed operations from Washington, assisted by a seasoned group of media consultants.

Kerry, who had used two political advertising firms during his quest for the Democratic Party's presidential nomination, relied on Bill Knapp (Squire, Knapp, and Dunn) and Michael Donilon (Shrum, Devine, and Donilon) for creative development. Knapp had also directed Clinton's 1996 and Gore's 2000 campaign advertising.[36] Another firm handled the placement and timing of the ads, primarily on local stations.

Designing and airing political commercials constitutes the principal expense of contemporary presidential campaigns. In 2000, the total advertising by the candidates, parties, and nonparty groups on the race for the presidency amounted to $263 million; in 2004, the price tag was $620, an increase of 235 percent.[37] The Democrats enjoyed an advantage in overall advertising spending, $358 million to the Republicans' $262 million.[38] Kerry, however, actually spent a little less than Bush because his media consultants bought time at the lowest rate, whereas the Bush campaign bought at a fixed (and more expensive rate) to insure that their ads would be run at the time they wanted.[39]

FORMAT AND TYPE OF ADS

Political commercials take many forms. Short spots are interspersed with other commercials in regular programming. Longer advertisements that preempt part of the standard broadcast fare and full-length productions, such as interviews, documentaries, and campaign rallies, have also been employed, although less in recent elections because of their expense. The benefits of the short spots are that they make a point, are cheaper to produce and air, and are usually viewed by a larger audience. Longer programs, which may go into greater detail about the candidate's career, qualifications, and beliefs, are generally seen by fewer people, although Ross Perot's novel media campaign in 1992 attracted and maintained a sizable audience even though most of his programs lasted thirty minutes or longer.[40]

From the perspective of their content, there are basically three types of political commercials: those that praise candidates and their accomplishments (positive ads), those that contrast candidates to the obvious advantage of the ad's sponsor (contrast ads), and those that just criticize candidates on the grounds of their policy preferences or personal behavior (negative ads). In most campaigns, candidates use all three types, although of late, the emphasis has been on contrast and negativity.

Positivity

Positive campaign advertisements emphasize the strengths of a candidate. For presidents seeking reelection, or even vice presidents running for the top office, one of those strengths is clearly experience in high office, which incumbents always emphasize. One of Jimmy Carter's most effective commercials in 1980 showed him in a whirl of presidential activities ending as darkness fell over the White House. A voice intoned, "The responsibility never ends. Even at the end of a long working day, there is usually another cable addressed to the chief of state from the other side of the world where the sun is shining and something is happening." As a light came on in the president's living quarters, the voice concluded, "And he's not finished yet." Ronald Reagan in 1984 and George Bush in 1992 used a variation of the president-at-work ad.

Challengers need to stress their qualifications. They have to define themselves or risk having their opponents do it for them. Thus, the first task of most challengers is usually to present themselves to the American people by designing and airing biographical ads that feature their life story in a positive and compelling way.

A related task is to distinguish themselves from their opponents using comparison ads. In 1976, Carter emphasized his unusual leadership abilities. His slogan, "A leader, for a change," as well as his less formal appearance and even his decision to use green as the color of his literature in contrast to the traditional red, white, and blue, conveyed "freshness" and set him apart from old-style Washington politicians in general and the two Republican presidents who preceded him in particular.

In 1980, Reagan stressed different kinds of solutions to the nation's old and persistent policy problems, as did Perot in 1992. Perot's ads that year were among the most distinctive ever seen in a presidential campaign. Their amateurish quality was purposely designed to set them apart from the slick, smooth, professional commercials of his Republican and Democratic opponents. It was precisely this contrast that Perot wanted to convey to the American people.[41]

In 2000, Bush's ads emphasized his likeability and trustworthiness; Gore's stressed his knowledge, experience, and caring and crusading spirit as a fighter for the working class. Both candidates ran more positive than negative

BOX 8.1	A POSITIVE AD: THE DEMOCRATS REINTRODUCE THEIR TEAM

Script: Narrator: "One is a combat veteran with over thirty years of experience handling the toughest issues facing America. The other is the son of a mill worker who all his life has stood up for ordinary people against powerful interests. Today they're a new team for America with a plan to make us stronger at home and respected in the world. John Kerry and John Edwards. President. Vice President. A new team for a new America."

Picture: Kerry saluting the American flag and then speaking with people with phrases "combat veteran," "30 years experience," and "fighting for Americans" printed on screen. Then comes a picture of Edwards addressing a crowd and interacting with voters with phases "from a working family," "stood up for people," and "fought powerful interests" printed on screen. The two of them are then pictured together, followed by a shot of Kerry alone before an applauding crowd and then greeting voters. The ad ends with the two of them shaking hands and looking straight at each other with the phrases, "a new team for America," and "stronger at home, respected in the world," superimposed on screen.

commercials until the final two weeks of the campaign. Their national party organizations, however, went negative earlier.

The 2004 campaign was more negative than in 2000. Bush began attacking Kerry in March of the election year and continued to do so until election day. Only twenty-three of his eighty ads were positive.[42]

The Democratic National Committee and the 527s that supported their ticket went after Bush, but the Kerry campaign stayed positive in an effort to build up the candidate's resume. Box 8.1 "A Positive Ad: The Democrats Reintroduce Their Team," presents a positive Kerry ad.

The Bush campaign began and ended with the president's response to 9/11. The first ads aired in March 2004, and the final ones near the end of the campaign recalled the president's strong leadership after the terrorist attacks. But it was a commercial by a 527 group supporting Bush that received the most attention and seemed to have the greatest emotional impact. The ad showed the president giving a big hug to Ashley, a little girl whose mother died in the collapse of the World Trade Center. "I know that's hard. Are you all right?" Ashley replied, "He's the most powerful man in the world and all he wants to do is make sure I'm safe." Ashley's father added: "What I saw was what I want to see in the heart and in the soul of the man who sits in the highest elected office in our country."

Twenty million dollars was spent on the air buys for "Ashley." There were 7,000 showings in Ohio alone. Seventy percent of the people polled in that state remember seeing the ad.[43] Said Kerry's media adviser, Bob Strum, "'Ashley' was real, was human, people could relate to it. 'Ashley' probably cost us Ohio and cost us the presidency!"[44]

Negativity

Most of Bush's ads were negative as were Reagan's in 1984 and Clinton's in 1996. When presidents run for reelection, they try to cast doubts in voter's minds about the qualifications of their opponent. According to Mark McKinnon, director of media for the 2000 and 2004 Bush campaigns, close to 50 percent of Reagan's ads in 1984 and 70 percent of Clinton's in 1996 were negative.

> People really knew George Bush—both our supporters and our detractors. . . . People have a very firm notion about who he is. . . . We tested a lot of this positive stuff; it just didn't move the dial much. Kerry was just not as well known. So our opportunity to get a return on our investment was much greater by talking about the problems that we saw with the Kerry presidency—what he was proposing and his record.[45]

Negative ads exploit a candidate's weaknesses by focusing on character deficiencies, issue inconsistencies, and/or false leadership claims. They are not new. There has always been much negativity in American political campaigns. George Washington was called a philanderer and a thief; Andrew Jackson was accused of marrying a prostitute; at the outset of the Civil War, Abraham Lincoln was charged with being illegitimate and black; Theodore Roosevelt was said to be a drunkard; Herbert Hoover, a German sympathizer during World War I; and Franklin D. Roosevelt, a lecher, lunatic, and a closet Jew whose real name was Rosenfeldt.

What seems to be different today is the increasing emphasis placed on negative advertising and the use of fear to heighten its effect. Most negative ads provide contrasts that benefit the ad's sponsor. Clinton' 1996 ads against Robert Dole are a good illustration. Instead of criticizing Dole personally, the ads criticized the policy positions he took and the votes he cast in the Senate. One ad, "Wrong in the Past," went through a litany of popular education and health care programs that Dole ostensibly opposed. The announcer ended the ad by repeating the theme, "Bob Dole, wrong in the past, wrong for our future." This ad was shown 6,780 times in seventy-five media markets.[46]

In the negative ads of 2000, Democrats challenged George W. Bush's record in Texas, accused him of being a captive of special interests, and chided him for proposing policies that would help the rich, bankrupt Social Security, and take away badly needed funds from public schools for private school vouchers. Republicans, in turn, characterized Al Gore as a proponent of big government, big spending, and big give-away programs.

The 2004 Bush campaign was designed to contrast Bush's proven leadership skills with Kerry's policy inconsistencies, using Kerry's words and votes against him. One ad pictured Kerry windsurfing, going back and forth on the waves. It was a perfect metaphor—Kerry the patrician, the elitist candidate who claimed he represented the common person, and Kerry the flip-flopper, the candidate who couldn't make up his mind. Box 8.2, "A Negative Ad: Republicans Contrast the Candidates," presents a contrast ad designed by the Bush campaign.

BOX 8.2	A NEGATIVE AD: REPUBLICANS CONTRAST THE CANDIDATES

Script: Narrator: "President Bush and Congressional allies: strong leadership to protect America; tax relief; common sense health care; strengthen and protect Social Security. John Kerry and liberal allies: higher taxes; voting to tax Social Security benefits; government-run health care; a record of slashing intelligence; and reckless defense cuts. Alone in the booth, why take the risk?"

Screen: Begins with the picture of a presidential ballot. Under the words:

"President Bush and his Congressional Allies" are the choices (left), boxes with check marks (center), and happy people (right):

Strong Leadership

Tax Relief

Common Sense Healthcare

Strengthen and Protect Social Security

Then the words "**John Kerry and liberal allies in Congress**" with the choices (left):

Higher Taxes

Voting to Tax Social Security

Government-Run Health Care

Slashing Intelligence

Reckless Defense

The people who are shown on the right are unhappy. The ad ends with a picture of the President and his wife.

EMOTIVE CONTENT

The Bush ads also played on the fear generated by the terrorist attacks. One ad, entitled "Risk" included pictures of terrorist attacks, frightened children, and a warning:

> After September 11, our world changed. Either we fight terrorists abroad or face them here. John Kerry and liberals in Congress have a different view. They opposed Reagan as he won the Cold War, voted against the first Gulf War, voted to slash intelligence after the first Trade Center attack, repeatedly opposed weapons vital to winning the war on terror. John Kerry and his liberal allies: Are they a risk we can afford to take today?[47]

The negative ads against Bush were less effective, and for the most part, less scary, although one of them showed a soldier shooting into the air, a car bursting into flames with the announcer saying, "Now Americans are being kidnapped, held hostage—even beheaded."[48] Most of the anti-Bush ads were produced by the Democratic National Committee (DNC) and the nonparty 527 groups. In the words of a member of the DNC's advertising team:

We all understood that John Kerry was going have to make the case for John Kerry. It is very hard for 527 independent campaigns to carry the positive piece of the candidate message. . . . Our basic feeling was that the Kerry campaign had to define Kerry and it was up to us to define Bush."[49]

CONTENT ACCURACY

Since the 1988 election, the public has become more leery of the negative ads. Part of their skepticism stems from the legacy of negative advertising, particularly in that year. Part of it results from exaggeration and hyperbole that are contained in shrill accusations.

The 2004 campaign was no exception. Bush charged that Kerry had proposed "government-run health care," wanted "higher taxes," and had voted in favor of "slashing intelligence" and "reckless defense cuts." Kerry in turn accused Bush of having "the worst economic record since Hoover"; he also claimed that Bush "intended to reinstitute the draft" and "cut Social Security benefits by 30 to 45 percent."

Although these accusations did not go unchallenged by the campaigns at which they were directed and by reporters covering them, the repetition of the claims in speeches and in the ads themselves drowned out the press' attempt to set the record straight. Reports on the accuracy of speeches and ads are usually single stories, but the speeches and the ads are voiced and shown many times over, which gives them greater impact.[50]

TACTICAL CONSIDERATIONS

Targeting

Another characteristic of contemporary political advertising is the degree to which it is targeted to individual groups within the most competitive states. Clinton directed his 1996 ads toward twenty-four key states, very similar in composition to the group of states he targeted four years earlier.[51]

Targeting was even more concentrated in 2000 and 2004 with both candidates and their parties dueling over the airways in the battleground states. Initially, each side focused on about one-third of the states, relying on public opinion polls to gauge the continuing competitiveness of the states and the impact of their advertising efforts. As states became less competitive, they were dropped from the list.

The targeting meant that most of the country did not see ads for the presidential election. In their study of advertising in the 2004 national election, Michael M. Franz, Joel Rivlin, and Kenneth Goldstein describe the geographic focus:

> . . . only 21 states received *any* advertising at all during the 2004 presidential campaign. More than half of all Americans—57 percent of the electorate—did not see a single ad broadcast in their home media market. And during the final month of the campaign, 87 percent of all presidential ads were concentrated in just 44 media markets in a shrinking number of battleground states, home to only 27 percent of the electorate.[52]

Most of the commercials in 2004 were aired on local broadcast stations or specialized cable media. Buying time on the national broadcast networks was too expensive and the broadcast audience too diffuse.

Newsworthiness

The most effective ads are those that reinforce or become news. Since the beginning of television advertising, three political commercials have made news, which extended their reach and potential impact. The first one to do so was the Democrats' 1964 ad suggesting that Barry Goldwater might get the country involved in a nuclear war. Designed to reinforce the impression that Goldwater was a trigger-happy zealot who would not hesitate to unleash nuclear weapons against a communist foe, the ad pictured a little girl in a meadow plucking petals from a daisy. She counted to herself softly. When she reached nine, the picture froze on her face, her voice faded, and a stern-sounding male voice counted down from ten. When he got to zero there was an explosion, the little girl disappeared, and a mushroom-shaped cloud covered the screen. Lyndon Johnson's voice was heard: "These are the stakes—to make a world in which all of God's children can live, or go into the dark. We must either love each other, or we must die." The ad ended with an announcer saying, "Vote for President Johnson on November 3. The stakes are too high for you to stay home."

The commercial was run only once. Goldwater supporters were outraged and protested vigorously, but their protestations actually kept the issue alive. Parts of the ad were shown on television newscasts. The Democrats had made the point, and the news made it stick.[53]

"A 30-Second Ad on Crime," New York Times, November 3, 1988, B20.

The second infamous ad, "Willie Horton," featured a mug shot of an African-American prisoner who had raped a white woman while on a weekend furlough from a Massachusetts jail. Aimed at those who were fearful of crime, and especially of African-American males, the ad, sponsored by a PAC supporting Vice President George H. W. Bush in 1988, was supplemented by other prisoner ads designed by the Bush campaign. The cumulative impact of these ads left the impression that Dukakis was a liberal, do-gooder. By the end of the 1988 presidential campaign, 25 percent of the electorate knew who Willie Horton was, what he did, and who furloughed him; 49 percent thought Dukakis was soft on crime.[54]

The third ad that became news was run in August 2004, right after the Democratic Convention in which Kerry had emphasized his Vietnam military record in his acceptance speech. He had been awarded two purple hearts and a bronze star for his valor in commanding a Navy gunboat under attack. A group, consisting of some Vietnam veterans, calling themselves Swift Boat Veterans for Truth, disputed Kerry's claims and brought attention to his antiwar efforts after his release from active duty.

Shown in August during the lull between major party conventions, the ads captured national attention. The decision of the Kerry campaign not to respond to them gave the ads credibility and undermined the image that the Democrats were trying to project about Kerry—a much decorated veteran who had demonstrated his qualification to be Commander-in-Chief.

The reach and potential impact of the first Swift Boat ad, which was shown in just seven small media markets (Charleston, Dayton, Green Bay, La Crosse,

| BOX 8.3 | SWIFT BOAT VETERANS FOR TRUTH—ANTI-KERRY AD |

Script: "Even before Jane Fonda went to Hanoi to meet with the enemy and mock America, John Kerry secretly met with enemy leaders in Paris though we were still at war and Americans were being held in North Vietnamese prison camps. Then he returned and accused American troops of committing war crimes on a daily basis. Eventually, Jane Fonda apologized for her activities. But John Kerry refuses to. In a time of war, can America trust a man who betrayed his country?"

Picture: Jane Fonda in Hanoi in 1972 with clapping North Vietnamese soldiers in the background; the scene then shifts to John Kerry with scenes of war in the background and then turns to Kerry testifying before the Senate committee investigating the Vietnam War. Jane Fonda is then pictured at a news conference, followed by Kerry before the Senate committee with the words "betrayed his country," superimposed on him.

Toledo, Wassau, and Youngstown) was enormous. The Swift Boat Veterans gave over 1,000 interviews on talk radio, appeared on network newscasts, and raised $19 million, which they used to run other anti-Kerry ads. Although news reporters raised questions about the validity of the allegations, the attention that they gave to the charges actually extended and may have enhanced their effect. Kerry's credibility suffered as a result. Box 8.3, "Swift Boat Veterans for Truth—Anti-Kerry Ad," contains a clip from one of the Swift Boat advertisements.

The Kerry campaign tried to create news of its own by running ads on its Web site that were designed for television but not shown to the public. The ads directly responded to charges leveled against Kerry by the Bush campaign, Republican National Committee, and Republican-oriented 527 groups. After discovering that the ads were not aired, the press complained bitterly about these fake video releases.[55]

Timing and Sequencing
The timing of the Swift Boat ads after the Democratic convention and during the period when the Kerry campaign went dark caught Kerry and his media handlers off guard. Since both Democratic and Republican nominees planned to accept federal funds, the Kerry team, which had to stretch their dollars over five more weeks than the Republicans, decided to stay off the air in August to save money and also not compete with the summer Olympics.[56]

In the words of media adviser, Michael Donilon:

> Our hands were tied in the August period. If we spent early, no one knows what would happen in October—especially with the heavy spending of the Republican 527s at the end. Money mattered.[57]

Kerry's advisers hoped that nonparty groups would fill the void, but the BCRA prohibited them from coordinating campaign efforts with the Kerry campaign or the Democratic National Committee. The 527s did run ads during this period, but only one of them responded to the accusations made by the Swift Boat Veterans for Truth; the rest of the ads were anti-Bush.

Most advertising content is sequenced. At the outset, it is necessary to provide biographical information about family, experience, and qualifications for the office. The Clinton biographical ads were particularly effective in 1992. His biography, entitled "The Man from Hope," presented the personal Clinton from his childhood in Hope, Arkansas, the town in which he was born and initially raised, to his governorship of that state. The film used the town's name to convey Clinton's optimism and his life story to demonstrate his ability to achieve his dreams and the country's.

Gore, Kerry, and Bush (in 2000) ran biographical ads in their nomination campaigns. They continued these ads and supplemented them with other information about the candidate's life history; the ads were run primarily at the beginning of the general election period. Gore's ads stressed his career as a journalist, military service during the Vietnam War, and twenty-four years of public service as a representative, senator, and vice president. Bush's 2000 ads pointed to his popularity as governor of Texas and his ability to bring people together.

Once the personal dimension has been established, the policy orientations of the candidates and their priorities for the coming years are articulated. In this phase of advertising, themes are presented and policy positions noted. The second stage of the Kerry campaign ads presented his agenda, the principal issues and what he wanted to do about them. These ads were designed to position Kerry for his debates with Bush. They provided him with a pro-grammatic foundation upon which to stand.

In the third stage, the candidate frequently goes on the offensive by running a series of ads in which the reasons not to vote for the opponent are stressed. Candidates who are behind frequently "go negative" earlier. Thus, the final stage of Kerry advertising, which occurred after the presidential debates, presented new policy directions as the choice for the voters. Bob Knapp described the plan as follows:

> People wanted a change in policy domestically; they didn't necessarily want a change in leadership because it was a risky, uncertain time. So we tried to thread the needle by making the case for change without saying it is time for change.[58]

Both the 2000 and 2004 campaigns contained an especially heavy dosage of negative advertising in their final weeks.[59]

By going negative at the end, the advertising campaigns had come full circle. From initially trumpeting their candidate's strengths, the campaigns ended by blasting their opponent's weaknesses. The choice had come down to which candidate was the lesser of two evils.

THE IMPACT OF ADVERTISING ON TURNOUT AND VOTING BEHAVIOR

People get a lot of information from advertisements, both positive and negative, even *more* than most people get from newscasts. Thomas Patterson and Robert McClure found that voters in 1972 did not learn and retain much information about the substantive issues from television news. They concluded:

1. Most election issues are mentioned so infrequently that viewers could not possibly learn about them.
2. [M]ost issue references are so fleeting that they could not be expected to leave an impression on viewers.
3. [T]he candidates' issue positions generally were reported in ways guaranteed to make them elusive.[60]

Their findings, which occurred during the golden era of broadcast network television when the ABC, CBS, and NBC news organizations dominated the air waves and commanded public attention, have not been refuted by contemporary scholars. Even though there are many alternative sources of news about the campaign available to the electorate, there is little evidence to suggest these alternative news sources have produced a more informed public than in the past.

With the preponderance of negative ads and negative news, has the electorate become more cynical? According to two political scientists, Stephen Ansolabehere and Shanto Iyengar, it has. Their experimental studies on negative political commercials found that these ads adversely affected turnout, increased cynicism, and decreased feelings of efficacy, especially for those with no partisan allegiances. In other words, the ads were a turnoff; people who saw them lost interest in voting.[61]

Other political scientists, however, are not so sure. In fact, much of the theoretical and empirical evidence suggests quite the opposite effect, that negative ads stimulate turnout. For knowledgeable partisans, their primary effect is to reinforce rather than challenge their inclinations to support their party's nominees. Negative advertisements, in particular seem to generate a strong response from partisans, which solidifies their vote and energizes them to do so. In this sense, the ads "work." They prime the electorate; they provide clues for seeing and images for evaluating; and they turn out party voters.[62]

Do ads change opinions? The evidence here is less clear. With the increase in partisan loyalties within the electorate and the relatively small number of independent voters, the audience that watches the campaign on television, hears it on radio, or follows it in newspapers or on the Internet, is a tough group to convince, much less change their minds.

THE CUMULATIVE EFFECT OF THE MASS MEDIA ON ELECTIONS

The time, money, and energy spent on media by the candidates suggest that the mass media do condition campaigns and affect voting behavior. Why else would so many resources be devoted to them? Yet it is difficult to document the media's precise effect.

Much of the candidates' concern focuses on news coverage. The negativism of the press, the tendency to highlight inconsistencies and misstatements, even the propensity to interpret rather than report events, has led many people, especially candidates and their handlers, to conclude that this coverage is biased, has adversely affected their campaigns, and unduly influences the electorate.

Are the media, particularly the news media, really that powerful? Do they affect voter choice? The answer is probably yes, although their impact may depend on the level of public knowledge, strength of partisan attitudes of the electorate, and the initial judgments voters make even before the campaign begins.

There is evidence that voters do learn from campaigns and use that knowledge to make an informed judgment on election day. They learn from the candidates, from the conventions, from the debates, from the ads, and from the news media's analyses, the statements that are reported by partisan and non-partisan sources, and the information that is discovered by investigative reporting.

What they learn tends to reinforce their political attitudes because people are more attracted to news sources that reflect their beliefs rather than challenge them. Not only has the proliferation of news networks facilitated the selective exposure of political partisans, but it has also widened the levels of knowledge between activists and others who are less interested, involved, and informed about campaign politics.

Despite the discernible orientations of news sources and the distortion and bias of political commercials, voters still assert that they have enough information to make an enlightened voting decision. When asked if they learned enough from the 2000 and 2004 campaigns to make an informed choice, over 80 percent said they had.[63] Of course, how much information people *really* need to make such a judgment continues to be subject to much debate.[64]

The watchdog function is performed less well by the news media in campaigns because of the pace of the campaign and the time and resources necessary for effective investigative reporting. As a consequence, the news media also serves as a vehicle for communicating opposition research collected by the campaigns and given or leaked to the press. The fact checks, performed by major news organizations, are important, but usually do not get the attention that the original statement or claim received. And as noted previously, the attention given to an inaccurate statement, exaggerated claim, or an unsupported charge can often reinforce the allegations or claims, rather than set the record straight.

Another function of the news media is to identify the key issues, frame them, force the candidates to address them, and help the public to evaluate candidate and party responses. This too is a critical role because it provides an issue agenda that carries over into the new government.

Still another role of the news media is explanation, discerning the meaning of the election. The outcome of the vote indicates who wins but not why they have won or what is expected of them in government. Exit polls and media interpretations provide such analyses. We turn to those studies in the next chapter.

SUMMARY

The mass media have a profound effect on presidential elections: on the organization, strategy, and tactics of the campaign, the distribution of resources, and directly or indirectly on the electorate's voting decisions. That is why so much of presidential campaign is devoted to media-related activities.

First newspapers, then radio and television, and more recently, the Internet, have provided the primary channels through which information about the campaign is transmitted to voters. The multiplication of news networks on cable, the increasing importance (and length) of local news shows, and the entertainment/news format have provided additional, and for the most part, more favorable opportunities for candidates to reach the electorate than they had when the broadcast news networks monopolized campaign coverage. Nonetheless, the candidates still need to take media bias into account when trying to affect the coverage they receive; a bias that political scientists believe is more journalistic than ideological.

The news media see and report the campaign as a game, fitting statements, events, and activities into various story lines. Their schema highlights drama and gives controversial statements and events the most attention but also downplays in-depth discussions of policy issues. Campaign coverage also plays up personalities and gives disproportionate attention to blunders, factual errors, personal exaggerations, and slips of the tongue; reporters focus on conflict and emphasize the contest.

Candidates naturally try to improve the coverage they receive by planting stories, leaking opposition research, scripting their speeches with sound bites, orchestrating events with the mass media in mind, minimizing spontaneity to prevent embarrassing words or situations, and creating good visuals. But even with all this preparation and staging, the news of their campaign may not be accurate or complete, and from the candidates' perspective, it is never good enough.

For this reason, candidates also try to circumvent the national news media to reach the voters directly. People like to be entertained, so candidates have resorted to various popular interview and even comedy shows to convey a message, project a personal image, energize their supporters, and extend their appeals to those who do not regularly tune in to national news programming.

In the past, parades, rallies, and other campaign events were the principal vehicles by which these objectives were achieved. The party conventions and presidential debates also provide large-audience opportunities and format-friendly environments for candidates to make appeals, look presidential, and expand and excite their partisan base. Debates, especially, facilitate candidate comparisons that usually work to the advantage of challengers who need to present themselves as the equal of their incumbent opponents. The news media play a role here as well, covering the debates, and often participating in them by asking questions, and reporting the candidates' responses, public's reaction, and their own evaluations in terms of winners and losers. They then integrate the debate into the ongoing story of the campaign.

In a very close race, debates can make a difference. Usually, however, they do not. Partisans disproportionately comprise the debate audience; they tend to root for their candidates while handlers from the campaigns and significant others "spin" the results to their political advantage. As a consequence, bounces from the debates tend to be short-lived and fade into the political environment that helps shape the election and condition its outcome.

Since campaign news is often bad from the candidate's perspective, campaigns try to make their own news and direct their messages through advertising. More money is spent on this campaign activity than any other. Although political commercials tap both positive and negative leadership dimensions, the amount of negativity has increased in recent elections.

Voters have become increasingly leery about the claims of these ads, but the political commercials still seem to have an impact, particularly on the partisan base. Reinforcing issue positions and leadership images turns out partisans; it also tends to clarify the differences between the candidates and their parties, and in that process, may affect the votes of a relatively small group of undecided voters. The partisan polarization of the American electorate has made *mobilization,* not *persuasion,* the name of the game.

For strong partisans, the cumulative impact of the media is to reinforce their political predispositions and attitudes, energize them during the campaign, and facilitate efforts to get them out to vote; for weaker partisans and independents, however, the impact is less clear. Over the course of an election campaign, news media coverage can alter opinions of less partisan voters and help those who are not partisan and may not be even interested in politics arrive at an informed voting decision. Although one election campaign does not usually change partisan attitudes on a permanent basis, it may cause them to shift, and over a period of time, to change.

WHERE ON THE WEB?

In addition to the media outlets mentioned in previous chapters, here are some others to explore.

- **Associated Press**
  www.ap.org

The largest news service in the United States provides fast-breaking information on its wire service and Web site.

- **Center for Media and Public Affairs**
  www.cmpa.com
  Conducts studies on television coverage of the campaign and the "spin" that the candidates and their stands on the issues get.

- **Commission on Presidential Debates**
  www.debates.org
  Plans the debates, selects the cities, decides which candidates can participate, and moderates the discussion format between the principal candidates. The Commission also provides transcripts of past and present presidential debates.

- **The Freedom Forum**
  www.freedomforum.org
  Provides information on freedom of the press issues, with links to the Newseum, the Media Studies Center, and the First Amendment Center, all sponsored by the Gannett news organization.

- **Factcheck.org**
  www.factcheck.org
  A nonpartisan, nonprofit group organized by the Annenberg Public Policy Center at the University of Pennsylvania that evaluates the accuracy of political advertising.

- **National Annenberg Election Survey**
  www.annenbergpublicpolicycenter.org
  Conducts ongoing national surveys over the course of the campaign that measures information acquisition, voters' attitudes, and the news media and advertising's impact.

- **Newspaperlinks.com**
  www.newspaperlinks.com
  Provides links to the online editions of local newspapers across the country.

- **The Pew Research Center for the People & the Press**
  www.people-press.org
  A nonpartisan research organization sponsored by the Pew Charitable Trusts that surveys public opinion on politics and the media.

- **Politics Online**
  www.politicsonline.com
  Tracks presidential campaigning on the Internet.

- **Washington Post**
  www.washingtonpost.com
  A good source of information about the campaign and the mindset of the Washington political establishment.

EXERCISES

1. Contrast the advertisements of the presidential candidates on the basis of their messages, presentations, and target groups. Note also the media on which the advertisements ran. These ads should also be available on the candidates' Web sites.

2. Check the accuracy of the ads you have discussed in question 1 by using Factcheck.org. Which ads appear to be more accurate? Do you think that these ads are also more effective? Explain.

3. Compare the amount of television coverage given to the horse race and to issues of candidate personality, policy, and strategy and tactics by examining the analysis performed by the Center for the Media and Public Affairs (www.cmpa.com). Do you feel the coverage was balanced or unbalanced? Did it provide voters with sufficient information to make an intelligent judgment on election day? Did the press display an ideological bias?

4. Take any major event in the presidential campaign and compare coverage of it by a national newspaper, television broadcast network, a national news magazine, and a major source of information on the Internet. Which coverage was better? Which was more interesting? Why?

5. View one of the presidential debates and note the principal points the candidates made. If elected, did the candidate follow through on the positions he/she advocated? (These tapes should be available in the C-SPAN archives and at the Commission on Presidential Debates web site at www.debates.org.)

6. Compare the blogs of the principal candidates running for president. Which one do you find the most interesting? Which do you think is the most informative? Which one generates the most enthusiasm among bloggers? Which campaign organizations do you think has best been able to convert this web-based enthusiasm into a grassroots movement?

SELECTED READINGS

Ansolabehere, Stephen, and Shanto Iyengar. *Going Negative*. New York: Free Press, 1995.

Buchanan, Bruce. *Renewing Presidential Politics: Campaigns, Media, and the Public Interest*. Lanham, M.D.: Rowman & Littlefield, 1996.

Davis, Richard, and Diana Owen. *New Media and American Politics*. New York: Oxford University Press, 1998.

Denton, Robert E. Jr. *The 2004 Presidential Campaign: A Communication Perspective*. Lanham, M.D.: Rowman & Littlefield, 2005.

Devlin, L. Patrick. "Contrasts in Presidential Campaign Commercials of 2000." *American Behavioral Scientist,* 44 (Aug. 2001): 2338–2369.

———— "Contrasts in Presidential Campaign Commercials of 2004," *American Behavioral Scientist,* 49 (Oct. 2005): 279–313.

Farnsworth, Stephen J., and S. Robert Lichter. *The Nightly News Nightmare: Network Television Coverage of Presidential Elections, 1988–2004*. Lanham, M.D.: Rowman & Littlefield, 2006.

Geer, John G. *In Defense of Negativity: Attack Ads in Presidential Campaigns*. Chicago: University of Chicago Press, 2006.

Goldstein, Ken, and Paul Freedman. "Campaign Advertising and Voter Turnout: New Evidence for a Stimulation Effect." *The Journal of Politics,* 64 (Aug. 2002): 721–740.

Hart, Roderick. *Campaign Talk: Why Elections Are Good for Us.* Princeton, N.J.: Princeton University Press, 2000.

Iyengar, Shanto, and Donald Kinder. *News That Matters: Television and American Opinion.* Chicago: University of Chicago Press, 1987.

Jamieson, Kathleen Hall. *Everything You Think You Know about Politics and Why You're Wrong.* New York: Basic Books, 2000.

———. *Packaging the Presidency: A History and Criticism of Presidential Campaign Advertising.* Oxford: Oxford University Press, 1996.

———. *Dirty Politics: Deception, Distraction, Democracy.* Oxford: Oxford University Press, 1996.

———. and David S. Birdsell. *Presidential Debates.* New York: Oxford University Press, 1988.

Kaid, Lynda Lee, and Anne Johnston. "Negative versus Positive Television Advertising in U.S. Presidential Campaigns, 1960–1988." *Journal of Communications,* 41 (Summer 1991): 53–64.

Kerbel, Matthew Robert. *Edited for Television: CNN, ABC, and the American Presidential Campaign.* Boulder, C.O.: Westview Press, 1998.

Kraus, Sidney. *Televised Presidential Debates and Public Policy.* 2nd ed. Mahwah, N.J.: Erlbaum, 2000.

Mark, David. *Going Dirty: The Art of Negative Campaigning.* Lanham, M.D.: Rowman & Littlefield, 2006.

Mutz, Diana C. "How the Mass Media Divide Us," in Pietro S. Niola and David W. Brady, eds. *Red and Blue Nation? Characteristics and Causes of America's Polarized Politics.* Washington, D.C.: Brookings/Hoover, 2006: 223–262.

Patterson, Thomas E. *Doing Well and Doing Good: How Soft News and Critical Journalism Are Shrinking the News Audience and Weakening Democracy—And What News Outlets Can Do about It.* Cambridge, M.A.: Joan Shorenstein Center on the Press, Politics, and Public Policy, 2000.

———. *Out of Order.* New York: Knopf, 1993.

Schroeder, Alan. *Presidential Debates: Forty Years of High-Risk TV.* New York: Columbia University Press, 2000.

West, Darrell M. *Air Wars: Television Advertising in Election Campaigns, 1952–2004,* 4th ed. Washington, D.C.: CQ Press, 2005.

NOTES

1. The term *yellow journalism* comes from the comic strip, "The Yellow Kid," which first appeared in Joseph Pulitzer's *New York World* in 1896. The kid, whose nightshirt was colored yellow in the paper, was an instant hit and sparked a bidding war for the comic strip between Pulitzer and William Randolph Hearst. Although the strip's popularity lasted only a few years, the competition between these two media titans continued for decades.

2. David Stebenne, "Media Coverage of American Presidential Elections: A Historical Perspective," in *The Finish Line: Covering the Campaign's Final Days,* ed. Martha FitzSimon (New York: Freedom Forum Media Studies Center, 1993), p. 83.

3. 2007 Statistical Abstract of the United States, "Utilization of Selected Media, 1970–2005." Table 111. www.census.gov.

4. Brian Faler, "Presidential Ad War Escalates Online," *Washington Post* (May 30, 2004), p. A5.

5. Thomas E. Patterson, *Out of Order* (New York: Knopf, 1993), pp. 53–133.

6. Thomas E. Patterson, "Television and Election Strategy," in *The Communications Revolution in Politics,* ed. Gerald Benjamin (New York: Academy of Political Science, 1982), p. 30.

7. Michael J. Robinson and Margaret A. Sheehan, *Over the Wire and on TV: CBS and UPI in Campaign '80* (New York: Russell Sage Foundation, 1983), p. 148.

8. When running for their party's nomination, candidates receive coverage roughly in proportion to their popular standing, with the front-runners getting the most attention. After the conventions are over, it becomes primarily a two-person contest. The amount of speaking time candidates receive on the national news is roughly proportional to their media coverage. In 2000, Gore was heard on the broadcast networks for fifty-three minutes, Bush for forty-two, and Nader for three. Stephen J. Farnsworth and S. Robert Lichter, "*The Nightly News Nightmare* Revisited: Television's Coverage of the 2004 Presidential Election." Paper presented at the annual meeting of the American Political Science Association, Washington D.C., (Sept. 2005).

9. See Diana C. Mutz, "How the Mass Media Divide Us," in Pietro S. Nivola and David W. Brady, eds. *Red and Blue Nation? Characteristics and Causes of America's Polarized Politics.* (Washington, D.C.: Brookings/Hoover, 2006), pp. 224–240.

10. S. Robert Lichter, Stanley Rothman, and Linda S. Lichter, *The Media Elite* (Bethesda, M.D.: Adler & Adler, 1986).

11. Farnsworth and Lichter, "*The Nightly News Nightmare* . . . ," p. 15.

12. Kiku Adatto, "The Incredible Shrinking Sound Bite," *New Republic* (May 28, 1990): p. 22.

13. David R. Runkel, ed., *Campaign for President: The Managers Look at '88* (Dover, M.A.: Auburn House, 1989), p. 136.

14. Adatto, "Sound Bite," p. 22.

15. Mutz, "How the Mass Media Divide Us," p. 246.

16. Center for Media and Public Affairs, "Journalists Monopolize TV News." p. 21; Thomas E. Patterson, *Out of Order,* p. 106.

17. Patterson, *Out of Order,* p. 106.

18. Ibid., pp. 119–120.

19. Ibid., pp. 118–119.

20. Paul Lazarsfeld, Bernard Berelson, and Hazel Goudet, *The People's Choice* (New York: Columbia University Press, 1948); Bernard Berelson, Paul Lazarsfeld, and William McPhee, *Voting: A Study of Opinion Formation in a Presidential Campaign* (Chicago: University of Chicago Press, 1954).

21. Martin Kaplan, Ken Goldstein, and Matthew Hale, "Local News Coverage of the 2004 campaign: An Analysis of Nightly Broadcasts in Eleven Markets," Lear Center, Local News Archives, February 15, 2005. www.localnewsarchive.org.

22. Michael J. Robinson, "Mass Media and the Margins of Democratic Politics: Non-Transformations in the USA," (unpublished paper, March 1993), pp. 81–83.

23. "Media: More Voices, Less Credibility," Pew Research Center for the People and the Press, *Trends 2005*, pp. 49–52.

24. Dan Balz, "Democratic Senator Dodd Enters Presidential Race," *Washington Post* (Jan. 12, 2007), p. A6.

25. In his initial quest for the presidency in 2000, George W. Bush spoke for thirteen minutes on a single appearance on the *Late Show with David Letterman*—longer than the total time he appeared on the evening news of three television broadcast networks during the *entire* month of October. Similarly, Gore appeared on Letterman's show in September for more time than he appeared on the three evening news shows during that whole month combined. Center for Media and Public Affairs, "Journalists Monopolize TV News." p. 27.

26. Matthew A. Baum, "Talking the Vote: Why Presidential Candidates Hit the Talk Show Circuit," *American Journal of Political Science*, 49 (April 2005), pp. 213–234.

27. Peter Goldman, Thomas M. DeFrank, Mary Miller, et al., *Quest for the Presidency: 1992* (College Station: Texas A&M Press, 1994), p. 535.

28. Admiral Stockdale had not been briefed by Perot's handlers prior to the debate. He was unable to answer questions about Perot's policy positions At one point when the moderator asked him a question, he said that he could not hear it because his hearing aid was not on. Viewers did not come away with confidence that he could be an effective vice president, much less president.

29. Perot complained bitterly, first appealing to the Federal Communications Commission and then instituting legal action to prevent the debates from being held if he could not participate. Although he failed to stop the debates, he used his exclusion to emphasize one of his campaign themes—the self-serving nature of the two-party system and the need to reform it. The reason that Perot was so agitated was that participating in the debates was part of his 1996 campaign strategy. He had boosted his popularity significantly in 1992 by his performance in the presidential debates and hoped to do so again in 1996.

30. In 2000, the Commission on Presidential Debates proposed four 90-minute debates, three involving the presidential candidates and one, the vice presidential nominees. Al Gore accepted immediately, but George W. Bush did not. Instead, Bush proposed debates on two network talk shows, *Meet the Press* and *Larry King Live*, and wanted only to participate in one of the commission's debates. With Gore enjoying a better reputation as a skilled and knowledgeable debater than Bush, the press interpreted the Republican candidate's counterproposal as an attempt to make the debates less formal, limit the size of the viewing audience, and reduce their impact on the electorate. Although the vice president had stated that he would debate his opponent in any venue, including news shows, he refused to accept Bush's invitation unless and until the governor agreed to accept the Bipartisan Commission's entire debate proposal, which Bush eventually did.

31. Nixon had closeted himself alone in a hotel before his first debate with Kennedy. He received only a ten-minute briefing. Moreover, he had bumped his knee on a car door going into the television studio and was in considerable pain. Theodore H. White, *The Making of the President, 1960* (New York: Atheneum, 1988), p. 285.

32. Helped by the low expectations that accompanied his appearance and his opponents' aggressive style and factual embellishments, Bush seemed the equal of his opponent on the issues and the nicer person in the give and take, especially during their first debate when Gore's sighs and expressions of dismay, heard while Bush was talking, produced a negative public reaction among viewers, particularly women. In the words of Bush adviser, Matthew Dowd, "His 'sighs' and bearing made him look like he wasn't a nice person, and at points, when he answered questions, he lectured. He actually did more damage to himself than we did to him." Kathleen Hall Jamieson and Paul Waldman, *Electing the President 2000: The Insiders' View* (Philadelphia: University of Pennsylvania Press, 2001), p. 22.

33. Kennedy Institute of Politics, *Campaign for President: The Managers Look at 2004* (Lanham, M.D.: Rowman and Littlefield, 2006), p. 147.

34. *Campaign for President, 2004*, p. 144.

35. Moreover, Kemp was not particularly critical of the vice president or the incumbent president, something a challenger has to be to make the case for change. His performance so dismayed Republican strategists who were watching it on television that Haley Barbour, the chair of the Republican National Committee was heard to remark, "I told you we should have kept the ball game [the National League playoffs] on one channel!" Haley Barbour, quoted in Evan Thomas, *Back from the Dead* (New York: Atlantic Monthly Press, 1997), p. 184.

36. L. Patrick Devlin, "Contrasts in Presidential Campaign Commercials of 2004," *American Behavioral Scientist*, 49 (Oct. 2005), pp. 281–282, 298–299.

37. Ibid., pp. 279–281.

38. Ibid., p. 281.

39. Ibid., pp. 280–281.

40. In 1996, he was less successful. His audience was only about one-third the size of the one he had in 1992.

41. His ads in 1996 lacked the visual appeal and uniqueness of those he aired in 1992.

42. Devlin, "Contrasts in Presidential Campaign Commercials of 2004," p. 283.

43. The poll was conducted by Public Opinion Strategies. Devlin, "Contrasts in Presidential Campaign Commercials of 2004," p. 296.

44. Ibid.

45. Ibid., p. 283.

46. L. Patrick Devlin, "Contrasts in Presidential Campaign Commercials of 1996," *American Behavioral Scientist*, 40 (Aug. 1997): p. 1064.

47. Lynda Lee Kaid, "Videostyle in the 2004 Presidential Advertising," in Robert E. Denton Jr. ed. *The 2004 Presidential Campaign: A Communication Perspective.* Lanham, M.D.: Rowman & Littlefield, 2005, p. 292.

48. Jim Rutenberg, "Scary Ads Take Campaign to a Grim New Level," *New York Times* (Oct. 17, 2004), p. A1.

49. Devlin, "Contrasts in Presidential Campaign Commercials of 2004," p. 305.

50. The Annenberg Center for Public Policy at the University of Pennsylvania maintains a Web site called FactCheck, which lists the exaggerated and false claims and provides information to refute or modify them.

51. A little less than half of the commercials ran in five of the largest, most competitive states: California, Florida, Michigan, Pennsylvania, and Ohio. Since Clinton advertised early and often, his media consultants avoided the big and expensive news media markets in New York, Washington, D.C., and Los Angeles in the hope that this unusually early advertising campaign would not become a campaign issue. It didn't. Only two stories about Clinton's ads appeared in the mainstream press during this period. Dick Morris, *Behind the Oval Office* (New York: Simon & Schuster, 1996), p. 139.

52. Michael M. Franz, Joel Rivlin, and Kenneth Goldstein, "Much More of the Same: Television Advertising Pre-and Post-BCRA" in Michael J. Malbin, ed. *The Election after Reform* (Landam, M.D.: Rowman and Littlefield, 2006), p. 147.

53. A daisy girl look-alike advertisement was aired in several battleground states in 2000 by a nonprofit, Republican-oriented group from Texas. Like its famous predecessor, the ad featured a young girl plucking the petals of a daisy, a countdown, and a nuclear explosion. The message was that the Clinton–Gore administration had jeopardized the nation's security by providing nuclear secrets to China in exchange for campaign contributions, thereby giving China the capacity to unleash a nuclear attack against the United States. The ad ended with the words, "Don't take a chance, please vote Republican." Leslie Wayne, "Infamous Political Commercial Is Turned on Gore," *New York Times* (Oct. 27, 2000), p. A26.

54. Edwin Diamond and Adrian Marin, "Spots," *American Behavioral Scientist,* 32 (March/April 1989), p. 386.

55. Howard Kurtz, "Some Kerry Spots Never Make the Air," *Washington Post* (Oct. 20, 2004), p. A6.

56. Gore had run into trouble in 2000 when early spending by the Democrats in that election left them unable to match the funds the Bush campaign put into Florida and the other key battleground states at the end. The Kerry advertising team was determined not to repeat this mistake again.

57. Devlin, "Contrasts in Presidential Campaign Commercials of 2004," p. 301.

58. Ibid., p. 299.

59. According to a study by the Brennan Center for Social Justice at New York University, nearly 90 percent of the candidate ads in the three weeks before the 2000 election were negative. Craig B. Holman and Luke P. McLoughlin, *Buying Time 2000: Television Advertising in the 2000 Federal Elections* (New York: Brennan Center for Social Justice at New York University, 2001), pp. 54–56.

60. Thomas E. Patterson and Robert D. McClure, *The Unseeing Eye* (New York: Putnam, 1976), p. 58.

61. Stephen Ansolabehere and Shanto Iyengar, *Going Negative: How Political Advertisements Shrink and Polarize the Electorate* (New York: Free Press, 1995), pp. 147–150.

62. Ken Goldstein and Paul Freedman, "Campaign Advertising and Voter Turnout: New Evidence for a Stimulation Effect," *Journal of Politics* 64 (Aug. 2002), pp. 122–123. See also Steven Finkel and John Geer, "A Spot Check: Casting Doubt on the Demobilizing Effect of Attack Advertising," *American Journal of Political Science,* 42 (June 1988), pp. 573–595; Paul Freedman and Ken Goldstein, "Measuring

Media Exposure and the Effects of Negative Campaign Ads," *American Journal of Political Science*, 43 (Sept. 1999), pp. 1189–1208; Kim Fridkin Kahn and Patrick Kenney, "Do Negative Campaigns Mobilize or Suppress Turnout? Clarifying the Relationship between Negativity and Participation," *American Political Science Review*, 93 (Dec. 1999), pp. 877–890; Martin Wattenberg and Craig Brians, "Negative Campaign Advertising: Demobilizer or Mobilizer?" *American Political Science Review*, 93 (Dec. 1999), pp. 891–900; John G. Geer, *In Defense of Negativity: Attack Ads in Presidential Campaigns* (Chicago: University of Chicago Press, 2006).

63. Pew Research Center for the People & the Press, "Despite Uncertain Outcome, Campaign 2000 Highly Rated," November 16, 2000; "Voters Liked Campaign 2004, But Too Much 'Mud-Slinging'" November 11, 2004.

64. For a very interesting article on this subject, see Larry M. Bartels, "Uniformed Votes: Information Effects in Presidential Elections," *American Journal of Political Science*, 40 (Feb. 1996), pp. 194–230. Princeton professors, Bartel and Chris Achen are currently involved in a research project on the thought processes of people when they evaluate political issues and make voting decisions.

THE ELECTION

UNDERSTANDING PRESIDENTIAL ELECTIONS

INTRODUCTION

Predicting the results of an election is a favorite American practice. Politicians do it; the news media do it; even the public tries to anticipate the outcome far in advance of the event. It is a form of entertainment—somewhat akin to forecasting the winner of a sporting contest.

Presidential elections are particularly prone to such predictions. National surveys report on the opinions of the American public at frequent intervals during the campaign. On election night, television news commentators project a winner before most of the votes are counted. Election day surveys of voters exiting the polls assess the mood of the electorate and present the first systematic analysis of the results. Subsequently, more in-depth studies reveal shifts in opinions and attitudes.

Predictions and analyses of the electorate based on survey data are not conducted solely for their entertainment or news value, although many are. They provide important information to candidates running for office and to those who have been elected. For the nominees, surveys of public opinion indicate the issues that can be effectively raised and those that should be avoided. They also suggest which audience might be most receptive to specific policy positions, even the words and expressions they should use. For the successful candidates, analyses of voter preferences, opinions, and attitudes provide an interpretation of the vote, indicate the range and depth of public concern on the key issues, and signal the amount of support newly elected presidents are likely to receive as they begin their term in office.

This chapter examines the presidential vote from three perspectives. The first anticipates the vote by examining the environment and public opinion as the election approaches. There are many ways to assess the electoral environment. The first part of this section looks at how political scientists have tried to do so, the models they have used, and the success that they have had in predicting the outcome of the popular vote. The focus then shifts to the public, its attitudes, beliefs, and opinions. Here we look at snapshots of the public over the course of the election campaign. This part of the chapter discusses national opinion polls, describes their methodologies, and evaluates their predictive success. We then turn to the news media's election forecasts and analyses based on the large exit poll that is taken on election day.

The second section turns to an examination of the vote itself. After discussing election day surveys, it reports on the American National Election Studies (ANES), which have been conducted since 1952 by researchers at the University of Michigan. These studies, which survey voters before and after the election, provide basic data that scholars have used to analyze elections and understand voting behavior. The principal findings of these analyses are summarized for each presidential election since 1952.

The final section of the chapter turns to the relationship between campaigning and governing, between issue debates and public policy making, between candidate evaluations and presidential style. Do the campaign issues determine the new agenda of the government building? Does the projected or perceived image of the candidates affect the tone of the presidency or the actions of the one who is elected? Can an electoral coalition be converted into a governing party? Does the selection process help or hinder the president in meeting the expectations it creates? These questions are explored in an effort to determine the impact of the election on the operation of the presidency, the behavior of the president, and the functioning of the political system.

PREDICTING PRESIDENTIAL ELECTIONS

Political scientists have had a long-running debate about how much campaigns really matter. Do they dictate, influence, or have relatively little impact on the election results?

There are two principal schools of thought. One argues that campaigns usually do not matter all that much and that the environment in which elections occur shapes the electorate's judgment and augurs the outcome of the vote; another suggests that it is the preexisting political views that matter; a third alternative is that campaigns can be decisive, particularly when the electorate is closely divided. These contending positions are not necessarily inconsistent with one another, but they do reflect differences in the perceptions of what are the most important influences on voting—economic, social, and political conditions, attitudes, issues, and personalities, or the campaign itself?

FORMAL MODELS

Those in the environment-conditions-the-results school have constructed formal models by which they forecast election outcomes. They identify critical variables that measure or reflect the economic, social, and political environment in which an election occurs; place these variables in their model; and use them to predict the percentage of the popular vote that the winning candidate should receive. To ensure that they have the right combination of factors in their model, the researchers usually test its accuracy on the basis of how their model would have worked in past elections.

Since economic performance is a major criterion by which the electorate evaluates the party in power and its candidates for office, especially if the incumbent is running for reelection, almost all the election models contain measures of the economy; some modelers also try to anticipate how it will perform in the year of the election and how the public thinks it will perform.[1] Economic indicators include the Gross National Product (GNP), the Gross Domestic Product (GDP), the rate of economic growth, the level of unemployment, the number of new jobs created since the previous election, the rate of inflation, consumer confidence index, and forecasts about the country's economic future.

If the indicators are favorable, models assume that the electorate will make a retrospective judgment and reward the party in control of the White House and the incumbent; if they are unfavorable, the expectation is that the electorate would vote for the other party's candidates in the hopes that they will improve conditions. When an incumbent president is not on the ticket, the electorate looks more to future and makes a prospective judgment based on the promises and qualifications of the candidates seeking the White House. In making a prospective voting decision, people need to have knowledge of the candidates, their parties, and their policies in order to judge them.

In the 2004 election, the electorate was more informed about the positions of the candidates than it was in the previous election, according to data collected by the National Annenberg Election Surveys. The survey also found that President Bush was advantaged. The less informed people were in 2004, the more likely they perceived the president's position as closer to their own.[2]

A second set of variables concern the political environment: the public's evaluation of the current president, the electability of the candidates running for the nomination, and the party that has been in control of the White House, sometimes for an extended period of time. The principal measure for judging the president is job approval, revealed by the question, do you approve or disapprove of the job the president is doing? High job approval (over 50 percent) is normally considered a positive sign for an incumbent seeking reelection. Similarly, the success of a candidate seeking the nomination is predictive of how that candidate will do in the general election.[3] People like to support a winner or at least a candidate who has a reasonable chance of winning.

Another variable is the number of terms a party controls the White House. Assuming that the public tires of one-party control for an extended period, the "get-tired-effect" should kick in after two or more presidential terms, thereby reducing the vote of the candidate of the party in power. However, the candidate of a party that has recently gained control of the White House should not be affected in a quest for reelection. In the twentieth century, of the presidents who were elected, only Jimmy Carter was defeated after his and his party's first term in the White House; the other incumbents who lost, William Howard Taft (1912), Herbert Hoover (1932), and George H. W. Bush (1992), did so after an extended period of their party controlling the presidency.

Models forecast election results. Their success in doing so depends on the relevance of the measures they use as criteria by which the voters will decide, the timeframe in which they have collected data for these measures, and the assumption that the campaigns of the two major candidates will effectively cancel each other out. If the measures do not incorporate the principal issues of the campaign, if the data on which they are based is collected too early, then the forecast may not be accurate, particularly if other events, including the campaign itself, affect the judgment of the voters.

Prior to the 2000 presidential election, all the models predicted a Gore victory from 52.8 percent to 60.3 percent of the popular vote. They did so because the measures they used reflected the booming economy, the absence of a national security threat and the position of the United States as the only superpower, and President Bill Clinton's high job approval ratings, although his personal favorability ratings were much lower. Nonetheless, Al Gore seemed to be in a strong position to take advantage of these favorable factors, or so the models forecast. What went wrong? Why were the modelers' forecasts off by so much?

Some critics attributed the incorrect estimates of the final popular vote to ideological bias. They see political scientists as liberal-leaning and Democratic—hence favorable for Gore. Others, however, contended that the 2000 election was unique, or at least different from previous elections. Bill Clinton's personal digressions may also have been a factor that none of the models included. Perhaps the economy didn't help the Democrats because the prosperity had lasted too long, and people had gotten used to it. Or perhaps, a good economy is not nearly as beneficial to the party in power as a bad economy is harmful.

The electorate believed that either of the candidates could and would continue the good economic times, thereby decreasing the incumbent vice president's initial advantage. Finally, and most importantly, the vice president's inability or unwillingness to take credit for the successful economic policies of the Clinton years may also have contributed to his narrow popular vote victory but Electoral College defeat.

In their postmortems following the election, the modelers pointed to a variety of factors that impaired their collective judgment: They used the wrong combination of variables; they calculated presidential approval but not Clinton's personal unfavorability; they overemphasized economic factors and underestimated moral and social ones; and finally, they failed to consider the uniqueness of the 2000 election. Dr. Christopher Wlezien concluded an analysis of why his and other models did not capture the final result with greater accuracy with the following admonition:

> All that forecasting models can offer well in advance of an election is some sense of the advantage or disadvantage candidates have as the campaign begins. They offer a starting point of sorts, not the final resting place. Campaigns matter. They always have and always will. If this wasn't already clear before the 2000 election, it is now.[4]

In 2004, the modelers did better. They all forecast that Bush would win the popular vote, receiving anywhere from 49.9 percent to 57.6 percent of the two party vote. The medium forecast was 53.8 percent; Bush actually received 50.7 percent of the total vote.[5]

Why did most of the models overestimate the incumbent's vote? Although the models used different measures and collected data at different points in time, none of them considered the campaign itself and its potential impact on the electorate. Most of them did not account for the partisan polarization of the electorate or the larger turnout of voters. Nor did they anticipate the Electoral College strategies that directed campaign resources to the principal battleground states. None of these campaign-related variables figured prominently, if at all, in the modelers' calculations. Campaigns can make a difference, particularly when the economic and political factors do not overwhelmingly favor one side or the other.

PUBLIC OPINION POLLS

In addition to using formal models to forecast the vote, political scientists and journalists also depend heavily on public opinion surveys to anticipate election outcomes and gain information about the political views of the electorate. The public is naturally interested in who is going to win. The news media and candidates are obsessed with the answer to the question of who will win.

In focusing on the campaigns, the news media report which candidate is ahead, how the candidates are perceived, and what issues are dividing the voters. In forging a winning coalition, candidates and their organizations need to know how the electorate is reacting to them and their issue positions. Waiting for this information until after the election is over is obviously too late. That is the reason there are so many public opinion polls.

In recent elections, there have been literally hundreds of polls. Published in newspapers, broadcast by the television networks, and available online, they monitor daily shifts in perceptions and opinions, and anticipate voting decisions of the electorate. Polls also provide the major party campaigns with information about how their messages are being received, the type of appeals that seem to resonate most effectively with different groups of voters, and the electoral opportunities that present themselves over the course of the campaign.

Although the number of polls has mushroomed in recent years, polling itself is not a new phenomenon. There have been nationwide assessments of public opinion since 1916. The largest and most comprehensive of the early surveys were the straw polls conducted by the *Literary Digest,* a popular monthly magazine. The *Digest* mailed millions of ballots and questionnaires to people who appeared on lists of automobile owners and in telephone directories. In 1924, 1928, and 1932, the poll correctly predicted the winner of the presidential election. In 1936, it did not: A huge Alfred Landon victory was forecast, and a huge Franklin Roosevelt victory followed.

What went wrong? The *Digest* mailed 10 million questionnaires over the course of the campaign and received 2 million back. As the ballots were returned, they were tabulated. This procedure, which provided a running count, blurred shifts in public opinion that may have been occurring over the course of the campaign. But that was not its only problem. The principal difficulty with the *Digest*'s survey was that the sample of people who responded was not representative of the voting public. Automobile owners and telephone subscribers were simply not typical voters in 1936, since most people did not own cars or have telephones. This distinction mattered more in 1936 than it had in previous years because of the Great Depression. There was a socio-economic cleavage within the electorate. The *Literary Digest* sample did not reflect this cleavage; thus its results were inaccurate.

While the *Digest* was tabulating its 2 million responses and predicting that Landon would be the next president, a number of other pollsters were conducting more scientific surveys and correctly forecasting Roosevelt's reelection. The polls of George Gallup, Elmo Roper, and Archibald Crossley differed from the *Digest*'s in two principal respects: they were considerably smaller, and their samples approximated the characteristics of the population as a whole, permitting more accurate generalizations of public opinion to be made.

The *Digest* went out of business, but Gallup, Roper, and Crossley continued to poll and to improve their sampling techniques. In 1940, Gallup predicted Roosevelt would receive 52 percent of the vote; he actually received 55 percent. In 1944, Gallup forecast a 51.5 percent Roosevelt vote, very close to his actual 53.2 percent. Other pollsters also made predictions that closely approximated the results. As a consequence, public confidence in election polling began to grow.

The confidence was short-lived, however. In 1948, all major pollsters forecast a victory by Republican Thomas E. Dewey. Their errors resulted from poor sampling techniques, from the premature termination of polling before the end of the campaign, and from incorrect assumptions about how the undecided would vote.

In attempting to estimate the population in their samples, the pollsters had resorted to filling quotas. They interviewed a certain number of people with different demographic characteristics until the percentage of these groups in the sample resembled that percentage in the population as a whole. Simply because the percentages were approximately equal, however, did not mean that the sample was representative of the population. For example, interviewers avoided certain areas in cities, and their results were consequently biased.

Moreover, the interviewing stopped several weeks before the election. In mid-October, the polls showed that Dewey was ahead by a substantial margin. Burns Roper, son of Elmo Roper, polling for *Fortune* magazine, saw the lead as sufficiently large to predict a Dewey victory without the need for further surveys. A relatively large number of people, however, were undecided. Three weeks before the election, Gallup concluded that 8 percent of the voters had still not made up their minds. In estimating the final vote, he and other pollsters assumed that the undecided would divide their votes in much the same manner as the electorate as a whole. This assumption turned out to be incorrect. Most of those who were wavering in the closing days of the campaign were Democrats. In the end, most of them voted for Truman or did not vote at all.

The results of the 1948 election once again cast doubt on the accuracy of public opinion polls. Truman's victory also reemphasized the fact that surveys reflect opinion at the time they are taken, not necessarily days or weeks later. Opinion and voter preferences may change.

To improve the monitoring of shifts within the electorate, pollsters changed their method of selecting people to be interviewed. They developed a more effective means of anticipating who would actually vote and polled continuously to and through election day to identify more precisely and quickly any shifts that occurred in public sentiment and any reactions to campaign events. Obviously, polls conducted closer to the day on which people vote are more likely to come closer to forecasting the actual results than polls taken months before.[6] The closer to the election, the more likely that public opinion has solidified; more people have made up their minds; and pollsters can usually anticipate what their decision will be on election day.

These changes, plus the continued refinement of the questions, have produced better and more accurate polls, particularly in the 100 days before the election. Between 1936 and 1950, the average error of the final Gallup preelection poll was 3.6 percent; since then it has usually been 2 percent or less. (Table 9.1 indicates the final Gallup Polls and the election results since 1936. Table 9.2 lists the final preelection polls and results in 2004.)

Very close elections in 1960, 1968, and 1976, however, resulted in several pollsters' making wrong predictions. In 1980, the size of Reagan's victory was substantially underestimated in some nationwide polls; in 1992 and 1996, Clinton's margin was overestimated; whereas in 2000, Gore's was underestimated by some pollsters (see Table 9.2).

Why do pollsters underestimate or overestimate the results? Although opinions can change between a poll and the actual vote, that change should be small since most pollsters now conclude their surveys on election day. They also try to identify the voting patterns of people who tell interviewers that they plan to vote early or by absentee ballot. There are, however, two other variables that pollsters must consider: turnout and undecided voters. Who is likely to vote, whether the undecided will vote, and if so, for whom, are factors that can result in a discrepancy between the sample result and the popular vote.

TABLE 9.1	GALLUP POLL ACCURACY RECORD, 1936–2004 (IN PERCENTAGES)

Year	Final Survey	Election Results	Deviation
2004	Bush 49	Bush 50.7	−2
	Kerry 49	Kerry 48.3	+1
2000	Bush 48	Bush 47.9	+0
	Gore 46	Gore 48.4	−2
	Nader 4	Nader 2.7	+1
1996	Clinton 52	Clinton 50.1	+1
	Dole 41.0	Dole 41.4	−0
	Perot 7	Perot 8.5	−1
1992	Clinton 49	Clinton 43.3	+5
	Bush 37	Bush 37.7	−0
	Perot 14	Perot 19.0	−5
1988	Bush 56	Bush 53.0	+2
	Dukakis 44	Dukakis 46	−2
1984	Reagan 59	Reagan 59.2	0
	Mondale 41	Mondale 40.8	0
1980	Reagan 47	Reagan 50.8	−3
	Carter 44	Carter 41	+3
	Anderson 8	Anderson 6.6	+1
	Other 1	Other 1.6	−0
1976	Carter 48	Carter 50.1	−2
	Ford 49	Ford 48.1	+0
	McCarthy 2	McCarthy .9	+1
	Other 1	Other .9	+0
1972	Nixon 62	Nixon 61.8	+0
	McGovern 38	McGovern 38.2	−0
1968	Nixon 43	Nixon 43.5	−0
	Humphrey 42	Humphrey 42.9	−0
	Wallace 15	Wallace 13.6	+1
1964	Johnson 64	Johnson 61.3	+2
	Goldwater 36	Goldwater 38.7	−2
1960	Kennedy 51	Kennedy 50.1	+0
	Nixon 49	Nixon 49.9	−0
1956	Eisenhower 59.5	Eisenhower 57.8	+1
	Stevenson 40.5	Stevenson 42.4	−1
1952	Eisenhower 51	Eisenhower 55.4	−4
	Stevenson 49	Stevenson 44.6	+4
1948	Truman 44.5	Truman 49.5	−5
	Dewey 49.5	Dewey 45.1	+4
	Wallace 4	Wallace 2.4	+1
	Other 2	Other 3	−1
1944	Roosevelt 51.5	Roosevelt 53.8	−2
	Dewey 48.5	Dewey 46.2	+2
1940	Roosevelt 52	Roosevelt 55	−3
	Willkie 48	Willkie 45	+3
1936	Roosevelt 55.7	Roosevelt 62.5	−6
	Landon 44.3	Landon 37.5	+6

Source: "Election Poll Accuracy," The Gallup Poll. http://www.gallup.com/content/default.aspx?ci=9442&pg=1 (accessed August 10, 2006).

TABLE 9.2 | ACCURACY OF THE FINAL 2004 PREELECTION POLLS

Poll*	Bush	Kerry	Nader	Unsure/ Others
Actual Results	50.7	48.3	.4	.6
ABC News/Washington Post	49	48	1	3
CBS	49	47	1	3
CNN/USA Today	49	47	–	4
Harris	49	48	2	1
NBC News/Wall Street Journal	48	47	1	4
Pew Research Center	51	48	1	–
TIPP†	50.1	48.0	1.1	.8
Zogby	49.4	49.1	–	–

*All polls include the allocated undecided vote.
†*Investor's Business Daily, Christian Science Monitor,* TIPP poll conducted by TechnoMetrica Market Intelligence.
Source: Polling Report, "Election 2004." http://www.pollingreport.com/2004.htm (accessed August 10, 2006).

Anticipating likely voters is a tricky business. Simply asking people whether they plan to vote is not sufficient because more people will say that they intend to vote than actually do so. Pollsters usually ask a battery of questions to determine the likelihood of the respondent actually voting: Are you currently registered to vote? Did you vote in the last election? By the way, where do people vote around here?

Similarly, it is necessary for pollsters to anticipate who is really undecided, whether they will vote, and if so, for whom. The wording of preference questions can be critical. Researchers at Harvard's Shorenstein Center found that presenting people with a list of choices and asking them for whom they would vote if the election were held today results in a lower percentage of undecideds than if they are given the additional option of choosing an alternative response such as "or haven't you picked a candidate yet?"[7]

As election day approaches, pollsters need to allocate the undecided vote if they are to accurately forecast the results. If their allocation formula proves to be incorrect, then their sample is likely to deviate from the actual vote. This happened in 2000 when some pollsters split the undecided vote between Gore and Bush. As a consequence, they failed to capture the extent of the late surge for Gore.[8] Similarly in 1992, pollsters made an incorrect judgment about the Perot vote. Based on the experience of other third-party and independent candidates whose support had declined as election day neared, pollsters underestimated the popular vote that Perot received. Not only did Perot's support not decline, but his campaign also succeeded in attracting a large number of first-time voters whose turnout was difficult to predict.

Typically, most voters decide well before the campaign's final week. In fact, in a normal election, one-half to two-thirds of the electorate make their decision before or during the national nominating conventions. In 2004, it was two-thirds. (See Chapter 7, Table 7.2.) The polarized nature of the American electorate facilitated an easy choice for most voters.

If most people decide before Labor Day, the polls conducted in September are likely to be close to the final election results. And they have been. In "trial heats" conducted by the Gallup organization, the candidate who was ahead in early September won in twelve of fifteen elections between 1948 and 2004. During this period, the person ahead at the end of September won all but two of these elections. The exceptions were Truman in 1948 and Gore in 2000. Both trailed at the end of September but eventually won the popular vote.[9]

There is obviously a relationship between the incumbent's job approval and reelection. Since the end of World War II, presidents whose approval ratings have been 50 percent or higher prior to the election have won reelection; those whose ratings have been 50 percent and below have lost.[10] George W. Bush's approval rating hovered between 52 and 48 percent in the months leading up to the vote, making if difficult for pollsters to anticipate whether he would win or lose the election. According to the final poll conducted before the election, Bush' approval rating stood at 48 percent.[11]

TELEVISION FORECASTS

Forecasts continue right to the end, until all the votes are tabulated. The final projections are presented by the major television broadcast and cable networks during the night of the election. In airing the results, the news media have four objectives: to report the vote, to forecast the winners, to analyze the returns, and to do so ahead of the other networks.

Beginning in the 1980s, the major networks and news services established a consortium to pool their resources in reporting the vote count. Thousands of reporters were assigned to precincts and county election boards around the country to communicate the presidential, congressional, and gubernatorial votes as soon as they were tallied.

If all the news media wanted to do was report the results, this type of reporting would suffice. But they want to do more. They want to analyze the vote and explain its meaning. To do so, they consolidated their data-gathering operations in 1992 and conducted a large exit poll in which thousands of people were surveyed after they left their voting places.

Exit polling has continued since then although the organization that runs the polls has changed. Here's how these polls work. A large number of precincts across the country are randomly selected. The random selection is made within states in such a way that principal geographic units (cities, suburbs, and rural areas), size of precincts, and their past voting records are taken into account. Approximately 1,200 representatives of the polling organization administer the poll to voters who are chosen in a systematic way (for example, every fourth or fifth person) as they leave the voting booths. Voters are asked to complete a short questionnaire (thirty to forty items) that is designed to elicit information on their voting choices, political attitudes, and candidate evaluations and feelings, as well as their demographic characteristics. Several times over the course of the day, the questionnaires are collected, tabulated, and their results telephoned to a central computer bank where they are analyzed using various statistical measures.

A variety of models are used to compare the returns from the precincts to those of past elections and to returns from other parts of the state. The sequence of the votes, the order in which they are received, is also considered in the analysis. Then, after most or all of the election polls in a state have been completed, the findings of the exit poll are made public by the news media. Over the course of the evening, the networks adjust the exit poll data to reflect the actual results as they are tabulated.

The exit poll is usually very accurate. Because it is conducted over the course of the day, there may be a little bias that would under-represent or over-represent certain types of voters who cast their ballots at different times of the day. By the end of the day, however, this bias should be eliminated.

Only voters are sampled and in large numbers, thereby reducing the error to much less than that of the national surveys conducted before the election. In addition, the exit poll provides a sample of sufficient size to enable analysts to discern the attitudes, opinions, and choices of smaller groups and subgroups (such as white southern Protestants; African-American males; and unmarried, college-educated women) within the electorate. In 2004, 13,110 people exiting hundreds of polling places around the country participated in this survey. In addition, 500 people who voted early were interviewed on the telephone. (See Table 9.3 later in this chapter.)

Early projections of the winner on election night based on exit polling have generated considerable criticism, primarily on the grounds that they discourage turnout and affect voting in states in which the polls are still open. This controversy was heightened in 1980. When the early returns and polls conducted for the networks and major newspapers all indicated a Reagan landslide, the networks projected his victory early in the evening while voting was still occurring in some parts of the country. At 9:30 PM. Eastern Standard Time (EST), President Jimmy Carter appeared before his supporters and conceded defeat. Almost immediately, Carter's early announcement incurred angry protests, particularly from defeated West Coast Democrats, who alleged that the president's remarks discouraged many Democrats from voting. It is difficult to substantiate their claim, however.[12] Researchers who have studied the impact of the 1980 television projections on voting have found a small reduction in turnout in the West, but little evidence of vote switching or turnout bias toward or against the projected winner as a result of the early projections.[13]

The minimal effect of the election reporting on the outcome of the election seems to be related to the fact that relatively few people watch the broadcasts and then vote. Most people vote first and watch the returns later in the evening.

Perhaps this pattern of voting and then watching or listening to the returns explains why George H. W. Bush's projected victory on the networks in 1988 before the polls closed on the West Coast did little to change the results in three out of four Pacific states (Washington, Oregon, and Hawaii) that voted for Michael Dukakis. Nonetheless, sensitivity to the criticism that early returns affect turnout and voting behavior led the networks to agree prior to the 1992 election not to project winners in any election within a state until its polls had closed. In states with different time zones, a majority of its polls have to close before winners would be projected.

The networks amended their pledge to make a national prediction in 1996 even as people were voting on the West Coast. Promptly at 9 PM, EST, they forecast a Clinton victory. In anticipation of this early forecast, Republicans bitterly criticized the practice of calling the election before the polls had closed and warned of possible legislation to prevent it from happening again. No such legislation has been enacted, however, although congressional hearings were held.

Another prediction controversy in which speed and accuracy collided occurred in 2000. Early in the evening of the election (7:50 PM, EST), the television broadcast networks forecast a victory for Al Gore in Florida on the basis of exit polls even though residents in the central time zone living in the Florida Panhandle were still voting. The announcement elated Democrats. However, as the evening wore on, a discrepancy was noted between the actual returns and the exit polls. On the basis of this discrepancy, CNN retracted its prediction of a Gore victory. The other networks quickly followed suit. At 2:16 AM, EST, the Fox News channel declared Bush the winner on the basis of tabulated returns. Again, the other networks quickly followed.

Hearing the news, Vice President Gore called Governor George W. Bush to concede the election and was on his way to make a public announcement to his supporters. Before he did so, however, he learned that the election was still too close to call. Gore then telephoned Bush again and retracted his concession while the networks retracted their prediction of a Bush victory.[14] In the end, the closeness of the Florida vote combined with the voiding of thousands of improperly punched ballots precluded a valid exit poll prediction.

After much controversy over the inaccurate predictions of the Florida elections results in 2000, the networks' exit poll consortium did a substantial overhaul of its analytic models. In the 2002 midterm elections, the new system failed. Poll takers could not get through on the phone lines, the computers crashed, and the analysis could not be completed. Beginning in 2004, a new group consisting of Edison Media Research and Mitofsky International, conducted what became known as the National Election Poll (NEP). But its initial results were also controversial.

The first release of the exit data at 12:59 PM showed Kerry with a small but statistically insignificant lead.[15] By mid-afternoon, however, his lead had jumped to 3 percent, a percentage that was statistically significant. Democrats were gleeful; Republicans were puzzled because their poll watchers were reporting very high turnouts in Republican districts. Reporters began drafting their Kerry victory stories. Although Kerry's lead in the exit polls diminished over the rest of the day and into the evening, and the final exit poll at 1:33 AM confirmed Bush's popular and Electoral College wins, reporters and politicians were miffed at being misled.

Why would such a large sample of randomly selected voters be incorrect? Some NEP interviewers complained that they were kept at a distance from the polling centers (as prescribed by state law to prevent electioneering at the polls) and thus had difficulty interviewing the requisite number of voters. Moreover, in the morning, women voters seemed more willing to complete the interview and requisite questionnaire than men, skewing the results in Kerry's favor. The morning numbers may also have over-represented certain areas, such as cities and close-in suburbs, which tend to vote more Democratic. (Table 9.3 reports the results of the exit polls in the past three presidential elections.)

INTERPRETING THE ELECTION RESULTS

In addition to predicting the results, the television networks and major newspapers also provide instant analyses of results on election night and the morning after. This analysis, based primarily on exit polls, relates voting decisions to the issue positions, ideological perspectives, and partisan preferences of the electorate. Patterns among demographic groups, issue stands, and electoral perceptions and choices are noted and used to explain why people voted for particular candidates.

Although exit polls present a detailed picture of the electorate on election day (see Table 9.3), they do not provide a perspective over the course of the election. To understand changes in public attitudes and opinions during the campaign, it is necessary to survey people over the course of the election cycle, asking the same questions. The nationwide polls conducted by Gallup, Zogby, Pew, and the National Annenberg Election Survey, plus those designed for major news organizations, often repeat questions, but they do not do so with the same respondents. Nonetheless, they are able to measure aggregate opinion change and identify factors that may have contributed to it.

The American National Election Studies (ANES) conducted by researchers at the University of Michigan interview and reinterview many of the same respondents. As a consequence, they can analyze opinion change during the election. The wealth of data that these surveys have produced has served as a basis for political scientists to construct theories of why people vote as they do.

MODELS OF VOTING BEHAVIOR

There are two basic models of voting behavior: the *prospective,* which emphasizes the issues and looks to the future; and the *retrospective,* which emphasizes the candidates and their parties and looks to the past.[16]

In the prospective voting model, voters compare their beliefs and policy preferences with those enunciated by the parties and their nominees. They make a determination of which party and which candidates espouse positions that are closer to their own and thus would more likely pursue those positions if elected. In other words, voters make a judgment on the prospects of obtaining future policy they desire based on the current positions of the candidates and their parties and the policies they promise to pursue.

To make a prospective judgment, voters must have discernible beliefs and opinions of their own; they must be able to differentiate the candidates on the basis of their beliefs and opinions; and finally, they must be able to make a judgment about which party and candidate is closer to their own views on the issues they deem most important. If people were only concerned with a single issue, the choice might be easy. But alas there are usually multiple issues upon which the voters are interested and candidates and parties take positions. To simplify the task for voters, the issues are frequently bundled together by the parties and their nominees and given an ideological label. Contemporary voters have no difficulty discerning the Democratic Party as liberal and the Republican Party as conservative. To decide which party and candidate are more likely to pursue desired policy goals, voters rely on their perceptions of current conditions and on the party and candidate more responsible for them. The judgment is retrospective. In other words, history serves as a prologue for the future.

If the economy is strong, society harmonious, and the nation secure and at peace, people assume that their leaders, particularly the president, must be doing a good job. If conditions are not good, then the president gets much of the blame.[17] Thus, the key question that voters ask themselves when making a retrospective evaluation is "Am I and my country better off now than before the party now in power and its candidates won control of the White House?"

If an incumbent president or even vice president is running, then this retrospective judgment should be closely related to the voting decision, especially if the electorate sees the most important problems the country is facing as similar to those that occurred during the incumbent's term. If, however, there is no incumbent seeking reelection (such as in 1952 and 2008), then the retrospective judgment is less relevant for voters, but partisan affiliation remains important.

Another component of retrospective voting decisions involves a comparison between the principal contenders and their parties. Which of them is more likely to do well in the future?[18] Thus, in any one voting decision, voters weigh the parties and candidates' past performance as well as the promise offered by the challengers and their party for the future.

In both the prospective and retrospective models, partisanship is apt to be an important influence on the evaluations people make to arrive at their voting decision. As noted in Chapter 3, political attitudes are relatively stable, although they tend to be activated and may be modified over the course of an election cycle.[19] They also can be changed, but how quickly and under what circumstances has been subject to some dispute.[20] A partisan orientation provides voters with a lens through which campaigns can be filtered, candidates and issues evaluated, and electoral judgments made.

In the retrospective model, partisanship itself is the consequence of evaluations of the past performance of parties. It therefore functions as a summary judgment of how the parties and the candidates have done, and as a basis for anticipating how they will do in the future. Partisans who make a retrospective evaluation are more apt to rate presidents of their party more favorably before, during, and after the election and those of the other party less favorably. They also tend to see themselves as closer to the positions of their candidate and party than to the opposition.

Since the identification people have with political parties is the most stable and resilient factor affecting the voting decision, it is considered to be the single most important long-term influence on voting. Orientations voters have toward the candidates and issues are short-term factors that fluctuate from election to election.

One of the most significant developments within the American political environment has been the growing polarization of the parties and their elected officials. This polarization has produced greater policy differences between the parties and more issue consistency within them, guided by the party's ideological orientation. In reinforcing partisanship, ideology has also linked more tightly a collection of issue positions to political attitudes, making the issues less of an independent factor in determining election outcomes. In other words, the partisan prism through which most voters view the election is more compelling than it was two or three decades ago. That prism exerts more influence on their evaluation of the candidates, the issues, and subsequently, the voter's electoral choice.

EXPLAINING CONTEMPORARY PRESIDENTIAL ELECTIONS: 1952–2004

Since a majority of the electorate continues to identify with a political party or leans in a partisan direction, the candidate of the dominant party should have an advantage—all things being equal. But as we noted throughout this book, the major parties are at rough parity with one another, and all things are not usually equal. Candidates change, issues come and go, and the public mood shifts in intensity and direction. Thus, it is important to understand how the electorate evaluates these changes, how people feel about the candidates, how they perceive and evaluate candidates and their issue stands, and how the electorate's perceptions and evaluations affect their voting decisions and the election outcomes.[21] This section discusses the interplay of these components in presidential elections since 1952.

1952–1956: The Impact of Personality
In 1952, the Democrats were the dominant party, but the Republicans won the presidential election and gained a majority in both houses of Congress. The issues of that election—the fear of communism at home and abroad, the presence of corruption in high levels of government, and the United States involvement in the Korean War—benefited the GOP, as did the popularity of its

presidential candidate, former General Dwight D. Eisenhower. These short-term factors offset the Democrats' longer-term, partisan advantage and enabled the Republicans to win.[22] The electorate saw the Republicans as better able to deal with the problems of fighting communism, promoting efficiency in government, and ending the war.[23]

President Eisenhower's reelection four years later was also a consequence of his personal popularity, not his party's. He was evaluated favorably by the voters, while his opponent, Adlai Stevenson, was not. The Republicans did not win control of Congress, however, as they had in 1952. Their failure to do so in 1956 testified to the continuing partisan advantage that the Democrats enjoyed among the American electorate at that time.

1960–1972: The Increasing Importance of Issues
Beginning in 1960, the issues of the campaign seemed to play a more important role in the election's outcome than they had since the New Deal realignment. Noneconomic policy issues undercut the impact of partisanship forged on economic ties. In general, these issues contributed to the defection of Democrats from their party's presidential candidates in 1960, 1968, and 1972, and to defections by Republicans (and Southern Democrats) in 1964.

John Kennedy's Catholicism was a primary concern to many voters in 1960 and helps explain the closeness of that election as a whole. Despite the Democrats' dominance within the electorate, Kennedy received only 115,000 more votes than Richard Nixon, 0.3 percent more of the total vote. Kennedy's Catholicism cost him votes in the heavily Protestant South. Outside the South, Kennedy actually picked up Democratic votes because of the massive support he received from Catholics and the concentration of this religious group in the cities in the large industrial states.[24]

Although Kennedy barely won in 1960, Lyndon Johnson won by a landslide four years later. Short-term factors contributed to the magnitude of the Johnson victory.[25] Barry Goldwater was perceived as a minority candidate within a minority party, ideologically to the right of most Republicans. Moreover, he did not enjoy a favorable public image as Johnson did. Policy attitudes also favored the Democrats, even in foreign affairs. Goldwater's militant anticommunism scared many voters. They saw Johnson as the peace candidate.

Two groups of voters began to change their voting preferences and eventually their partisan orientation. White, Southern Democrats, opposed to their party's civil rights initiatives, cast a majority of their votes for Goldwater, and moderate, northern Republicans, who disagreed with Goldwater's conservative policy positions, voted for Johnson. For the first time since the New Deal, five states in the solidly Democratic South (plus Goldwater's home state of Arizona) went Republican, auguring the major regional realignment that was to occur in the elections that followed.

In addition to civil rights, a new set of foreign policy issues also split the Democrats in 1968. The Vietnam War and the campus unrest and protests that followed from it increased Democratic defections as that party's share of the vote declined 19 percent. The Republican vote, however, increased by only 4 percent.

The third-party candidacy of George Wallace accounted for much of the difference between Democratic defections and the Republican vote. Wallace's support was issue based. Although he did not have much personal appeal himself, his policy positions did, particularly among white southerners, young new voters, and some blue-collar workers.[26] Had Wallace not run, the Republican presidential vote undoubtedly would have been larger because Nixon was the second choice of most Wallace voters.

The results of the 1968 presidential election thus deviated from the partisan alignment of the electorate. A significant number of voters had grievances against the Democratic Party and against Lyndon Johnson's conduct of the Vietnam War. Some of these voters supported Wallace and, to a lesser extent, Nixon. The Democratic candidate, Hubert H. Humphrey, suffered accordingly.

A decline in the intensity of partisanship and a growth in the number of independents contributed to issue voting. Had it not been for the Democrats' large partisan advantage and the overwhelming African-American vote that Humphrey received, the presidential election would not have been nearly so close.

The trend away from partisan presidential voting for the majority party's candidate continued in 1972. With a nominee who was ideologically and personally unpopular, the Democrats suffered their worst presidential defeat since 1920. Richard Nixon enjoyed a better public image than George McGovern. He was seen as the stronger of the two presidential candidates. These perceptions, positive for Nixon and negative for McGovern, contributed to Nixon's large victory in the 1972 election. More of the electorate saw the Republican standard-bearer as closer to its own positions than the Democratic candidate. McGovern was perceived as liberal on all issues and ideologically to the left of his own party. Democrats defected in considerable numbers; Republicans voted for their nominee.[27]

1976–1996: The Evaluation of Performance

Issue differences narrowed in 1976. Neither Gerald Ford nor Jimmy Carter emphasized the social and cultural concerns that played a large role in the previous presidential contest. Both focused their attention on trust in government and on domestic economic matters. In the wake of Watergate and a recession that occurred during the Ford presidency, it is not surprising that these issues worked to the Democrats' advantage.

Carter was also helped by a slightly more favorable personal assessment than that given to Ford.[28] The latter's association with the Nixon administration, highlighted in the public mind by his pardon of the former president, his difficult struggle to win his own party's nomination, and his seeming inability to find a solution to the country's economic woes adversely affected his presidential image.[29]

With sociocultural issues muted and the Vietnam War over, economic concerns divided the electorate along partisan lines. This division put the candidate of the majority party back into the driver's seat. Carter won primarily because he was a Democrat and secondarily because his personal evaluation was more favorable than Ford's. Carter was also helped by being a Southerner. He received the electoral votes of every southern state except Virginia. In an otherwise divided Electoral College, this southern support proved to be decisive.

When Carter sought reelection four years later, being a Democrat, an incumbent, and a southerner was not sufficient to win. Poor performance ratings overcame the advantage that partisanship and incumbency normally bring to a president of the majority party. In 1976, Carter was judged on the basis of his potential *for* office, and he beat Ford. In 1980, Carter was judged on the basis of his performance *in* office, and he lost badly to challenger, Ronald Reagan. Carter's vote fell behind his 1976 percentages in every single state, and in approximately half the states, it dropped at least 10 percent. Why did he lose so badly?

Personal evaluations of Carter and assessments of his policies were not nearly as favorable as they had been four years earlier. Personal assessments of Ronald Reagan were also low, but in contrast to Carter's, they improved over the course of the campaign. Economic conditions—high inflation, large-scale unemployment, and the decreasing competitiveness and productivity of American industry—worked to the advantage of the party out of power. For the first time in many years, the Republicans were seen as the party better able to invigorate the economy, return prosperity, and lower inflation.

In addition, dissatisfaction with the conduct of foreign affairs, culminating in frustration over the Soviet Union's invasion of Afghanistan and especially, in the failure of the United States to obtain the release of American hostages held in Iran, contributed to Carter's negative evaluation and to changing public attitudes toward defense spending and foreign affairs. In 1980, most Americans supported increased military expenditures, a position with which Reagan was closely identified, combined with a less conciliatory approach and a tougher, more militant posture in dealing with problems abroad. These issues, together with the negative assessment of Carter as president, explain why the Democratic candidate lost in 1980.

John Anderson, a former Republican member of Congress, also ran in that election as an independent. A protest candidate who drew equally from Democrats and Republicans, Anderson was unable to attract a solid core of supporters. Nor was he able to differentiate his policy positions sufficiently from Carter's and Reagan's to generate an issue-oriented vote. In the end, his failure to win any electoral votes and only 6.5 percent of the popular vote demonstrated the resiliency of the major parties and the legitimacy that their labels provided candidates for national office.

In summary, in 1980, Carter was repudiated by the voters because of their negative retrospective evaluation of his presidency. Reagan appeared to offer greater potential for leadership.[30]

Four years later, voters rewarded President Reagan for a job well done with a huge victory. It is interesting to note that ideology did not work to Reagan's advantage in either 1980 or 1984. It was conditions more than Reagan's positions on the issues that apparently influenced the electorate's judgment. A resurgent economy, strengthened military, and renewed feelings of national pride brought the president broad support. Although voters agreed with Mondale more than with Reagan on many of the specific problems confronting the nation, they viewed Reagan as the person better able to deal with those issues.

Leadership was a dominant concern. Voters evaluated Reagan much more highly than Mondale in this regard. It was a retrospective vote. The electorate supported Reagan primarily for his performance in office. In other words, they voted *for* him in 1984 just as they had voted *against* Carter four years earlier.

The trend of retrospective voting continued in 1988 with the election of Reagan's vice president, George H. W. Bush. Bush won because the electorate evaluated the Reagan administration positively, associated Bush with that administration, and concluded that he, not Michael Dukakis, would be better able and more likely to maintain the Reagan revolution and the good times people associated with Reagan's presidency.[31] That Bush was not as favorably evaluated as Reagan had been four years earlier partially accounts for his narrower victory.[32]

Partisanship affected voting behavior more in 1988 than it had in any election since 1960.[33] In the past, a high correlation between partisan identities and voting behavior worked to the Democrats' advantage. In 1988, it did not. An increase in Republican allegiances and a decline in Democratic partisan support produced an almost evenly divided electorate. There were slightly more Democrats but greater turnout and less defection among Republicans. In the end, neither candidate enjoyed a partisan advantage, but among independents, Bush held a solid lead.

Ideological orientations worked to reinforce partisan voting patterns in 1988, with Republican candidate George H. W. Bush winning overwhelmingly among Republicans and conservatives, and Democratic candidate Dukakis doing almost as well among Democrats and liberals. The problem for Dukakis, however, and any liberal for that matter, was that the proportion of people that considered themselves liberal declined substantially. In 1988, almost twice as many voters considered themselves conservative rather than liberal.

Four years later, with the economy in recession, budget and trade deficits rising, and layoffs of white-collar managers and blue-collar workers dominating the news, Bush was judged on his own performance in office, and that judgment was negative. He received only 37.4 percent of the popular vote in a three-person contest and 168 electoral votes (only 31 percent of the total). His 1992 vote declined among every population group.

Clinton was clearly helped by his partisan affiliation and his southern heritage in 1992. With slightly more Democrats in the electorate than Republicans, Clinton received the votes of three out of four Democrats. For the first time since 1964, Republican defections actually exceeded those of Democrats. Turnout, traditionally seen to advantage the Republicans, was neutralized in 1992. Democratic turnout was up, and Republican turnout was down.

Still, Clinton's partisan advantage could have been offset by a lopsided vote of independents against him, but they divided their support among the three candidates, giving Clinton a plurality of their vote (38 percent) with Perot and Bush splitting the rest. (Refer to Table 9.3.) Nor did ideology work to the president's advantage as it had in previous elections. Although liberals and conservatives continued to support Democratic and Republican candidates respectively, Perot cut into both groups, dropping Bush's support among conservatives about 15 percent from his 1988 level. Moreover, Clinton did comparably better among moderates than previous Democratic candidates, substantially leading Bush and Perot among self-identified moderates.

Although Bush was credited with a successful foreign policy, the lower salience of foreign policy issues in 1992 undercut Bush's achievements in this policy realm and even served to highlight his inattention to domestic matters. The economy was the principal issue, and Clinton its principal beneficiary.[34]

In short, Clinton won a solid victory. Although he received only 43 percent of the vote, his popular vote margin over the president was 5.6 percent. In the Electoral College, he won thirty-two states and the District of Columbia for a total of 370 votes.

By 1996, domestic concerns were still dominant, but the economy was stronger, crime had decreased, and the nation remained at peace—all conditions that favored the incumbent. Voters responded accordingly, reelecting the Democratic president but also the Republican congressional majority. Clinton's popular and electoral vote exceeded his 1992 totals, although the regional composition of his vote was essentially the same as it had been four years earlier.

Despite misgivings about some aspects of the president's character, notably his personal integrity, honesty, and willingness to stand up for his beliefs, voters saw Clinton as more caring, more in touch with the times, and more visionary than his Republican opponent. But it was the nation's economy, not the president's character, which proved to be the critical factor in determining the outcome of the election. Those who perceived themselves to be better off (about one-third of the electorate) supported the president; those who saw themselves as worse off (about 20 percent) supported his opponent.

In short, the 1996 election was a referendum on the Clinton presidency, and Clinton won. Not only did the electorate evaluate his first term favorably, but they saw the president as more capable of understanding and handling the challenges of the 1990s and building a bridge to the twenty-first century than either Dole or Perot.

2000–2004: Party Polarization and Personal Performance

Although the 2000 election could have been another referendum on the Clinton presidency, it was not for many voters. Vice President Al Gore's decision to emphasize the differences between himself and Governor George W. Bush rather than contrast the economic, social, and international conditions at the end of 2000 with those of 1992, the last time the Republicans controlled the White House and a Bush was in the presidency, focused the attention of the electorate on the future, not the past. Encouraging voters to make more of a prospective choice than a retrospective judgment turned out to be a poor strategic decision for the vice president. Gore's proportion of the Democratic vote dropped below Clinton's. By severing his ties with the Clinton administration, Gore hurt his own candidacy.[35]

Nonetheless, many of the same voting patterns emerged in 2000 that were evident in previous presidential elections, particularly during the 1990s. (Refer to Table 9.3.) The electorate was clearly and evenly divided. Parity between the major parties contributed to this division. Partisans overwhelmingly supported their party's nominee, while independents were almost evenly split between Bush and Gore.

A large, persistent gender gap increased in size to 11 percent in 2000, with a majority of women supporting Gore and Lieberman and a majority of men backing Bush and Cheney. Other groups within each party's electoral coalitions also voted in record proportions and along party lines with African Americans, Latinos, and organized labor voting Democratic, and Christian fundamentalists and evangelicals voting Republican.

Other past voting trends were also evident. Jews voted heavily for Gore and his Jewish running mate, Joseph Lieberman; Catholics gave Gore slightly more support than Bush, the consequence of a strong Hispanic vote. There was also a sectarian-secular divide with people who attended religious services more regularly voting more Republican than those who attended less regularly or not at all.

Bush's vote varied directly and Gore's varied indirectly with income and education, with the exception of those with a postgraduate education who leaned toward Gore. Contributing to the size of Bush's vote was the increasing proportion of upper-income voters (with family incomes of $50,000 or more) who cast ballots in 2000. This group constituted 53 percent of the 2000 electorate compared to 39 percent four years earlier.

There was also a regional divide, with Gore doing well in the Northeast and Pacific Coast, and Bush doing well in the South and Rocky Mountain areas, and in the agricultural heartland in the Midwest. The vote in the other regions of the country was more evenly split between the major party two candidates.

Ralph Nader and Pat Buchanan attracted much less attention and support than in the years when Perot ran on the Reform Party ticket. Neither candidate had funds that were comparable to Perot's in 1992 or even 1996. However, the closeness of the 2000 election enhanced the influence of these third-party candidacies, especially Nader's.[36] Had Nader not been on the Florida ballot, Gore would have probably won that state and thereby the Electoral College. In the exit polls conducted on election day, 70 percent of those who said that they voted for Nader indicated that they would still have voted had he not run. Of this group, Gore was preferred over Bush by a margin of two to one.

The nation's bitter political divisions that emerged during the Clinton presidency continued through the 2000 election and fueled the political controversy over the Florida vote. Were it not for the strong economy, the general contentment of the society, and people's optimism about the future, these divisions might have generated the same level of intensity within the population as they had among the political elites in Washington during the 1990s. Fortunately, however, they did not, and the electorate was able to get over its angst from the Florida vote controversy as the new president took office and began to exercise power. Politics returned to normal until the terrorist's attacks of September 11, 2001.

The election of 2004 extended and reinforced most these cleavages within the body politic. The major parties remained at parity with one another, divided by ideology. The president was viewed as a highly polarizing figure with Republicans overwhelmingly supporting him, and Democrats overwhelming disapproving of his presidency. With the proportion of independents shrinking and the intensity of party allegiances increasing, the election outcome turned on efforts to maximize partisan bases and persuade the relatively few undecided for whom to vote.

There were few surprises in the partisan, regional, and demographic composition of the vote. With the parties evenly divided, the size and loyalty of each party's electoral base became a critical factor in the outcome of the election. The Republicans bested the Democrats on both counts: They turned out a larger vote in the key battleground states (4.4 percent to the Democrats' 3.6 percent), and their partisans were slightly more loyal (93 percent of Republicans for Bush compared to 89 percent Democrats for Kerry).

The geographic trends evident in 2000 continued in 2004. Only three states, Iowa, New Hampshire, and New Mexico, switched their presidential vote from 2000 to 2004.

Familiar cleavages within the electorate on religion, marital status, and gender persisted although the gender gap was reduced. The president received a larger proportion of the vote of married women than he did four years earlier, thereby increasing his proportion of the female vote.[37]

The religious divide remained with attendance at places of worship a key factor differentiating Bush and Kerry voters. Within the religious community, there was an additional distinction between traditionalists and modernists. Protestant fundamentalists and evangelicals, Latter-day Saints, traditional Catholics, and orthodox Jews gave more support to the president than those with more nuanced and moderate sectarian beliefs.[38] That Kerry was Catholic seemed to have little impact on Catholic voters who cast their ballots along partisan rather than religious lines.[39]

Minority racial and ethnic groups continued their support of the Democratic candidate. African Americans voted overwhelmingly for Kerry. Hispanics also favored the Democrat but by a lesser amount.[40]

The reasons for Bush's victory are more speculative than the findings about who voted for him. The president and his supporters benefited from a strong campaign that activated and extended the Republican base, the incumbency factor, the continued salience of terrorism as a principal issue, and perceptions of the president's strong personal leadership following the attacks on September 11, 2001.

TABLE 9.3 | PORTRAIT OF THE AMERICAN ELECTORATE, 1992–2004 (IN PERCENTAGES)

Percentage of 2004		1996			2000			2004		
		Clinton	Dole	Perot	Bush	Gore	Nader	Bush	Kerry	Nader
	Total Vote	49%	41%	8%	48%	48%	3%	50%	49%	1%
46	Men	43	44	10	53	42	3	54	45	1
54	Women	54	38	7	43	54	2	47	52	1
77	Whites	43	46	9	54	42	3	57	42	1
11	Blacks	84	12	4	9	90	1	11	89	0
9	Hispanics	72	21	6	35	62	2	42	55	2
2	Asians	43	48	8	41	55	3	41	59	–
63	Married	44	46	9	53	44	2	56	43	1
37	Unmarried	57	31	9	38	57	4	40	59	1
17	18–29 Years	53	34	10	46	48	5	44	54	1
28	30–44 Years	48	41	9	49	48	2	51	47	1
30	45–59 Years	48	41	9	49	48	2	50	49	1
25	60+ Years	48	44	7	47	51	2	53	46	0
4	Not H.S. Grad	59	28	11	38	59	1	49	50	0
22	H.S. Grad	51	35	13	49	48	1	51	48	1
31	Some College	48	40	10	51	45	3	53	46	0
26	College Grad	44	46	8	51	45	3	51	47	1
17	Postgraduate	52	40	5	44	52	3	43	55	1
53	White Protestant+	36	53	10	56	42	2	58	41	0

Catholic	27	53	37	9	47	50	2	51	48	1
Jewish	3	78	16	3	19	79	1	24	76	–
White Born-Again Christian@	22	26	65	8	80	18	1	77	22	1
Union Household	24	59	30	9	37	59	3	39	60	1
Family Income Under $15,000	8	59	28	11	37	57	4	36	63	1
$15,000–$29,999	15	53	36	9	41	54	3	41	58	0
$30,000–$49,999	22	48	40	10	48	49	2	48	51	0
$50,000–$74,999	23	44	48	7	51	46	2	55	44	1
$75,000–$99,999	14	41	51	7	52	45	2	53	46	0
$100,000+	11	38	54	6	54	43	2	56	43	1
Family's Financial Situation is										
Better Today	31	61	35	3	36	61	2	79	20	0
Same Today	39	46	45	8	60	35	3	48	50	1
Worse Today	28	27	57	13	63	33	4	19	80	1
Northeast	22	55	34	9	39	56	3	43	56	1
Midwest	25	48	41	10	49	48	2	51	48	1
South	31	46	46	7	55	43	1	58	41	0
West	21	48	40	8	46	48	4	45	53	2
Republicans	37	13	80	6	91	8	1	93	7	0
Independents	26	43	35	17	47	45	6	47	50	2
Democrats	37	84	10	5	11	86	2	10	89	0
Liberals	21	78	11	7	13	80	6	13	86	1

(continued)

TABLE 9.3 | CONTINUED

		1996			2000			2004		
Percentage of 2004		Clinton	Dole	Perot	Bush	Gore	Nader	Bush	Kerry	Nader
45	Moderates	57	33	9	44	52	2	44	55	0
33	Conservatives	20	71	8	81	17	1	83	16	1
60	Employed#	48	40	9	48	49	2	52	46	1
40	Unemployed#	49	42	8	48	47	3	49	50	1
11	First-Time Voters	54	34	11	43	52	4	45	54	1
52	Approve of Clinton's/Bush's Performance				20	77	2	90	9	1
46	Disapprove of Clinton's/Bush's Performance				88	9	2	5	93	1
	Most Important Issue for Voting									
5	Taxes							56	44	0
4	Education							25	75	–
15	Iraq							25	74	0
19	Terrorism							84	14	0
20	Economy/Jobs							18	80	1
22	Moral Values							79	18	2
8	Health Care							22	78	–

*N = 13,660

@Includes all Protestants in 2000 and 2004.

+Includes all people who identified themselves as part of the religious right in 2000 and 2004.

#The 1996 question: Are you employed full time? In 2000 and 2004: Do you work full-time for pay? "Yes" answers were categorized as "employed"; "no" answers as "unemployed."

Source: General Exit Poll in 1996 and 2000 conducted by VNS for the National Election Pool, a consortium of the major news networks; General Exit Poll in 2004 conducted by Edison Media Research and Mitofsky International for the National Election Pool.

By turning the presidential election into a contest of leadership during crisis, mounting a negative campaign against Kerry's leadership skills, and emphasizing the threat of terrorism, Bush maximized the advantage of the attributes that he had demonstrated following the terrorists' attacks: strength, vision, conviction, reliability, and moral character.[41] Although half the electorate had qualms about Bush's presidency, his conservative policies, his ties to the Christian right, and the war in Iraq, people still trusted him more than Kerry to handle domestic terrorism.

CONVERTING ELECTORAL CHOICE INTO PUBLIC POLICY

It is not unusual for the meaning of the election to be ambiguous. The reasons that people vote for presidents vary. Some do so because of their party affiliation, some because of issue stands, and some because of their assessment of the candidates' potential or their past performance. For most people, a combination of factors contributes to their voting decision. This combination makes it difficult to discern exactly what the electorate means, desires, or envisions by its electoral choice.

THE PRESIDENT'S IMPRECISE MANDATE

The president is rarely given a clear mandate for governing. For a mandate to exist, the presidential candidates must take discernible and compatible policy positions, and the electorate must vote for them because of those positions. Moreover, the results of the election must be consistent. If there is a discrepancy between the popular and the electoral vote or if one party wins the White House and another wins the Congress, it is difficult for a president to claim a mandate for governing.

Few elections meet the criteria for a mandate. Presidential candidates usually take a range of policy positions, often waffle on a few highly divisive and emotionally charged issues, may differ from their party and its other candidates for national office in their priorities and their stands, and rarely have coattails long enough to sweep in others with them. In fact, they tend to run behind the congressional candidates of their own party in those candidates' legislative districts.

Mandates may not exist, but that has not prevented presidents from claiming them. They do so largely for political reasons. Winning a large popular and electoral vote and gaining control of Congress creates opportunities and expectations that a newly elected president might want to seize to change national policy. Such an incentive would be enhanced if the victor defeated an incumbent.

Professor Patricia H. Conley argues that the elections of 1952, 1964, and 1980 encouraged the winners to claim a policy mandate. Eisenhower's campaign promise to go to Korea, Goldwater's strong opposition to Johnson's domestic legislative program, and Reagan's rejection of the ideology, policies, and programs of the Carter administration provided the electorate with a clear choice of which policy direction it preferred. The winners' sizable victories were interpreted as mandates for these presidents to pursue their policy orientation and achieve their stated goals.[42]

The election results in 1948 and 1992 were not quite as clear, according to Conley, but they still offered Truman and Clinton opportunities to claim a mandate and use it as evidence of popular support.[43] Democratic majorities in both houses of Congress furthered the claim that the voters had made a policy choice in their electoral decisions. Clinton's failure to achieve many of his promises, such as to cut middle-class taxes, stimulate the economy, "change welfare as we know it," reform the nation's health care system, and eliminate discrimination on the basis of sexual orientation, shows the flip side of a mandate claim—the magnification of failure, if expectations are not met.

George W. Bush was careful not to claim a mandate in 2000 as he pursued his campaign promises. However, prior to September 11, 2001, he had achieved only one legislative campaign promise—a large tax cut. After his reelection in 2004, however, the president expressed more confidence. At a press conference held two days after his reelection, Bush said:

> . . .when you win there is a feeling that the people have spoken and embraced your point of view. And that's what I intend to tell the Congress. That I made it clear what I intend to do as the president. . . .I've earned capital in this election. And I'm going to spend it for what I told the people I'd spend it on, which is, you've heard, the agenda: Social Security and tax reform, moving this economy forward, education, fighting and winning the war on terror.[44]

But did the people embrace the president's point of view on Social Security, tax reform, and the economy? Did he really have more political capital?

Data collected from the exit polls and postelection surveys reveal a mixed electoral message at best. On the issues such as fighting the war on terror and supporting family values, the electorate expressed more confidence in Bush than Kerry; on the economy and a range of other domestic issues, voters said that they had more confidence in Kerry. Neither Social Security nor tax reform was cited as principal reasons for voting for George W. Bush.

Did the increase in Republican seats in the House and Senate give the president political capital as he suggested in his news conference? Most election pundits attributed the GOP gain in the House to a controversial redistricting plan approved by the Republican-controlled legislature in Texas and in the Senate to five seats in southern states in which the incumbent Democrat retired from office. Only one Democratic incumbent, Tom Daschle, was defeated for reelection, and then by only 1 percent of the vote.

If the analysis presented in this chapter is correct, Bush had strong public support to lead the country in the war against terrorism; his base continued to back his position on social issues. The electorate, however, did not provide the president with a blank check to pursue other policy initiatives. When he tried to do so, he failed, reducing rather than increasing his political capital for the remainder of his term.

Confusing hope with fact, claiming a mandate when none exists, contending that the electorate supports most or all of the winner's policy agenda, and assuming that members of Congress will dutifully follow a president's lead are fraught with danger as Bush found out. Even when there is electoral support for specific policies, that support can wane quickly in the face of unexpected events, changing conditions, and shifts in public sentiment. Presidents must adapt to these changes or their job approval will suffer and their political influence will decline. Bill Clinton's insistence on redeeming his campaign promises to stimulate the economy and reform health care in the light of a recovering economy and public unease with big government programs got him off to a shaky start. Similarly, George W. Bush's unwillingness to acknowledge mistakes in his postwar policies in Iraq, much less change those policies in the light of news reports of the continuing resistance, and sectarian violence, undermined confidence in his leadership during his second term.

In short, elections provide a window of opportunity for presidents but not much more than that. And the timeframe for that opportunity may be short. The longer the period after the election, the less the election will serve as a guide to priorities and policy decisions for the government.

PARTY PLATFORMS, CAMPAIGN PLEDGES, AND THE NEW AGENDA

Assuming that party is an influence on voting behavior, what cues can presidents cull from their partisan connection in defining their programmatic mandate? As described in Chapter 6, party platforms normally contain a large number of positions and proposals, but there are problems in using the platform as a guide for a new administration. Presidential candidates may not have exercised a major influence on the platform's formulation, although in contemporary conventions they have. However, they may have had to accept certain compromises in the interests of party unity. It is not unusual for a nominee to disagree with one or several of the platform's positions or priorities. Carter personally opposed his party's abortion stand in 1980 and had major reservations about a $12 billion jobs program that the Democratic platform endorsed. Dole made little mention of the Republican Party's abortion plank once his 1996 campaign began. Kerry played down the Democrat's position on gun control.

In addition to containing items the president-elect may oppose, the platform may omit some items that the new president favors, particularly if they are controversial. There was no mention of granting amnesty to Vietnam draft dodgers and war resisters in the 1976 Democratic platform, although Carter had publicly stated his intention to do so if he was elected.[45] Similarly, the 2004 Republican platform did not pledge to create a guest worker program or a path to citizenship for illegal aliens as the president had proposed.

Nonetheless, there seems to be a correlation between campaign promises, party platforms, and presidential performance. Political scientist Jeff Fishel found that from 1960 to 1984, presidents "submitted legislation or signed executive orders that are broadly consistent with about two-thirds of their campaign pledges." Of these, a substantial percentage was enacted into law, ranging from a high of 89 percent of those proposed during the Johnson administration to a low of 61 percent during the Nixon years.[46] Although these figures do not reveal the importance of promises, their scope, or their impact, they do suggest that, in general, campaign platforms and candidate pledges are taken seriously by those in power. They provide a foundation from which an administration's early policy initiatives emanate.[47]

EXPECTATIONS AND PERFORMANCE

When campaigning, candidates also try to create an aura of leadership, conveying such attributes as assertiveness, decisiveness, compassion, and integrity. Kennedy promised to get the country moving, Johnson to continue the New Frontier–Great Society programs, Nixon to "bring us together," and George H. W. Bush to maintain the Reagan policies that produced peace and prosperity for the eight previous years but in "a kinder and gentler" way. In 1992, Clinton pledged policy change in a moderate direction and an end to gridlock between Congress and the presidency; in 1996, he promised to build a bridge to the twenty-first century. In 2000, George W. Bush promised to defuse the strident partisan political climate in Washington, and in 2004, to "do whatever it takes" to win the war on terror.

These promises created performance expectations. In the 1976 election, Jimmy Carter heightened these expectations by his constant reference to the strong, decisive leadership he intended to exercise as president. His decline in popularity stemmed in large part from his failure to meet these leadership expectations. Similarly, when George W. Bush, reelected in large part because voters saw him as a stronger leader than his Democratic opponent, did not exercise such leadership in the aftermath of Hurricane Katrina, his job approval suffered significantly.

All new administrations, and to some extent most reelected ones, face diverse and often contradictory desires. By their ambiguity, candidates encourage voters to see what they want to see and believe what they want to believe. Disillusionment naturally sets in once a president begins to make decisions. Some supporters feel deceived as Senator Jim Jeffords (Republican of Vermont) did in June 2001 when he defected from the GOP and became an independent.

One political scientist, John E. Mueller, has referred to the disappointment groups may experience with an administration as "the coalitions of minorities variable." In explaining declines in popularity, Mueller notes that presidents' decisions inevitably alienate parts of the coalition that elected them. This alienation, greatest among independents and supporters who identify with the other party, can produce a drop in popularity over time, although as the Reagan and Clinton presidencies demonstrate, such a drop is not inevitable, particularly if good times prevail.[48]

The campaign's emphasis on personal and institutional leadership also inflates performance expectations. By creating the aura of assertiveness, decisiveness, and potency, candidates help shape what the public anticipates they will do in office. Most presidents contribute to the decline in their own popularity by promising more than they can deliver. The question is, can the promise of leadership be conveyed during the campaign without creating unrealistic and unattainable expectations for the new president? For most candidates, especially challengers, the answer clearly seems to be no.

THE ELECTORAL COALITION AND GOVERNING

Not only does the selection process inflate performance expectations and create a set of diverse policy goals, but also it may decrease the president's power to achieve them. Moreover, the anti-Washington, anti-government mood of the electorate, evident since the mid-1970s, has given outsiders, who are less experienced in national politics and may as a result be less able to meet the demands of the office when they first assume it, an electoral advantage. Carter in 1976 and Clinton in 1992 made much of the fact that they did not owe their nomination to the power brokers within their own party nor did they owe their election to members of Congress. George W. Bush also distanced himself from congressional Republicans in his 2000 campaign. Carter and Clinton's electoral ploy soon became a governing handicap. Almost as soon as they took office, they had difficulty getting Democratic Congresses to follow their lead. Bush did not encounter such difficulties after the September 11th attacks due to the national unity that those attacks produced and the limited policy agenda that followed from them.

But even an experienced Washington hand would face difficulties. The political muscle of the White House has been weakened by the growth of autonomous state and congressional electoral systems; the proliferation of well organized, well funded, and well led interest groups that pursue their own policy goals; and the decentralization and compartmentalization of power within the government.

Presidential candidates begin their quest for office largely on their own. They essentially designate themselves to run. They create their own organizations, choose certain professionals to run them, mount their own campaigns, and make their own promises. So do most members of Congress. Moreover, the coattails that tied party partisans to the winning presidential candidate have all but dissipated. Safe seats and incumbency advantage have given members of Congress more independence. They can choose to follow the president's lead or choose not to do so; either way, it is their partisan constituency that will decide their fate, not the president.

The recent increase in party unity has offset some of this independence, but it hasn't eliminated it entirely. Moreover, a unified party in Congress can exercise more influence on a president than can individual members. Partisan unity encourages presidents to adopt a partisan strategy, which gives members of the president's party more leverage with the president than they might otherwise have. Clinton in his first two years had great difficulty keeping Democrats in line, as did Bush with Republicans during his second term.

To win elections, presidential candidates have to mobilize a broad constituency. Nonparty groups play a large role in that mobilization process; they run campaigns within campaigns—contributing and spending money, communicating with their members and sympathizers, and turning out the vote. But they do so with strings attached. They encourage candidates to take policy positions they favor, and if elected, to pursue policies they advocate. Presidents who deviate from their campaign agenda do so at the risk of alienating these support groups. The interest groups' struggle enlarges the arena of policy making, raises the political stakes, and contributes to the multiplicity of forces that converge on most presidential decisions. They limit a president's policy options.

Presidential campaigns encourage candidates to promise new programs and project an image of leadership. Normally, they indicate what they will do if elected, but rarely do they add the caveat, "if Congress is willing to do so, if the bureaucracy follows my lead, or if the courts deem it constitutional." There is a disconnect between the campaign promises and leadership images of those who run for the presidency and the reality of the American constitutional system, which divides powers to prevent any one institution from dictating public policy on its own.

PERSONALITY POLITICS AND PRESIDENTIAL LEADERSHIP

What are presidents to do under these circumstances? How can they lead, achieve their goals, and satisfy pluralistic interests at the same time? Obviously, there is no set formula for success. Forces beyond the president's control may affect the course of events. Nonetheless, presidents would be wise to follow certain maxims in their struggle to convert promises into performance and perhaps also to get reelected.

1. Initially, they must convert their campaign promises into a governing agenda without enflaming the political divisions within the electorate, and simultaneously, maintain their credibility as they move from candidate to president.
2. They must also prioritize their policies, limiting them to what is feasible within the current political environment without overwhelming or disappointing Congress and the American people.
3. They must convert their electoral coalition into a governing coalition, one that can be sustained over a range of issue areas. If government is divided, they must make across-the-aisle appeals without compromising their principal objectives; if government is unified, they have to be careful that

they are not pulled by their own partisans to the edge of the ideological divide. Above all, they must not take their own partisans for granted. Egos matter, especially when dealing with members of Congress.

4. Presidents must be flexible enough to adjust to changing conditions and public moods, yet consistent enough to provide direction and stability in their policy orientation and credibility for their words, decisions, and actions. People want to know the direction in which their president is heading and become unnerved when they perceive indecision and inconsistency. But they also become impatient and increasingly critical when the policy a president is pursuing does not seem to be working. President George W. Bush's steadfastness in maintaining his policy in Iraq despite the evidence of increasing sectarian violence reported by the American news media illustrates how unsuccessful policy decisions can weaken a president's reputation and political clout over time.

5. Presidents must be sensitive to public opinion, but they must also try to mold that opinion as well, using it to inform their rhetoric, affect their timing, and shape their policies. Leadership often requires interpreting public opinion and making policy decisions that are consistent with it, although the president must not be perceived as a captive of the polls. Promoting public relations has become an important component of the contemporary presidency.

6. Finally, presidents must grow and learn in office, utilizing the status of their position to enhance their personal esteem in the eyes of the public and using the lessons of the past as guides to the future. To counter the increasingly negative media coverage, the White House must utilize information about policies, actions, and personnel at its disposal to its advantage. The ceremonial and symbolic aspects of the office can enhance a president's public status and increase his political power.

Priority setting is a necessary presidential task. Without it, an administration appears to lack direction and leadership. People question what presidents are doing and have difficulty remembering what they have done. The absence of clear, achievable priorities at the beginning of the Carter administration, combined with the president's perceived inconsistency in some of his economic and foreign policy decisions, affected President Carter's approval ratings in the public opinion polls and contributed to his defeat four years later.

The Reagan administration understood the lessons of the Carter experience, but the Clinton administration did not, at least not initially. Reagan limited the issues, controlled the agenda, and, most importantly, focused the media on his principal policy objectives during his first term in office. Clinton did not. He had too many goals, too little public support, and took on too much himself. All of these factors adversely affected his leadership image and his opportunities to achieve his policy initiatives during his first two years in office. But to his credit, Clinton learned from this experience and became more focused in his words, decisions, and actions after that.

George W. Bush maintained his initial focus on cutting taxes, reforming education, and rebuilding the military until the events of September 11th forced him to redefine his role and readjust his priorities. That redefinition and readjustment provided a new focus to his presidency and initially, bipartisan support. Over time, however, partisan support waned as the president got mired in a costly, lengthy, and increasingly unpopular occupation of Iraq. By the end of his third year in office, he became a highly polarizing figure, reflecting rather than moderating the country's partisan division.

Despite his reelection, the leadership style that enhanced Bush's presidency over the course of the first four years detracted from it in the second term. Instead of strength, many Americans saw cockiness, arrogance, and bullying; instead of good judgment, many saw incompetence and a blindness to reality; instead of confidence, they saw stubbornness; and instead of courage, Americans saw recklessness and an unwillingness to acknowledge errors.[49]

Presidents have discretion in deciding on their priorities. Reagan used this discretion at the beginning of his first term when he jettisoned his conservative social agenda in favor of major economic reforms. George H. W. Bush chose to emphasize foreign policy and deemphasize domestic issues in the first three years of his administration, despite his campaign's emphasis on domestic concerns. Clinton stuck with his principal priority of stimulating the economy (even though the economy was recovering) but added a host of other policies from deficit reduction to child immunization to ending discrimination against homosexuals in the military to comprehensive health care and welfare reform. By doing so, he overwhelmed Congress and dissipated much of its energy and his public support. George W. Bush was careful not to overload the Congress, but he had few accomplishments to trumpet as well until the events of September 11th strengthened his hand, fortified his resolve, and changed his policy focus from domestic to national security, a policy arena in which the president is usually advantaged.

Beyond establishing priorities and positions, presidents have to get them adopted. Their electoral coalition does not remain a cohesive entity within the governing system as George W. Bush found out during his second term. The inevitable shifting of that coalition for governing forces presidents to build and rebuild their own alliances.

Public appeals are often necessary to do so. The Reagan administration effectively marshaled public support in 1981 and 1982. President Reagan took to the airwaves to explain his economic program to the American people and rally them behind it. Taking no chances, the White House orchestrated the public's favorable response, directing it toward members of Congress. George H. W. Bush and Bill Clinton initially were much less successful in convincing the public to support controversial domestic policies, but Clinton was able to gain backing for his trade policies (NAFTA and GATT) and mobilize opposition to Republican budget proposals in 1995 and 1996. The George W. Bush White House was extremely successful in controlling the news media's agenda until conditions in Iraq spiraled out of control, the Democrats began their nomination process, national security and corruption scandals erupted, and

Hurricane Katrina took a terrible toll. These events put the administration on the public relations defensive.[50]

In addition to building an external coalition, presidents need to employ other inducements and tactics to convince public officials, who have their own constituencies and must be responsive to them, to back presidential policy. This effort requires time, energy, and help. The president cannot do it alone.

As campaign organizations are necessary to win elections, so, too, are governing organizations necessary to win support for presidential policies. Several offices within the White House have been established to provide liaison and backing for the president on Capitol Hill, in the bureaucracy, and with interest groups and the public. By building and mending bridges, presidents can improve their chances for success. They can commit, convince, cajole, and otherwise gain cooperation despite the constitutional and political separation of institutions and powers.

Unlike winning the general election, making and implementing public policy are not all-or-nothing propositions. Assessments of performance are based on expectations, somewhat as they were in the elections. Part of the image problem all presidents face is the contrast between an idealized understanding of the institution's powers and the president's actual ability to get things done. The gap between expectations and performance explains why presidents need a public relations staff and why constant campaigning seems inevitable.

If presidents cannot achieve their goals, they can at least look good trying, and perhaps they can even claim partial success. Finally, they can always change their priorities as conditions change. Failure to do so, however, makes them look increasingly out of sync and may erode what public support and political capital they had.

SUMMARY

Americans are fascinated by presidential elections. They want to know who will win, why the successful candidate has won, and what the election portends for the next four years. Their fascination stems from four interrelated factors about elections: elections are dramatic, decisive, participatory, and affect future political leadership, public policy, and coalition building.

Using past elections as a guide, political scientists have tried to construct models to anticipate how the electorate will react to economic, political, and to a lesser extent, social conditions. The models provide formulas for calculating the percentage of the vote the winning candidate is likely to receive on the basis of a combination of quantifiable indicators such as per capita GDP, level of employment, rate of inflation, popularity of the president, and the number of terms the president's party has controlled the White House. In the past, these models have been reasonably accurate; in 2000 and 2004, however, they substantially overestimated the size of Gore's and Bush's popular vote.

Whatever the reasons for the models' overestimation, most political scientists still agree that campaigns do matter, and that they can affect voting behavior and thereby alter the conventional wisdom of who is likely to win.

To see how campaigns affect the electorate, researchers monitor public opinion over the course of an election. They do so by analyzing data from national and state opinion polls of likely voters. Polls are also important to candidates for discerning what to emphasize and how to prioritize, articulate, and direct their policy and personal appeals.

National opinion polls have become fairly accurate measures of the public mood and candidate preferences at the time the polls are taken. They provide data that can be employed to help explain the meaning of an election: the issues that are most salient, the positions that are most popular, and the hopes and expectations that are initially directed toward the elected leaders of government.

The personality of the candidates, the issues of the campaign, and the evaluation of the administration in power have dominated recent elections and the voting decisions of the electorate. Singularly and together, these factors, as seen through the prism of partisanship, explain the outcome of the vote. In 1960, it was Kennedy's Catholic religion that seemed to account for the closeness of the popular vote despite the large Democratic majority in the electorate. In 1964, it was Goldwater's uncompromising ideological and issue positions that helped provide Johnson with an overwhelming victory in all areas but the deep South. In 1968, it was the accumulation of grievances against the Democrats that spurred the Wallace candidacy and resulted in Nixon's triumph. In 1972, ideology, issues, and the public's perception of McGovern's incompetence split the Democratic Party and culminated in Nixon's landslide. In 1976, however, partisanship was reinforced by issue, ideological, and personal evaluations to the benefit of the majority party's nominee, Jimmy Carter. Dissatisfaction with Carter's performance in 1980 and satisfaction with Reagan's in 1984 overcame the Democrats' decreasing numerical advantage within the electorate, leading voters to cast their ballots for Reagan as the person they thought would be best qualified to lead. By 1988, the Democrats appeared to lose their partisan advantage entirely. The retrospective evaluation of the Reagan years gave the incumbent vice president an advantage that his campaign maximized.

In a certain sense, the 1992 election was a rerun of 1980. The incumbent was rejected on the grounds that his performance in dealing with the nation's most pressing issue, the economy, was unsatisfactory. In choosing between his two opponents, the public voted for Clinton primarily because of his partisan affiliation. Perot ran a strong race, but independent candidates are disadvantaged because the electorate does not think that they can win, a perception that has its roots in the operation of the Electoral College system and the dominance of the two major parties.

If the 1992 election was a rejection of George H. W. Bush, the 1996 election marked the approval of Bill Clinton. Helped by a strong economy, a skilled campaign, and effective use of the presidential office, Clinton augmented his partisan support from Democrats with a successful appeal to moderates and to independent voters.

Partisan divisions, issue differences, and mixed performance evaluations of the Clinton presidency carried over into the 2000 election, although the focus tended to be more on future policies and leadership than on past performance. The electorate was evenly divided between the major parties. Disputes over the vote count and the discrepancy between the popular and electoral vote heightened these partisan divisions, clouded the election results, and delayed the designation of a president-elect.

The 2004 election continued to reveal cleavages evident since the 1980s. The parties remained evenly divided with each retaining the bulk of its core supporters. Contributing to the president's victory was a larger Republican turnout and a slightly more loyal Republican electorate. The ideological divide also worked to the Republican's advantage as conservatives continued to outnumber liberals.

A key element in Bush's victory was his campaign's ability to keep the focus on leadership against terrorism. By tying Iraq to the war on terrorism, the Bush–Cheney strategy limited the impact of negative news about the postwar occupation in Iraq; by raising questions about Kerry's leadership skills and his policy inconsistencies, the Republican campaign provided a contrast that favored the president. Although the American people did not agree with all or even most of Bush's policies, they acknowledged his strong leadership after the terrorist attacks of September 11, 2001 and expressed more confidence in his ability to handle the terrorism challenge than in his Democratic opponent's ability to do the same.

The closeness of the vote indicated that the partisan composition of the electorate had not changed very much, a political fact that the incumbent should have considered when determining his agenda for the second term. Instead of maintaining his focus on terrorism, however, the president turned to domestic issues upon which his support was more fragile; and he was unsuccessful. As a result, Bush's popularity declined; his political capital withered; and partisan "politics as usual" returned with a vengeance to the nation's capital as political scandals within the administration, accusations of government ineptitude by it, and the persistence of the Iraq issue took its toll on the Bush presidency and the Republican congressional majority.

The president had misread the results of the 2004 election. He assumed that his victory meant that the public would support his entire policy agenda; he was wrong. Most elections do not provide a mandate, much less a clear message. Moreover, the public usually has a diverse and inflated set of expectations about the president and the policies he will pursue, expectations that may be conflicting, unrealistic, or in other ways, unattainable. Yet presidents are still expected to take the lead and fulfill them.

Not only does the election provide mixed messages, but also it rarely gives a contemporary president the necessary political clout to get things done that were promised. This situation has presented serious governing problems for second-term presidents. To overcome these problems, presidents must establish priorities consistent with public sentiment, construct their own governing alliances, not take them for granted, provide policy directions while flexibly moving among options, and use the office to enhance their image and their programs' chances for being enacted into law. It is not an easy task, but it is one that presidents are expected to undertake.

 WHERE ON THE WEB?

PUBLIC OPINION

Access the latest polls about the election from the following sites:

- **Gallup Organization**
  www.gallup.com
- **CBS News Poll**
  www.CBSNews.com
- **The Pew Research Center for the People & the Press**
  www.people-press.org
- **Pollingreport.com**
  www.pollingreport.com
- **Roper Center for Public Opinion Research at the University of Connecticut**
  www.ropercenter.uconn.edu
- **Zogby International**
  www.zogby.com

ELECTION RESULTS

The Web sites of most major news organizations will have the unofficial results as collected by the Associated Press just as soon as the election is over and the results have been tabulated. These results usually do not include absentee ballots, which are counted later or the results of any vote challenges. The official results are available from the Federal Election Commission (www.fec.gov) later in the year.

For presidential election results by states from 1860–2004, see *Atlas of U.S. Presidential Elections* (www.uselectionatlas.org).

ELECTION ANALYSIS

Most major news organizations usually carry the final election exit poll in whole or part on their web sites. In addition, data from the American National Election Studies (ANES) conducted by researchers at the University of Michigan (www.electionstudies.org) are made available to faculty and students at universities and colleges that are members of the Inter-University Consortium for Political and Social Research about six months after the election is completed.

EXERCISES

1. Look at polls over the course of the election, and try to explain opinion shifts on the basis of events in the campaign or in the country as a whole. You can obtain a graph of Gallup polling over the course of the election at that organization's Web site (www.gallup.com).
2. Look at the results of several national polls at different points in the election cycle to determine how they contrast and compare to one another. If the polls show different results for the same period, try to ascertain who the respondents were (the general public, the electorate, registered voters, or most likely voters), whether the same questions were asked in the polls, how many people were surveyed, and the extent to which the results were within the margin of error.
3. After the election has concluded, access the large exit poll that will appear on the Web sites of the major news networks. Analyze the election results on the basis of this poll. In your analysis, note how major demographic groups voted, what the primary issues were, how important partisanship and ideology seemed to be, and the feelings voters had toward the candidates and their parties. Are the divisions, evident in past elections, continuing, or do you see changes in the voting patterns of the American electorate?
4. On the basis of the results of the presidential election, write a memo for the winning candidate explaining the meaning (mandate) of the election for governance. In your memo, indicate what the people expect the new president to do and the order in which they expect the president to do it.

SELECTED READINGS

Abramson, Paul R., John H. Aldrich, and David W. Rohde. *Change and Continuity in the 2004 Elections.* Washington, D.C.: CQ Press, 2006.

————. "The 2004 Presidential Election: The Emergence of a Permanent Majority?" *Political Science Quarterly,* 120 (Nov. 2005): 33–57.

Campbell, James E. "The Presidential Election of 2004: The Fundamentals and the Campaign," *The Forum,* 2 (2004): 1–15.

Conley, Patricia Heidotting. *Presidential Mandates: How Elections Shape the National Agenda.* Chicago: University of Chicago Press, 2001.

Crotty, William. ed. *A Defining Moment: The Presidential Election of 2004.* Armonk, N.Y.: M. E. Sharpe, 2005.

Dahl, Robert A. "Myth of the Presidential Mandate." *Political Science Quarterly,* 105 (Fall 1990): 355–372.

Erikson, Robert S. "The 2000 Presidential Election in Historical Perspective." *Political Science Quarterly,* 116 (Spring 2001): 29–52.

Fiorina, Morris. *Retrospective Voting in American National Elections.* New Haven, C.T.: Yale University Press, 1981.

Fishel, Jeff. *Presidents and Promises.* Washington, D.C.: Congressional Quarterly, 1985.

Leal, David L., Matt A. Barreto, Jongho Lee, and Rodolfo O. de la Garza. "The Latino Vote in the 2004 Election." *PS: Political Science and Politics* (Jan. 2005): 41–49.

Miller, Arthur H., and Martin P. Wattenberg. "Throwing the Rascals Out: Policy and Performance Evaluations of Presidential Candidates, 1952–1980." *American Political Science Review,* 79 (1985): 359–372.

Nelson, Michael. ed. *The Elections of 2004*. Washington, D.C.: CQ Press, 2005.

Popkin, Samuel L. *The Reasoning Voter*. Chicago: University of Chicago Press, 1991.

Wattenberg, Martin P. ed., "2004 Presidential Election," *Presidential Studies Quarterly*, 36 (June 2006): 137–296.

Wayne, Stephen J., and Clyde Wilcox, eds. *The Election of the Century and What It Tells Us about the Future of American Politics*. New York: M. E. Sharpe, 2002.

Weiner, Marc D. and Gerald M. Pomper, "The 2.4% Solution: What Makes a Mandate?" *The Forum*, 4 (2006). www.bepress.com/forum/vo4/iss2/art4

Notes

1. Public expectations about the economy may be revealed by survey data, such as responses to the following question: "Now looking ahead, do you think that a year from now you (and your family living here) will be better off financially, or worse off, or about the same as now?"

2. Kate Kenski and Kathleen Hall Jamieson, "Issue Knowledge and Perceptions of Agreement in the 2004 Presidential General Election," *Presidential Studies Quarterly*, 36 (June 2006), pp. 243–259.

3. According to political scientist Helmut Norpoth, "How well presidential candidates do in primary elections foretell their prospects in the November election with great accuracy." Using a measure of the primary vote as his independent variable, Norpoth claims that his model predicted the winner of every presidential election since 1912 with the exception of the election of 1960. Helmut Norpoth, "From Primary to General Election: A Forecast of the Presidential Vote," *Political Science and Politics*, 37 (Oct. 2004), pp. 737–740.

4. Christopher Wlezien, "On Forecasting the Presidential Vote," *PS*, 34 (March 2001), p. 30. For an extended discussion by the modelers of what went wrong, see the March 2001 edition of *PS*, 9–75 and Christopher Wlezien, "Presidential Election Polls in 2000: A Study in Dynamics," *Presidential Studies Quarterly*, 33 (March 2003): pp. 172–187.

5. For a discussion and synopsis of the 2004 model forecasts, see Alan I. Abramowitz, James E. Campbell, Robert S. Erikson, Thomas M. Holbrook, Michael S. Lewis-Beck, Helmut Norpoth, Charles Tien, and Christopher Wiezien, "Forecasting the 2004 Presidential Election," *Political Science and Politics*, 37 (Oct. 2004), pp. 733–767.

6. There are two types of problems here. One is to determine the likelihood of respondents' actually voting; to do so, pollsters must ask a series of questions and make some assumptions. The other problem concerns the representative character of the sample. Respondents are chosen by a system of random digit dialing. Most of the calls are made between 6:00 PM and 9:00 PM, a busy time in most households. There is a very high rate of nonresponses; people who do not want to be bothered or become impatient and do not complete the survey. Pollsters have to try to determine whether these people have different attitudes and opinions from those answer the questions.

7. Joan Shorenstein, Center on the Press, Politics, and Public Policy, "One in Seven Likely Voters Still Undecided on a Presidential Candidate," Harvard University, October 18, 2000. www.vanishingvoter.org (accessed October 30, 2000).

8. The results of Gallup's final unallocated poll was 47 percent for Bush, 45 percent for Gore, 4 percent for Nader, less than 1 percent for Buchanan, and 4 percent undecided. Anticipating that half of the undecided would not vote, Gallup split the remaining 2 percent between Bush and Gore. Either because more than half the undecided voters voted and/or voted more heavily for Gore, the final Gallup poll underestimated Gore's vote by more than 2.5 percent.

9. James E. Campbell and Kenneth A. Wink, "Trial-Heat Forecasts of the Presidential Vote," *American Politics Quarterly,* 18 (July 1990): p. 257. Updated by author.

10. Jeffrey M. Jones, "Bush Approval Average at 50% in Volatile Quarter," Gallup Poll, October 19, 2004. www.brain.gallup.com/content/defaultaspx?ci=13687 (accessed December 17, 2006).

11. Frank Newport and David W. Moore, "Key Insights From Election," Gallup Poll, November 8, 2004. www.gallup.com/poll/content/default.aspx?ci=13963 (accessed November 9, 2004).

12. In general, turnout declined more in the East and Midwest than it did in the West in 1980. Even if there was a decline after Carter's concession, there is little evidence to suggest that Democrats behaved any differently from Republicans and Independents. Hawaii, the last state to close its polls, voted for Carter.

13. Raymond Wolfinger and Peter Linquiti, "Tuning In and Turning Out," *Public Opinion,* 4 (Feb./March 1981): pp. 57–59. Harold Mendelsohn and Irving Crespi, *Polls, Television, and the New Politics* (Scranton, P.A.: Chandler, 1970), pp. 234–236.

14. Sandra Sobieraj, "The Story Behind the Near-Concession." Associated Press, November 8, 2000, www.ap.org.

15. Although voters are questioned throughout the day of the election, the poll data are not supposed to be released until voting in a state has been completed. Early results, however, have been made available to the news organizations that subscribe to the poll to give reporters a head start in writing their stories. In 2004, these early voting trends spread quickly on the Internet.

16. Morris P. Fiorina, *Retrospective Voting in American National Elections* (New Haven, C.T.: Yale University Press, 1981).

17. Presidents will not be blamed for natural disasters or even acts of terrorism over which they have no control, but they will be evaluated on how quickly and effectively they react to cataclysmic events, empathize with the victims, and provide the help from the federal government.

18. This view of retrospective voting was advanced by Anthony Downs, *An Economic Theory of Democracy* (New York: Harper & Row, 1957). Downs suggests that people evaluate the past performance of parties and elected officials in order to anticipate how they will perform in the future compared with their opponents.

19. Kenneth Winneg and Kathleen Hall Jamieson, "Elections: Party Identification in the 2004 Elections," *Presidential Studies Quarterly,* 35 (Sept. 2005): pp. 576–589.

20. Among political scientists, there are two schools of thought. One believes that partisan change results from revolutionary events and government actions to deal with them. These events and policies divide and realign the electorate. The Depression of the 1930s and the Roosevelt administration's New Deal policies resulted in such a realignment along economic lines with the Democrats becoming

the majority party. The civil rights movement of the 1950s and 1960s, the Democrats' embrace of that movement, and the civil rights and voting rights laws that followed produced a new division within the electorate, particularly in the South, that led to the Republicans gaining ascendancy in that region of the country and reduced Democratic support among blue-collar workers.

There have been no major realigning events since then, yet partisan attitudes have continued to shift, prompting some to postulate that partisan loyalties are also subject to evolutionary change. As the product of a collective body of political experience, these attitudes can strengthen or weaken as a consequence of how well the parties deal with contemporary conditions and events and how well they reflect the public moods and beliefs. However partisanship takes hold, both schools of thought agree that party allegiances do affect voting behavior; the stronger the allegiances, the greater the effect.

21. For a very interesting, albeit sophisticated article on the impact of emotions on learning, perceptions, and voting, see George E. Marcus and Michael B. Mackuen, "Anxiety, Enthusiasm, and the Vote: The Emotional Underpinnings of Learning and Involvement during Presidential Campaigns," *American Political Science Review,* 87 (Sept. 1993): pp. 672–685.

22. For an analysis of the components of the 1952 presidential election, see Angus Campbell, Philip E. Converse, Warren E. Miller, and Donald Stokes, *The American Voter* (New York: Wiley, 1960), pp. 524–527.

23. Eisenhower was also perceived in a more favorable light than his opponent, Adlai Stevenson. Although the public still regarded Democrats as more capable of handling domestic problems, the appeal of Eisenhower, combined with the more favorable attitude toward the Republican Party in the areas of foreign affairs and government management, resulted in the victory of the minority party's presidential candidate.

24. Kennedy's Catholicism may have enlarged his Electoral College total by 22 votes. See Ithiel de Sola Pool, Robert P. Abelson, and Samuel Popkin, *Candidates, Issues, and Strategies* (Cambridge, M.A.: MIT Press, 1965), pp. 115–118.

25. For a discussion of the 1964 presidential election, see Philip E. Converse, Aage R. Clausen, and Warren E. Miller, "Election Myth and Reality: The 1964 Election," *American Political Science Review,* 59 (June 1965): pp. 321–336.

26. Philip E. Converse, Warren E. Miller, Jerrold G. Rusk, and Arthur C. Wolfe, "Continuity and Change in American Politics: Parties and Issues in the 1968 Election," *American Political Science Review,* 63 (Dec. 1969): p. 1097.

Wallace claimed that there was not "a dime's worth of difference" between the Republican and Democratic candidates and their parties. He took great care in making his own positions distinctive. The clarity with which he presented his views undoubtedly contributed to the issue orientation of his vote. People knew where Wallace stood and liked him or didn't like him because of it.

27. Arthur H. Miller, Warren E. Miller, Alden S. Raine, and Thad A. Brown, "A Majority Party in Disarray: Policy Polarization in the 1972 Election," *American Political Science Review,* 70 (1976): pp. 753–778.

28. Arthur H. Miller and Warren E. Miller, "Partisanship and Performance: Rational Choice in the 1976 Presidential Elections" (paper presented at the annual

meeting of the American Political Science Association, Washington, D.C., September 1–4, 1977).

29. Nonetheless, Ford was probably helped more than hurt by being the incumbent. He gained in recognition, reputation, and stature. He benefited from having a podium with a presidential seal on it. His style and manner in the office contrasted sharply with his predecessor's—much to Ford's advantage. As the campaign progressed, his presidential image improved. It just did not improve quickly enough to allow him to hold on to the office.

30. Warren E. Miller, "Policy Directions and Presidential Leadership: Alternative Interpretations of the 1980 Presidential Election" (paper presented at the annual meeting of the American Political Science Association, New York: September 3–6, 1981).

31. J. Merrill Shanks and Warren E. Miller, "Alternative Interpretations of the 1988 Election," (paper presented at the annual meeting of the American Political Science Association, Atlanta, Georgia, August 31-September 3, 1989), p. 58.

32. Paul R. Abramson, John H. Aldrich, and David W. Rohde, *Change and Continuity in the 1988 Elections*, (Washington, D.C.: CQ Press, 1990), p. 195.

33. Ibid., p. 212.

34. Had Perot not run, it is unlikely that the results of the election would have been any different. Exit polls of Perot voters indicate that they would have divided their votes fairly evenly between Clinton and Bush, although the number voting would undoubtedly have declined.

35. Gore's advisers contended that they had no choice. Their surveys indicated that Clinton was a liability, that he turned off swing voters, and that the electorate was tired of his scandal-plagued administration and wanted a change. What they did not calculate was the extent to which Clinton energized the Democratic base.

36. For an excellent discussion on the influence of third-party candidates, see Samantha Luks, Joanne M. Miller, and Lawrence R. Jacobs, "Who Wins? Campaigns and the Third Party Vote," *Presidential Studies Quarterly,* 33 (March 2003): pp. 9–30.

37. See Susan J. Carroll, "Security Moms and Presidential Politics: Women Voters in the 2004 Election," (paper prepared for delivery at the 2005 annual meeting of the American Political Science Association, Washington, DC, September 1–4, 2005).

38. James L. Guth, Lyman A. Kellstedt, Corwin E. Smidt, and John C. Green, "Religious Influences in the 2004 Presidential Election," *Presidential Studies Quarterly,* 36 (June 2006), pp. 223–242.

39. For an analysis and explanation of the Catholic vote, see Mark M. Gray, Paul M. Perl, and Mary E. Bendyna, "Camelot Only Comes But Once? John F. Kerry and the Catholic Vote," *Presidential Studies Quarterly,* 36 (June 2006), pp. 203–222.

40. According to the exit poll, the president gained a larger proportion of the Hispanic vote (44 percent) than he received in 2000 (35 percent). However, experts disagree over the size of the increase because of the small subset of self-identified Hispanic voters.

41. Martin P. Wattenberg, "Elections: Reliability Trumps Competence: Personal Attributes in the 2004 Presidential Election," *Presidential Studies Quarterly,* 26 (Dec. 2006), pp. 705–713.

42. Patricia Heidotting Conley, *Presidential Mandates: How Elections Shape the National Agenda* (Chicago: University of Chicago Press, 2001), pp. 77–115.

43. Ibid., pp. 116–145

44. George W. Bush, "Press Conference," November 4, 2004 as quoted in *New York Times* (Nov. 5, 2004), p. A16.

45. Another limitation to using a platform as a guide to the partisan attitudes and opinions of the public is that many people, including party rank and file, are unfamiliar with most of its contents. The platform per se is not the reason people vote for their party's candidates on election day.

46. Jeff Fishel, *Presidents and Promises* (Washington, D.C.: Congressional Quarterly, 1994), pp. 38, 42–43.

47. One reason campaign promises are important is that they are part of the public record; candidates and parties can be held accountable for them. Another is that they represent the interests of a significant portion of the population. To gain public approval, presidents must respond to these interests. In addition, organized groups, to whom promises have been made, have clout in Congress and in the bureaucracy. Presidents can either mobilize these groups to help them achieve their campaign promises or be thwarted by them if they fail to do so. George Bush ran into this problem in 1990 when he recanted on his pledge not to raise taxes. Conservative Republican members of Congress, who opposed tax increases in their own campaigns for office, voted against the budget compromise that contained a tax increase, a compromise that the president supported.

48. John E. Mueller, *War, Presidents, and Public Opinion* (New York: Wiley, 1973), pp. 205–208, 247–249.

49. "Bush Approval Falls to 33%, Congress Earns Rare Praise," Pew Research Center for the People and the Press, March 15, 2006.

50. The national security scandal was a leak to the news media by a high administration official that revealed the identity of a covert CIA operative whose husband had been very critical of the president's claim that Saddam Hussein was trying to get uranium from an African country to develop nuclear weapons. The corruption scandals involved a Washington lobbyist, Jack Abramoff, and favors he provided members of Congress in exchange for legislative "earmarks" (special provisions in the law) they obtained for his clients. Other members of Congress were also accused of accepting payoffs for "services rendered." There was also a member, Mark Foley, who wrote sexually explicit e-mail to young male congressional pages; the Speaker's office was notified of the problem member but did nothing about it until the incident became public.

Reforming the
Electoral System

CHAPTER 10

INTRODUCTION

The American political system has evolved significantly since the second half of the twentieth century. Party rules, finance laws, and media coverage are now very different from what they were before the 1960s. The composition of the electorate has changed as well, with the expansion of suffrage to all citizens eighteen years of age or older and the continuing reduction of legal obstacles to voting. Campaigning for president has changed, and new communications technologies have enabled the parties and their nominees to measure public opinion, focus resources in the most competitive states, and target appeals to specific groups of voters within the electorate.

Have these changes been beneficial or harmful? Have they improved the democratic character of the political system? Have they made the electoral process operate more efficiently and represent more effectively the interests of the population? These questions have elicited a continuing, and sometimes spirited, debate.

Critics have alleged that the electoral process is too long, too costly, too burdensome, too error prone, and too easily subject to discretionary decisions by state election officials and to manipulation by the parties, candidates, and their supporters. They claim that it wears down candidates and numbs voters, and that it results in too many personal accusations and too little substantive discussion, too much name-calling and "sound bite" rhetoric, and too little real debate on the issues. They have said that many qualified people are discouraged from running for office, and much of the electorate is uninformed, uninterested, and uninvolved as evidenced by the fact that a large number of people do not vote on a regular basis.

Other criticisms are that the system benefits the wealthy and the special interests, encourages factionalism, weakens the party's control over the campaign and its outcome, overemphasizes personality and underemphasizes policy, and that it is unduly influenced by a news media motivated more by economic gain than public service.

In contrast, proponents argue that the political system is seen as more legitimate and operates more democratically than ever before. There are relatively few disputed elections; people abide by the results; more, not fewer people, vote; and more, not fewer partisans, participate in the nomination phase. Candidates, even lesser-known ones, now have an opportunity to run for office and in the process, demonstrate their competence, endurance, motivation, and leadership capabilities. Parties remain important as vehicles through which the system operates and by which governing is accomplished. Those who defend the electoral system believe voters do receive as much information as they desire and enough to make informed and reasoned judgments.

The old adage "where you stand influences what you see" is applicable to the debate about electoral reform. No political process is completely neutral. There are always winners and losers. To a large extent, the advantages that some enjoy are made possible by the disadvantages that others encounter. Rationalizations aside, much of the debate about the system—about equity, representation, and responsiveness—revolves around a very practical, political question: Who gains, and who loses?

Proposals to change the system need to be assessed in the light of this question. They should also be judged on the basis of how such changes would affect the operation of the electoral system, the agenda and composition of government, and the public policy that results from those elected to government. This chapter discusses some of these proposals and the effect they could have on the road to the White House. The chapter is organized into two sections: the first deals with the more recent developments and proposals in party rules, campaign finance, and media coverage; and the second examines the long-term, democratic issues of citizen participation, representation, and equity in the electoral process. Throughout this discussion, basic questions, central to a democratic electoral process are asked and answered.

MODIFYING RECENT CHANGES IN PARTY RULES

Of all the changes that have recently occurred, the reforms in the nomination process, particularly the selection of delegates, engender the most controversy and have resulted in the most persistent fine-tuning. Designed to encourage grassroots participation and broaden the base of representation, these reforms have also extended the nominating period, made the campaign more expensive, and made the need for early money more critical. They have generated candidate-based organizations, weakened the influence of some state and local party leaders, converted conventions into coronations, and loosened the ties between the parties and their nominees. All of these consequences have made governing more difficult.

Since 1968, when the Democrats began to rewrite their rules for delegate selection, the parties have suffered from unintended repercussions of the rules changes. Each succeeding presidential election has seen reforms to the reforms, modifications that have attempted to reconcile expanded participation and representation with the traditional need for party unity and campaign oversight. Although less reform conscious than the Democrats, the Republicans have also tried to steer a middle course between greater rank-and-file involvement and more equitable representation on the one hand and the maintenance of successful electoral and governing coalitions on the other.

How to balance these often competing goals has been a critical concern. Those who desire greater public participation have lauded the trend toward having more primaries and a larger percentage of delegates selected in them. Believing that the reforms have opened up the process and made it more democratic, they favor the continued selection of delegates based on the proportion of the popular vote that they or the candidate to whom they are pledged receive. In contrast, those who believe that greater control by state and national party leaders is desirable argue that the reforms have gone too far. They would prefer fewer primaries, a smaller percentage of delegates selected in them, more unpledged delegates and party leaders participating in the nominating conventions, and a larger role for state and national party organizations during the entire presidential campaign.

WHO SHOULD PARTICIPATE IN THE CAUCUSES AND PRIMARIES?

Democratic Party rules have consistently sought to limit participation in its primary elections to registered or self-declared Democrats, although such restrictions are difficult to enforce in practice. Crossover voting by the partisans of one party in the other's primary has remained a contentious issue and a strategic choice that candidates for the nomination must consider. Do they direct their appeals to independent and independent-minded partisan voters as John McCain and Bill Bradley did in 2000 or appeal primarily to their own party partisans?

From the party's perspective, the issue of crossover voting is critical. To allow nonpartisans to participate dilutes the influence of party regulars and creates the possibility of selecting a nominee who does not best reflect the interests, needs, or ideological views of most of the party's rank and file. A particular fear is that adherents of the other party will cross over to vote for the weaker opposition candidate in order to enhance their own nominee's chances in the general election. There is little empirical data to support this fear, however.

On the other hand, from the perspective of the citizenry, a primary closed to all but registered partisans precludes much of the population from participating and reduces the incentive for nonparticipants to become informed and get involved during the election. Moreover, it allows party activists, who tend to have the strongest ideological convictions, to exercise more influence. It also encourages candidates to appeal to the beliefs and issue positions of a narrower group of partisan activists rather than a broader cross-section of the party and the electorate. Political parties can benefit from an open primary system if it leads to the recruitment of more active supporters or makes their nominees more electable.

How Should the Votes be Allocated?

Another rules issue concerns the allocation of votes in primaries. Since 1992, the Democrats have used a straight proportional voting system that allocates pledged delegates according to the percentage of the popular vote they or the candidate to whom they are committed receives. The Republicans permit the states to decide on the method of allocation, which could be proportional or winner-take-all within districts or on an at-large basis.

Proportional voting more closely reflects the view of a state's primary electorate, but it also could have the effect of extending the nomination, delaying a consensus on the eventual nominee, and costing more money, although it has not done so in contemporary nominations. The more divided the party is going into its nominating convention, the weaker its candidates are likely to be in the general election, or so the thinking has been within the national leadership of both major parties.[1]

Should the Nomination Process be Shortened?

There has been widespread public support for condensing the nomination campaign, which Professor Thomas E. Patterson has argued "disrupts the policy process, discourages the candidacies of responsible officeholders, and wears out the voters."[2] It also diverts public attention from issues of government to campaign-related controversies and does so many months before the general election campaign begins. Moreover, Patterson notes that a long election cycle generates more negative news about the candidates as the campaign progresses, thereby souring voters on the choices they have on primary day and creating image problems for the candidates in the general election.[3]

Several proposals have been made for addressing the issue of excessively long campaigns. Some have even been introduced in the form of legislation in Congress. A simple change would be to limit the period in which caucuses and primaries can be scheduled to two or three months; it presently extends from mid January to early June. A second proposal would cluster primaries and caucuses, forcing states in designated regions or groups to hold their elections on the same day. A third plan, which is already in effect, provides incentives for states to schedule their contests later in the spring, but there have been few takers. A fourth idea is to create a national primary.

Spreading out the caucuses and primaries would reduce the impact of front loading. It might also weaken the news media's influence on public opinion, which is greatest at the beginning of the nomination process, but it also probably enhances the press' influence at the end.

The Democratic Party has attempted to frame its nomination process by specifying the period during which primaries and caucuses can be held. Opposition from several states, however, including Iowa and New Hampshire, has forced the party to grant exceptions to its imposed time frame, much to the consternation of other states that also want exceptions. In the 2008 nominations, Nevada is scheduled to hold its caucus right after Iowa's, and South Carolina will have a primary following New Hampshire's. But other states have moved their primaries closer to the beginning of the calendar during which party caucuses and primaries may be held, thereby unbalancing the process even more, starting the campaign earlier and earlier—in some cases up to two years before the election—and creating a Super-Duper Tuesday in early February almost six months before the parties hold their nominating conventions.

The Republicans face the same front-loading problem as the Democrats or worse, because the GOP has not imposed a time frame on its state parties. As a consequence, the Republican Party has encountered even more front-loading than the Democrats with many of the same unhappy consequences.

CAN FRONT-LOADING BE PREVENTED?

Front-loading creates inequities. It gives greater influence to those states that hold their contests earlier and less to those that hold them later. To the extent that partisans in the early states are not representative of the party's rank and file, much less the general population, they can generate momentum for a candidate who may not be the first or most acceptable choice for the party as a whole.

Front-loading helps well-known and well-financed candidates. Conversely, it hurts long shots who must raise more money more quickly and must also enter more contests before they have had ample opportunity to demonstrate their electability. The stepping-stones to the nomination have become more compressed, and as a result, the prospects that a nonfront-runner can win the nomination have become more remote.

Front-loading moves the campaign forward, well into the year before the general election. Not only does it lengthen the nomination process, it also shortens its competitive phase. In 2004, the competitive period lasted only six weeks. Thus candidates have to begin their quest for the nomination earlier, and if successful, continue it longer.

Front-loading also forces candidates to campaign in many states simultaneously. They must do so through the mass media and at considerable expense to their campaigns. Retail politics, in which candidates interact with voters in small groups and informal settings, suffers as a consequence.

From the perspective of a democratic political system, perhaps the most negative aspect of front-loaded campaigns is that the decisive stage of the nomination process occurs before most people are paying attention to it. By the time the party's electorate tunes in, many of the candidates may have dropped out.[4] Moreover, there is little incentive for the public to stay attentive or even turn out to vote in later primaries once the winner has been effectively determined.

Inequitable state representation and declining overall participation, particularly after the competitive phase of the nominations are over, are two of the reasons that both major parties established commissions to examine the impact of the nomination calendar on the party, its candidates, and its partisan electorate.

The state parties, however, have resisted pressures to limit their scheduling discretion. Nor have they accepted party incentives of receiving more convention delegates in exchange for agreeing to hold their nomination contests later in the spring.

SHOULD REGIONAL PRIMARIES BE INSTITUTED?

Nomination contests could be formally regionalized with states in different regions required to hold their nomination contests on the same day. Since the 1980s, there have been agreements between states in some regions to do so. The case for regional primaries is based on the assumption that such a system would be more equitable for the states and provide more focus for the candidates.

As long as the regions adopted some plan to rotate their nomination dates, which they do not do at present, each region over time would be able to exercise approximately equal influence over the selection of a party's nominees. Moreover, candidates would be forced to address regional concerns and appeal to regional interests. A nomination that extended to the four regional primaries would probably ensure that the winning candidate had broad-based geographic support, the kind of support that is necessary to win in the Electoral College.

But regionalization is not without its critics who fear that it would exacerbate sectional rivalries, encourage local or area candidates, and produce more candidate organizations to rival those of the state and national parties. Moreover, like straight proportional voting, a regional primary system could impede the emergence of a consensus candidate, thereby extending the process to the convention and increasing, not decreasing, costs, time, and media attention. In addition, regional primaries help the best-organized and best-financed candidates because they require more resources to be devoted to the mass media.

Should a National Primary be Held?

Another option, and the one that represents the most sweeping change, would be to hold a national primary. The heavily front-loaded schedule in 2008 creates a *de facto* jumbo primary on February 5th, much to the dismay of the leaders of both major parties, including members of the reform commissions, who object to the early date and the concentration of so many contests on the same day.

Congress has been cool to idea of a national primary, but the general public seems to favor it. Gallup Polls taken over the past two decades indicate that almost two-thirds of the electorate prefers such an election to the present patchwork system.[5]

Most proposals for a national primary call for it to be held in the late spring or early summer, followed by party conventions. Candidates who wanted to enter their party's primary would be required to obtain a certain number of signatures. Any aspirant who won a majority of that party's vote would automatically receive the nomination. In some plans, a plurality would be sufficient, provided it was at least 40 percent. In the event that no one received 40 percent, a runoff election would be held several weeks later between the top two finishers, or the national nominating convention could choose from among the top two or three candidates. In any event, nominating conventions would continue to be held to select the vice presidential candidates, to decide on the platforms, and determine rules.

A national primary would be consistent with the "one person, one vote" principle that guides most aspects of the U.S. electoral system. All participants would have an equal voice in the selection. No longer would those in the states that held the early caucuses and primaries exercise more influence.

It is also likely that a national primary would stimulate turnout. The attention given to such an election would provide greater incentives for voting than currently exists, particularly in those states that hold their nomination contests after the apparent winner has emerged. A national primary would probably result in a nomination by a more representative electorate than is currently the case.

A single primary election for each party would accelerate a nationalizing trend. Issues that affect the entire country would be the primary focus of attention. Thus, candidates for the nation's highest office would be forced to discuss the problems they would most likely address during the general election campaign and would most likely confront as president.

Moreover, the results of the election would be clear-cut. The person with the most votes would be the winner. The media could no longer interpret primaries and caucus returns as they see fit. An incumbent's ability to garner support through the timely release of grants, contracts, and other spoils of government might be more limited in a national contest, but it would not be eliminated entirely.

On the other hand, such an election would undoubtedly discourage challengers who lacked national reputations. No longer could an early victory catapult a relatively unknown aspirant into the position of serious contender or jeopardize a president's chances for renomination. In fact, lesser-known candidates, such as George McGovern, Jimmy Carter, Michael Dukakis, and even Bill Clinton in 1992, might find it extremely difficult to raise money, build an organization, and mount a national campaign. John McCain would have had more difficulty challenging George W. Bush if he had had to campaign in all fifty states.

From the standpoint of the major parties, a national primary would further weaken the ability of party leaders to influence the selection of the nominees. Successful candidates would probably not owe their victory to state party officials. Moreover, a post-primary convention could not be expected to tie the nominee to the party, although it might tie the party to the nominee, at least through the election.

Such nominees, if elected, might also find governing much more difficult. They could not count on the support of party leaders if those leaders played little or no role in their nomination. Party leaders and members of Congress that have no stake in the election of the president would be harder to mobilize and quicker to jump ship should the president get into political difficulty.

Whether a national primary winner would be the party's strongest candidate is also open to question. With a large field of contenders, those with the most devoted or ideological supporters might do best. On the other hand, candidates who do not arouse the passions of the diehards, but who are more acceptable to the party's mainstream, might not do as well. Everybody's second choice might not even finish second, unless systems of approval voting or cumulative voting were used.[6] Approval or cumulative voting systems, however, complicate the election, confuse the electorate, question the result, undercut its legitimacy, and perhaps add to its costs.

In addition to weakening the party, a national primary could lessen the ability of states to determine when and how their citizens would participate in the presidential nomination process, although they would still be responsible for holding caucuses and primaries for other candidates for federal and state office. Finally, a national primary would in effect produce two presidential elections every four years. Could public attention be maintained throughout such an elongated election cycle? Could sufficient money be raised? If so, by which candidates, those who are personally wealthy or who have the reputation and position to attract money? Could the candidates' grassroots organizations handle such a task, not once but twice? These questions have tempered widespread support within the parties for such a plan despite the general appeal of the idea to the public.

THE PERILS OF CAMPAIGN FINANCE

Closely related to the delegate selection process are the laws governing campaign finance. These laws were first enacted in the 1970s in reaction to the secret and sometimes large illegal bequests to candidates, the disparity in contributions and spending among the candidates, and the spiraling costs of modern campaigns, particularly television advertising. These laws were designed to improve accountability, reduce spending, subsidize nominations, and fund the general election. Some of these objectives have been achieved, but unintended consequences have also resulted, and campaign finance remains a persistent issue.

The laws have taken campaign finance out of the back rooms and put much of it into the public spotlight. They have also, however, created a nightmare of compliance procedures and reporting requirements. Detailed records of practically all contributions and expenditures of the presidential campaign organizations must now be kept and periodically reported to the Federal Election Commission.[7]

Good accountants and attorneys, specializing in election law, are now as necessary as pollsters, image makers, and grassroots organizers.

Can Campaign Contributions and Expenditures be Effectively Limited?

The hard money, soft money, independent spending conundrum remains. There are still loopholes in the law of which nonparty groups (527s and 501c), stimulated by the party officials and their partisan supporters, have taken advantage. The biggest is the familiar soft-money route by which stealth party groups escape the federal contribution and spending limits to achieve partisan advantage. These limits, which the Federal Election Campaign Act imposed and the Bipartisan Campaign Reform Act tried to reinforce, have been undercut by the political ingenuity of party leaders, the refusal or inability of the Federal Election Commission to issue a general ruling that would prohibit or regulate this practice, and by the Supreme Court's insistence that independent spending is a protected form of freedom of speech.

Soft money is likely to continue to be a problem in 2008. Not only does it give wealthy individuals and groups more influence, but nonparty groups that solicit and spend the large contributions and independent spenders cannot coordinate their campaign activities with the candidates and their parties. The result is that three campaigns are now being waged at the same time: one by the candidates in partial coordination with the parties, one by the parties spending independently, and one by the nonparty groups and wealthy individuals on their own.

One fear, however, has not come to pass. The ban on the national parties soliciting soft money contributions has not hurt party fund-raising. In 2004 and in 2006, the major parties raised more in hard money than they had in hard money and soft money previously. And the 2008 candidates for their party's nomination have raised record amounts.

Is there anything that Congress can and should do about soft money and independent expenditures? Congress could extend the prohibition on soft money to nonparty groups, but it cannot control the expenditures of these groups or of individuals as long as the Supreme Court's ruling that "campaign spending equals free speech" stands.

The Republican-controlled 109th Congress evidenced little interest in enacting further campaign finance legislation, nor does such legislation top the priorities for the Democratically-controlled 110th Congress. And even if Congress were to act, the more conservative Roberts Court would probably be less likely to accept restrictions on this activity than the Rehnquist Court was. In 2006, the Roberts Court held in *Randall v. Sorrell* that Vermont's strict contribution and expenditure limits violated candidates' free speech protection as enunciated in its *Buckley v. Valeo* decision.[8]

CAN ISSUE ADVOCACY BE CONSTRAINED?

Another objective of the BCRA was to reform the practice of issue advocacy serving as a vehicle for candidacy advocacy. The law did so by prohibiting ads that pictured or mentioned candidates by name thirty days or less before a primary and sixty days or less before the general election. The Supreme Court upheld this provision in *McConnell v. FEC* in 2003 despite the claim of non-party groups that it restricted their freedom of speech.[9] However in 2007, the Supreme Court heard a case in which the FEC had fined a group that mentioned the name of a candidate in its advertising during the 2004 election. The case involved a pro-life organization that aired a commercial urging viewers to write to their Senators (whose names were included in the ad) to protest the filibuster of President Bush's judicial nominations. One of the Senators in question, Russ Feingold, was running for reelection although the commercial did not refer to his pro-choice position and/or voting record on judicial appointments or on aiding groups interested in controlling population. The Court's decision, expected at the end of its 2006–2007 term, will likely limit still further the government's ability to restrict issue advocacy.

CAN THE ACCUSATIONS IN ADVERTISEMENTS BE ADEQUATELY POLICED?

In addition to limiting surreptitious candidate advertising in issue ads, the sponsors of the BCRA also wanted to reduce the negativity of so many campaign commercials.[10] Members of Congress had attributed the increasing prevalence of negative ads to the failure of candidates to take responsibility for the ads. Beginning in 2004, the BCRA required a picture of the candidate and statement acknowledging responsibility in each candidate-sponsored political commercial.

This requirement has not been challenged in the courts, but it also seems to have had little, if any, impact on the content of the advertising, the trend toward negativity, or even public recognition of the ad's sponsor.

CAN PUBLIC FUNDING BE SAVED?

The BCRA did not intend to cripple the public-funding provision, but it may have done so inadvertently by doubling the individual contribution limits and then adjusting them to the rate of inflation. The increase in the size of contributions has made it easier for candidates to raise more private funds. Bush, Kerry, and Dean's success in doing so increased their incentive for rejecting federal funds and not being subject to the spending limits that accepting those funds imposed. Today, the ability and desire of most campaigns to raise and spend more money than accepting public funds permits has rendered this provision of the FECA inoperative for most front-running candidates for their party's nomination and probably for the two major party candidates in the general election.[11]

Despite the benefits of public funding—it has made presidential elections more equitable, broadened the field of potential contenders by giving nonfront-runners a chance, increased competition at the beginning of the process, lessening to some extent candidates' dependence on large contributions from wealthy donors and people with access to them, and at least initially, reduced the amount of time candidates had to spend raising funds—there has been little public outcry about the demise of public funding and even less pressure on candidates to accept government funding and abide by the spending limitations. Suspicion of politicians, opposition to federal "give away programs," fears of tax increases and/or larger budget deficits that would be required to replenish the campaign fund, and the general but pervasive cynicism about campaigns and elections have all contributed to public indifference, even hostility to federal funding. At present, only 10 to 11 percent of taxpayers authorize $3 of their taxes go into the election fund, and a majority of people prefer candidates to raise and spend their own funds rather than use public money.[12]

However, there are various ways that Congress could save the public funding system for presidential elections if it chose to do so. The easiest way to do so would be to raise or eliminate the spending limit that accepting the funds imposes on candidates.[13] Increasing the size of the match for small or all contributions; providing federal funds earlier, in the year before the election; having an escape clause that allows candidates to raise and spend additional private funds if they face a privately funded candidate with a large war chest; or even permitting the candidate's organization to coordinate its campaign with independent spending by party and nonparty groups would help retain the federal system of matching funds and government grants.[14]

Congress could even follow the lead of several European countries by prohibiting private contributions entirely and providing the parties or their candidates with a specified amount of money to campaign. But none of these changes, with the possible exception of coordinate independent spending and joint candidate/party expenditures, seem likely at this time.[15]

The discouraging news is that the "I-owe-you" problem, which the public perceives successful candidates may have after the election is over, is not likely to go away, thereby contributing to cynicism about the electoral system and mistrust of the motives of elected officials in their policy making decisions.

The campaign finance quandary at its most basic level is one of competing values: the freedom to spend on behalf of one's interests, beliefs, and opinions versus the equality of citizens in affecting campaign issues, debate, and election outcomes. In a democratic political system in which the vote and presumably the voice of all citizens should be equal, the wealthy should not have an advantage, but in a free and open society, everyone should be able to voice their opinions and spend their own resources as much as they desire. Here is the problem: How to ensure that candidates have sufficient funds, that freedom of speech is protected, that political equality is promoted, and that the public has sufficient information to make an informed judgment. No wonder campaign finance reform has proven to be so difficult, so controversial, and seemingly insoluble.

PUBLIC AWARENESS AND KNOWLEDGE

Is the amount and type of information sufficient for people to make an informed judgment when voting? Most voters answer this question "yes"; political scientists and other students of election behavior are not so sure. Almost everyone agrees that the more information that people have about the candidates, issues, and parties, the better able they will be to cast an enlightened vote. But how much information is necessary and desirable?

How Can People Become Better Informed?

Legislation could be enacted to require television stations that operate over the public airways to give candidates more free time to respond to political advertising, debate, or simply state their policy positions and equal time to respond to charges in editorials and op ed pieces. Candidates might also get reduced rates for mailing campaign literature to the voters. Naturally, these proposals are opposed by profit-making media and would require a federal subsidy if they applied to the U.S. Postal Service, much less private carriers such as United Parcel Service and Federal Express.

A law that forced the news media to provide free time might even be counterproductive, reducing rather than increasing the amount of public communications during the campaign. Television and radio stations would undoubtedly be discouraged from selling time to nonparty groups and individuals if they were under obligation to provide it free to the person or party who was the object of the commercial. A decrease in media advertising would reduce the information available to the public and increase the electorate's dependence on the news media.

Besides, the appearance of candidates on talk-entertainment shows beginning in 1992 and the proliferation of all-news cable channels have given major candidates more "free" time to respond to questions about their policy positions and personal character. But it has also given the producers, hosts, and commentators on these shows subtle ways of influencing the amount and content of the information by the wording and sequencing of questions to the candidates, by the choice of whom to interview and when to do so, and by the comments they make after the candidates respond to their questions.

IS CAMPAIGN NEWS COVERAGE SATISFACTORY?

Critics say "no." They point to media bias and spin and to the emphasis on the horse race, campaign strategy, and personal behavior at the expense of more substantive discussion of policy issues.

To augment public knowledge, scholars have suggested that the major news networks and wire services assign special correspondents to cover the policy issues of the campaign, much as they assign people to report on its color, drama, and personal aspects. Others have suggested that the press place greater emphasis on campaign coverage, that they assess the accuracy of the statements and advertising claims of the candidates, and that they indicate the potential costs and benefits of the policy proposals the candidates offer.

To their credit, some newspapers, such as the *Washington Post* and the *New York Times;* major television networks; and public interest groups have begun to do ad checks on a regular basis. They have also provided analyses of the campaign issues, although mostly, it is to differentiate the candidates and parties on the basis of the positions they take rather than present an in-depth discussion.

In addition to criticizing the news media's coverage of the campaign, academicians and others have called into question the amount and accuracy of election reporting. Other than requiring fairness, preventing obscenity, and ensuring that public service commitments are met, there is little the government can do to regulate the news media without impinging on the constitutional protections implicit in freedom of the press. The news media are free to choose which elections and candidates to cover, what kind and how much coverage to provide, how to interpret the results of primaries and caucuses, and even to predict who will win before the election is concluded. These choices tend to be exercised by the news networks with public preferences in mind. Not only do corporations that own media affiliates engage in constant private polling to discern the interest of the viewing, listening, and reading public, but people "vote" every day when they turn on a particular program on radio or television or buy a particular newspaper or magazine.

There is much that candidates can do, however, to affect the coverage they receive. If their words are unreported or not reported correctly, or if their ideas are misinterpreted or their motives suspected, they can seek other mass media formats for reaching the general public, as they have done by using the entertainment and talk shows, and maintain Web sites on which they provide information on themselves and their opponents. They can also employ satellite technology to reach local and regional audiences directly and thereby circumvent the national networks and news services. And they can agree to other "competitive" formats such as debates that will get national coverage because these formats fit into the game motif that the news media use.

DOES EXIT POLL REPORTING AFFECT VOTING DECISIONS AND ELECTION OUTCOMES?

Another media-related issue is the election night forecasts based on exit polling data that the networks air before all voting has been completed. Beginning in

1984, the networks promised not to forecast the results in any state until a majority of its polls had closed, although they violated that promise in reporting the exit poll results and projecting the winner in Florida in 2000.

Opponents of the early reporting and predictions claim that it discourages turnout in states in which the polls are still open. The networks respond that the election night forecasts are news; they have a right to report them; and people want to know the winners and losers as soon as possible.

Is there really a problem with the early forecasts? After all, public opinion polls on the election's probable outcome are being reported right up to election day. Political scientists have found that the early forecasts may depress turnout in states in which the polls are still open, but they have not found evidence that the predictions affect the overall results of the election.[16] Nonetheless, the perception that a problem exists is itself a problem, one that has forced Congress several times to hold hearings on the matter.

One proposed solution is to prevent the networks from making any forecasts about the outcome in a state until all its polls have closed; similarly, national predictions could not be made until all the voting in the United States has been completed. However, the number of time zones would effectively prevent any national prediction until the next morning Eastern Standard Time.

Some have even suggested a uniform closing hour for the entire country, but even if there were one, could Congress compel the news networks to abide by it before reporting their exit poll results, given the competitive character of news reporting? Besides, people enjoy the election night broadcasts and are eager to learn the results and celebrate or commiserate, accordingly.

Moreover, exit polls have considerable value in the information they provide about the beliefs, attitudes, and motivations of the voters. Much of the initial analyses of presidential elections and their meaning are based on that poll data. In a democracy, it is essential to get as clear a reading of the pulse of the electorate as possible.

ENHANCING THE DEMOCRATIC CHARACTER OF PRESIDENTIAL ELECTIONS

How can the structure and conduct of presidential elections be more consistent with a democratic electoral process? Increasing voter turnout, improving the quantity and quality of information that is available to the electorate, and making the results mirror public opinion more closely would help promote democratic values and produce a more democratic electoral process.

Is Nonvoting a Problem in U.S. Elections?

Many political scientists would say "yes."[17] They would point to the gap between those eligible to vote and those who actually do so. This gap, which will always exist in a system that does not compel voting, widened during the last forty years of the twentieth century. In 1996, for the first time since 1920, more than half of those eligible chose *not* to vote; in 2004, 43 percent of the voting-age population did not do so; in the 2006 midterm elections, almost six in ten people of voting age did not participate.

Low turnout in a free and open electoral system has been a source of embarrassment to the United States and of concern to its political leaders for several reasons. It weakens their credibility when promoting democracy abroad if it is practiced so lackadaisically at home.

Moreover, the demographic differences between voters and nonvoters—those in the electorate are more educated with higher incomes than the general population—increase the influence gap within the political arena, advantaging the advantaged. Those with more education and higher incomes regularly exercise more influence over the outcome of elections, the agenda of government, and its public policy decisions. Disparities in political participation reinforce and even widen the division between the "haves" and "have nots," resulting in alienation, apathy, and cynicism among people at the lower end of the socioeconomic continuum.

If nonvoting is a problem, then what can and should be done about it? Should people be encouraged to vote? Should they be forced to do so?

How Can More Citizens be Encouraged to Vote?

The national government and many of the states have been trying to make it easier for people to vote. We have discussed some of the ways in which Congress has tried to facilitate voting.

Ease Government-Imposed Regulations
The enactment of the "motor-voter" bill in 1993 has made registration easier. The Help America Vote Act (HAVA) in 2002 provides money to computerize and consolidate voter registration lists, make voting more accessible to the disabled and to non-English speakers, protect the integrity of the voting process, and permit provisional voting for people whose registration is challenged at the time they vote. The law also created the U.S. Electoral Assistance Commission (EAC) to oversee its implementation. Thus far, the law has helped improve accuracy of registration lists, provided money for new voting machines, and has reduced the number of incidences of voter intimidation and fraudulent voting practices.

More needs to be done, however, according to the Commission on Federal Election Reform, which studied voting problems and electoral issues following the 2004 election. The Commission recommended a series of measures: a universal system of voter registration for the entire country, uniform procedures for counting provisional ballots and determining voter eligibility, a country-wide system of voter identification, and civic education programs for the general public. It also urged states to restore voting rights to ex-felons who have served their sentences.[18] Other suggestions include electronic voting machines with a paper ballot backup system.[19]

Although the Commission's proposals would improve the integrity of voting in the United States, might make it easier for people (especially minorities) to vote, and could reduce the economic discrepancies between voters and nonvoters, it is unlikely that the proposals would eliminate these problems entirely or vastly increase turnout. Making it easier to vote is not the same thing as encouraging people to vote. Besides, Congress has not acted on the Commission's report.

Other proposals to make registration automatic, as it is in many European countries, or extending it to election day itself, as is already permitted in a few states, have also been advanced. Counties or states which have facilitated registration in these ways have considerably higher levels of turnout than those that do not. But whether these states are better governed and/or their elections are perceived as more legitimate by the people is another question, one on which there may not be sufficient data to answer.

Make Election Day a Holiday or Nonworkday

Another idea to enhance turnout would be to make election day a national holiday or move it to Veterans Day, which comes later in the month. Presumably, either change would prevent work-related activities from interfering with voting as much as they do now for the bulk of the population.

Many countries follow the practice of holding their elections on a holiday or Sunday. The problem here is that an additional national holiday would cost employers millions of dollars in lost revenue and productivity, with no guarantee that turnout would increase. Moreover, veterans would probably oppose having politics obscure the meaning for which the holiday was intended—to honor those who served and died for their country in the two World Wars. For workers in certain service sectors, the holiday might be a workday anyway.

Some states have extended the period for voting up to twenty-one days prior to the election to increase the number of voters. Others have enacted a "no fault" absentee ballot system for those who find it difficult or inconvenient to get to the polls on election day. Under a liberalized absentee voting procedure, any eligible voter can obtain an absentee ballot with no questions asked. Twenty states currently provide one or both of these options, and voting turnout in those states has increased.[20] Oregon has gone so far as to institute a mail ballot, and turnout in that state now exceeds the national average.

But extending the voting period and balloting by mail are not without their costs. Fear of fraud if the ballots get into the wrong hands is one concern. Voting without all pertinent information is another. People who vote early do so without knowing what may be revealed or happen at the end of the campaign. And for the candidates themselves, there is the added cost of mailing thousands of sample ballots or other information to voters and appealing to the electorate to use them when voting. Nonetheless, the benefit of increasing turnout has motivated more states to modify their single-day voting tradition.

However, political scientist Adam J. Berinsky claims that electoral reforms that have already occurred have actually reinforced rather than reduced the education and income gap between the electorate and the population as a whole. He writes:

> No matter how low the direct costs to casting a ballot are set, the only way to accomplish both goals of increasing turnout and eliminating socioeconomic biases in the voting population is to increase the engagement of the broader mass public with the political world. Political information and interest, not the high tangible costs of the act of voting, are the real barriers to a truly democratic voting public.[21]

Conduct Citizen Education Campaigns

Educating the people on the merits of participating and the responsibilities of citizenry might also generate greater involvement and a higher turnout. If the public better understood what difference it makes who wins, if people had greater confidence that elected officials would keep their promises and that government would address salient issues, then more people might vote.

But invigorating the electoral environment and encouraging more people to participate is not an easy task. If it were, it would have already occurred. It is difficult to convince nonvoters to spend the time and effort necessary to educate themselves on the candidates and the issues, to donate money or get involved in the campaign, and to vote unless they can see what is in it for them and what might happen if they acted in this manner.

If, however, more people voted on a regular basis, the parties and candidates would have to broaden, not narrow, their appeals. They would have to address the needs and desires of all the people and not concentrate on those who are most likely to vote for their candidates. Those who have not participated as frequently in the current voluntary system of voting—the poorer, less educated, less fortunate, and younger—would receive more attention not only from candidates but from elected officials. More equitable public policies might result.

Encourage Grassroots Campaigns

Another way to increase turnout is for party and nonparty groups to continue to devote more resources to get-out-the-vote activities as was done in 2004. Turnout increased by nearly 5 percent in that election in the battleground states. In the nonbattleground states, the increase was more modest. Nonetheless, by bringing out the base rather than appealing to the relatively small number of independent voters, the major parties produced a larger vote because partisans have more motivation to vote than do nonpartisans.

But combining a partisan appeal with greater grassroots organizing, voter targeting, and turnout efforts may also divide the electorate into warring camps and give party activists, who tend to have the strongest ideological views, more influence, thereby turning off moderate voters, especially those without strong partisan allegiances. Such a result would further polarize the electorate, create a more contentious political environment, and perhaps result in a government in which public officials are less open to compromise and to incremental policy decisions. In a contentious political environment, shifts in party control are apt to be more disruptive and result in greater shifts in public policy.

Finally, a more partisan political environment might exacerbate rather than reduce the economic and social divisions within the body politic because these divisions are already evident within the parties' electoral coalitions. Is there any other way to increase turnout without creating deeper cleavages within the electorate?

Change the Electoral System Entirely

The Electoral College does not encourage turnout in the noncompetitive states. Neither does having noncompetitive, single-member, legislative districts. Replacing the Electoral College with a direct popular vote and either making single-member districts more competitive or converting them into multimember districts in which congressional candidates would be chosen on the basis of the vote that they or their party receive, would increase turnout.

But systemic changes are difficult to accomplish. They upset the established political order and are likely to generate opposition from those who fear change and those who like and gain from the current arrangement. Moreover, reforming the electoral system in this manner would probably require a constitutional amendment, which is always more difficult than enacting legislation. As a consequence, these proposals are not likely to be implemented in the short run or in the absence of other changes.

Require Voting as an Obligation of Citizenship

Another proposal would be to compel people to vote as an obligation of citizenship. Penalties could be imposed on those who refused to do so. Australia, Belgium, and Chile require voting, and their turnout is very high.

One obvious problem with forcing people to vote is the compulsion itself. Some may be physically or mentally incapable of voting. Others may not care, have little interest, and have very limited information. They might not even know the names of the candidates. Would the selection of the best-qualified person be enhanced by the participation of uninformed, uninterested, and uncaring voters? Might demagogy be encouraged, or even slicker and more simplistic advertising designed? Would government be more responsive and more popular, or would it be more prone to what British philosopher John Stuart Mill referred to as "the tyranny of the majority?"

Finally, is it democratic to force people to vote? If the right to vote is an essential component of a democratic society, then what about the right *not* to vote; isn't that an important right that should be protected as well? Would the democracy be better served and a better judgment made in the election if people who lacked interest and information voted? Wouldn't political divisions likely run even deeper if the entire society were forced to participate?

In short, the turnout issue is a difficult one to resolve. There are costs and benefits in enlarging the electorate as well as in the ways that this enlargement is achieved. Greater participation would probably produce a more representative election outcome but not necessarily a more informed or enlightened electorate. It would reduce the bias that now exists between the voters and nonvoters, but it might also result in a more contentious political environment that spills over into the operation of government. It would probably result in a more representative government but not necessarily a more efficient one or better public policy decisions.

SHOULD THE ELECTORAL COLLEGE BE MODIFIED OR ABOLISHED?

In addition to the problem of who votes, another source of contention is how the votes should be aggregated. Theoretically, the Constitution allows electors chosen by the states to vote as they please. In practice, all votes are cast for the popular vote winner of the state. Electors are chosen for their partisan allegiances and are expected to vote for their party's nominees.

This *de facto* system has been criticized as undemocratic, unrepresentative of minority views within states, and potentially unreflective of the nation's popular choice. Candidate strategies to win the electoral vote focus on the key battleground states in which less than one-third of the population lives. The proportion of minorities who reside in these states is even lower.[22]

The campaign's concentration on the competitive states not only excludes most Americans from seeing the presidential candidates up close or in television advertising, but it also skews the campaign toward the issues in the battleground states, discourages people in the nonbattleground states from voting, and creates the false impression that the results of the election represent a national voting decision and, correspondingly, give the winner a national mandate.

Over the years, there have been numerous proposals to alter the presidential voting system. The first was introduced in Congress in 1797. Since then, there have been more than 500 others. In urging changes, critics have pointed to the Electoral College's archaic design, its electoral biases, and the undemocratic results it can produce (see Chapter 1).

Abolish the Electors
The electors in the Electoral College have been an anachronism since the development of the party system. Their role as partisan agents is not and has not been consistent with their exercising an independent judgment. In fact, sixteen states plus the District of Columbia prohibit such a judgment by requiring electors to cast their ballots for the winner of the state's popular vote. Although probably unenforceable because they seem to clash with the Constitution, these laws strongly indicate how electors should vote.

One idea is to do away with the electors entirely and the danger that they may exercise their personal preferences rather than the preferences of the public that elected them. First proposed in 1826, this suggestion has received substantial support, including the backing of Presidents John Kennedy and Lyndon Johnson. The Automatic Plan, as it is called, keeps the Electoral College intact but eliminates the electors. Electoral votes are automatically given to the candidate who has received the most popular votes within the state.

Other than removing the potential problem of faithless or unpledged electors, which have not been a major problem to date, the plan would do little to change the system as it currently operates. There have in fact been only a few faithless electors who failed to vote for their party's nominees—eight since 1948.[23] In 2000, one District of Columbia elector submitted a blank ballot to protest the District's lack of voting representation in Congress. Four years later, one Democratic elector from Minnesota made a mistake and voted for John Edwards for president and John Kerry for vice president.[24] In short, the problem of the faithless electors has not been much of a problem, nor one of sufficient magnitude to justify a constitutional amendment.

Apportion the Electoral Vote to the Popular Vote
Electing the entire slate of presidential electors has also been the focus of considerable attention. If the winner of a state's popular vote takes all the electoral votes, the impact of the dominant party is increased within that state, and the larger, more competitive states, where voters tend to be more evenly divided, benefit.

From the perspective of the other major party and minor parties within the state, this winner-take-all system is neither desirable nor fair. In effect, it disenfranchises people who do not vote for the winning candidate. And it does more than that: it discourages a strong campaign effort by a party that has little chance of winning the presidential election in that state, such as Democrats in Utah or Alaska or Republicans in Hawaii or Rhode Island. Naturally the success of other candidates of that party is affected as well. The winner-take- all system reduces voter turnout.

One way to rectify this problem would be to have proportional voting. Such a plan has been introduced on a number of occasions in Congress; in 2004, it appeared as an initiative on the Colorado ballet. But the voters of that state wisely rejected it because it would have reduced Colorado's influence in the Electoral College. A proportional voting system only makes sense for individual states if *all* states adopt such a system.

Under a proportional system, the electors would be abolished, the winner-take-all principle would be eliminated, and a state's electoral vote would be divided in proportion to the popular vote the candidates received within the state. A majority of votes in the Electoral College would still be required for election. If no candidate obtained a majority, most proportional plans call for a joint session of Congress to choose the president from among the top two or three candidates.

The proportional proposal would have a number of major consequences if adopted on a nationwide basis. It would decrease the influence of the most competitive states and increase the relative importance of the least competitive ones, where the voters are likely to be more homogeneous.

Having the electoral vote proportional to the popular vote provides an incentive to all the parties, not simply the dominant one, to mount a more vigorous campaign and to establish a more effective organization. This incentive could strengthen the other major party within the state, but it might also help third parties as well, thereby weakening the two-party system. Ross Perot, who received no electoral votes under the present winner-take-all system, would have received approximately 102 under the proportional plan in 1992 and 49 in 1996. More important, Bill Clinton would not have received a majority in 1992 or 1996 if electoral votes were distributed according to the proportion of the vote candidates received in individual states. (See Table 10.1.) Under these circumstances, third-party candidates, such as Perot and Nader, might have the power to influence the election between the major party candidates by instructing their electors to support one of the other candidates or by forcing the House of Representatives to determine the winner.

Selection by the House weakens a president's national mandate and might encourage the major party candidates to make promises or grant favors to legislators in exchange for their support. Such actions could decrease presidential influence during the initial period of an administration and reward regional or state interests at the expense of the national interest. And what happens if the leading candidate is of one party and the House is controlled by the other party? Would legitimacy of the result be enhanced under that arrangement?

Operating under a proportional plan would in all likelihood make the Electoral College vote much closer, thereby reducing the claim most presidents want to make that they have received broad public backing for themselves, their new administration, and the policy proposals they have advocated during their campaign. George H. W. Bush would have defeated Michael Dukakis by only 43.1 electoral votes in 1988, Jimmy Carter would have defeated Gerald Ford by only 11.7 in 1976, and Richard Nixon would have won by only 6.1 in 1968. The election of 2000 would have been even closer with Bush winning by less than 1 electoral vote; in 2004, he would have won by 16.9. And in at least one recent instance, a proportional electoral vote in the states might have changed the election results. Had this plan been in effect in 1960, Richard Nixon would probably have defeated John Kennedy by 266.1 to 265.6.12.

Choose Electors in the Same Way as Members of Congress
Another proposal aimed at reducing the effect of winner-take-all voting is to choose electors in the same way a state chooses its members of Congress. Instead of selecting the entire slate on the basis of the statewide vote for president, only two electoral votes would be decided in this manner. The remaining votes would be allocated on the basis of the popular vote for president within individual districts (probably congressional districts). Maine and Nebraska currently employ such a district voting system.

A majority of the electoral votes would still be necessary for election. If the vote in the Electoral College were not decisive, then most district plans call for a joint session of Congress to make the final selection.

For the very smallest states, those with three electoral votes, all three electors would have to be chosen on a statewide basis. For others, however, the

TABLE 10.1 | VOTING FOR PRESIDENT, 1956–2004: FOUR METHODS FOR AGGREGATING THE VOTES

Year	Electoral College	Proportional Plan	District Plan	Direct Election (Percentage of Total Votes)
1956				
Eisenhower	457	296.7	411	57.4
Stevenson	73	227.2	120	42.0
Others	1	7.1	0	0.6
1960				
Nixon	219	266.1	278	49.5
Kennedy	303	265.6	245	49.8
Others (Byrd)	15	5.3	14	0.7
1964				
Goldwater	52	213.6	72	38.5
Johnson	486	320.0	466	61.0
Others	0	3.9	0	0.5
1968				
Nixon	301	231.5	289	43.2
Humphrey	191	225.4	192	42.7
Wallace	46	78.8	57	13.5
Others	0	2.3	0	0.6
1972				
Nixon	520	330.3	474	60.7
McGovern	17	197.5	64	37.5
Others	1	10.0	0	1.8
1976				
Ford	240	258.0	269	48.0
Carter	297	269.7	269	50.1
Others	1	10.2	0	1.9
1980				
Reagan	489	272.9	396	50.7
Carter	49	220.9	142	41.0
Anderson	0	35.3	0	6.6
Others	0	8.9	0	1.7
1984				
Reagan	525	317.6	468	58.8

(continued)

Year	Electoral College	Proportional Plan	District Plan	Direct Election (Percentage of Total Votes)
Mondale	13	216.6	70	40.6
Others	0	3.8	0	0.4
1988				
Bush	426	287.8	379	53.4
Dukakis	111	244.7	159	45.6
Others	1	5.5	0	1.0
1992				
Bush	168	203.3	214	37.5
Clinton	370	231.6	324	43.0
Perot	0	101.8	0	18.9
Others	0	1.3	0	0.6
1996				
Clinton	379	262.0	345	49.2
Dole	159	219.9	193	40.7
Perot	0	48.8	0	8.4
Others	0	7.3	0	1.7
2000				
Gore	266*	259.9@	250	48.4
Bush	271	260.3	288	47.9
Nader/Others	0	17	0	2.7
2004				
Kerry	251+	258.3	221	48.3
Bush	286	275.2	317	50.7
Nader	0	4.5	0	1.0

*One Democratic elector in the District of Columbia cast a blank electoral vote to protest the District's absence of voting representation in Congress.

@If the vote were divided just between the two major candidates in 2000, the respective vote received would be Gore 268.77 and Bush 269.23.

+A Minnesota elector mistakenly voted for Edwards for president and Kerry for vice president.

Sources: Figures on proportional and district vote for 1952–1980 were supplied to the author by Joseph B. Gorman of the Congressional Research Service, Library of Congress. Calculations for 1984–1992 were made on the basis of data reported in the *Almanac of American Politics* (Washington, D.C.: National Journal, annual) and by the Federal Election Commission. Calculations for 1996 were made on the basis of official returns as reported by the FEC. For 2000, they are based on the official returns as reported by the FEC. Proportional and District plan figures come from *Every Vote Equal: A State-Based Plan for Electing the President by National Popular Vote* (Los Altos, C.A.: National Popular Vote Press, 2006), 106–109, 177. The figures for 2004 were calculated by the author on the basis of the election results as reported in the "Official General Election Results for United States President, November 2, 2004," Federal Election Commission. www.fec.gov/pubrec/fe2004/2004pres.pdf

combination of district and at-large selection would probably result in a split electoral vote, especially in the larger states. On a national level, this change should make the Electoral College more reflective of the partisan division of the newly elected Congress rather than of the popular division of the national electorate.

The losers under such an arrangement would be the large, competitive states and, most particularly, the cohesive, geographically concentrated groups within those states. The winners would include small states. Third parties, especially those that are regionally based, might also be aided to the extent that they were capable of winning specific legislative districts.

It is difficult to project whether Republicans or Democrats would benefit more from such an arrangement, since much would depend on how the legislative districts within the states were apportioned and how those districts tended to vote. If the 1960 presidential vote were aggregated on the basis of one electoral vote to the popular vote winner of each congressional district and two to the popular vote winner of each state, Nixon would have defeated Kennedy 278 to 245, with 14 unpledged electors. In 1976, the district system would have produced a tie, with Carter and Ford receiving 269 votes each (see Table 10.1).

Elect the President by Direct Popular Vote
Of all the plans to alter or replace the Electoral College, the direct popular vote has received the most attention and support. Designed to eliminate the College entirely and count the votes on a nationwide basis, it would elect the popular vote winner provided the winning candidate received a certain percentage of the total vote. In most plans, 40 percent of the total vote would be necessary. In some, 50 percent would be required.[25] In the event that no one got the required percentage, a runoff between the top two candidates would be held to determine the winner.[26]

A direct popular vote would, of course, remedy a major problem of the present system—the possibility of electing a nonplurality president. It would better equalize voting power both among and within the states. The large competitive states would lose some of their electoral clout by the elimination of the winner-take-all system. Party competition within the states and perhaps even nationwide would be increased.

A direct election would force the candidates to campaign in population centers, appeal to urban-suburban voters and their interests, and provide more justification for claiming a national mandate.

Critics, however, see a direct, popular vote, particularly a close one, as more likely to nationalize and thereby aggravate such problems as determining voter eligibility, possible vote fraud, and vote tabulation errors like the ones in Florida in 2000. A national election would probably cost more and might take longer. Less populated, rural areas, particularly in the Mountain states, Hawaii, and Alaska might be neglected. An election decided primarily by voters concentrated on the Atlantic and Pacific coasts would not provide the geographic balance and federal character that the current system provides.

Finally, a plurality winner might not receive a majority of the votes as the Electoral College requires today. In seven out of the twenty-five elections in the twentieth century and one out of two in the twenty-first century, the winner did not receive 50 percent of the popular vote.

A direct election, however, might also encourage minor parties to enter and compete more vigorously, which could weaken the two-party system. The possibility of denying a major party candidate 50 percent of the popular vote might be sufficient to entice a proliferation of candidates and produce a series of bargains and deals in which support was traded for favors with a new administration. The new administration might even look more like a coalition government in a multiparty system than one that existed in a two-party system.

The organized groups that are geographically concentrated in the large industrial states would have their votes diluted by a direct election. Jewish voters, for example, highly supportive of the Democratic Party since World War II, constitute only about 2.5 percent of the total population but 14 percent in New York, one of the largest states. Thus, the impact of the New York Jewish vote is magnified under the present Electoral College arrangement, as is that of Hispanic voters in Florida, Texas, and California, and the Christian fundamentalists and evangelicals in the South.[27]

There are partisan issues as well. Republicans perceive that they benefit from the current arrangement, which provides more safe Republican states than Democratic ones. They also fear that demographic trends, especially the increase in the Hispanic population, might work against them. The last two nonplurality presidents, Benjamin Harrison and George W. Bush, were both Republicans.

A very close popular vote could also cause problems in a direct election. The winner might not be evident for days, even months. Voter fraud could have national consequences. Under such circumstances, large-scale challenges by the losing candidate would be more likely and would necessitate national recounts rather than confining such recounts to individual states, as the current Electoral College system does.

The provision for the situation in which no one received the required percentage of the popular vote has its drawbacks as well. A runoff election would extend the length of the campaign and add to its cost. Considering that some aspirants begin their quest for the presidency a year or two before the election, a further protraction of the process might unduly tax the patience of the voters and produce an even greater numbing effect than currently exists. Moreover, it would also cut an already short transition period for a newly elected president and would further drain the time and energy of an incumbent seeking reelection.

There is still another difficulty with a contingency election. It could reverse the order in which the candidates originally finished. This result might undermine the ability of the eventual winner to govern successfully. It might also encourage spoiler candidacies. Third parties and independents seeking the presidency could exercise considerable power in the event of a close contest between the major parties. Imagine what Perot's influence would have been in a runoff between Clinton and Bush in 1992.

TABLE 10.2 | PUBLIC OPINION AND THE ELECTORAL COLLEGE

Year	Favor Direct Election	Oppose Direct Election	No Opinion
1944	65%	23%	13%
1967	58	22	20
1968			
May	66	–	–
November	80	–	–
1977	73	–	–
1980	67	–	–

Year*	Amend the Constitution	Keep the Current Electoral System	Neither/Both/ No Opinion
2000			
November 11–12	61	35	4
December 15–17	59	37	4
2004 October 11–14	61	35	4

*Gallup changed the question in 2000: "Thinking for a moment about the way in which the president is elected in this country, which would you prefer: to amend the Constitution so the candidate who receives the most total votes nationwide wins the election, or to keep the current system, in which the candidate who wins the most votes in the Electoral College wins the election?"

Source: Frank Newport, "Americans Support Proposal to Eliminate Electoral College System," Gallup Poll, January 5, 2001, www.gallup.com/poll/releases/pr010105.asp; Darren K. Carlson, "Public Flunks Electoral College System," Gallup Poll, November 2, 2004. www.galluppoll.com/content/Default.aspx?ci=13918 (accessed December 27, 2006).

Nonetheless, the direct election plan is supported by public opinion and has been ritualistically praised by contemporary presidents. Gallup Polls conducted over the past three decades have consistently found the public favoring a direct election over the present electoral system by substantial margins as indicated in Table 10.2. Former presidents Carter and Ford have both urged the abolition of the Electoral College and its replacement by a popular vote.

In 1969, the House of Representatives actually voted for a constitutional amendment to establish direct election for president and vice president, but the Senate refused to go along. Despite public opinion, it seems unlikely that sufficient impetus for a change that requires a constitutional amendment will occur until the issue becomes salient to more people, and states that believe that they currently are at an advantage with the Electoral College system decide to forego their perceived advantage in the interest of a larger democratic objective. Don't hold your breath!

With the likelihood of a constitutional amendment remote, proponents of a direct popular vote have come up with another plan to achieve the same goal—an interstate compact in which states would agree to join together to pass identical laws that awarded all of their electoral votes to the presidential candidate who won the most popular votes in the country as a whole. The compact would not take effect, however, until it was agreed to by states that constituted a majority of the Electoral College. Otherwise, there would be no assurance that the candidate with the most popular votes would win in the Electoral College.[28]

The practical merit of such a plan is that it would not require a constitutional amendment; it would also allow states to retain their authority for choosing their electors and for deciding how they should vote. The problem thus far is that only one state, Maryland, has formally agreed to join such a compact. The California legislature enacted a bill supporting the plan but Governor Schwarzenegger vetoed it.

SUMMARY

There have been changes and continuities in the way we select a president. In general, the changes have made the system more democratic. The continuities link the system to its constitutional roots and its republican past.

The nomination process has been affected more than the general election. Significant modifications have occurred in the rules for choosing delegates, in the laws and judicial decisions regulating contributions and expenditures, and in ways in which campaign appeals are made, targeted, and evaluated; voters are informed; and elections reported to the public.

Supporters of the parties' rules changes contend that they have taken the nomination out of the back rooms and into the public arena, provided more opportunities for more candidates to compete, and given partisans more of a voice in choosing their party's nominees. In contrast, critics allege that the party rules still favor nationally recognized candidates, allow activists to exercise more influence over the selection of delegates and the eventual standard-bearer, and do not encourage participation in most of the states that hold their contests later in the process.

The campaign finance system has also been problematic. Many of the undemocratic features of the private funding system remain even though the size of individual and group contributions to candidates and parties have been limited, spending restrictions have been imposed on federally funded candidates, public funding has provided greater opportunities for more candidates to run for their party's nomination and has also helped to equalize campaign expenditures, and most campaign financial activity is now subject to full public disclosure. However, inequities continue to exist; loopholes in the law have permitted groups to skirt the federal funding contributions limits; Supreme Court decisions allow unlimited independent spending; federal funding is now jeopardized by candidates' abilities to raise large amounts of private money;

and each presidential campaign is more expensive than the last one, often by significant amounts.

The public's ability to make an informed, enlightened judgment has also been called into question by the amount and quality of the communications received from the candidates and parties and coverage of the election by the news media. The channels of communication have increased, but the bulk of the communication is skewed toward those in the battleground states. In addition to being highly targeted, political commercials have become increasingly negative and emotionally charged with very little evaluation of their claims and allegations by nonpartisan, neutral sources. The news media seem more concerned with reporting entertaining campaign news than educating the public on the principal issues of the day, the way candidates would deal with these issues, and the impact that their policies would have on the country in the short term or long term. Moreover, the constitutional protections of freedom of the press severely limit what government can do to improve the coverage and ensure that the people get the information they need to make an informed judgment on election day.

Have these changes been beneficial or harmful? Have they functioned to make the system more efficient, more responsive, and more likely to result in the choice of a well-qualified candidate? Politicians, journalists, and political scientists disagree in their answers.

Who votes and how votes should be aggregated continues to prompt debate and elicit concern. The expansion of suffrage has made the election process more democratic in theory, but the actual rates of participation have reduced this theoretical gain. Although the failure to vote of nearly half of the adult population has been a source of embarrassment and dismay to proponents of a democratic electoral process, there is also little agreement on how to deal with the problem in a federal system that values individual initiative, civic responsibility, and states' rights simultaneously.

Finally, the equity of the Electoral College has also been challenged once again by the results of the 2000 election, but none of the proposals to alter or abolish it, except the direct election of the president, has received much public backing. With no outcry for reform, Congress has been reluctant to alter the system by initiating an amendment to the Constitution and seems unlikely to do so until another electoral crisis and/or unpopular result creates public pressure to force its hand. Proponents of direct election have thus recommended that states form an interstate compact among themselves and agree to have their electors support the popular vote winner, but thus far, only one state has done so.

Does the electoral process work? Yes. Can it be improved? Of course, it can. Will it be changed? Probably, but if the past is any indication, there is no guarantee that legally imposed changes will produce only, or even, their desired effect. If politics is the art of the possible, then success is achieved by those who can adjust most quickly to the legal and political environment and turn it to their electoral advantage.

WHERE ON THE WEB?

Public Interest Groups

- **Center for Responsive Politics**
  www.opensecrets.org
- **Common Cause**
  www.commoncause.org
- **Public Citizen**
  www.citizen.org

Think Tanks

- **The American Enterprise Institute for Public Policy**
  www.aei.org
  A moderate, Republican-leaning institute interested in public policy.
- **The Brookings Institution**
  www.brookings.org
  Washington's oldest think tank; it has a moderate, centrist orientation.
- **Cato Institute**
  www.cato.org
  A libertarian-oriented institute that examines contemporary public policy issues.
- **Center for American Progress**
  www.americanprogress.org
  A liberal-oriented, Democratic-leaning think tank that examines contemporary issues and provides reports and op ed articles.
- **Heritage Foundation**
  www.heritage.org
  A conservative group concerned with salient public policy issues.
- **Joint Center for Political and Economic Studies**
  www.jointctr.org
  A liberal-oriented think tank specializing in issues of particular concern to minority groups.
- **Urban Institute**
  www.urban.org
  A nonpartisan institute for the study of domestic public policy.

Government Sources

- **Congress**
  www.thomas.gov or www.house.gov and www.senate.gov
- **Presidency**
  www.whitehouse.gov

EXERCISES

1. From the perspective of American democracy, explain what you consider to be the major problem facing the presidential electoral system today and why you think it is such a problem. Then describe whether (and if so, how) liberal, moderate, and conservative groups as well as the Democratic, Republican, and minor parties see the issue you have identified and indicate any solutions they have proposed to fix it. Which of their proposals do you think is best and why? If you do not think any of their proposals will be effective, then propose one of your own.

2. Examine the legislation Congress has recently enacted to reform the electoral system. Indicate the major provisions of the legislation and how they have been implemented to date. What else do you think that Congress should do?

3. From the perspective of the presidential candidates, what is the most odious feature of the current presidential electoral system? Under the existing law, advise the candidates how to deal with this problem and/or propose reforms to reduce or eliminate it.

SELECTED READINGS

Bennett, Robert W. *Taming the Electoral College*. Stanford, C.A.: Stanford University Press, 2006.

Best, Judith. *The Case against Direct Election of the President: A Defense of the Electoral College*. Ithaca, N.Y.: Cornell University Press, 1975.

Center for Voting and Democracy. *The Shrinking Battleground: The 2008 Presidential Election and Beyond*. 2005. www.fairvote.org/shrinking

Edwards, George C. III. *Why the Electoral College is Bad for America*. New Haven, C.T.: Yale University Press, 2004.

Issacharoff, Pamela S. Karlan, and Richard H. Pildes. *When Elections Go Bad: The Law of Democracy and the Presidential Election of 2000*. New York: Foundation Press, 2001.

Koza, John R. et al. *Every Vote Equal: A State-Based Plan for Electing the President by National Popular Vote*. Los Altos, C.A.: National Popular Vote Press, 2006.

Longley, Lawrence D., and Alan G. Braun. *The Politics of Electoral College Reform*. New Haven, C.T.: Yale University Press, 1975.

Peirce, Neal R., and Lawrence D. Longley. *The People's President*. New Haven, C.T.: Yale University Press, 1981.

Polsby, Nelson W. *Consequences of Party Reform*. New York: Oxford University Press, 1983.

Schumaker, Paul D., and Burdett A. Loomis, eds. *Choosing a President: The Electoral College and Beyond*. New York: Chatham House, 2002.

Sundquist, James L. *Constitutional Reform*. Washington, D.C.: Brookings Institution, 1983.

Wayne, Stephen J. *Is This Any Way to Run a Democratic Election?* 3rd ed. Washington, D.C.: CQ Press, 2007.

NOTES

1. Although Democrats Michael Dukakis in 1988 and Bill Clinton in 1992 had amassed large leads early and seemed headed toward easy nominations, opponents Jesse Jackson and Jerry Brown were able to contest primaries and caucuses until the

very end of the nomination process, garnering headlines and criticizing the front-runners. Although they eventually agreed to support the national ticket, their extended campaign had the effect of weakening their party's nominees, effectively undercutting the impact of their own endorsements, and in the case of African Americans who supported Jackson in 1988, reducing turnout in the general election. Robert Dole also had to endure a costly and divisive nomination process in contrast to Clinton's clear sailing to his 1996 renomination—a disadvantage that started Dole far behind his Democratic opponent in the 1996 general election.

2. Thomas E. Patterson, *Out of Order* (New York: Knopf, 1993), p. 210.

3. Ibid.

4. This was the situation in which the Republicans found themselves in 2000 when six of the twelve serious candidates withdrew before the first state selected its delegates; three additional candidates dropped out shortly thereafter.

5. Darren K. Carlson, "Public Flunks Electoral College System," Gallup Poll, November 2, 2004. www.galluppoll.com/content/Default.aspx?ci=13918 (accessed December 27, 2006).

6. Approval voting allows the electorate to vote to approve or disapprove each candidate who is running. The candidate with the most approval votes is elected. In a system of cumulative voting, candidates are rank ordered, and the ranks may be averaged to determine the winner.

7. It normally takes the Federal Election Commission up to two years to complete an audit of the expenses and determine which of them may not have been in compliance with the law.

8. *Randall v. Sorrell* (Nos. 04-1528, 04-1530 and 04-1697), 382 F.3rd 91 (June 2006). *Buckley v. Valeo* 424 U.S. 1 (1976).

9. *McConnell v. FEC* 540 U.S. 93 (2003).

10. Studies of campaign advertising have documented increasing negativity in political commercials.

11. The front-loading of the nomination process, the four to five month period between the time a candidate effectively wins the nomination and the national nominating conventions are held, and the increasing costs of high tech communications and other aspects of campaigning have also contributed to the advantage that well-financed, privately funded candidates have over their publicly funded challengers.

12. Nor do voters believe that the large amounts of revenue and expenditures will adversely affect the character of the next president. Lydia Saad, "American Prefer Presidential Candidates to Forgo Public Funding," Gallup Poll, April 27, 2007.

13. The Campaign Finance Institute, a nonprofit, nonpartisan think tank that is oriented toward campaign finance reform, has proposed raising the overall limit during the nomination period to equal that of the general election. The Institute claims that the additional monies are needed by candidates to distinguish themselves from one another, run in multiple states, and do so for an extended period of time. "So the Voters May Choose: Reviving the Presidential Matching Fund System," Campaign Finance Institute, 2005. www.CampaignFinanceInstitute.org.

14. The Campaign Finance Institute proposes a three to one match for all contributions up to $100. Such a change would encourage candidates to seek more small donors and would encourage donors to give if they knew that their $100 contribution would be worth $400 to the candidate of their choice.

15. In a series of recent decisions, *Colorado Republican Federal Campaign Committee v. FEC* 518 U.S.604 (1996) and *McConnell v. FEC* 540 U.S.93 (2003)], the Supreme Court has ruled that parties can spend unlimited amounts of money independently on behalf of their candidates for federal office. At present, their coordinated spending with their candidates is limited, however. These decisions forced the FEC to rescind its rule against independent spending by parties in the general election. As a consequence, the amount of such spending increased markedly in 2004.

16. Raymond Wolfinger and Peter Linquiti, "Tuning In and Turning Out," *Public Opinion,* 4 (Feb./Mar., 1981), pp. 57–59. See also Harold Mendelshon and Irving Crespi, *Polls, Television, and the New Politics* (Scranton, P.A.: Chandler, 1970), pp. 234–236.

17. APSA Task Force on Inequality and American Democracy, "American Democracy in an Age of Rising Inequality," *Perspectives on Politics,* 2 (Dec., 2004), pp. 647–690.

18. Excluded would be those convicted of a capital crime and sex offenders. "Building Confidence in U.S. Elections," Report of the Commission on Federal Election Reform, September 2005.

19. There have been accuracy and security problems with electronic voting. Computer scientists contend that the current system is vulnerable to hidden programming by the designers of such systems as well as to outside hacking. A small error in the programming could switch hundreds, if not thousands of votes. They also claim that the voting machines have not been adequately tested, a claim which the Election Assistance Commission supported when it decertified the main company testing the machines on the grounds that it did not adequately document the tests it was doing on the equipment. Christopher Drew, "Citing Problems, U.S. Bars Lab From Testing Electronic Voting," *New York Times* (Jan. 4, 2007), pp. A1, A14.

    Another issue has been the absence of a paper trail to use when determining the accuracy of electronic machines in tabulating the vote. Without such a trail, it is difficult to check whether all the votes have been properly recorded and tabulated.

    Voting on the Internet is even more suspect. Problems with security prompted the Department of Defense to cancel the implementation of a Web-based system to allow members of the armed forces stationed abroad to vote via the Internet.

20. Eleven states currently allow early voting; sixteen have liberal absentee voting rules. Lois Romano, "Growing Use of Mail Voting Puts Its Stamp on Campaigns," *Washington Post* (Nov. 29, 1998), pp. A1, 6, 7.

21. Adam J. Berinsky, "The Perverse Consequences of Electoral Reform in the United States," *American Politics Research,* 33 (July, 2005), pp. 471–491.

22. According to a report by Center for Voting and Democracy, more than 30 percent of the nation's white population lives in the battleground states compared to just 21 percent of African Americans and Native Americans, 18 percent of Latinos, and 14 percent of Asian Americans. "Presidential Election Inequality: The Electoral College in the 21st Century," *A Report by the Center for Voting and Democracy* (Takoma Park, M.D.: 2006), p. 13.

23. There is some controversy over whether three other electors in 1796 might also have gone against their party when voting for president. They supported John Adams although they were selected in states controlled by the other party. However, the fluidity of the party system in those days, combined with the weakness of party identification, makes their affiliation (if any) hard to establish.

24. The same problem occurred in 1988, although in that case, the reversal of presidential and vice presidential votes was done purposefully by a Democratic West Virginia elector.

25. Abraham Lincoln was the only plurality president who failed to attain the 40 percent figure. He received 39.82 percent in 1860, although he probably would have received more had his name been on the ballot in nine southern states.

26. Other direct election proposals have recommended that a joint session of Congress decide the winner. The runoff provision was contained in the resolution that passed the House of Representatives in 1969. A direct election plan with a runoff provision failed to win the two-thirds Senate vote required to initiate a constitutional amendment in 1979.

27. John Kennedy carried New York by approximately 384,000 votes. He received a plurality of more than 800,000 from precincts that were primarily Jewish. Similarly, in Illinois, a state he carried by less than 9,000, Kennedy had a plurality of 55,000 from the so-called Jewish precincts. Mark R. Levy and Michael S. Kramer, *The Ethnic Factor* (New York: Simon & Schuster, 1972), p. 104.

28. *Every Vote Equal: A State-based Plan for Electing the President* (Los Angeles: National Popular Vote Press, 2006), pp. 243–274.

APPENDICES

APPENDIX | **A**

2000 AND 2004 ELECTORAL VOTE DISTRIBUTION

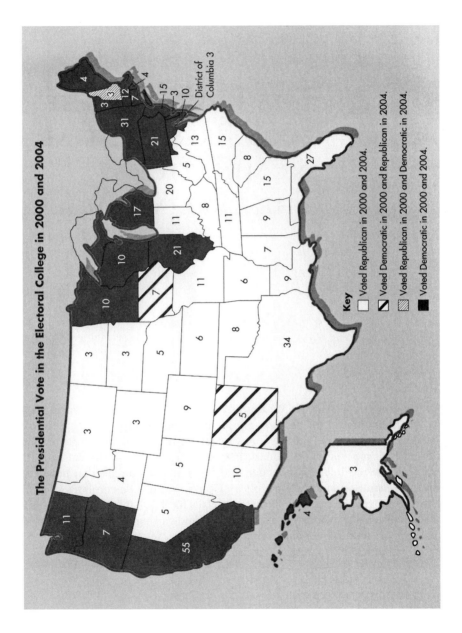

The Presidential Vote in the Electoral College in 2000 and 2004

Key

☐ Voted Republican in 2000 and 2004.

◪ Voted Democratic in 2000 and Republican in 2004.

▨ Voted Republican in 2000 and Democratic in 2004.

■ Voted Democratic in 2000 and 2004.

District of Columbia 3

B APPENDIX | THE RACE FOR THE 2008 PRESIDENTIAL NOMINATIONS: THE PRELIMINARIES

From the moment of George W. Bush's reelection, potential candidates were assessing their chances for the next presidential election cycle. As the political environment within the United States began to change with the increasing sectarian violence and loss of American lives in Iraq, the government's inadequate response to Hurricane Katrina, and the political scandals that beset the Bush administration and the Republican Congress, aspirants on both sides of the partisan divide began to position themselves for a possible presidential run.

They tested the waters to discern their fund-raising potential, organizational support within the national and state parties, leadership endorsements, and their abilities to generate enthusiasm for their own candidacy.

GETTING STARTED

The first step in getting started was creating a campaign organization and hiring staff. Most potential candidates already had some structural entities in place upon which they could build: their campaign staff from their last election campaign; their office personnel, if they currently held a position in government; their leadership and/or policy-oriented PACs; and their family, friends, and advisers.

The first announcement for presidential candidates is usually the establishment of an exploratory committee, or in some cases, an official campaign committee. Creating one of these committees allows candidates to raise money, develop donor lists, hire staff, travel to the early caucus and primary states, and line up party leaders and sympathetic groups behind their efforts.

The formation of these committees has come earlier and earlier in the election cycle. Bill Clinton declared his candidacy for the 1992 Democratic nomination in the fall of 1991, three months before the year of the election. The first candidate to throw his hat into the ring for 2008 was former Alaska Senator Mike Gravel who indicated his desire to run on April 17, 2006. The Democratic field, however, did not begin to take shape until the fall of 2006 when Governor Tom Vilsack (Iowa), Congressman Dennis Kucinich (Ohio), and former vice presidential nominee, John Edwards, announced their intention to seek their party's presidential nomination. They were quickly followed by others afraid to wait for fear that the best fund-raisers, pollsters, media consultants, and party officials in the states that hold the first contests would have already committed themselves to work for others.

Republicans were a little slower in making their announcements and setting up their committees for their 2008 nomination than Democrats, but most of them established exploratory committees in the winter of 2006, a full year before the first caucus and primary were scheduled. Table B.1 indicates the dates when 2008 candidates got started, and in some cases, ended their campaigns.

FUND-RAISING

Money is the life-blood of American politics. The costs of seeking a party's nomination have become greater and greater. Early estimates for 2008 range from a minimum of $50 million to about $100 million for a vigorous campaign run against well-financed opponents.

The need for money upfront was magnified in 2008 by the heavily front-loaded nomination schedule, forcing candidates to try to amass as large a war chest as soon as possible. Anticipating a presidential run, some candidates purposely raised more money than they needed in their previous federal campaign to transfer it to their presidential effort. Hillary Rodham Clinton is a good example. She received $10 million more than she spent for her 2006 Senate campaign and transferred it to her presidential effort. Other 2008 candidates who transferred substantial sums include Democrats Joe Biden ($2 million), Chris Dodd ($5 million), Barack Obama ($516,000), and Republican, John McCain ($492,000).

TABLE B.1	GETTING IN AND OUT		
	IN	OUT	
	Announced	Announced	Announced
	Candidate Exploratory Committee	Official Candidate Committee	Termination of Candidacy
Democrats			
Mike Gravel	Apr. 17, 2006		
Mark Warner	Oct. 12, 2006		
Tom Vilsack	Nov. 9, 2006	November 30, 2007	Feb. 23, 2007
Russ Feigold	Nov. 12, 2006		
Tom Daschle	Dec. 2, 2006		
Dennis Kucinich	Dec. 12, 2006		
Birch Bayh	Dec. 3, 2006	Dec. 16, 2006	
John Edwards	Dec. 28, 2006		
Chris Dodd	Jan. 11, 2007		
Barack Obama	Jan. 16, 2007	Feb. 10, 2007	
Hillary Rodham Clinton	Jan. 20, 2007		
Bill Richardson	Jan. 21, 2007		
John Kerry	Jan. 24, 2007		
Joe Biden	Jan 7, 2007	Jan. 31, 2007	
Republicans			
John Cox	March 9, 2006		
Duncan Hunter	Oct. 30, 2006	Jan. 25, 2007	
Rudy Giuliani	Nov. 10, 2006		
Mike Huckabee	Jan. 26, 2007		
John McCain	Nov. 12, 2006	April 25, 2007	
Tommy Thompson	Nov. 15, 2006	April 4, 2007	
Bill Frist	Nov. 29, 2006		
Jim Gilmore	Dec. 20, 2006		
Mitt Romney	Jan. 3, 2007	February 13, 2007	
Ron Paul	Jan. 11, 2007	March 12, 2007	
Frank Keating	Jan. 16, 2007		
Tom Tancredo	Jan. 16, 2007	April 2, 2007	
Sam Brownback	Dec. 4, 2006	Jan. 20, 2007	

The candidates' leadership and policy PACs have also been a source for initial funding. Contributors to these groups are targets for additional fund-raising appeals. Staff and travel expenses to the early states can also be paid by PACs. Finally, candidate PACs provide a pot of gold from which to distribute donations to others seeking office and collect "I-owe-you's" for future use. The candidates who gave the most money to other federal candidates in their party during the 2006 election were Democrats Hillary Rodham Clinton ($277,000), Chris Dodd ($259,000), and Barack Obama ($576,769), and Republicans Rudy Guiliani ($363,500), John McCain ($325,809), and Mitt Romney ($200,250).[1]

A third critical early step on the road to the White House is identifying wealthy donors who not only will give the maximum amount but also can persuade at least 100 of their family, friends, and professional acquain-tances to do so. For Republican candidates, the task for 2008 was to woo the Pioneers and Rangers who worked on George W. Bush's successful presidential campaigns; for the Democrats, the objective was to appeal to major party donors, many of whom contributed the maximum amount and raised additional money for the Kerry–Edwards campaign, as well as identify new targets of opportunity. In 2008, Hillary Rodham Clinton set the highest goal for her principal financial backers; she asked them to raise $1 million each!

Courting these big-money solicitors requires personal contacts and donor-oriented events. George W. Bush's successful fund-raising for his two presi-dential campaigns provides the model that most contemporary candidates follow. They host small dinner parties, sports outings, and even donor trips to the early states. The purpose of the events is to befriend the contributors, conduct off-the-record conversations with them, address their policy concerns, and sometimes present personally, or have a senior adviser do so, a general campaign strategy, ending with an invitation to join the team. Sometimes these events precede the creation of an exploratory committee such as with Senator Barack Obama who made a much-publicized trip to New York in early December 2006 to meet with potential donors at the home of billionaire George Soros.[2] Sometimes the events are designed to launch that committee with a big financial bang as Mitt Romney did in January 2007, raising $6.5 million on the first day in which his exploratory campaign held a fund-raiser.[3]

Meeting with the large donors is only one phase of the early fund-raising effort; tapping small donors is another. Previously outreach to small contrib-utors was accomplished by early and frequent direct mail appeals. Candidates used lists of past or likely donors to previous campaigns and leadership and policy PACs. However, Howard Dean's successful use of the Internet to raise a large number of modest-size contributions provided an additional and inex-pensive communication channel for raising money as well as involving people in the campaign. Today, the creation of a Web site with a blog is essential. (See "Where on the Web" at the end of this Appendix for the sites of the 2008 candidates.) In the first quarter of 2007, Barack Obama led all the candidates in the amount of money raised on the Internet, $6.9 million, compared to $4.2 million for Clinton and $3 million for Edwards.

During the same period, the Obama campaign also received contributions from more people, 104,000, while Hillary Rodham Clinton received donations from 50,000. However, about three-fourths of Clinton's contributors gave the maximum amount compared to half of Obama's, thereby giving Obama a potential fund-raising advantage by going back to a larger percentage of his contributors for additional contributions.

It takes money to raise money. The candidates spent substantial portions of what they raised by hiring firms to identify large donors, holding fund-raising events, and designing ads to trumpet their credentials and encourage more contributions. More money was raised during the first quarter of 2007 than during any other first quarter. Barack Obama received almost $25 million in contributions and Mitt Romney almost $21 million. Although not raising as much new money as Obama, Clinton still had the largest war chest because of the funds she transferred from her 2006 Senate campaign. Combined, the candidates raised $117 million in the first quarter of 2007 compared to $49 million four years earlier. Table B.2 lists the amount of money candidates raised and spent in the first quarter of the 2007–2008 election cycle.

TABLE B.2 | REVENUE AND EXPENDITURES, JANUARY–MARCH, 2007 (IN THOUSANDS)

Democratic Candidates

Candidate	Home State	Raised/ Transferred	Spent	Cash on Hand	Debts
Clinton, Hillary	NY	$36,054,568	$5,079,789	$30,974,779	$1,582,639
Obama, Barack	IL	$25,797,721	$6,605,200	$19,192,520	$190,560
Edwards, John	NC	$14,031,662	$3,299,781	$10,733,641	$0
Dodd, Chris	CT	$8,795,706	$1,313,239	$7,482,467	$0
Richardson, Bill	NM	$6,249,354	$1,226,881	$5,022,473	$19,579
Biden, Joe	DE	$4,013,089	$1,174,174	$2,838,915	$0
Kucinich, Dennis	OH	$344,891	$194,217	$163,887	$0
Gravel, Mike	AK	$15,534	$18,304	$498	$88,516

(continued)

Republican Candidates

Candidate	Home State	Raised/ Transferred	Spent	Cash on Hand	Debts
Romney, Mitt	MA	$23,434,634	$11,570,981	$11,863,652	$2,350,000
Giuliani, Rudy	NY	$16,623,410	$5,688,207	$11,949,734	$88,862
McCain, John	AZ	$13,087,559	$8,379,214	$5,180,799	$1,812,636
Brownback, Sam	KS	$1,871,057	$1,064,431	$806,626	$0
Tancredo, Tom	CO	$1,256,090	$711,012	$575,078	$15,000
Paul, Ron	TX	$639,989	$115,070	$524,919	$0
Huckabee, Mike	AR	$544,157	$170,239	$373,918	$52,502
Hunter, Duncan	CA	$538,524	$265,971	$272,552	$0
Thompson, Tommy	WI	$391,628	$252,404	$139,723	$129,194
Gilmore, Jim	VA	$203,896	$113,789	$90,107	$88,013

Source: Center for Responsive Politics. April 30, 2007, www.opensecrets.org/Pres08/index.asp?cycle=2008.

POLITICAL TRAVELS

Gaining and maintaining visibility is very important to the candidates; political contacts matter. Travel to Iowa and New Hampshire and the other early states is a must to meet the electorate, become a news item, begin to lay out a message, and create a leadership image. Republican candidates made 78 trips to Iowa and 57 to New Hampshire *prior* to the beginning of the 2007–2008 election cycle; Democratic candidates made 63 visits to Iowa and 72 to New Hampshire during the same period. The pace of visits picked up in 2007. In the first four months, Republicans traveled to Iowa 59 times and to New Hampshire 30 times compared to 29 and 19 respectively for the Democratic candidates.[4]

One problem that many candidates encounter is how to meet the obligations of their current position and still do the campaigning necessary to gain visibility, meet voters, and raise money. Days on the road, missed votes, and canceled campaign appearances all create difficulties that can damage a leadership image.[5]

As a consequence, elected officials running for the presidency constantly have to juggle their campaign needs and obligations with their job requirements.

IMAGE AND POLICY APPEAL

Initially, the race for the nomination is about positing partisan credentials. All candidates need to articulate a basic appeal to their party activists. For the Democrats, it was criticism of the Bush administration, particularly the war in Iraq, the politicization of the administration of justice, as evident by the firing of seven U.S. Attorneys, and the president's position on a host of social issues ranging from abortion to same sex marriage to stem cell research. For the Republicans, it was adherence to traditional conservative beliefs, the free enterprise, capitalistic system; a strong national security posture; and the pursuit of traditional family values. Although most of the Republican candidates supported the wars in Afghanistan and Iraq, they did not heap praise on the postwar strategy of the Bush administration in Iraq. Instead, at the first presidential debate held at the Reagan library in May 2007, the Republican candidates praised President Reagan and cited their credentials as Reagan Republicans.

In addition to emphasizing their conservative credentials, the GOP candidates pointed to their character strengths and policy orientations: McCain as a well-known Senator, Vietnam prisoner of war, and good government advocate; Guiliani as a tough law and order mayor who rallied New York after the terrorist attacks; Romney as a successful businessman and governor; Hunter as an expert in defense; T. Thompson and Huckabee as strong managers with expertise in health policy; Tancredo as a strong critic of the Bush administration's immigration policies; and Paul as a libertarian.

The Democratic candidates also tried to present a distinctive presidential image and policy appeal. Hillary Rodham Clinton emphasized her experience as First Lady and New York Senator, moderate policy positions and knowledge of the issues, and strength of character. With greater public recognition and a lead in the early prenomination polls, her campaign presented Senator Clinton as the inevitable Democratic nominee. In contrast, Senator Barack Obama was the new guy on the block, the fresh young leader, a junior Senator with new ideas and a message of hope. He presented himself as the personification of the American melting pot and dream. John Edwards repeated the popularist theme he had voiced in his previous quest for the Democratic presidential nomination. Pointing to the growing gap between the rich and the middle and lower classes, Edwards urged a fairer and more equitable government that promoted social policies such as universal health care. The other Democratic candidates stressed their areas of expertise: Biden, foreign affairs; Dodd, banking and finance; and Richardson, foreign policy and executive management. Kucinich rekindled his liberal activist, no-holds-barred rhetoric.

Targets are also important. Republicans Romney and Brownback directed their appeals to the religious conservatives, while McCain targeted more generally the Republican establishment, and Guilani appealed to Republican moderates who desired a proven, no-nonsense leader and manager.

On the Demcoratic side, Clinton made a special appeal to women for financial support, public relations, and involvement in her campaign. Obama stayed visible on the Internet and college campuses. By the end of April 2007, more than 325,000 people had signed onto his Facebook.com network, and over 300 college organizations supported his candidacy.[6] Obama also built and solidified his backing within African-American communities. Edwards and Kucinich focused on liberal activists within their party. Richardson made a more general partisan appeal.

MEDIA COVERAGE AND ADVERTISING

Candidates need media attention from the outset. Travel to the early states is one way to get local coverage and occasionally some national attention as well. Participating in media and party-sponsored debates is another. Those debates begin in the year before the election and continue through the caucuses and primaries.[7] The first Democratic debate for the 2008 presidential nomination was held April 2007 in South Carolina; the first Republican debate occurred in May 2007 at the Ronald Reagan Library in California.[8]

Early advertising is also necessary to gain recognition or reverse a public image. Mitt Romney was the first of the GOP candidates to run biographical ads in Iowa, a state in which he was not well known. He spent $1.7 million on the design, production, and airing of ads in the first quarter of 2007 alone.[9] Bill Richardson was the first Democrat to do so. In commercials that aired in the early caucus and primary states, Richardson pointed to his experience as a cabinet member, UN ambassador, foreign policy negotiator, and state governor. John Edwards also ran early ads that opposed the war in Iraq and urged the president to bring the troops home.

Another media-related issue is whether to commit time and resources necessary to compete in the straw votes that occur in the year prior to the nomination. These votes generate publicity as the first indication of how the candidates are being evaluated by the voters. As such, they could provide a momentary boost and added visibility if the candidate does well but can also be costly if the candidate does not finish near the top of the pack and has put a lot of effort into getting supporters to vote.

SUMMARY

Initially, the race for the nomination is about money, media, and momentum. Money provides the resources to campaign early, continually, and extensively. It is also a sign of strength and viability. Media provide visibility; it is the medium through which candidates point to their credentials, demonstrate their leadership attributes, and extend their policy appeals. Momentum is achieved by doing well, exciting partisans, and gaining status as the front-runner. It is previewed in the postnomination polls and boosted or undercut by the early straw polls and initial caucuses and primaries. The heavily front-loaded schedule, however, leaves little time for repositioning and retooling once the nomination process begins. Candidates need to run flat-out from the opening bell.

WHERE ON THE WEB

THE CANDIDATES FOR THE 2008 REPUBLICAN AND DEMOCRATIC PARTY NOMINATIONS

	Campaign Committees	Leadership PACs
Democrats		
Joe Biden	joebiden.com	uniteourstates.com
Hillary Clinton	hillaryclinton.com	
Chris Dodd	chrisdodd.com	
John Edwards	johnedwards.com	oneamericacommittee.com
Mike Gravel	gravel2008.us	
Dennis Kucinich	kucinich.us	
Barack Obama	barackobama.com	
Bill Richardson	richardsonforpresident.com	
Republicans		
Sam Brownback	brownback.com	
John Cox	cox2008.com	
Rudolph Giuliani	joinrudy2008.com	solutionsamerica.com
Mike Huckabee	explorehuckabee.com	
Duncan Hunter	gohunter08.com	
John McCain	johnmccain.com	
Ron Paul	ronpaulexplore.com	
Mitt Romney	mittromney.com	thecommonwealthpac.com
Tom Tancredo	teamtancredo.org	teamamericapac.org
Tommy Thompson	tommy2008.com	
Potential Candidates		
Michael Bloomberg (Independent)	mikebloomberg.com	
Wes Clark (Democrat)	securingamerica.com	
Newt Gingrich (Republican)	newt.org	
Chuck Hagel (Republican or Independent)		hagel.senate.gov
George Pataki (Republican)	georgepataki.com	freedompac.com
Fred Thompson (Republican)	draftfredthompson.com	

NOTES

1. Receipts from 2005 to midyear of 2006, Democracy in Action: The Race for the White House. www.gwu.edu/~action/2008/leadershippac08.html; Contributions to Federal Candidates, 2005–2006, Center for Responsive Politics, January 27, 2007. www.opensecrets.org/pacs/industry.asp?txt+Q03&cycle=2006.

2. Chris Cillizza and Michael A. Fletcher, "Candidates Woo Bush Donors for 'Invisible Primary'," *Washington Post* (Dec. 10, 2006), p. A15.

3. Glen Johnson, "Romney Kicks Off Presidential Campaign With Fundraising Blitz," *Boston Globe* (Jan. 9, 2007) www.boston.com/news/local/massachusetts/articles/2007/01/09/romney_kicks_off_presidential_campaign_with_fundraising_blitz.

4. "Iowa Caucus and New Hampshire Primary," Democracy in Action: Presidential Campaign 2008. www.P2008.org (accessed May 6, 2007).

5. McCain missed 60 Senate roll call votes in the first four months of 2008 compared to 41 for Biden, 37 for Brownback, 26 for Dodd, 7 for Obama, and 3 for Clinton. "McCain Leads In Missed Votes," *Washington Post* (April 29, 2007), p. A2.

6. Heidi Przybyla, "Obama's 'Youth Mojo' Sparks Student Activism, Fueling Campaign." Bloomberg News. www.bloomberg.com/apps/news?pid=washingtonstory&sid=a (accessed May 7, 2007).

7. **Democratic Debates:**

   -April 26, 2007—South Carolina Democratic Party/NBC News debate at South Carolina State University in Orangeburg, SC.

   -June 3, 2007 (initially April 5, 2007)—CNN/WMUR/New Hampshire Union Leader Democratic debate at Saint Anselm College in Manchester, NH.

   -June 28, 2007—PBS Democratic presidential forum at Howard University in Washington, D.C.

   -Aug. 19, 2007—ABC News and ABC5/WOI-TV/Iowa Democratic Party forum in Des Moines, IA.

   -After Labor Day 2007—Yahoo!, The Huffington Post and Slate online—only Democratic presidential debate.

   -Sept. 23, 2007—Congressional Black Caucus Political Education and Leadership Institute (CBC Institute)/FOX debate in Detroit, MI.

   -Sept. 26 or 27, 2007—NECN, NBC News, Dartmouth College, and NHPR debate at Dartmouth College in Hanover, NH.

   -Oct. 21, 2007—ABC News/WMUR-TV/Union Leader Democratic debate in Manchester, NH.

   -Nov. 4, 2007—CNN/Nevada Democratic Party Nevada Democratic Presidential Debate at UNLV in Las Vegas, NV.

   -Jan. 9 or 10, 2008—NPR/Iowa Public Radio debate in Des Moines, IA.

   -Jan. 2008—Congressional Black Caucus Political Education and Leadership Institute (CBC Institute)/CNN debate in SC.

   -Jan. 31, 2008—CNN/Los Angeles Times debate in Los Angeles, CA. *also:* DNC will sanction six debates.

Republican Debates:

-May 3, 2007—Reagan Presidential Library Foundation/MSNBC/THE POLI-TICO debate in Simi Valley, CA.

-May 15, 2007—South Carolina Republican Party/FOX News debate at the University of South Carolina in Columbia, SC.

-June 5, 2007 (initially April 4, 2007)—CNN/WMUR/New Hampshire Union Leader Republican debate at Saint Anselm College in Manchester, NH.

-Aug. 5, 2007—ABC News and ABC5/WOI-TV Republican forum in Des Moines, IA.

-Sept. 6, 2007—FOX News/NHGOP Republican debate in NH.

-After Labor Day 2007—Yahoo!, The Huffington Post, and Slate online—only Republican presidential debate.

-Sept. 26 or 27, 2007—NECN, NBC News, Dartmouth College and NHPR debate at Dartmouth College in Hanover, NH.

-Sept. 27, 2007—PBS Republican presidential forum at Morgan State University in Baltimore, MD.

-Oct. 14, 2007—ABC News/WMUR-TV/Union Leader Republican debate in Manchester, NH.

-Oct. 21, 2007—Florida Republican Party/FOX News debate in Orlando, FL.

-Nov. 6, 2007—MSNBC Republican debate at Iowa State University in Ames, IA.

-Jan. 9 or 10, 2008—NPR/Iowa Public Radio debate in Des Moines, IA.

-Jan. 30, 2008—CNN/Los Angeles Times debate in Los Angeles, CA.

-Jan. 30, 2008—Reagan Presidential Library Foundation debate in Simi Valley, CA.

8. After a comment by Fox News President, Roger Ailes, directed at Barack Obama, and a petition campaign organized by the liberal group, Moveon.com, Democratic candidates decided not to participate in a Nevada debate sponsored by Fox News in 2007.

9. Chris Cillizza and Shailagh Murray, "In This Race, There's No Starting Gun," *Washington Post* (May 13, 1007), p. A2.

INDEX